# A SIP THROUGH TIME

## A COLLECTION OF OLD BREWING RECIPES

*In A Single Illustrated Volume,*
*Containing Hundreds of Old Recipes for*
*Ale, Beer, Mead, Metheglin, Cider, Perry, Brandy, Liqueurs,*
*Distilled Waters, Hypocras, Wines, Etc.,*
*dating from 1800 B.C. to Modern Times.*

by

## Cindy Renfrow

*This book is humbly dedicated to*
*George, the Duke of Clarence,*
*murderously drowned in a butt of malmsey wine*
*in the Tower of London,*
*February 18, 1478.*
*What a way to go!*

1st Printing   - June, 1995
2nd Printing  - February, 1996
3rd Printing   - May, 1997

Also By This Author:

"Take a Thousand Eggs or More," A Collection of Fifteenth Century Recipes.

Library of Congress Card Catalog Number TX 4-019-890.

# TABLE OF CONTENTS

# PERMISSIONS ACKNOWLEDGEMENTS

RECIPES from *The First American Cookbook*, by Amelia Simmons. Dover Publications, Inc. New York, 1958. Reprinted by permission of Dover Publications.

RECIPES from *Le Viandier de Taillevent*, translated by James Prescott, Second Edition. Alfarghaugr Publishing Society. Eugene, Oregon, 1989. Reprinted with the kind permission of the translator.

RECIPES from *The Dyer's Companion*, by Elijah Bemiss, 1815. Dover Publications, Inc. New York, 1973. Reprinted by permission of Dover Publications.

RECIPES from *Martha Washington's Booke of Cookery, and Booke of Sweetmeats: being a Family Manuscript, curiously copied by an unknown Hand sometime in the seventeenth century, which was in her Keeping from 1749, the time of her Marriage to Daniel Custis, to 1799, at which time she gave it to Eleanor Parke Custis, her grandaughter, on the occasion of her Marriage to Lawrence Lewis.* Edited by Karen Hess. Columbia University Press. New York, 1981. Reprinted by permission of The Historical Society of Pennsylvania.

RECIPES from *Penn Family Recipes, Cooking Recipes of Wm. Penn's Wife, GULIELMA.* Edited by E. A. Benson. George Shumway, Publisher. York, Pennsylvania, 1966. Reprinted by permission of The Historical Society of Pennsylvania.

RECIPES from *The Country Housewife and Lady's Director*, by Richard Bradley. 1736 edition. Reproduced in facsimile by Prospect Books. London, 1980. Reprinted by kind permission of Prospect Books.

RECIPE from *The Forme of Cury*. A Roll of Ancient English Cookery, Compiled, about A.D. 1390, by the Master-Cooks of King Richard II, London, Printed by J. Nichols, Printer to the Society of Antiquaries, 1780. Rpt. the Early English Text Society, Supplementary Series 8, 1985. Reprinted by kind permission of the Council of the Early English Text Society.

# ACKNOWLEDGEMENTS

My thanks go out to the people who helped me to complete this book: to Christina Krupp, Bill Gillen, and Douglas Brainard for supplying source material, counsel, and editing; to David Ovitt for recipes; to the Wrights for information about honeybees; and to Paul O'Rourke for Egyptian material and advice. Thanks to Bob Renfrow for lending me source material and support, and to Mindy Godfrey for her enthusiasm and offers of help. Thanks also to those many authors and bibliophiles who have preserved these precious links to our past so that we might one day read and enjoy them.

Last, but by no means least, I owe special thanks to my husband, Richard, for once again keeping me typing by telling me to "stop working on that stupid book." When will he learn?

The distillation of herbs. From *Le Proprietaire des Choses*, Paris, 1500.

# INTRODUCTION

This book contains a representative sampling of brewing recipes from earliest times to the present, and is meant for those of you who enjoy not only poring over old recipes, but also pouring out and sharing the results. It is intended to be a convenient reference tool, and to this end it includes: over 400 period brewing recipes for ale, beer, wine, cider, mead, metheglin, brandy, hypocras, etc.; a glossary of unfamiliar terms; an Appendix of the herbs and fruits called for in the recipes; a list of these same plants which also produce cloth dyes; an annotated bibliography; an index; numerous illustrations; and a list of sources for materials, services, and information which may be of use to you. Modernized directions have been intentionally omitted in order to keep this book affordable – instruction books may readily be found at any library, beer and wine-making supply store, or through your local agricultural extension service.

The recipes in this book have been gathered from the works of many authors, some of whom may be known to you. The recipes are organized first by the type of recipe (ale, mead, etc.), and then by the date of publication, with the earlier works coming first. In order to assist you in preparing these recipes, I have taken the liberty of adding a list of ingredients after the title and date, and offering clarification where the meaning of the recipe is unclear. While very few of you will be brewing several hogsheadsful at a time, the original measurements have been retained in these lists of ingredients so that you may reduce the recipes to the volume you desire and convert to your favorite system of measurement. Most conversions can be found in the glossary.

The numbers preceding the recipes from Plat and Digby refer to the position of the recipe in the original manuscripts; the numbers have been added in order to facilitate reference to the original texts.

Beverages whose sole purpose was purely medicinal have been intentionally omitted. However, some recipes which call for ingredients now known to be poisonous or harmful *have been included* so that you may learn caution when dealing with older recipes. Please take the time to consult the Appendix of Herbs and Fruits before making any recipe that has the note: "CAUTION! (See Appendix.)"

You will find that a large gap exists between the works of Apicius and those of the fourteenth century. It is regrettable that so few recipes from this time have survived, and those that have are being hoarded in closely guarded collections. I believe the more often these older recipes are printed and reprinted, the less likely it is that they will be lost to us forever. Would that more collectors shared this sentiment!

The purpose of this work has been to make a great many period recipes more widely available to the modern brewing enthusiast for enjoyment, study, and re-discovery. I hope that I have succeeded in this endeavor. Enjoy!

# ALES & BEERS

**\*\*\*\*\*\*\***

Ale is made of malte and water
and they the which do put any other thynge to ale
than is rehersed, except yest, barme or godesgood,
doth sofysticat theyr ale.

Bere is made of malte, of hoppes, and water;
it is the naturall drynke for a Dutche man,
and nowe of lete days it is much used in England
to the detryment of many Englysshe people...
(Andrew Boorde, 1547.)

## SUMERIAN ALE – c. 1800 B.C.

*Our earliest recipe, which is for ale made with a bappir (a loaf of bread made of aromatic barley), comes from an Ancient Sumerian clay tablet and dates to circa 1800 B.C. It is, of course, the famous "Hymn to Ninkasi," the Sumerian goddess of brewing. A commercial brew has been derived from this recipe and is available under the name "Ninkasi Sumerian Beer."*[1]

| | |
|---|---|
| water | honey or date juice |
| malt, soaked in water | toasted barley |
| grapes or unsulphured raisins | |
| barley bread made with sweet aromatic herbs and date honey | |

Briefly, the recipe calls for: fresh spring water; a *bappir* of barley bread made with sweet aromatic herbs and date honey, which is baked in a large oven; malt soaked in hot or boiling water, stirred with the *bappir* and additional toasted barley.

The malt mixture is spread on reed mats and cooled. The liquid is then drained off into a large vat, and is sweetened with honey or date juice. Grapes or unsulphured raisins are added in order to introduce naturally occurring yeast to the wort. The vat is then covered and the liquid is allowed to ferment.

When ready, the liquid is poured out through a coarse filter, not a siphon. It is then drunk using straws, presumably because there is still a large amount of sediment in the brew. As can be expected, no measurements or timings are specified in the hymn/recipe, nor are the herbs identified.

---

[1] The complete text of the "Hymn to Ninkasi," illustrated on a clay tablet, as well as the translation by Miguel Civil and the quest to reproduce the recipe for "Ninkasi Sumerian Beer," can be found in an article by Solomon H. Katz, and Fritz Maytag (president of Anchor Brewing Company), in *Archaeology* magazine, July/August, 1991, pp. 24-33.

There are two Egyptian papyri, known as the Rhind Mathematical Papyrus and the Moscow Mathematical Papyrus, which allude to the brewing of beer in confusing mathematical word problems. The calculations are so complex, and the errors in them so numerous, that the papyri have generated a great deal of scholarly debate and many research papers. Some people, who have assumed these problems represent actual measurements and proportions of ingredients, have tried to use the problems as recipes (using emmer wheat, spelt, barley, water, and dates) in an attempt to re-construct Egyptian beer. (*See Nims and Spalinger for more information.*)

*As you will see, there is a large time gap between the preceding and following recipes. While thousands of extant artifacts as well as literary references prove without doubt that brewing took place, it is unfortunate that little is known of the specific recipes used by our forebears during this period. References such as the following are quite common, but alas are useless for one intent on re-creating a specific beverage:*

### 1st Century A.D. – Roman

The nations of the west also have their own intoxicant, made from grain soaked in water; there are a number of ways of making it in the various provinces of Gaul and Spain and under different names, although the principle is the same. The Spanish provinces have by this time even taught us that these liquors will bear being kept a long time. Egypt also has devised for itself similar drinks made from grain, and in no part of the world is drunkenness ever out of action, in fact they actually quaff liquors of this kind neat and do not temper their strength by diluting them, as is done with wine...[1]

### 3rd Century A.D. – Greek

"For they place in the wine-jar dough made from spelt, first mixing it with honey, so that the wine gets its fragrance from itself, but its sweetness from the dough."[2]

### 9th Century – Anglo-Saxon

Then to the feast they went to sit in pride
At the *wine-drinking*, all his warriors...
So the wicked one
Through the day drenched his followers with *wine*,
The haughty gift-lord, till they lay in swoon;
His nobles all o'erdrenched as they were struck
To death, and every good poured out of them.[3]

### 12th Century – Irish

"...*Wine* in well rose sparkingly, *Beer* was rolling darkingly, *Bragget* brimmed the pond. Lard was oozing heavily, Merry malt moved wavily, Through the floor beyond..."[4]

### 13th Century

"He had us asked what we wanted to drink, wine or *terracina*, which is rice wine (*cervisia*), or *caracosmos*, which is clarified mare's milk, or *bal* which is honey mead. For in winter they make use of these four kinds of drinks."[5]

---

[1] Pliny the Elder, *Natural History*, Book XIV, section XXIX, p. 285.

[2] Athenaeus, Book I, p. 141.

[3] *Judith*, c. 850 to 940 A.D., found in Cook, p. 122.

[4] *The Vision of Viands*, 12th century, found in Ross, p. 497.

[5] *A Mission to the Great Khan*, by William of Rubruck, c. 1253-4 A.D., *ibid.*, p. 469.

> Greet sokene hath this millere, out of doute,
> With whete and malt of al the land aboute...
> For which this millere stal bothe mele and corn
> An hundred tyme moore than biforn;
> For therbiforn he stal but curteisly,
> But now he was a theef outrageouosly...[1]

***

## BEER – 1577

*This is a recipe for two different drinks which begin with the same steps. The numbers in brackets have been added to help differentiate the two recipes.*

| [1] <u>Beer</u>: | [2] <u>Brackwort or Charwort</u>: |
|---|---|
| 8 bushels malt, ground | 8 or 9 gallons of this unfermented beer, set aside |
| 160 gallons water, boiling | 1 handful wheat flour |
| 1/2 bushel wheat meal | 1/2 ounce orache (or orris root?[2]) |
| 3 1/2 to 4 lbs. English hops | 1/8 ounce bay laurel berries, powdered |
| 1/2 bushel oats, ground | *optional*: use long pepper in place of orache and bay laurel berries |

"Nevertheless," he says, "sith I have taken occasion to speake of bruing, I will exemplifie in such a proportion as I am best skilled in, bicause it is the usuall rate for mine owne familie, and once in a moneth practised by my wife and hir maid servants, who proceed withall after this maner, as she hath oft informed me.

[1] Having therefore groond eight bushels of good malt upon our querne, where the toll is saved,[3] she addeth unto it half a bushel of wheat meale, and so much of otes small groond, and so tempereth or mixeth them with the malt, that you cannot easily discerne the one from the other, otherwise these later would clunter, fall into lumps, and thereby become unprofitable. The first liquor which is full eightie gallons according to the proportion of our furnace, she maketh boiling hot, and then powreth it softlie into the malt, where it resteth (but without stirring) untill hir second liquor be almost ready to boile. This doone she letteth hir mash run till the malt be left without liquor, or at the leastwise the greater part of the moisture, which she perceiveth by the staie and softe issue thereof, and by this time hir second liquor in the furnace is ready to seeth, which is put also to the malt as the first woort also againe into the furnace, whereunto she addeth two pounds of the best English hops, and so letteth them seeth together by the

---

[1] Chaucer, *The Reeve's Tale*, lines 3987-3996.

[2] CAUTION! (*See Appendix.*)

[3] That is, she frugally saves the miller's fee by grinding her own malt with a hand quern.

*4*

space of two hours in summer, or an houre and a halfe in winter, whereby it getteth an excellent colour and continuance without impeachment, or anie superfluous tartnesse. [2] But before she putteth her first woort into the furnace, or mingleth it with the hops, she taketh out a vessel full, of eight or nine gallons, which she shutteth up close, and suffereth no aire to come into it till it become yellow, and this she reserveth by it selfe unto further use, as shall appeare hereafter, calling it Brackwoort or Charwoort, and as she saith it addeth also to the colour of the drinke, whereby it yeeldeth not unto amber or fine gold in hew unto the eie. [1] By this time also hir second woort is let runne, and the first being taken out of the furnace and placed to coole, she returneth the middle woort into the furnace, where it is striken over, or from whence it is taken againe.

"When she hath mashed also the last liquor (and set the second to coole by the first) she letteth it runne and then seetheth it againe with a pound and a half of new hops or peradventure two pounds as she seeth cause by the goodness or baseness of the hops; and when it hath sodden in summer two hours, and in winter an houre and a halfe, she striketh it also and reserveth it unto mixture with the rest when time doth serve therefore. [2] Finallie when she setteth hir drinke together, she addeth to hir brackwoort[1] or charwoort halfe an ounce of arras[2] and halfe a quarterne of an ounce of baiberries[3] finelie powdered, and then putteth the same into hir woort with an handful of wheate floure, she proceedeth in such usuall order as common bruing requireth. Some in steed of arras and baies add so much long peper onely, but in hir opinion and my lyking it is not so good as the first, [1] and hereof we make three hoggesheads of good beere, such (I meane) as is meet for poore men as am I to live withall whose small maintenance (for what great thing is fortie pounds a yeare *computatis computandis*, able to performe?) may indure no deeper cut, the charges whereof groweth in this manner.

I value my malt at ten shillings, my wood at foure shillings which I buie, my hops at twenty pence, the spice at two pence, servants wages two shillings sixpence, both meat and drinke, and the wearing of my vessell at twentie pence, so that for my twenty shillings I have ten score gallons of beer or more, notwithstanding the loss in seething. The continuance of the drinke is always determined after the quantitie of the hops, so that being well hopped it lasteth longer. For it feedeth upon the hop and holdeth out so long as the force of the same endureth which being extinguished the drinke must be spent or else it dieth and becometh of no value.

(From *The Description of England*, by William Harrison, 1577. *This recipe is cited in many sources, but the spelling and punctuation vary.*)

---

[1] Brackwort is not the same as *Braggot*, or *Bragawd*, a Welsh drink that is a combination of ale and metheglin. No honey is added to the brackwort.

[2] Arras is a city in Northern France. Perhaps the pot herb Arrach, or Orache, is being called for here; or, as Edelen suggests, it could be a misspelling of Orris. (CAUTION! *See Appendix.*)

[3] Berries of bay laurel (*Laurus nobilis* L.), not bayberries (*Myrica* spp.).

"'The liquor drunk in the houses of the rich [Celts] is wine brought from Italy and the country round Marseilles, and is unmixed; though sometimes a little water is added. But among the needier inhabitants a beer is drunk made from wheat, with honey added; the masses drink it plain. It is called *corma*.'"[1]

✳✳✳

## 74. THE MAKING OF A BRAGGOT, WHICH IS MANY TIMES MISTAKEN FOR A MUSKADEL BY THE SIMPLE SORT OF PEOPLE – 1594

*Braggot, or Bragawd, is a Welsh drink that is a combination of ale and metheglin. There are two interpretations possible for this recipe depending on how you read the first sentence:*

*1- We could use 9 gallons alewort + 9 gallons raw honey and reduce it to 9 gallons clarified honey as per recipe #75.*

*2- Alternately, we could mix 4 1/2 gallons alewort with 4 1/2 gallons of already clarified honey (recipe follows) to make the 9 gallons called for in recipe #74.*

*Thanks to Douglas Brainard for supplying and clarifying this recipe.*

| | |
|---|---|
| 59 gallons Ale | 1 ounce licorice |
| 3 ounces cinnamon | 3 ounces ginger root |
| 1 ounce cloves | 3 ounces grains of paradise |
| 1 ounce whole nutmegs | 1 ounce coriander seed |
| 1/2 ounce long pepper | 1 1/2 ounce cardamom |

*either:* 9 gallons raw honey + 9 gallons alewort, *or* 4 1/2 gallons alewort + 4 1/2 gallons clarified honey

Put one part of smal Alewort that is bloud warm with one part of clarified hony according to the manner set down, num. 75, but put no Cloves therein in the clarifying. For the making of one Hogshead of this Braggot which is about 63 gallons, you must take nine gallons of this clarified honey, and 54 gallons of strong new ale: when your clarified honey hath stood one day, then mingle the same with your new ale in a Hogshead, first filling your Hogshead half full before you put in your honey, and then hang this aromatical composition in a long slender bag in the midst of the vessel, viz. of Cinamon 3 ounces, Ginger 3 ounces, Greins 3 ounces, Colianders one ounce, Cloves 1 ounce, Nutmegs 1 ounce, long Pepper half an ounce, Cardamomum one ounce and a half, Liquorice 1 ounce, then fill up the vessel almost full with the best of the new ale (yet some commend rather the putting in of the spices confusedly then in a bag) be sure

---

[1] Poseidonius, quoted in Athenaeus, Book IV, p. 193.

to have 4 or 5 gallons or more of the same new ale to fill up the hogshead as it purges over continually. There is a lesser hole near the bung hole in beer Hogsheads, which must stand open whilest it purgeth, you must also be carefull in the beginning to give some little vent to the hogshead whilest it worketh: in three or four moneths it will be ready to drink. You must have a hazel stick of the bigness of a good cudgel, so great as may well enter in at the round bung hole, and when your Hogshead is about three quarters full, put in this stick, being sawed crosse wise at the end about one cubit in length (the Vintners call it their parelling staffe) as the aptest tool for this pupose. Beat with the said staffee the new ale and the honey together a good pretty while, and when you have finished this agitation, fill up the vessel with the rest, and let it purge as before. If you find your muskadel too thick after it hath stood 2 or 3 moneths, you may take a cane or pipe, made of tin plates, that will reach into the midst of the hogshead or somewhat more, stop the end thereof, and make some holes in the sides, and with a funnel you may pour more new ale into the Cane, and so make it thinner. The cane is an apt instrument to convey any liquor or composition into a vessel of wine without troubling of the same, or turning up the lees, whereby you may draw the same fine presently.

(From *The Jewel House of Art and Nature*, by Sir Hugh Plat, 1594.)


## 75. HOW TO CLARIFIE HONEY SO THAT THE TASTE THEREOF SHALL BE MUCH ALTERED – 1594

*This recipe is for the clarified honey called for above. Although it is not perfectly clear, the phrase "boil... till all the water be consumed" means to reduce the volume by half. So that:*

*1 gallon water + 1 gallon honey + heat = 1 gallon clarified honey.*

1 gallon water          1/2 ounce cloves
1 gallon honey

Put a gallon of water blood warm to a gallon of hony, put in your honey first, and with a stick take the depth thereof in the vessel wherein you boil it, and then put half an ounce of beaten cloves bound in a linnen cloth therein, and let them boil with the water and honey on a gentle fire till all the water be consumed, which you shall guesse as by this mark on the stick. Your hony must be pure and simple, not mingled with wort, flower, or other bad compsition, even as it is gathered upon the breaking up of the hives. It is a work of two or three hours, and the elder the honey is, the better it serveth for this purpose: you must remember to take away the skum as it riseth. Some boil this hony a little higher to a more consistency, and preserve fruit therewith instead of sugar... (*ibid.*)

## ON SAGE ALE

"Sage is much vſed of many in the moneth of May faſting, with butter and Parſley, and is held of moſt much to conduce to the health of mans body. It is alſo much vſed among other good herbes to bee tund vp with Ale, which thereupon is termed Sage Ale, whereof many barrels full are made, and drunke in the ſaid moneth chiefly for the purpoſe afore recited: and alſo for teeming women, to helpe them the better forward in their childebearing, if there be feare of abortion or miſcarrying." [1]

"No man needeth to doubt of the wholeſomneſſe of Sage ale, being brewed as it ſhoulde be, with Sage, Scabious, Betonioe, Spikenard, Squinanth, and Fennell ſeedes." [2]

SAGE

## 32. DIVERS EXCELLENT KINDES OF BOTTLE-ALE – 1609

*This is really five different recipes for flavoring previously brewed ales with Sage, Mace, Nutmeg, Hypocras, or Roasted Oranges and Cloves. The numbers in brackets have been added to help differentiate the five recipes.*

1 or 2 quarts ale
oil of sage, *or* oil of mace, *or* oil of nutmeg, *or* 1/2 pint white hypocras, *or* roasted oranges stuck with cloves

I cannot remember, that euer I did drinke the like [1] Sage-ale at any time, as that which is made by mingling two or three droppes of the extracted oyle of Sage with a quart of Ale, the same being well brewed out of one pot into another: and this way a whole stand of Sage ale is very speedily made. [2,3] The like is to bee done with the oyle of Mace or Nutmegs. [4] But if you will make a right Gossips cup that shall farre exceede all the Ale that euer mother *Bunch* made in her life time, then in the bottling vp of your best aile, runne half a pinte of white Ipocrasse that is newly made, and after the best receit, with a pottle of Ale: stoppe your bottle close, and drink it when it is stale. [5] Some commend the hanging of roasted Orenges prickt full of Cloues in the vessell of Ale till you finde the taste thereof sufficiently graced to your own liking.
(From *Delightes for Ladies*, by Sir Hugh Plat, 1609.)

---

[1] Parkinson, 1629, p. 478.

[2] Gerard, 1597, p. 624.

***

Touching ordinary Beere, which is that wherewith either Nobleman, Gentleman, Yeoman, or Husbandman ſhall maintaine his family the whole yeere; it is meet firſt that our *Engliſh Huſ-wife* reſpect the proportion or allowance of mault due to the ſame, which amongſt the beſt Huſbands is thought moſt conuenient, and it is held that to drawe from one quarter of good malt three Hogſheads of beare is the beſt ordinary proportion that can be allowed, and hauing age and good caske to lie in, it will be ſtrong enough for any good mans drinking.[1]

***

## OF BREWING ORDINARY BEERE – 1615

| | |
|---|---|
| 8 bushels malt | 1 1/2 lbs. hops |
| 3 hogsheads water | yeast |

Now for the brewing of ordinary Beere, your mault being well ground and put in your Maſh-fat, and your liquor in your leade ready to boile, you ſhall then by little and little with ſcopes or pailes put the boiling liquor to the mault, and then ſtirre it euen to the bottome exceedingly well together (which is called the maſhing of the mault) then the liquor ſwimming in the top couer all ouer with more mault, and ſo let it ſtand an howre & more in the maſh-fat, during which ſpace you may if you pleaſe heate more liquor in your leade for your ſecond or ſmall drinke; this done, pluck vp your maſhing ſtroame, and let the firſt liquour runne gently from the mault, either in a cleane trough or other veſſels prepared for the purpoſe, and then ſtopping the maſh-fat againe put the ſecond liquor to the mault and ſtirre it well together; then your leade being emptied put your firſt liquour or wort therein and then to euery quarter of mault put a pound and a half of the beſt hops you can get, and boile them an hower together, till taking vp a diſhfull thereof you ſee the hops ſhrinke into the bottome of the diſh; this done put the wort through a ſtraight ſiue which may draine the hoppes from it into your cooler, which ſtanding ouer the Guil-fat you ſhall in the bottome therof ſet a great bowle with your barme and ſome of the firſt wort (before the hops come into it mixt together, that it may riſe therein, and then let your wort drop or run gently into the diſh with the barme which ſtands in the Guil-fat, and this you ſhal do the firſt day of your brewing letting your cooler drop all the night following, and ſome part of the next morning, and as it droppeth if you finde that a blacke skumme or mother riſeth vpon the barme, you ſhall with your hand take it off and caſt it away, then nothing being left in the cooler, and the beere well riſen, with

---

[1] Markham, p. 121.

[2] 'Lead' refers to a cauldron, not the metal.

your hand ſtirre it about and ſo let it ſtand an hower after, and then beating it and the barme exceeding well together, tunne it vp in the Hogſheads being cleane waſht and ſcaulded, and ſo let it purge, and herein you ſhall obſerue not to tun your veſſels too full for feare thereby it purge too much of the barm away, when it hath purged a day and a night you ſhall cloſe vp the bung-holes with clay, and only for a day or two after keepe a vent-hole in it, and after cloſe it vp as cloſe as may be.

(From *The English Huſ-wife, etc.*, by Gervase Markham, 1615, pp. 121-122.)

## [OF SMALL BEER] – 1615

*This recipe uses the malt and hops left over from the preceding recipe.*

8 bushels leftover malt
1 hogshead water
1 1/2 lbs. leftover hops

From *Eygentliche Beschreibung aller Stande auf Erden*
by Hans Sachs.

Time to completion: 2 weeks.

Nor for your ſecond or ſmall drinke which are left vpon the graines you ſhall offer it there to ſtay but an hower or a little better, and then drain it off alſo, which done put it into the lead with the former hops and boile the other alſo, then cleere it from the hops and couer it very cloſe till your firſt beere bee tunn'd, and then as before put it alſo to barme and ſo tunne it vp also in ſmaller veſſels, and of this ſecond beere you ſhall not drawe aboue one Hogſhead to three of the better. Now there be diuers other waies & obſeruations for the brewing of ordinary Beere but none ſo good, ſo eaſie, ſo ready and quickly performed as this before ſhewed: neither will any beere laſt longer or ripen ſooner, for it may bee drunke at a fortnights age and will laſt as long and liuely.

(*ibid.*, p. 122.)

# #105 SCOTCH ALE FROM MY LADY HOLMBEY – 1669

1+ hogshead water                     1 quart ale barm
malt

Time to completion: 1 year.

The Excellent Scotch Ale is made thus. Heat Spring-water; it must not boil, but be ready to boil, which you will know by leaping up in bubbles. Then pour it to the Malt; but by little and little, stirring them strongly together all the while they are mingling. When all the water is in, it must be so proportioned that it be very thick. Then cover the vessel well with a thick Mat made on purpose with a hole for the stick, and that with Coverlets and Blankets to keep in all the heat. After three or four hours, let it run out by the stick (putting new heated water upon the Malt, if you please, for small Ale or Beer) into a Hogshead with the head out. There let it stand till it begin to blink, and grow long like thin Syrup. If you let it stay too long, and grow too thick, it will be sowre. Then put it again into the Caldron, and boil it an hour or an hour and a half. Then put it into a Woodden-vessel to cool, which will require near forty hours for a hogshead. Then pour it off gently from the settling. This quantity (of a hogshead) will require better then a quart of the best Ale-barm, which you must put to it thus. Put it to about three quarts of wort, and stir it, to make it work well. When the barm is risen quick scum it off to put to the rest of the wort by degrees. The remaining Liquor (that is the three quarts) will have drawn into it all the heavy dregs of the barm, and you may put it to the Ale of the second running, but not to this. Put the barm, you have scummed off (which will be at least a quart) to about two gallons of the wort, and stir it to make that rise and work. Then put two Gallons more to it. Doing thus at several times, till all be mingled, which will require a whole day to do. Cover it close, and let it work, till it be at it's height, and begin to fall, which may require ten or twelve hours, or more. Watch this well, least it sink too much, for then it will be dead. Then scum off the thickest part of the barm, and run your Ale into the hogshead, leaving all the bung open a day or two. Then lay a strong Paper upon it, to keep the clay from falling in, that you must then lay upon it, in which you must make a little hole to let it work out. You must have some of the same Liquor to fill it up, as it works over. When it hath done working, stop it up very close, and keep it in a very cold Cellar. It will be fit to broach after a year; and be very clear and sweet and pleasant, and will continue a year longer drawing; and the last glass full be as pure and as quick as the first. You begin to broach it high. Let your Cask have served for Sweet-wine.[1]
(From *The Closet of the Eminently Learned Sir Kenelme Digby Kt. Opened*, 1669.)

---

[1] Wooden casks which had contained Sack wine were often re-used in this manner. The cask absorbed the flavor of the wine, and, unless scoured clean, imparted the wine's flavor to any liquid subsequently stored in the cask.

# # 112  SMALL ALE FOR THE STONE – 1669

*The hops have been included in this recipe for their diuretic virtues. Hops "opens obstructions of the liver and spleen, cleanses the blood, opens the bowls, cleanses the reins from gravel and provokes urine."*[1]

14 or 15 gallons water          1/2 pint beer barm
1/2 ounces hops          1 to 1 1/2 pecks malt, coarsely ground

Time to completion:  4 or 5 days.

The Ale, that I used to drink constantly of, was made in these proportions.  Take fourteen Gallons of Water, and half an Ounce of Hops; boil them near an hour together. Then pour it upon a peck of Malt.  Have a care the Malt be not too small ground; for then it will never make clear Ale.  Let it soak so near two hours.  Then let it run from the Malt, and boil it only one walm or two.  Let it stand cooling till it be cool enough to work with barm, which let be of Beer rather than Ale, about half a pint.

After it hath wrought some hours, when you see it come to it's height, and is near beginning to fall in working, Tun it into a barrel of eight Gallons; and in four or five days it will be fit to broach to drink.  Since I have caused the wort to be boiled a good half hour; since again I boil it a good hour, and it is much the better; because the former Ale tasted a little Raw.  Now because it consumes in boiling, and would be too strong, if this Malt made a less proportion of Ale; I have added a Gallon of water at the first, taking fifteen Gallons instead of fourteen.  Since I have added half a peck of Malt to the former proportions, to make it a little stronger in Winter.
(From *The Closet ...Opened*, 1669.)

*Hops*
From Gerard's
*Herball*, 1597.

"The flowers [of hops] are vſed to ſeaſon Beere or Ale with, and ouermany do cauſe bitternes therof, and are ill for the head.  The manifold vertues in Hops do manifeſtly argue the holſomneſſe of Beere aboue Ale; for the Hops rather make it a Phiſicall drinke to keepe the body in health, then an ordinarie drinke for the quenching of our thirſt."[2]

---

[1] Culpeper, pp. 156-7.
[2] Gerard, p. 738.

# # 111  ALE WITH HONEY – 1669

*The second part of this recipe is for re-fermenting beer that has gone flat.  The numbers in brackets have been added to separate the recipes.*

[1]
40 gallons small ale                    5 gallons honey
ale barm

Sir Thomas Gower makes his pleasant and wholesom drink of Ale and Honey thus. Take fourty Gallons of small Ale, and five Gallons of Honey.  When the Ale is ready to Tun, and is still warm, take out ten Gallons of it; which, whiles it is hot, mingle with it the five Gallons of Honey, stirring it exceeding well with a clean arm till they be perfectly incorporated.  Then cover it, and let it cool and stand still.  At the same time you begin to dissolve the honey in this parcel, you take the other of thirty Gallons also warm, and Tun it up with barm, and put it into a vessel capable to hold all the whole quantity of Ale and Honey, and let it work there; and because the vessel will be so far from being full, that the gross foulness of the Ale cannot work over, make holes in the sides of the Barrel even with the superficies of the Liquor in it, out of which the gross feculence may purge; and these holes must be fast shut, when you put in the rest of the Ale with the Honey:  which you must do, when you see the strong working of the other is over; and that it works but gently, which may be after two or three or four days, according to the warmth of the season.  You must warm your solution of honey, when you put it in, to be as warm as Ale, when you Tun it; and then it will set the whole a working a fresh, and casting out more foulness; which it would do too violently, if you put it in at the first of the Tunning it.  It is not amiss that some feculence lie thick upon the Ale, and work not all out; for that will keep in the spirits.  After you have dissolved the honey in the Ale, you must boil it a little to skim it; but skim it not, till it have stood a while from the fire to cool; else you will skim away much of the Honey, which will still rise as long as it boileth.  If you will not make so great a quantity at a time, do it in less in the same proportions.  He makes it about Michaelmas for Lent.

[2]
1 hogshead flat beer                    5 pounds honey

When strong Beer groweth too hard, and flat for want of Spirits, take four or five Gallons of it out of a Hogshead, and boil five pounds of honey in it, and skim it, and put it warm into the Beer; and after it hath done working, stop it up close.  This will make it quick, pleasant and stronger.
(From *The Closet ...Opened*, 1669.)

# # 116 MR. WEBB'S ALE AND BRAGOT – 1669

*This is three recipes in one; the numbers in brackets have been added to differentiate the recipes. Mr. Webb's mead recipe may be found on pp. 37-40.*

[1] Ale:
5 bushels malt
2+ hogsheads water
1/4 lb. hops
beer yeast

[2] Bragot:
1 hogshead of this ale
1 lb. honey to every 2 gallons ale
6 ounces ginger, sliced
3 ounces stick cinnamon
*optional*: add cloves and mace.
<u>1 1/2 handful total</u>: rosemary, thyme, sweet marjoram, 3 mint sprigs.
1 1/2 handful sweetbrier leaves

[1] Five Bushels of Malt will make two Hogsheads. The first running makes one very good Hogshead, but not very strong; the second is very weak. To this proportion boil a quarter of a Pound of Hops in all the water that is to make the two Hogsheads; that is, two Ounces to each Hogshead. You put your water to the Malt in the Ordinary way. Boil it well, when you come to work it with yest, take very good Beer-yest; not Ale-yest.

[2] To make Bragot, He takes the first running of such Ale, and boils a less proportion of Honey in it, then when He makes His ordinary Meath; but dubble or triple as much spice and herbs. As for Example to twenty Gallons of the Strong-wort, he puts eight or ten pound, (according as your taste liketh more or less honey) of honey; But at least triple as much herbs, and triple as much spice as would serve such a quantity of small Mead as He made Me (For to a stronger Mead you put a greater proportion of Herbs and Spice, then to a small; by reason that you must keep it a longer time before you drink it; and the length of time mellows and tames the taste of the herbs and spice). And when it is tunned in the vessel (after working with the barm) you hang in it a bag with bruised spices (rather more then you boiled in it) which is to hang in the barrel all the while you draw it.

[3] He makes also Mead with the second weak running of the Ale; and to this He useth the same proportions of honey, herbs and spice, as for his small Mead of pure water; and useth the same manner of boiling, working with yest, and other Circumstances, as in making of that.
(From *The Closet ...Opened*, 1669.)

### # 268 TO MAKE CAPON ALE – c. 1550 to 1625

*These next four recipes for Cock Ale are rather disgusting, but informative. Personally, I'd much rather have my chicken soup and ale separately, thank you.*

| | |
|---|---|
| 1 capon, plucked and gutted | sugar |
| 1 ounce caraway seeds | 1 ounce anise seeds |
| 2 ounces hart's horn[1] | 1 handful rosemary |
| 1 or 2 mace blades | 1 lemon peel |
| hot water | 2 gallons strong working ale |

Take an old capon with yellow leggs.  pu[ll] him & crush ye bones, but keep ye scin whol[e], & then take an ounce of carraway seeds, and an ounce of anny seeds, and two ounces of har[ts] horne, and one handfull of rosemary tops, a piece or 2 of mace, and a leamon pill.  sow all these into ye bellie of your capon and chop [*put*] him into a hot mash, or hot water, and put him into two gallons of strong ale when it is working. after, let it stand two or three dayes, & then drink it.  or you may bottle it after it hath stood 4 or 5 dayes, & put a lump of sugar into every bottle [wch] will make it drink brisker.  this ale is good for any who are in a consumption, & it is restorative for any other weakness.
(From *Martha Washington's Booke of Cookery*, ed. by Karen Hess.)


### # 173 TO MAKE COCK-ALE – 1669

| | |
|---|---|
| 8 gallons Ale | 2 or 3 whole nutmegs |
| 1 capon, boiled | 3 or 4 mace blades |
| 4 lbs. raisins | 1/2 lb. dates |
| 2 quarts Sack wine | |

Time to completion:  1 month.

Take eight Gallons of Ale; take a Cock and boil him well; then take four pounds of Raisins of the Sun well stoned, two or three Nutmegs, three or four flakes of Mace, half a pound of Dates; beat these all in a Mortar, and put to them two quarts of the best Sack; and when the Ale hath done working, put these in, and stop it close six or seven days, and then bottle it, and a month after you may drink it.
(From *The Closet ...Opened*, 1669.)

---

[1] The hart's horn called for here is most likely the Wind-flower, *Pulsatilla*, which was once used as a remedy for lung diseases (*see Appendix*).  Stuffing the bird with deer antler shavings (in order to make gelatine), or with ammonium carbonate, does not make sense here.

*15*

## TO MAKE COCK ALE – 1762

10 gallons ale                   1 large old cock
2 quarts Sack wine          3 lbs. seedless raisins
mace blades                  cloves

Take ten gallons of ale and a large cock, the older the better; parboil the cock, flay him and stamp him in a stone mortar till his bones are broken (you must craw him and gut him when you flay him); then put the cock into two quarts of sack, and put to it three pounds of raisins of the sun stoned, some blades of mace, and a few cloves; put all these into a canvas bag, and a little before you find the ale has done working, put the ale and bag together into a vessel; in a week or nine days' time bottle it up; fill the bottle but just above the neck, and give the same time to ripen as other ale.
(From *The London Cook, etc.* by W. Gelleroy.)

## COCK ALE – 1780

10 gallons ale
1 large old cock
unspecified spices

Pounding herbs in a mortar.
From *Hortus Sanitatis,* c. 1497.

Take 10 gallons ale, a large cock (the older the better). Slay, caw and gut him, and stamp him in a stone mortar. Add spice and put all into a canvas bag. Lower him into the ale while still working. Finish working and bottle.[1]

---

[1] Hartley (p. 547) dates this recipe to 1780, but does not give a proper citation for it. It is likely that this recipe was derived from the preceding recipe. I have included Hartley's recipe here because in this version the cock is *raw*. Another recipe for Cock Water, found in Hess (pp. 414-5), calls for the cock to be *whipped and plucked alive* and put in a still with leaf gold, spices and wine, etc., with the resultant liquid being a remedy for consumption. Hess speculates that these and earlier recipes for Cock Water, which she notes all call for *red* cocks, are holdovers from the days of ritual sacrifices and witchcraft. It is unclear whether the birds in these recipes are meant to be eaten.

A similar 17th century recipe for a spring tonic says to "take a quart of earthworms, scour with salt, slit open, wash with their own filth, put in a stone mortar and beat" (Foley, p. 16). The worms were mixed with herbs and toasted snails; the water derived from this mess was then drunk with strong beer. Presumably *very strong* beer, indeed!

# 95 [APPLE BEER] – c. 1674

1 hogshead apple cider         3 lbs. sugar
beer yeast         hops
malt

stamp apels and strain them as usuly for Cyder, then take the Liquor and warm it and put it upon the malt, then when it is Com throu boyle it, and then worke it Like other bere, when it is put into vesells put 3 pound of hard suger in to the quantaty of an hogsheed, a few hops should bee boyled in it –
(From *Penn Family Recipes, etc.,* c. 1674.)

ALE, HOMEBREWED – HOW IT IS MADE – 1869

72 gallons water         12 lbs. hops
8 or 9 bushels malt         5 quarts yeast

...The middle classes of the English people usually make their ale in quantities of two barrels, that is, seventy-two gallons. For this purpose a quarter of malt, (8 bus.) is obtained at the malt-house – or, if wished to be extra strong, nine bushels of malt – are taken, with hops, 12 lbs.; yeast, 5 qts.

The malt, being crushed or ground, is mixed with 72 gals. of water at the temperature of 160 degrees, and covered up for 3 hours, when 40 gallons are drawn off, into which the hops are put, and left to infuse. Sixty gallons of water at a temperature of 170 degrees are then added to the malt in the mash-tub, and well mixed, and after standing 2 hours, sixty gallons are drawn off. The wort from these two mashes is boiled with the hops for 2 hours, and after being cooled down to 65 degrees, is strained through a flannel bag into a fermenting tub, where it is mixed with the yeast and left to work for 24 or 30 hours. It is then run into barrels to cleanse, a few gallons being reserved for filling up the casks as the yeast works over. Of course when the yeast is worked out it must be bunged...
(From *Dr. Chase's Recipes, etc.,* 1869.)

*Harvesting apples and making cider.*
From *The Cyder Feast* by Edward Calvert.

## TO BREW ALE IN SMALL FAMILIES – 1829

| | |
|---|---|
| 1 3/4 bushels pale malt, ground | 1 pint yeast |
| 18 gallons water | 1 lb. hops |

A bushel and three quarters of ground malt, and a pound of hops, are sufficient to make 18 gallons of good family ale. That the saccharine[1] matter of the malt may be extracted by infusion, without the farina, the temperature of the water should not exceed 155 or 160 deg. Fahrenheit's thermometer. The quantity of water should be poured on the malt as speedily as possible, and the whole being well mixed together by active stirring, the vessel should be closely covered over for an hour; if the weather be cold, for an hour and a half. If hard water be employed, it should be boiled, and the temperature allowed, by exposure to the atmosphere, to fall to 155 or 160 degrees Fahrenheit; but if rain water is used, it may be added to the malt as soon as it arrives to 155 degrees. During the time this process is going on, the hops should be infused in a close vessel, in as much boiling water as will cover them, for two hours. The liquor may then be squeezed out, and kept closely covered.

The hops should then be boiled for about ten minutes, in double the quantity of water obtained from the infused hop, and the strained liquor, when cold, may be added with the infusion, to the wort, when it has fallen to the temperature of 70 deg. The object of infusing the hop in a close vessel previously to boiling, is to preserve the essential oil of the hop, which renders it more sound, and, at the same time, more wholesome. A pint of good thick yeast should be well stirred into the mixture of wort and hops, and covered over in a place of the temperature of 65 deg. Fahrenheit; and when the fermentation is completed, the liquor may be drawn off into a clean cask previously rinsed with boiling water. When the slow fermentation which will ensue has ceased, the cask should be loosely bunged for two days, when, if the liquor be left quiet, the bung may be properly fastened. The pale malt is the best, because, when highly dried, it does not afford so much saccharine matter. If the malt be new, it should be exposed to the air, in a dry room, for two days previously to its being used; but if it be old, it may be used in 12 or 20 hours after it is ground. The great difference in the flavour of ale, made by different brewers, appears to arise from their employing different species of the hop.

(From *Five Thousand Receipts in All the Useful and Domestic Arts: constituting A Complete Practical Library*, by Mackenzie, 1829.)

---

[1] The word "saccharine" means "sweet," and is <u>not</u> a reference to the commercial sweetener.

> Ther spryngen herbes grete and smale,
> The lycorys and the cetewale,
> And many a clowe-gylofre;
> And notemuge to putte in ale,
> Wheither it be moyste or stale,
> Or for to leye in cofre.[1]

**✳✳✳**

## 97th.  TO MAKE BEER, WITHOUT MALT – 1815

13 gallons water                           a small quantity of yeast *or* lemon balm
2+ lbs. brown sugar                    2 lbs. molasses

Take thirteen gallons of water, boil and scum it, put two pounds of brown sugar and two pounds of treacle to it; boil them together half an hour, strain the liquor thro' a sieve, and put to it a penny worth or two of baum,[1] when cold; work it a day and a night, then turn it:  let it stand in the barrel a day and a night, then bottle it, and put into each bottle a tea-spoon full of brown sugar.
(From *The Dyer's Companion*, by Elijah Bemiss, 1815, p. 302.)

## TABLE BEER (EXCELLENT SUBSTITUTE) – 1819

*This recipe should have been called: 'how to stretch one bottle of porter to serve ten or more people, a recipe for the incredibly frugal housewife.'  The porter supplies the yeast.*

1 bottle porter                            1 lb. brown sugar or molasses
10 quarts water                          *optional*:  1 spoonful ginger root

As small beer is apt to become sour in warm weather, a pleasant beer may be made, by adding to a bottle of porter ten quarts of water, and a pound of brown sugar or molasses.  After they have been well mixed, pour the liquor into bottles, and place them, loosely corked, in a cool cellar.  In two or three days it will be fit for use.  A spoonful of ginger, added to the mixture, renders it more lively and agreeable to the taste.  This might be adopted in the navy instead of grog.
(*The Family Receipt Book, etc.*, 1819.)

---

[1] Chaucer, "Sir Thopas," lines 1950-1955.

[2] The manuscript says "baum," which most likely means barm (yeast), but could also be interpreted to mean balm (*Melissa officinalis*, L.), a common flavoring in older mead recipes.

## 1110.  TREACLE-BEER, A TABLE BEER – 1829

3 lbs. molasses or sugar
6 to 8 gallons water
1 pint beer yeast *or* 4 to 6 quarts fermenting beer wort
1 handful hops *or* gentian extract
*optional:* a little ginger root

Boil, for twenty minutes, three pounds of molasses, in from six to eight gallons of soft water, with a handful of hops tied in a muslin rag, or a little extract of gentian.  When cooled in the tub, add a pint of good beer-yeast, or from four to six quarts of fresh worts from the brewer's vat.  Cover the beer (and all fermenting liquids) with blankets or coarse cloths.  Pour it from the lees and bottle it.  You may use sugar for molasses, which is lighter.

N.B. – This is a cheap and very wholesome beverage.  A little ginger may be added to the boiling liquid if the flavour is liked.
(From *The Cook and Housewife's Manual: etc.,* by M. Dods, 1829, p. 472.)

*Home brewing.*
The housewife is pouring her hot wort into a cooling tub; the smoking furnace can be seen behind her.
From *Dictionarium domesticum* by N. Bailey. London, 1736.

## BEER – 1833

*This is not so much a recipe as a stream of related thoughts. Read it carefully before beginning.*

| | |
|---|---|
| 1 pailful water | 1 handful hops, *or* hops mixed with spruce |
| 1/2 pint molasses | 1 pint yeast per barrel |

*options*: boxberry,[1] feverbush, sweet fern, and horseradish; wintergreen; malt; 1 or 2 raw potatoes.

Beer is a good family drink. A handful of hops, to a pailful of water, and a half-pint of molasses, makes good hop beer. Spruce mixed with hops is pleasanter than hops alone. Boxberry, fever-bush, sweet fern, and horseradish make a good and healthy diet-drink. The winter evergreen, or rheumatism weed, thrown in, is very beneficial to humors. Be careful and not mistake kill-lamb[2] for winter-evergreen; they resemble each other. Malt mixed with a few hops makes a weak kind of beer; but it is cool and pleasant; it needs less molasses than hops alone. The rule is about the same for all beer. Boil the ingredients two or three hours, pour in a half-pint of molasses to a pailful, while the beer is scalding hot. Strain the beer, and when about lukewarm, put a pint of lively yeast to a barrel. Leave the bung loose till the beer is done working; you can ascertain this by observing when the froth subsides. If your family be large, and the beer will be drank rapidly, it may as well remain in the barrel; but if your family be small, fill what bottles you have with it; it keeps better bottled. A raw potato or two, cut up and thrown in, while the ingredients are boiling, is said to make beer spirited... Table beer should be drawn off into *stone* jugs, with a lump of white sugar in each, securely corked. It is brisk and pleasant, and continues good several months.
(From *The American Frugal Housewife*, by Mrs. Child, 1832, p. 86.)

---

[1] Box-berry is either *Mitchella repens* L. (partridge-berry), or *Gaultheria procumbens* L. (spicy wintergreen); the name is used for both species. Since wintergreen is called for specifically, Mrs. Child was probably referring to the former.

[2] Kill lamb is poisonous to sheep (*see Appendix*).

## HOP BEER – 1846

*In its use of toasted bread for flavor and body, this recipe from 1846 is similar to our earliest recipe for Sumerian Beer, which dates to 1800 B.C.[1]*

| | |
|---|---|
| 6 ounces hops | 2 quarts molasses |
| 9 quarts water | 1/2 lb. bread, toasted |
| 1 teacupful ginger root | 1 pint yeast |

Put to six ounces of hops five quarts of water, and boil them three hours – then strain off the liquor, and put to the hops four quarts more of water, a tea-cup full of ginger, and boil the hops three hours longer. Strain and mix it with the rest of the liquor, and stir in a couple quarts of molasses. Take about half a pound of bread, and brown it very slowly – when very brown and dry, put it in the liquor, to enrich the beer. Rusked bread is the best for this purpose, but a loaf of bread cut in slices, and toasted till brittle, will do very well. When rusked bread is used, pound it fine, and brown it in a pot, as you would coffee, stirring it constantly. When the hop liquor cools, so as to be just lukewarm, add a pint of new yeast, that has no salt in it. Keep the beer covered in a temperate situation, till it has ceased fermenting, which is ascertained by the subsiding of the froth – turn it off carefully into a beer keg, or bottles. The beer should not be corked very tight, or it will burst the bottles. It should be kept in a cool place.
(From *The Kitchen Directory, and American Housewife*, 1846.)

## COMMON BEER – 1849

| | |
|---|---|
| 2 gallons water | 1 pint yeast |
| 1 handful hops | 1 teacup molasses per gallon liquor |
| 1 quart wheat bran | *optional*: spruce *or* sweet fern |

Two gallons of water to a large handful of hops is the rule. A little fresh-gathered spruce or sweet fern makes the beer more agreeable, and you may allow a quart of wheat bran to the mixture; then boil it two or three hours. Strain it through a sieve, and stir in, while the liquor is hot, a teacup of molasses to every gallon. Let it stand till lukewarm, pour it into a clean barrel and add good yeast, a pint, if the barrel is nearly full; shake it well together; it will be fit for use the next day.
(From *The Way to Live Well, and To Be Well While We Live*, by Mrs. Sarah J. Hale, 1849.)

---

[1] See Phipps (p. 283) for an 18th century beer made with Persimmon Bread.

## DORCHESTER BEER – 1846

| | |
|---|---|
| 5 pailsful water | 1/2 pint rye meal |
| 1 quart hops | 2 quarts molasses |
| 1/2 pint yeast | |

1 handful sage, *or* <u>2 quarts total</u>: sassafras roots[1] and checkerberry[2]

To five pails of water put one quart bowl of hops, and one large handful of sage; or if you can procure them, about two quarts of sassafras roots and checkerberry, mixed, instead of the sage. Add a half pint of rye meal, and let all boil together three hours. Strain it through a sieve, while it is scalding hot, upon two quarts of molasses. There should be about four pails of the liquor when it is done boiling; if the quantity should be reduced more than that, add a little more water. When it is lukewarm, put to it a half pint of good yeast; then turn it into a keg and let it ferment. In two days or less it will be fit to bottle.

(From *The Young Housekeeper's Friend, etc.*, by Mrs. Cornelius, 1846.)

## GOOD, WHOLESOME SMALL BEER – 1850

*Small beer is an ideal beverage for hot summer days. It is fairly fizzy, but weak, since the fermentation is only allowed to proceed for a day or two. Historical recreationists are sure to find this just the thing for brewing demonstrations held "on site."*

| | |
|---|---|
| 2 ounces hops | 2 quarts molasses |
| 1/2 barrel water | yeast |

Time to completion: 1 day.

Take two ounces of hops, and boil them, three or four hours, in three or four pailfuls of water; and then scald two quarts of molasses in the liquor, and turn it off into a clean half-barrel, boiling hot; then fill it up with cold water; before it is quite full, put in your yeast to work it; the next day you will have agreeable, wholesome small beer, that will not fill with wind, as that which is brewed from malt or bran; and it will keep good till it is all drank out.

(From *The American Economical Housekeeper and Family Receipt Book*, by Mrs. Esther Allen Howland, 1850.)

---

[1] CAUTION! (*See Appendix.*)

[2] Two herbs are called checkerberry (*see Appendix*).

*"...for persons of a weak habit of body, and especially females, 1 glass of this with their meals is far better than tea or coffee, or all the ardent spirits in the universe."*

✳✳✳

## ENGLISH BEER, STRONG – 1869

| | |
|---|---|
| 6 lbs. brown sugar | water |
| 4 ounces hops | 1 peck malt *or* 1+ peck barley *or* 2 pecks oats |
| 1 teacupful yeast | |

Time to completion: 2 weeks.

Malt 1 peck; coarse brown sugar 6 lbs.; hops 4 oz.; good yeast 1 tea-cup; if you have not malt, take a little over 1 peck of barley, (twice the amount of oats will do, but are not as good,) and put it into an oven after the bred is drawn, or into a stove oven, and steam the moisture from them. Grind coarsely.

Now pour upon the ground malt 3 1/2 gals. of water at 170 or 172 degrees of heat. The tub in which you scald the malt should have a false bottom, 2 or 3 inches from the real bottom; the false bottom should be bored full of gimlet holes, so as not to act as a strainer, to keep back the malt meal. When the water is poured on, stir them well, and let it stand 3 hours, and draw off by a faucet; put in 7 gals. more of water at 180 to 182 degrees; stir it well, and let it stand 2 hours and draw it off. Then put on a gal. or two of cold water, stir it well and draw it off; you should have about 5 or 6 gals. Put the 6 lbs. of coarse brown sugar in an equal amount of water; mix with the wort and boil 1 1/2 to 2 hours with the hops; you should have eight gals. when boiled; when cooled to 80 degrees put in the yeast, and let it work 18 to 20 hours, covered with a sack; use sound iron hooped kegs or porter bottles, bung or cork tight, and in two weeks it will be good sound beer, and will keep a long time; and for persons of a weak habit of body, and especially females, 1 glass of this with their meals is far better than tea or coffee, or all the ardent spirits in the universe. If more malt is used, not exceeding 1/2 a bushel, the beer, of course, would have more spirit, but this strength is sufficient for the use of families or invalids. (From *Dr. Chase's Recipes, etc.*, 1869.)

## FOR BREWING SPRUCE BEER – 1796

*Spruce beer was another popular summertime drink. As in small beer and ginger beer, the fermentation goes on long enough to produce a fizzy drink, but not long enough to produce a high alcohol content.*

| | |
|---|---|
| 17 gallons water | 2+ gallons molasses |
| 1/2 pint yeast | 4 ounces hops |
| 8 ounces spruce essence in 1 quart water | |

Time to completion: 7 days.

Take four ounces of hops, let them boil half an hour in one gallon of water, ſtrain the hop water then add ſixteen gallons of warm water, two gallons of molaſſes, eight ounces of eſſence of ſpruce, diſſolved in one quart of water, put it in a clean caſk, then ſhake it well together, add half a pint of emptins, then let it ſtand and work one week, if very warm weather leſs time will do, when it is drawn off to bottle, add one ſpoonful of molaſſes to every bottle.
(From *The First American Cookbook, A Facsimile of "American Cookery,"* by Amelia Simmons, 1796, p. 47.)

## 98th. TO MAKE GOOD COMMON BEER – 1815

32 gallons water
1 gallon molasses
1 lb. spruce essence
1/2 lb. hops
yeast

Time to completion: 4 days.

*Spruce*

For a barrel of thirty two gallons take half a pound of hops, steep in four gallons of water two hours, strain off, then take one pound essence of spruce, and one gallon of molasses; mix them together, and put it in the barrel, and two cents worth of yeast, and fill with water: if it is summer it need not be warmed, but warm it in winter; when full shake it well, and stop it loosely and in four days it will be fit for bottling, and use.
(From *The Dyer's Companion*, by Elijah Bemiss, 1815, p. 302.)

## GINGER BEER – 1819

1 gallon water
1 ounce ginger root
1 lb. sugar

2 ounces lemon juice
yeast, 1/2 pint per 9 gallons liquor
isinglass, 1/2 pint per 9 gallons liquor

Time to completion: 2 weeks.

To every gallon of spring water add one ounce of sliced white ginger, one pound of common loaf sugar, and two ounces of lemon juice, or three large tablespoonfuls; boil it near an hour, and take off the scum; then run it through a hair sieve into a tub, and when cool (viz. 70 degrees) add yeast in proportion of half a pint to nine gallons; keep it in a temperate situation two days, during which it may be stirred six or eight times; then put it into a cask, which must be kept full, and the yeast taken off at the bung-hole with a spoon. In a fortnight add half a pint of fining (isinglass picked and steeped in beer) to nine gallons, which will, if it has been properly fermented, clear it by ascent. The cask must be kept full, and the rising particles taken off at the bung-hole. When fine (which may be expected in twenty-four hours) bottle it, cork it well, and in summer it will be ripe and fit to drink in a fortnight.
(From *The Family Receipt Book, etc.*, 1819.)

## GINGER BEER – 1832

1 cup ginger root
1 1/2 pails water
1 pint molasses
1 cup yeast

Time to completion: 1 day.

*Casks and leather bottles.*
From *The Vertuose Boke of Distillacyon*,
by Laurence Andrewe.

...Ginger beer is made in the following proportions: —One cup of ginger, one pint of molasses, one pail and a half of water, and a cup of lively yeast. Most people scald the ginger in half a pail of water, and then fill it up with a pailful of cold; but in very hot weather some people stir it up cold. Yeast must not be put in till it is cold, or nearly cold. If not to be drank within twenty-four hours, it must be bottled as soon as it works...
(From *The American Frugal Housewife*, by Mrs. Child, 1832, p. 86.)

## ENGLISH GINGER BEER – 1846

*The purpose of the cream of tartar in this recipe is to provide effervescence. According to Law's Grocer's Manual, for ginger beer of this type "two per cent of alcohol is the strict legal limit."* [1]

1 1/2 ounces ginger      1 lb. brown sugar or white sugar
1 ounce cream of tartar      4 quarts water, boiling
2 lemons, sliced      1 cup yeast

Time to completion: 1 day *or* 2 weeks.

Take one ounce and a half of ginger, one ounce of cream tartar, one pound of brown sugar, four quarts of boiling water, and two fresh lemons, sliced. It should be wrought twenty-four hours, with two gills of good yeast, and then bottled. It improves by keeping several weeks, unless the weather is hot, and it is a delightful beverage. If made with loaf instead of brown sugar, the appearance and flavour are still finer.
(From *The Young Housekeeper's Friend, or A Guide to Domestic Economy and Comfort*, by Mrs. Cornelius, 1846.)

## GINGER BEER, SUPERIOR – 1857

3 pints yeast      10 lbs. sugar
1/2 lb. honey      9 gallons water
1 egg white, beaten      9 ounces lemon juice
1/2 ounce lemon essence      11 ounces ginger root, bruised

Time to completion: 4 days.

Ten pounds of sugar. Nine ounces of lemon juice. Half a pound of honey. Eleven ounces bruised ginger root. Nine gallons of water. Three pints of yeast. Boil the ginger half an hour in a gallon and a half of water, then add the rest of the water and the other ingredients, and strain it when cold, add the white of one egg beaten, and half an ounce of essence of lemon. Let it stand four days then bottle it, and it will keep good many months.
(From *Miss Beecher's Domestic Receipt-Book: Designed as a Supplement to her Traetise on Domestic Economy*, 1857.)

---

[1] Simon, p. 142.

## MUM – 1723

*Many of these older recipes call for an enormous amount of water to be boiled down by a third or more before the other ingredients are added. This may have been done in order to purify the water. If so, then a step has been omitted here: the boiled water should settle, and the clear water should be drawn off into another vessel to prevent redissolution of the precipitate. If your water source is clean, use 1/3 less water here and in similar recipes.*

| | |
|---|---|
| 32 gallons water | 5 eggs |
| 3 1/2 bushels malt | 1/2 ounce barberries |
| 1/2 bushel oatmeal | 1 1/2 ounces cardamom |
| 1/2 bushel beans, ground | |
| 1 1/2 lb. spruce cambium *or* 1/2 lb. spruce and birch buds | |

<u>1 handful each</u>: sassafras,[1] ginger root, walnut cambium, elecampane root, water-cress, grated horseradish root, betony, burnet, marjoram, mother of thyme, pennyroyal,[1] elder flowers, blessed thistle

Take thirty-two gallons of water, boil it till a third part is wasted, brew it according to Art with three Bushels and a half of Malt, half a Bushel of ground Beans, and half a Bushel of Oatmeal when you put it into your Cask do not fill it too full and when it begins to work, put in a pound and a half of the inner rind of Fir, half a pound of tops of Fir and Birch instead of the inward Rind. Our English Mum-makers use Sassafras and ginger, the Rind of Walnut Tree, Elecampane Root, Water Cresses, and Horse Radish root rasp'd, Betony, Burnet, Marjoram, Mother of Thyme, Pennyroyal of each a small handful, Elder-flowers a handful, of Blessed Thistle a handful, of Barberries bruised half an ounce, of Cardamums bruised an ounce and a half. All these ingredients are to be put in when the liquor has wrought a while and after they are in let it work over the Vessel as little as may be when it has done working. Fill up the cask and put into it five new-laid eggs not broken nor crack'd, stop it close and it will be fit to drink in two years.
(From *The Receipt Book of John Nott*, 1723.)

---

[1] CAUTION! (*See Appendix.*)

"...a way was found among them [*the Egyptians*] to help those who could not afford wine, namely, to drink that made from barley... Now Aristotle declares that men who have been intoxicated with wine fall down face foremost, whereas they who have drunk barley beer lie outstretched on their backs; for wine makes one top-heavy, but beer stupefies."[1]

✳✳✳

MAPLE BEER – 1846

| | |
|---|---|
| 4 gallons water | 1 tablespoon spruce essence |
| 1 quart maple syrup | 1 pint yeast |

Time to completion: 3 days

To four gallons of boiling water, add one quart of maple molasses, and a small table spoonful of essence of spruce. When it is about milk warm, add a pint of yeast; and when fermented, bottle it. In three days it is fit for use.
(From *The Young Housekeeper's Friend, etc.*, by Mrs. Cornelius, 1846.)

NETTLE BEER – 1925

| | |
|---|---|
| 5 gallons water | 1/2 peck nettles |
| 2 pounds sugar | 1 pint yeast *or* 5 yeast cakes |

One-half peck of nettles, 5 gallons of water, 2 pounds of sugar, 1 pint of yeast or 5 yeast cakes. Boil the nettles 15 minutes; strain, sweeten and add the yeast; then, let it stand 12 hours; skim and bottle.
(From *The Kitchen Guide*, by Catherine V. Ferns, 1925, p. 124.)

DANDELION BEER – 1925

| | |
|---|---|
| 3 lbs. sugar | 1/2 peck dandelion flowers |
| 5 gallons water | 1 pint yeast *or* 5 yeast cakes |

Made the same as nettle beer, but put in 3 pounds of sugar instead of 2 pounds of sugar. They are both good spring tonics. (*ibid.*, p. 125.)

---

[1] Athenaeus, Book I, p. 149.

XCIX　　　*Inſtrumento per le Api*

"*They delight in the clash and clang of bronze,*
*and collect together at its summons...*"

(Pliny, Book XI, section XXII, p. 475.)

# MEADS,

# HYDROMELS,

# &

# METHEGLINS

*******

"On every hand I'm found and prized by men,
Borne from the fertile glades and castled heights
And vales and hills. Daily the wings of bees
Carried me through the air, and with deft motion
Stored me beneath the low-crowned, sheltering roof.
Then in a cask men cherished me. But now
The old churl I tangle, and trip, at last o'erthrow
Flat on the ground. He that encounters me
And sets his will 'gainst my subduing might
Forthwith shall visit the earth upon his back!
If from his course so ill-advised he fails
To abstain, deprived of strength, yet strong in speech,
He's reft of all his power o'er hand or foot,
His mind dethroned. Now find out what I'm called,
Who bind again the freeman to the soil,
Stupid from many a fall, in broad daylight!"
(*The Mead*, a riddle from the Exeter Book.)

"*Of Meade*: Meade is made of honny & water boyled both togyther; yf it be fyred and pure, it preserveth helth; but it is not good for them the whiche have the Ilyache or the Colycke."

"*Of Metheglyn*: Metheglyn is made of honny and water, & herbes, boyled and sodden togyther: yf it be fyred and stale, it is better in the regyment of helth than meade."[1]

✳✳✳

# 260  TO MAKE MEAD – c. 1550 to 1625

*As you will see in most of the following recipes, this distinction between meads and metheglins has been blurred, if indeed it was ever truly observed.*

| | |
|---|---|
| 8 or 9 lbs. raisins | 1/2 ounce whole nutmegs |
| 1/4 ounce whole cloves | 1/2 pint rosewater |
| 5 or 6 gallons water | 2 quarts honey |
| turnsole[2] | musk *or* ambergris |
| cinnamon sticks | 2 lemons *or* the peels of 2 lemons |

Take 8 or 9 pound of raysons of yᵉ sun, or els yᵉ best maligoe [*Malaga raisins*], & beat them. & take halfe an ounce of nutmegg, a quarter of an ounce of cloves, & one penny worth of cinnamon. beat & mix all these together. If yᵉ weather be hot, put in 2 leamons, If not, yᵉ pills of 2. & put to it 5 or 6 gallons of spring & 2 quarts of honey. then stir it 4 dayes together. & when it gathers to yᵉ top, then strayne out halfe yᵉ tubfull, & yᵉ other halfe, culler with turnesell strayned into it. & perfume it with muske or ambergreece & halfe a pinte of rosewater. & then bottle it up. yᵉ bottles you drink soon, fill not too full, but If you would keep them long, fill them full.
(From *Martha Washington's Booke of Cookery*, c. 1550 to 1625, ed. by Karen Hess.)

---

[1] Andrew Borde, *The Regyment, or a Dyetary of Helth*, 1542.

[2] CAUTION! (*See Appendix.*)

# # 261 TO MAKE MEAD – c. 1550 to 1625

| | |
|---|---|
| 1 quart honey | 1 sprig hyssop |
| 7 quarts water | yeast |
| bay leaves | 1 sprig rosemary |

Time to completion: 2 months.

Take a quart of honey & 7 quarts of water; of bay, rosemary, & hyssope, of each a sprigg. mix them together & boyle them halfe an houre, & then let it stand till it be clear. then put it up in a pot with a tap, & set new yeast on it, & let it worke untill it be clear, then bottle it up & let it be two moneths ould before you drink it. it may be drunk before, but ye keeping it soe long makes it brisker. (*ibid.*)

# # 6 A WEAKER, BUT VERY PLEASANT, MEATHE – 1669

| | |
|---|---|
| 1 quart honey | 6 quarts water |
| 1 egg | wine "mother" (yeast) |

Time to completion: 3 or 4 months.

To every quart of Honey take six of water; boil it till 1/3 be consumed, skiming it well all the while. Then pour it into an open Fat [*vat*], and let it cool. When the heat is well slakened, break into a Bowl-full of this warm Liquor, a New-laid-egge, beating the yolk and white well with it; then put it into the Fat to all the rest of the Liquor, and stir it well together, and it will become very clear. Then pour it into a fit very clean Barrel, and put to it some Mother of Wine, that is in it's best fermentation or working, and this will make the Liquor work also. This will be ready to drink in three or four Months, or sooner. (From *The Closet ...Opened*, 1669.)

# # 21 STRONG MEAD – 1669

| | |
|---|---|
| 1 part honey | 4 parts water |
| egg whites | |

Take one Measure of honey, and dissolve it in four of water, beating it long up and down with clean Woodden ladels. The next day boil it gently, scumming it all the while till no more scum riseth; and if you will clarifie the Liquor with a few beaten whites of Eggs, it will be the clearer. The rule of it's being boiled enough is, when it yieldeth no more scum, and beareth an Egge, so that the breadth of a groat is out of the water. Then pour it out of the Kettle into woodden vessels, and let it remain there till it be almost cold. Then Tun it into a vessel, where Sack hath been. (*ibid.*)

*MEADS*

"I observe that Meath requireth some strong Herbs to make it quick and smart upon the Palate; as Rose-mary, Bay-leaves, Sage, Thyme, Marjoram, Winter-savory, and such like, which would be too strong and bitter in Ale or Beer."[1]

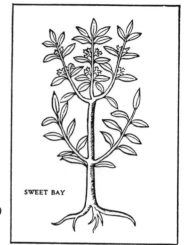

SWEET BAY

## # 4  MR. CORSELLISES ANTWERP MEATH – 1669

4 Holland pints water                    2 lbs. honey

To make good Meath, good white and thick Marsilian or Provence-honey is best; and of that, to four Holland Pints (the Holland Pint is very little bigger then the English Wine-pint:) of Water, you must put two pound of Honey; The Honey must be stirred in Water, till it be all melted; If it be stirred about in warm water, it will melt so much the sooner.[2]

When all is dissolved, it must be so strong that an Egge may swim in it with the end upwards.  And if it be too sweet or too strong, because there is too much Honey; then you must put more water to it; yet so, that, as above, an Hens Egge may swim with the point upwards:  And then that newly added water must be likewise well stirred about, so that it may be mingled all alike.  If the Eggs sink (which is a token that there is not honey enough) then you must put more Honey to it, and stir about, till it be all dissolved, and the Eggs swim, as abovesaid.  This being done, it must be hanged over the fire, and as it beginneth to seeth, the scum, that doth arise upon it, both before and after, must be clean skimed off.  When it is first set upon the fire, you must measure it first with a stick, how deep the Kettel is, or how much Liquor there be in it; and then it must boil so long, till one third part of it be boiled away.  When it is thus boiled, it must be poured out into a Cooler, or open vessel, before it be tunned in the Barrel; but the Bung-hole must be left open, that it may have vent.  A vessel, which hath served for Sack is best.

(From *The Closet of the Eminently Learned Sir Kenelme Digby Kt. Opened,* 1669.)

---

[1] Digby, #71.

[2] Note – A good many of our authors seem to have forgotten this point, and consequently they spend an inordinate amount of time dissolving honey in *cold* water. (*See note p. 257.*)

# #5 TO MAKE EXCELLENT MEATHE – 1669

1 quart honey                        4 quarts water
1 lb. raisins

Time to completion: 10 to 11 months.

To every quart of Honey, take four quarts of water. Put your water in a clean Kettle over the fire, and with a stick take the just measure, how high the water cometh, making a notch, where the superficies toucheth the stick. As soon as the water is warm, put in your Honey, and let it boil, skiming it always, till it be very clean; Then put to every Gallon of water, one pound of the best Blew-raisins of the Sun, first clean picked from the stalks, and clean washed. Let them remain in the boiling Liquor, till they be throughly swollen and soft; Then take them out, and put them into a Hair-bag, and strain all the juice and pulp and substance from them in an Apothecaries Press; which put back into your liquor, and let it boil, till it be consumed just to the notch you took at first, for the measure of your water alone. Then let your Liquor run through a Hair-strainer into an empty Woodden-fat,[1] which must stand endwise, with the head of the upper-end out; and there let it remain till the next day, that the liquor be quite cold. Then Tun it up into a good Barrel, not filled quite full, but within three or four fingers breadth; (where Sack hath been, is the best) and let the bung remain open for six weeks with a double bolter-cloth lying upon it, to keep out any foulness from falling in.[2] Then stop it up close, and drink not of it till after nine months...
(From *The Closet ...Opened*, 1669.)

---

[1] vat.

[2] Nowadays we use airlocks for this purpose.

## # 7  AN EXCELLENT WHITE MEATHE – 1669

| | |
|---|---|
| 1 gallon honey | 4 gallons water |
| cinnamon sticks | cloves |
| ginger root | mace blades |
| lemon peel | 1 slice of toast spread with yeast |

Time to completion:  2 or 3 months to 1 year.

Take one Gallon of Honey, and four of water; Boil and scum them till there rise no more scum; then put in your Spice a little bruised, which is most of Cinnamon, a little Ginger, a little Mace, and a very little Cloves. Boil it with the Spice in it, till it bear an Egge. Then take it from the fire, and let it Cool in a Woodden vessel, till it be but lukewarm; which this quantity will be in four or five or six hours. Then put into it a hot tost of White-bread, spread over on both sides, pretty thick with fresh barm; that will make it presently work. Let it work twelve hours, close covered with Cloves[1] [*sic*]. Then Tun it into a Runlet wherein Sack hath been, that is somewhat too big for that quantity of Liquor; for example, that it fill it not by a Gallon; You may then put a little Limon-pill in with it. After it hath remained in the vessel a week or ten days, draw it into Bottles. You may begin to drink it after two or three Months: But it will be better after a year. It will be very spritely and quick and pleasant and pure white. (From *The Closet ...Opened*, 1669.)

## # 30  SIR WILLIAM PASTON'S MEATHE – 1669

| | |
|---|---|
| 10 gallons water | 10 pints honey |
| yeast | lemon peel |
| | <u>1 handful each</u>:  rosemary, bay leaves. |

Time to completion:  13 days.

Take ten Gallons of Spring-water, and put therein ten Pints of the best honey. Let this boil half an hour, and scum it very well; then put in one handful of Rosemary, and as much of Bayleaves; with a little Limon-peel. Boil this half an hour longer, then take it off the fire, and put it into a clean Tub; and when it is cool, work it up with yest, as you do Beer. When it is wrought, put it into your vessel, and stop it very close. Within three days you may Bottle it, and in ten days after it will be fit to drink. (*ibid.*)

---

[1] This should probably read "close covered with <u>cloths</u>," not "cloves."

# #10  MR. WEBBES MEATH – 1669

*The following is really four recipes in one. These have been separated and numbered for your convenience.*

## [1 – THE KING'S MEATHE]

| | |
|---|---|
| 1+ hogshead water | 2 ounce ginger, sliced |
| 2 ounces hops | 1 ounce stick cinnamon |
| 1 part honey to 6 parts water | *optional*: cloves, mace. |
| 1/2 handful sweetbrier leaves | |

<u>1/2 handful total</u>: rosemary, thyme, sweet marjoram, 1 mint sprig, mixed.

Time to completion: 3 or 4 months.

Master Webbe, who maketh the Kings Meathe, ordereth it thus. Take as much of Hyde-park water as will make a Hogshead of Meathe: Boil in it about two Ounces of the best Hopp's for about half an hour. By that time, the water will have drawn out the strength of the Hopp's. Then skim them clean off, and all the froth, or whatever riseth of the water. Then dissolve in it warm, about one part of Honey to six of water: Lave and beat it, till all the Honey be perfectly dissolved; Then boil it, beginning gently, till all the scum be risen, and scummed away. It must boil in all about two hours. Half an hour, before you end your boiling, put into it some Rosemary-tops, Thyme, Sweet-marjorame, one Sprig of Minth, in all about half a handful, and as much Sweet-bryar-leaves as all these; in all, about a handful of herbs, and two Ounces of sliced Ginger, and one Ounce of bruised Cinamon. He did use to put in a few Cloves and Mace; But the King did not care for them. Let all these boil about half an hour, then scum them clean away; and presently let the Liquor run through a strainer-cloth into a Kiver of wood, to cool and settle. When you see it is very clear and settled, lade out the Liquor into another Kiver, carefully, not to raise the settlings from the bottom. As soon as you see any dregs begin to rise, stay your hand, and let it remain unstirred, till all be settled down. Then lade out the Liquor again, as before; and if need be, change it again into another Kiver: all which is done to the end no dregs may go along with the Liquor in tunning it into the vessel. When it is cold and perfect clear, tun it into a Cask, that hath been used for Sack, and stop it up close, having an eye to give it a little vent, if it should work. If it cast out any foul Liquor in working, fill it up always presently with some of the same liquor, that you have kept in bottles for that end. When it hath wrought, and is well settled (which may be in about two months or ten weeks) draw it into Glass-bottles, as long as it comes clear; and it will be ready to drink in a Month or two: but will keep much longer, if you have occasion: and no dregs will be in the bottom of the bottle.

[2]

| | |
|---|---|
| 1+ hogshead water | 1/2 lb. hops |
| 1 part honey to 6 parts water | 1 handful sweetbrier leaves |
| 6 ounces spices | |

1 handful total: rosemary, thyme, sweet marjoram, 1 mint sprig.

Time to completion: 1 to 2 years.

He since told me, that to this Proportion of Honey and water, to make a Hogshead of Meathe, you should boil half a pound of Hopps in the water, and two good handfuls of Herbs; and six Ounces of Spice of all sorts: All which will be mellowed and rotted away quite, (as well as the lushiousness of the Honey) in the space of a year or two. For this is to be kept so long before it be drunk.

[3]

same as [1] above                    yeast *or* 4 egg yolks plus 1/2 pint wheat flour

If you would have it sooner ready to drink, you may work it with a little yeast, when it is almost cold in the Kiver: and Tun it up as soon as it begins to work, doing afterwards as is said before; but leaving a little vent to purge by, till it have done working. Or in stead of yeast, you may take the yolks of four New-laid-eggs, and almost half a pint of fine Wheat-flower, and some of the Liquor you have made: beat them well together, then put them to the Liquor in the Cask, and stop it up close, till you see it needful, to give it a little vent.

Note, that yeast of good Beer, is better then that of Ale.

[4]

| | |
|---|---|
| 43 gallons water | 3 ounces ginger |
| 42 lbs. Norfolk honey | 1 1/2 ounces cinnamon |
| 1 handful hops | 5 whole nutmegs |
| 3 egg yolks | 1 spoonful white flour |
| 1/2 pint yeast | 7 or 8 small parsley roots |

*optional*: 1/2 ounce cloves.

Unspecified amounts of: rosemary, thyme, winter-savory, sweet-marjoram, sweetbrier leaves.

Time to completion: 3 weeks.

The first of Septemb. 1663. Mr. Webb came to my House to make some for Me. He took fourty three Gallons of water, and fourty two pounds of Norfolk honey. As soon as the water boiled, He put into it a slight handful of Hops; which after it had boiled a little above a quarter of an hour, he skimed off; then put in the honey to the boyling water, and presently a white scum rose, which he skimed off still as it rose;

which skiming was ended in little above a quarter of an hour more. Then he put in his herbs and spices, which were these: Rose-mary, Thyme, Winter-savory, Sweet-marjoram, Sweet-bryar-leaves, seven or eight little Parsley-roots: There was most of the Savoury, and least of the Eglantine, three Ounces of Ginger, one Ounce and a half of Cinnamon, five Nutmegs (half an Ounce of Cloves he would have added, but did not,) And these boiled an hour and a quarter longer; in all from the first beginning to boil, somewhat less then two hours: Then he presently laded it out of the Copper into Coolers, letting it run through a Hair-sieve: And set the Coolers shelving (tilted up) that the Liquor might afterwards run the more quietly out of them. After the Liquor had stood so about two hours, he poured or laded out of some of the Coolers very gently, that the dregs might not rise, into other Coolers. And about a pint of very thick dregs remained last in the bottom of every Cooler. That which ran out, was very clear: After two hours more settling, (in a shelving situation,) He poured it out again into other Coolers; and then very little dregs (or scarce any in some of the Coolers) did remain. When the Liquor was even almost cold, He took the yolks of three New-laid-eggs, a spoonful of fine white flower, and about half a pint of new fresh barm of good strong Beer (you must have care that your barm be very white and clean, not sullied and foul, as is usual among slovenly Brewers in London). Beat this very well together, with a little of the Liquor in a skiming dish, till you see it well incorporated, and that it beginneth to work. Then put it to a pailful (of about two Gallons and a half) of the Liquor, and mingle it well therewith. Then leave the skiming dish reversed floating in the middle of the Liquor, and so the yest will work up into and under the hollow of the dish, and grow out round about the sides without. He left this well and thick covered all night, from about eleven a clock at night; And the next morning, finding it had wrought very well, He mingled what was in the Pail with the whole proportion of the Liquor, and so Tunned it up into a Sack-cask.[1] I am not satisfied, whether he did not put a spoonful of fine white good Mustard into his Barm, before he brought it hither, (for he took a pretext to look out some pure clean white barm) but he protested, there was nothing mingled with the barm, yet I am in doubt. He confessed to me that in making of Sider, He put's in half as much Mustard as Barm; but never in Meathe. The fourth of September in the morning, he Bottled up into Quart-bottles the two lesser Rundlets of this Meathe (for he did Tun the whole quantity into one large Rundlet, and two little ones) whereof the one contained thirty Bottles; and the other twenty two. There remained but little settling or dregs in the Bottom's of the Barrels, but some there was. The Bottles were set into a cool Cellar, and He said they would be ready to drink in three weeks. The Proportion of Herbs and Spices is this; That there be so much as to drown the luscious sweetness of the Honey; but not so much as to taste of herbs or spice, when you drink the Meathe. But that the sweetnes [sic] of the honey may kill their

---

[1] Many of these recipes for mead call for the liquid to be fermented in a Sack cask, a wooden cask which has been used for storing *Sack*, a Spanish wine. You may wish to add a small amount of Sack to the liquid in order to simulate the flavor of this type of mead.

taste: And so the Meathe have a pleasant taste, but not of herbs, nor spice, nor honey. And therefore you put more or less according to the time you will drink it in. For a great deal will be mellowed away in a year, that would be ungratefully strong in three months. And the honey that will make it keep a year or two, will require a triple proportion of spice and herbs. He commends Parsley roots to be in greatest quantity, boiled whole, if young; but quarterred and pithed, if great and old. (From *The Closet ...Opened*, 1669.)

# # 11 MY OWN CONSIDERATIONS FOR MAKING OF MEATHE – 1669

*Read this recipe carefully before beginning; apart from being two recipes in one, the ingredients for the first part are given in a very confusing manner. The numbers in brackets have been added to separate the recipes.*

[1]
16 gallons water

1 gallon honey per 3 gallons flavored water
*Optional*: ale yeast, cardamom seeds, mint.

To every 16 gallons water take:

| | |
|---|---|
| 5 handfuls scabious | 2 handfuls bay leaves |
| 5 handfuls liverwort | 4 handfuls lemon balm |
| 4 handfuls rosemary | 1 handful thyme |
| 1 handful sweet marjoram | 5 eringo roots, split |
| 10 handfuls sweetbrier leaves | |

Also make a spice bag containing: two parts ginger root; one part cinnamon sticks; one part cloves; one part whole nutmegs.

Boil what quantity of Spring-water you please, three or four walms, and then let it set the twenty four hours, and pour the clear from the settling. Take sixteen Gallons of the clear, and boil in it ten handfuls of Eglantine-leaves, five of Liverwort, five of Scabious, four of Baulm, four of Rosemary; two of Bayleaves; one of Thyme, and one of Sweet-marjoram, and five Eringo-roots splitted. When the water hath drawn out the vertue of the herbs (which it will do in half an hours boiling,) let it run through a strainer or sieve, and let it settle so, that you may pour the clear from the Dregs. To every three Gallons of the Clear, take one of Honey, and with clean Arms stripped up, lade it for two or three hours, to dissolve the honey in the water; lade it twice or thrice that day. The next day boil it very gently to make the scum rise, and scum it all the while, and now and then pour to it a ladle full of cold water, which will make the scum rise more: when it is very clear from scum, you may boil it the more strongly, till it bear an Egge very high that the breadth of a groat be out of the water, and that it boil high with great walms in the middle of the Kettle: which boiling with great Bubbles in the middle is a sign it is boiled to it's height. Then let it cool till it be Lukewarm, at which time put some Ale yest into it, to make it work, as you would do Ale. And then put it up into a fit Barrel first seasoned with some good sweet White-wine (as Canary-sack) and keep the bung open, till it have done working, filling it up with some such honey-drink warmed, as you find it sink down by working over. When it hath almost done working, put into it a bag of thin stuff (such as Bakers use to bolt in) fastened by a Cord at the bung, containing two parts of Ginger-sliced, and one apiece of Cinamon, Cloves and Nutmegs, with a Pebble-stone in it to make it sink; And stop it up close for six Months or a year, and then you may draw it into bottles. If you like Cardamon-seeds, you may adde some of them to the spices. Some do like Mint exceedingly to be added to the other herbs. Where no yeast is to be had, The Liquor will work if you set it some days in the hot Sun (with a cover, like the roof of a house over it, to keep wet out, if it chance to rain) but then you must have great care, to fill it up, as it consumeth, and to stop it close a little before it hath done working, and to set it then presently in a Cool Cellar. I am told that the Leaven of bread will make it work as well as yest, but I have not tryed it.[1] If you will not have it so strong, it will be much sooner ready to drink; As if you take six parts of water to one of Honey. Some do like the drink better without either herbs or spices, and it will be much the whiter. If you will have it stronger, put but four Gallons and a half of water to one of honey.

You may use what Herbs or Roots you please, either for their tast or vertue, after the manner here set down.

If you make it work with yeast, you must have great care, to draw it into bottles soon after it hath done working, as after a fortnight or three weeks. For that will make it soon grow stale, and it will thence grow sower and dead before you are aware. But if it work singly of itself, and by the help of the Sun without admixtion of either Leaven or Yeast, it may be kept long in the Barrel, so it be filled up to the top, and kept very close stopp'd. [*Continued on next page.*]

---

[1] Bread yeast works just fine for mead (indeed, for centuries brewers and bakers supplied each other with yeast), but the flavor will be rougher than that of mead brewed using specialized wine or beer yeasts. Bread yeast works very quickly; two to three weeks fermentation is sufficient. The mead should then be bottled in champagne bottles (wine bottle glass is too thin and may break) and stored in a cool cellar or refrigerator. Handle the bottles carefully – the corks are likely to pop out, especially if the weather is warm. Plan to drink this mead within two weeks of its being bottled.

[2]

| | |
|---|---|
| 3 parts water | 1 part honey |

*optional*: yeast
1 or 2 handfuls trimmed clove gilliflowers per gallon of liquid
<u>distilled alcohols flavored with</u>: clove gilliflowers; ginger; rosemary; cinnamon.

I conceive it will be exceeding good thus: when you have a strong Honey-liquor of three parts of water to one of Honey, well-boiled and scummed, put into it Lukewarm, or better (as soon as you take it from the fire) some Clove-gilly-flowers, first wiped, and all the whites clipped off, one good handful or two to every Gallon of Liquor. Let these infuse 30 or 40 hours. Then strain it from the flowers, and either work it with yeast, or set it in the Sun to work; when it hath almost done working, put into it a bag of like Gilly-flowers (and if they are duly dried, I think they are the better) hanging it in at the bung. And if you will put into it some spirit of wine, that hath drawn a high Tincture from Clove-gillyflowers (dried I conceive is best) and some other that hath done the like from flowers and tops of Rosemary, and some that hath done the like from Cinnamon and Ginger, I believe it will be much the nobler, and last the longer.

I conceive, that bitter and strong herbs, as Rosemary, Bayes, Sweet-marjoram, Thyme, and the like, do conserve Meathe the better and longer, being as it were in stead of hops. But neither must they, no more than Clove-gillyflowers, be too much boiled: For the Volatil pure Spirit flies away very quickly. Therefore rather infuse them. Beware of infusing Gillyflower in any vessel of Metal, (excepting silver:) For all Metals will spoil and dead their colour. Glased earth is best.

(From *The Closet of the Eminently Learned Sir Kenelme Digby Kt. Opened*, 1669.)


# 42  A RECEIPT FOR MEATHE – 1669

| | |
|---|---|
| 7 quarts water | 2 quarts honey |
| 3 or 4 parsley roots | cloves |
| 3 or 4 fennel roots | 1/2 pint ale yeast |

Time to completion: 14 days.

To seven quarts of water, take two quarts of honey, and mix it well together; then set it on the fire to boil, and take three or four Parsley-roots, and as many Fennel-roots, and shave them clean, and slice them, and put them into the Liquor, and boil altogether, and skim it very well all the while it is a boyling; and when there will no more scum rise, then it is boiled enough: but be careful that none of the scum do boil into it. Then take it off, and let it cool till the next day. Then put it up in a close vessel, and put thereto half a pint of new good barm, and a very few Cloves pounded and put in a Linnen-cloth, and tie it in the vessel, and stop it up close; and within a fortnight, it will be ready to drink: but if it stay longer, it will be the better. (*ibid.*)

# 22  A RECEIPT FOR MAKING OF MEATH – 1669

1 quart honey
1/2 spoonful ale yeast
1 stick cinnamon
1 sprig rosemary
1 whole nutmeg

1 gallon water
6 cloves
2 egg whites
2 or 3 sprigs spikenard *or* spike lavender
ginger root

<u>1 handful total</u>:  strawberry and violet leaves, mixed.

Time to completion:  14 days.

Take a quart of honey, and mix it with a Gallon of Fountain-water, and work it well four days together, four times a day; The fifth day put it over the fire, and let it boil an hour, and scum it well.  Then take the whites of two Eggs, and beat them to a froth, and put it into the Liquor; stirring it well, till the whites of Eggs have raised a froth of Scum; then take it off, scumming the liquor clean.  Then take a handful of Strawberry-leaves and Violet-leaves together, with a little Sprig of Rosemary, and two or three little Sprigs of Spike; and so boil it again (with these herbs in it) a quarter of an hour.  Then take it off the fire, and when it is cold, put it into a little barrel, and put into it half a spoonful of Ale-yest, and let it work; which done, take one Nutmeg sliced, and twice as much Ginger sliced, six Cloves bruised, and a little stick of Cinamon, and sow these Spices in a little bag, and stop it well; and it will be fit for use within a fortnight, and will last half a year.  If you will have your Metheglin stronger, put into it a greater quantity of honey.
(From *The Closet ...Opened*, 1669.)

# 31  ANOTHER PLEASANT MEATHE OF SIR WILLIAM PASTON'S – 1669

1 gallon water
10 sprigs sweet marjoram

1 quart honey
5 bay leaves

Time to completion:  10 days.

To a Gallon of water put a quart of honey, about ten sprigs of Sweet-Majoram; half so many tops of Bays.  Boil these very well together, and when it is cold, bottle it up.  It will be ten days before it be ready to drink.  (*ibid.*)

# #27 MY LADY MORICES MEATH – 1669

2 or 3 gallons water

ginger root

2 spoonsful ale yeast per 10 gallons liquid

1 handful total: angelica, balm, borage and rosemary.

1 part honey to 3 parts liquid

1 porrengerful cloves (about 1/2 cup)

Time to completion: 1 to 2 years.

Boil first your water with your herbs. Those she likes best, are, Angelica, Balm, Borage, and a little Rosemary (not half so much as of any of the rest) a handful of all together, to two or 3 Gallons of water. After about half an hours boiling, let the water run through a strainer (to sever the herbs from it) into Woodden or earthen vessels, and let it cool and settle. To three parts of the clear, put one or more of honey, and boil it till it bear an Egge, leaving as broad as a shilling out of the water, skiming it very well. Then power [*pour*] it out into vessels, as before; and next day, when it is almost quite cold, power it into a Sack-cask, wherein you have first put a little fresh Ale-yest, about two spoonfuls to ten Gallons. Hang it in a bag with a little sliced Ginger, but almost a Porengerfull of Cloves. Cover the bung lightly, till it have done working; then stop it up close. You may tap and draw it a year or two after. It is excellent good.
(From *The Closet ...Opened*, 1669.)

# #43 MY LORD GORGE HIS MEATHE – 1669

water

1 sprig bay leaves

assorted spices

honey

2 or 3 sprigs sage

1 handful each: rosemary; sweetbrier; betony; strawberry leaves; wall-flowers; borage; and bugloss.

Time to completion: 3 or 4 months.

Take a sufficient quantity of Rain-water, and boil in it the tops of Rose-mary, Eglantine, Betony, Strawberry-leaves, Wall-flowers, Borage and Bugloss, of each one handful; one sprig of Bays; and two or three of Sage. Then take it off the fire, and put a whole raw Egge into it, and pour so much honey to it, till the Egge rise up to the top; then boil it again, skiming it very well, and so let it cool. Then Tun it up, and put Barm to it, that it may ferment well. Then stop it up, and hang in it such spices, as you like best. It will not be right to drink under three or four moneths. (*ibid.*)

# # 14 MY LADY GOWERS WHITE MEATHE USED AT SALISBURY – 1669

4 gallons water            3 or 4 egg whites
1 gallon honey             ale yeast
*optional*: rosemary, sweet marjoram, thyme, sweetbrier hips, ginger root, whole nutmegs.

Take to four Gallons of water, one Gallon of Virgin-honey; let the water be warm before you put in the honey; and then put in the whites of 3 or 4 Eggs well beaten, to make the scum rise. When the honey is throughly melted and ready to boil, put in an Egge with the shell softly; and when the Egge riseth above the water, to the bigness of a groat in sight, it is strong enough of the honey. The Egge will quickly be hard, and so will not rise; Therefore you must put in another, if the first do not rise to your sight; you must put in more water and honey proportionable to the first, because of wasting away in the boiling. It must boil near an hour. You may, if you please, boil in it, a little bundle of Rosemary, Sweet-marjoram, and Thyme; and when it tasteth to your liking, take it forth again. Many do put Sweet-bryar berries in it, which is held very good. When your Meath is boiled enough take it off the fire, and put it into a Kiver; when it is blood-warm, put in some Ale-barm, to make it work, and cover it close with a blancket in the working. The next morning tun it up, and if you please put in a bag with a little Ginger and a little Nutmeg bruised; and when it hath done working, stop it up close for a Moneth, and then Bottle it. (*ibid.*)

# # 32 ANOTHER WAY OF MAKING MEATH – 1669

4 gallons water            sweetbrier
ale yeast                raisins
1 gallon honey           sweet marjoram
mace                   cloves
lemon peel

*Norman beekeepers.*

Time to completion: 1 week.

Boil Sweet Bryar, Sweet Marjoram, Cloves and Mace in Spring-water, till the water taste of them. To four Gallons of water put one Gallon of honey, and boil it a little to skim and clarifie it. When you are ready to take it from the fire, put in a little Limon-peel, and pour it into a Woodden vessel, and let it stand till it is almost cold. Then put in some Ale-yest, and stir it altogether. So let it stand till next day. Then put a few stoned Raisins of the Sun into every bottle, and pour the Meath upon them. Stop the bottles close, and in a week the Meath will be ready to drink. (*ibid.*)

# 28 MY LADY MORICE HER
## SISTER MAKES HER'S THUS: – 1669

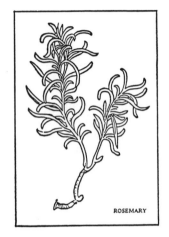

ROSEMARY

honey
10 gallons water
1 or 2 handfuls flour

<u>2 handfuls total</u>: sea-wormwood,[1]
rosemary, and sage, mixed.

Time to completion: 1 or 2 years.

Dissolve your honey in the water till it bear an Egge higher or lower, according to the strength you will have it of.    Then put into it some Sea-wormwood and a little Rosemary, and a little Sage; about too good handfuls of all together, to ten Gallons. When it hath boiled enough to take the vertue of the herbs, skim them out, and strew a handful or two of fine Wheat-flower upon the boyling Liquor.

This will draw all the dregs to it, and swim at the top, so that you may skim all off together.    And this she holdeth the best way of clarifying the Liquor, and making it look pale.    Then pour it into vessels as above to cool. Let it stand three days; then Tun it up into a Sack cask without yest or Spice, and keep it stopped till it work. Then let it be open, till it have done working, filling it up still with other honey-drink.   Then stop it up close for a year or two.    You may at first stop it so, that the strong working may throw out the stopple, and yet keep it close, till it work strongly.   She saith, that such a small proportion of wormwood giveth it a fine quick tast, and a pale colour with an eye of green.   The wormwood must not be so much, as to discern any the least bitterness in the taste; but that the composition of it with the honey may give a quickness.   The Rosemary and Sage must be a great deal less then the Wormwood.   Sometimes she stoppeth it up close as soon as she hath Tunned it, and lets it remain so for three moneths.    Then pierce it and draw it into bottles, which stop well, and tie down the stoppels. This will keep so a long time.   She useth this way most.   It makes the Mead drink exceeding quick and pleasant.   When you pierce the Cask, it will flie out with exceeding force, and be ready to throw out the stopper and spigot.
(From *The Closet ...Opened*, 1669.)

---

[1] CAUTION! (*See Appendix.*)

# # 29  TO MAKE WHITE MEATH – 1669

| | |
|---|---|
| 1 gallon water | 1 quart honey |
| 8 or 9 egg whites | cloves |
| mace blades | cinnamon sticks |
| whole nutmegs | shells of 6 eggs (for fining) |
| 1 spoonful yeast | 1 spoonful flour |

<u>1 handful each</u>:  rosemary, thyme, sweetbrier, pennyroyal,[1] bay leaves.

Take Rosemary, Thyme, Sweet-bryar, Penyroyal, Bayes, of each one handful; steep them 24 hours in a bowl of fair cold water covered close; next day boil them very well in another water, till the colour be very high; then take another water, and boil the same herbs in it, till it look green; and so boil them in several waters, till they do but just change the colour of the water. The first waters are thrown away.[2] The last water must stand 24 hours with the herbs in it. The Liquor being strained from them, you must put in as much fine honey till it will bear an Egge; you must work and labour the honey with the Liquor a whole day, till the honey be consumed; then let it stand a night a clearing. In the morning put your Liquor a boiling for a quarter of an hour, with the whites and shells of six Eggs. So strain it through a bag, and let it stand a day a cooling; so Tun it up, and put into the vessel in a Linnen bag, Cloves, Mace, Cinamon and Nutmegs bruised altogether. If you will have it to drink presently, take the whites of two or three Eggs, of barm a spoonful, and as much of Wheaten-flower. Then let it work before you stop it, afterwards stop it well with Clay and Salt. A quart of Honey to a Gallon of liquor, and so proportionably for these Herbs.
(From *The Closet ...Opened*, 1669.)

# # 57  A RECEIPT TO MAKE GOOD MEATH – 1669

| | |
|---|---|
| 1 gallon water | 1 quart honey |
| 2 whole nutmegs | yeast |
| 1 egg white | |

Take as many Gallons of water, as you intend to make of Meath; and to every Gallon put a quart of honey, and let it boil till it bear an Egg. To every Gallon you allow the white of an Egg, which white you must remove and break with your hands, and put into the Kettle, before you put it over the fire. Before it boileth, there will arise a skum, which must be taken off very clean, as it riseth. Put to every Gallon two Nutmegs sliced, and when it hath boiled enough, take it off, and set it a cooling in clean wort-vessels: And when it is as cold as wort, put in a little barm, and work it like Beer, and when it hath done working, stop it up, and let it stand two months.  (*ibid.*)

---

[1] CAUTION!  (*See Appendix.*)  [2] See note p. 61.

## # 33 SIR BAYNAM THROCKMORTON'S MEATHE – 1669

4 gallons water
2 or 3 spoonsful yeast

4 quarts honey
*optional*: ambergris.

<u>1/2 ounce each</u>: whole nutmegs, cloves, mace blades, ginger root.

Time to completion: 1 year.

Take four quarts of Honey, good measure; put to it four Gallons of water, let it stand all night, but stir it well, when you put it together. The next day boil it, and put to it Nutmegs, Cloves, Mace and Ginger, of each half an ounce. Let these boil with the honey and water till it will bear an Egge at the top without sinking; and then it is enough, if you see the Egge the breadth of a six-pence. The next day put it in your vessel, and put thereto two or three spoonfuls of barm; and when it hath done working, you may (if you like it) put in a little Amber-greece in a clout with a stone to it to make it sink. This should be kept a whole year before it be drunk; it will drink much the better, free from any tast of the honey, and then it will look as clear as Sack. Make it not till Michaelmas, and set it in a cool place. You may drink it a quarter old, but it will not taste so pleasant then, as when it is old. (*ibid.*)

## # 47 SIR JOHN ARUNDEL'S WHITE MEATH – 1669

3 + gallons honey
3 egg whites
*optional*: herbs.

12 gallons water
toast spread with yeast

Time to completion: 6 months.

Take three Gallons of Honey, and twelve Gallons of water: mix the honey and water very well together, till the honey is dissolved; so let it stand twelve hours. Then put in a New-laid-egg; if the Liquor beareth the Egg, that you see the breadth of a groat upon the Egg dry, you may set it over the fire: if it doth not bear the Egg, then you must adde a quart or three pints more [*honey*] to the rest; and then set it over the fire, and let it boil gently, till you have skimed it very clean, and clarified it, as you would do Suggar, with the whites of three New-laid-eggs. When it is thus made clear from all scum, let it boil a full hour or more, till the fourth part of it is wasted; then take it off the fire; and let it stand till the next day. Then put it into a vessel. When it hath been in the barrel five or six days, make a white tost, and dip it into new yeast, and put the tost into the barrel, and let it work. When it hath done working, stop it up very close. This keep three quarters of a year. You may drink it within half a year, if you please. You may adde in the boiling, of what herbs you like the taste, or what is Physical. (*ibid.*)

# #35 A RECEIPT FOR MAKING OF MEATH – 1669

| 100 gallons water | assorted spices |
| 20 to 25 gallons honey | toast spread with ale yeast |
| 2 handfuls hops | |

*optional*: 5 or 6 gallons raspberries *or* cherries; cardamom seeds; lemon peel; elderflowers.

Mistress Hebden telleth me, that the way of making Honey-drink in Russia is thus; Take for example, 100 Gallons of Spring water, boil it a little; then let it stand 24 hours to cool, and much sediment will fall to the bottom; from which pour the clear, and warm it, and put 20 or 25 Gallons of pure honey to it, and lade it a long time with a great woodden battle-dore, till it be well dissolved. The next day boil it gently, till you have skimed off all the scum that will rise, and that it beareth an Egge boyant. And in this Liquor you must put, in the due time, a little quantity of Hops, about two handfuls, which must boil sufficiently in the Liquor. Put this into the cooling fat to cool two or three days. When it is about milk-warm, take white-bread and cut it into tosts, upon which, (when they are hot) spread moderately thick some fresh sweet Ale-yest; and cover the superficies of the Liquor with such tosts; Then cover the Tub or Fat [*vat*] with a double course sheet, and a blancket or two, which tye fast about it. This will make your Liquor work up highly. When you find it is near it's height of working, and that the Liquor is risen to the top of the Tub (of which it wanted 8 or 10 Inches at first,) Skim off the tosts and yest, and Tun it up in a hogshead: which stop close; but after 24 hours draw it into another barrel: for it will leave a great deal of sediment. It will work again in this second barrel. After other 24 hours draw it into another barrel, and then it will be clear and pale like White-wine. Stop it up close, hanging a bag of bruised spice in the bung; and after five or six months, it will be fit to drink. If you would have your Meath taste of Raspes, or Cherries (Morello, sharp Cherries, are the best) prepare the water first with them; by putting five or six Gallons of either of these fruits, or more, into this proportion of water; in which bruise them to have all their juyce: but strain the Liquor from the Grains or Seeds, or Stones. And then proceed with this tincted water, as is said above. You may make your Liquor as strong, as you like, of the fruit. Cardamon-seeds mingled with the suspended spices, adde much to the pleasantness of the drink. Limon-peel, as also Elderflowers.
(From *The Closet ...Opened*, 1669.)

## # 36 MY LADY BELLASSISES MEATH – 1669

water

honey

toast spread with yeast

1 to 2 lbs. raisins per gallon of honey

1 cardamom pod per bottle of liquor

Time to completion: 3 or 4 months.

The way of making is thus. She boileth the honey with Spring-water, as I do, till it be cleer scumed; then to every Gallon of Honey, put in a pound or two of good Raisins of the Sun; boil them well, and till the Liquor bear an Egge. Then pour it into a Cowl or Tub to cool. In about 24 hours it will be cool enough to put the yest to it, being onely Lukewarm: which do thus: spread yest upon a large hot tost, and lay it upon the top of the Liquor, and cover the Tub well, first with a sheet, then with coverlets, that it may work well. When it is wrought up to it's height, before it begin to sink, put it into your barrel, letting it run through a loose open strainer, to sever the Raisins and dregs from it. Stop it up close, and after it hath been thus eight or ten days, draw it into bottles, and into every bottle put a cod [*pod*] of Cardamoms, having first a little bruised them as they lie in the cod; and opening the cod a little, that the Liquor may search into it. Stop your bottles close, and after three or four moneths you may drink, and it will be very pleasant and quick, and look like white wine.

(From *The Closet ...Opened*, 1669.)

## # 46 TO MAKE MEATH – 1669

3 gallons water

2 cloves per bottle

lemon peels

1+ quart honey

yeast

Take three Gallons of water, a quart of Honey; if it be not strong enough, you may adde more. Boil it apace an hour, and scum it very clean. Then take it off, and set it a working at such heat as you set Beer, with good yest. Then put it in a Runlet, and at three days end, draw it out in stone-bottles; into everyone put a piece of Limon-peel and two Cloves. It is only put into the Runlet, whilest it worketh, to avoid the breaking of the Bottles. (*ibid.*)

"The dryed rootes called *Orris* (as is ʃaid) is of much vʃe to make ʃweete powders, or other things to perfume apparrell or linnen. The iuice or decoction of the green roots doth procure both neezing to be ʃnuft vp into the noʃtrils, and vomiting very ʃtrongly being taken inwardly."[1]

✱✱✱

# #45 SEVERAL SORTS OF MEATH, SMALL AND STRONG – 1669

## 1. SMALL.

| | | |
|---|---|---|
| 10 gallons water | rosemary | sweetbrier |
| 5 quarts honey | lemon balm | burnet |
| cloves | ginger root | lemon peel |
| yeast | elder flowers | |

Take ten Gallons of water, and five quarts of honey, with a little Rosemary, more Sweet-bryar, some Balme, Burnet, Cloves, less Ginger, Limon Peel. Tun it with a little barm; let it remain a week in the barrel with a bag of Elder-flowers; then bottle it.

## 2. *Small.*

| | | |
|---|---|---|
| 10 quarts water | lemon balm | mint |
| 1 quart honey | ginger root | lemon peel |
| cloves | elder flowers | |
| yeast | | |

Take ten quarts of water, and one of honey, Balm a little; Minth, Cloves, Limon-peel, Elder-flowers, a little Ginger; wrought with a little yest, bottle it after a night working.

## 3. *Strong.*

| | | |
|---|---|---|
| 10 gallons water | borage | angelica |
| 13 quarts honey | bugloss | rosemary |
| 3 spoonsful yeast | sweetbrier | lemon balm |
| cloves | elder flowers | ginger root |

Take ten Gallons of water, thirteen quarts of honey, with Angelica, Borrage and Bugloss, Rosemary, Balm and Sweet-bryar; pour it into a barrel, upon three spoonfuls of yest; hang in a bag Cloves, Elder-flowers, and a little Ginger.

---

[1] Parkinson, p. 189.

4. *Very Strong.*

| 10 gallons water | sea wormwood[1] | sage |
| 4 gallons honey | rosemary | |

Take ten Gallons of Water, and four of honey, with Sea-worm-wood, a little Sage, Rosemary; put it in a barrel, after three days cooling. Put no yest to it. Stop it close, and bottle it after three or four months.

5. *Very Strong.*

| 10 gallons water | flour | angelica |
| 4 gallons honey | rosemary | bay leaves |
| lemon balm | cloves | elder flowers |
| ginger root | | |

To ten Gallons of water take four of honey. Clarifie it with flower; and put into it Angelica, Rosemary, Bayleaves, Balm. Barrel it without yest. Hang in a bag Cloves, Elder-flowers, a little Ginger.

6. *Very Strong.*

| 10 gallons water | lemon peel | elder flowers |
| 4 gallons honey | ginger root | cloves |
| orris root[2] | lily-of-the-valley[2] | |

*optional:* rosemary; betony; eyebright; wood sorrel;[1] sweetbrier; St. John's-wort.[1]

Take ten Gallons of water, and four of Honey. Boil nothing in it. Barrel it when cold, without yest. Hang in it a bag with Cloves, Elder-flowers, a little Ginger and Limon peel; which throw away, when it hath done working, and stop it close. You may make also strong and small by putting into it Orris-roots; or with Rose-mary, Betony, Eyebright and Wood-sorrel; or adding to it the tops of Hypericon with the flowers of it; Sweet-bryar, Lilly of the valley.
(From *The Closet ...Opened*, 1669.)

---

[1] CAUTION! (*See Appendix.*)

[2] CAUTION! Orris roots and Lily-of-the-valley are poisonous. Do not use them. (*See Appendix.*)

# #49  TO MAKE WHITE MEATH – 1669

| | |
|---|---|
| 6 gallons water | 6 quarts honey |
| 1/2 ounce whole nutmegs | 1/4 ounce mace blades |
| 1/4 ounce ginger root | |

<u>1 handful total</u>:  sweet marjoram, broad thyme, and sweetbrier.

Take six Gallons of water, and put in six quarts of honey, stirring it till the honey be throughly melted; then set it over the fire, and when it is ready to boil, skim it very clean. Then put in a quarter of ounce [*sic*] of Mace, so much Ginger, half an ounce of Nutmegs, Sweet-marjoram, Broad-thyme, and Sweet-bryar, of altogether a handful; and boil them well therein; Then set it by, till it be through cold, and then Barrel it up, and keep it till it be ripe.
(From *The Closet ...Opened*, 1669.)

# #52  A VERY GOOD MEATH – 1669

| | |
|---|---|
| 3 parts water | 1 part honey |
| 1/2 ounce whole nutmegs | assorted herbs |

*optional*:  yeast, pellitory of the wall, agrimony.[1]
<u>1 ounce each per 10 gallons water</u>:  ginger root; cinnamon sticks.

Put three parts of water to one of honey.  When the Honey is dissolved, it is to bear an Egge boyant.  Boil it and skim it perfectly clear.  You may boil in it Pellitory of the wall, Agrimony, or what herbs you please.  To every ten Gallons of water, take Ginger, Cinnamon, *ana*,[2] one Ounce, Nutmegs half an Ounce.  Divide this quantity (sliced and bruised) into two parts.  Boil the one in the Meath, severing it from the Liquor, when it is boiled, by running through a strainer; and hang the other parcel in the barrel by the bung in a bag with a bullet[3] in it.  When it is cold, Tun it.  And then you may work it with barm if you please; but it is most commended without.
(*ibid.*)

---

[1] CAUTION!  (*See Appendix*).

[2] *ana* (Latin) = use equal quantities of each.

[3] The bullet, most likely made of lead, was used as a weight, so that the spice bag would not float to the surface.  Use a clean pebble or glass marble if you wish to closely follow the original recipe.

# # 50  TO MAKE A MEATH GOOD FOR THE LIVER AND LUNGS – 1669

20 quarts water                     5 pints honey
coriander seeds                     cinnamon sticks

<u>4 ounces each roots of</u>: coltsfoot; fennel; fern;[1] licorice.

<u>2 ounces each roots of</u>: succory; wood sorrel; strawberry; bittersweet.[2]

<u>1 1/2 ounces each roots of</u>: scabious; elecampane.

<u>1 handful each</u>: alehoof; horehound; oak of Jerusalem; lungwort; liverwort; maidenhair; hart's-tongue.

<u>2 ounces each</u>: jujubes; raisins; currants.

Take of the Roots of Colts-foot, Fennel and Fearn [*sic*] each four Ounces. Of Succory-roots, Sorrel-roots, Strawberry-roots, Bitter-sweet-roots, each two Ounces, of Scabious-roots and Elecampane-roots each an Ounce and a half. Ground-ivy, Horehound, Oak of Jerusalem, Lung-wort, Liver-wort, Maiden-hair, Harts-tongue of each two good-handfulls. Licorish four Ounces. Jujubes, Raisins of the Sun and Currents, of each two Ounces; let the roots be sliced, and the herbs be broken a little with your hands; and boil all these in twenty quarts of fair running water, or, if you have it, in Rain water, with five Pints of good white honey, until one third part be boiled away; then pour the liquor through a jelly bag often upon a little Coriander-seeds, and Cinnamon; and when it runneth very clear, put it into Bottles well stopped, and set it cool for your use, and drink every morning a good draught of it, and at five in the afternoone. (*ibid.*)

1 *Capillus Veneris verus.*
True Maiden haire.

*Maidenhair fern.*
From Gerard's *Herball*, 1597.

---

[1] As maidenhair and hart's-tongue are called for specifically, the unnamed fern is probably a Spleen-wort, *Asplenium* species, which were used, of course, to cure ailments of the spleen.

[2] CAUTION! (*See Appendix.*) This is a reference to European Bittersweet, *Solanum Dulcamara* L., not the ornamental Climbing Bittersweet, *Celastrus scandens* L.

# #58 ANOTHER [*WAY*] TO MAKE MEATH – 1669

6 wine quarts water         1 quart honey
1/2 ounce whole nutmegs     pulp of 2 or 3 lemons
1 lemon peel              lemon juice

Time to completion: less than 1 month.

To every quart of honey allow six Wine-quarts of water; half an Ounce of Nutmegs, and the Peel of a Limon, and the meat of two or three, as you make the quantity. Boil these together, till the scum rise no more; It must stand till it be quite cold, and when you Tun it, you squeese into it the juyce of some Limons, and this will make it ripen quickly. It will be ready in less then a month.
(From *The Closet ...Opened*, 1669.)

# #63 ANOTHER WHITE MEATH – 1669

3 lbs. honey
1 gallon water
1/8 ounce ginger root
cloves
mace blades
agrimony[1]

*Hart's-tongue.*
From Gerard's
*Herball*, 1597.

Time to completion: 2 or 3 months.

Take three Pound of White-honey, or the best Hampshire-honey, and dissolve it in a Gallon of water, and then boil it; and when it beginneth first to boil, put into it half a quarter of an Ounce of Ginger a little bruised; and a very little Cloves and Mace bruised, and a small quantity of Agrimony. Let all this boil together a full hour, and keep it constantly skimmed, as long as any Scum will rise upon it. Then strain it forth into some clean Kiver or other vessel, and let stand a cooling; and when it is cold, let it stand, till it be all creamed over with a blackish cream, and that it make a kind of hissing noise; then put it up into your vessel, and in two or three months time it will be fit to drink.

    Look how much you intend to make, the same quantities must be allowed to every Gallon of water. (*ibid.*)

---

[1] CAUTION! (*See Appendix.*)

# #59 ANOTHER RECIPE – 1669

| | |
|---|---|
| 12 gallons water | 3 to 5 gallons honey |

<u>1 handful each</u>: muscovy; sweet marjoram; sweetbrier.
<u>1/4 ounce each</u>: mace blades; cloves; whole nutmegs; ginger root.

Time to completion: 4 years.

Take twelve Gallons of water, a handful of Muscovy (which is an herb, that smelleth like Musk), a handful of Sweet-Marjoram, and as much of Sweet-bryar. Boil all these in the water, till all the strength be out. Then take it off and strain it out, and being almost cold, sweeten it with honey very strong, more then to bear an Egg, (the meaning of this is, that when there is honey enough to bear an Egg, which will be done by one part of honey to three or four quarts of water: then you add to it a pretty deal of honey more, at least 1/4 or 1/3 of what you did put in at first to make it bear an Egg: then it is to be boiled and scummed: when it is thus strong, you may keep it four years before you drink it. But at the end of two years you may draw it out into bottles) just above it, else it will not keep very long: for the more honey the better. Then set it over the fire till it boils, and scum it very clean. Then take it from the fire, and let it stand, till it be cold: then put it into your vessel. Take Mace, Cloves, Nutmegs, Ginger, of each a quarter of an Ounce: beat them small, and hang them in your vessel (being stopped close) in a little bag.

Note, when any Meath or Metheglin grows hard or sower with keeping too long, dissolve in it a good quantity of fresh honey, to make it pleasantly Sweet; (but boil it no more, after it hath once fermented, as it did at the first Tunning) and with that it will ferment again, and become very good and pleasant and quick.
(From *The Closet ...Opened*, 1669.)

# #78 TO MAKE SMALL WHITE MEATH – 1669

| | |
|---|---|
| 6 quarts honey | 16 gallons water |

orris roots[1]

Take of the best white honey six quarts; of Spring-water sixteen Gallons; set it on a gentle fire at first, tell [sic] it is melted, and clean skimmed; then make it boil apace, until the third part be consumed. Then take it from the fire, and put it in a cooler, and when it is cold, Tun it up, and let it stand eight months, before you drink it. When you take it from the fire, slice in three Orris-roots, and let it remain in the Liquor, when you Tun it up. (*ibid.*)

---

[1] CAUTION! <u>Do not</u> add orris roots; they are poisonous. (*See Appendix.*)

# # 62  MY LORD HERBERT'S MEATH – 1669

10 gallons water
10 quarts honey
yeast
15 handfuls rosemary
15 ounces whole nutmegs
15 ounces cinnamon sticks
5 ounces cloves
10 ounces mace blades
12 egg whites and egg shells
2 1/2 lbs. ginger root

Time to completion:  3 weeks.

Gathering wild bees in a
straw hive or *skep.*

Take ten Gallons of water; and to every Gallon of water a quart of honey, a handful and
a half of Rosemary, one Ounce of Mace, one Ounce and a half of Nutmegs, as much
Cinamon, half an Ounce of Cloves, a quarter of a pound of Ginger scraped and cut in
pieces. Put all these into the water, and let it boil half an hour, then take it off the fire,
and let it stand, till you may see your shadow in it. Then put in the honey, and set it
upon the fire again. Then take the shells and whites of a dozen Eggs, and beat them
both very well together: and when it is ready to boil up, put in your Eggs,[1] and stir it;
then skim it clean, and take it off the fire, and put it into vessels to cool, as you do wort.
When it is cold, set it together with some barm, as you do Beer. When it is put together
leave the settlings behind in the bottom; as soon as it is white over, Tun it up in a vessel,
and when it hath done working, stop it up as you do Beer. When it is three weeks old,
it will be fit to bottle or drink.
(From *The Closet ...Opened*, 1669.)

---

[1] This method of clarifying the liquid is still used for broth. A preferable method in mead-making is to put
your herbs and spices in cheesecloth bags for the boiling process, remove the bags when done, and then to
filter the spiced liquid. Filter the liquid by placing a doubled piece of cheesecloth in a large funnel. Pour
the liquid through the cheesecloth so that it drips into the fermentation jug. This method is very effective
and also reduces the cost by 12 eggs.

# # 68  TO MAKE WHITE MEATHE – 1669

*Many of these recipes neglect to add yeast. This may be accidental, or, in some recipes, another substance, such as mustard seed, is used to begin fermentation (see his recipe #10). In older houses, where brewing and baking have been done for many years under less than sterile conditions, yeasts have taken up residence, their spores swirling freely in the air and falling into vats and kneading troughs, raising the bread and fermenting the beer without human intervention. It is possible that those recipes which leave out the yeast come from homes with such resident yeast colonies. Indeed, commercially brewed Belgian Lambic beers are fermented by allowing the wort to sit near open windows so that wild yeasts will fall into the vats and begin fermentation.[1]*

| | |
|---|---|
| 6 gallons water | 6 quarts honey |
| 1/4 ounce mace blades | 1/4 ounce ginger root |
| 1/2 ounce whole nutmegs | |

1 handful total:  sweet marjoram, broad thyme, and sweetbrier.

Take six Gallons of water, and put in six quarts of Honey, stirring it till the honey be throughly melted; then set it over the fire, and when it is ready to boil, skim it clean; then put in a quarter of an Ounce of Mace; so much Ginger; half an Ounce of Nutmegs; Sweet-marjoram, Broad-thyme and Sweet-Bryar, of all together a handful, and boil them well therein.  Then set it by, till it be throughly cold, and barrel it up, and keep it till it be ripe. (*ibid.*)


# # 69  ANOTHER [*WAY*] TO MAKE MEATHE – 1669

| | |
|---|---|
| 5 gallons water | 5 quarts honey |
| 1 handful sweet marjoram | 1/2 handful ginger root, sliced |
| 3 quarts yeast | raisins |
| sugar | |

Time to completion:  2 months.

To every Gallon of water, take a quart of Honey, to every five Gallons, a handful of Sweet-marjoram, half a handful of Sliced-ginger; boil all these moderately three quarters of an hour; then let it stand and cool:  and being Lukewarm, put to every five Gallons, about three quarts of Yest, and let it work a night and a day.  Then take off the Yest and strain it into a Runlet; and when it hath done working:  then stop it up, and so let it remain a month:  then drawing out into bottles, put into every bottle two or three stoned Raisins, and a lump of Loaf-sugar. It may be drunk in two months. (*ibid.*)

---

[1] Blue, pp. 24-25.

# # 70 ANOTHER VERY GOOD WHITE MEATH – 1669

| | |
|---|---|
| 1 gallon water | 1 quart honey |
| sweet marjoram | sweetbrier leaves |
| ginger root | cream of tartar |
| yeast | egg whites and egg shells |
| rosemary | |

*optional*:  violet leaves; strawberry leaves; agrimony; sweetbrier; borage; bugloss.

Take to every Gallon of water a quart of Honey:  boil in it a little Rose-mary and Sweet-marjoram:  but a large quantity of Sweet-bryar-leaves, and a reasonable proportion of Ginger:  boil these in the Liquor, when it is skimed; and work it in due time with a little barm.  Then tun it in a vessel; and draw it into bottles, after it is sufficiently settled.  Whites of Eggs with the shells beaten together, do clarifie Meath best.  If you will have your Meath cooling, use Violet and Straw-berry-leaves, Agrimony, Eglantine and the like:  adding Borage and Bugloss, and a little Rosemary and Sweet-Marjoram to give it Vigor.  Tartar makes it work well.
(From *The Closet ...Opened*, 1669.)

# # 91 ANOTHER [*MEATH*] – 1669

| | |
|---|---|
| 1 quart honey | 1 gallon water |
| 1 or 2 sprigs winter savory | 1 or 2 sprigs sweet marjoram |
| mace blades | whole nutmegs |

Take a quart of honey to a Gallon of water; set the Kettle over the fire, and stir it now and then, that the honey may melt; let it boil an hour; you must boil in it, a Sprig or two of Winter-savory, as much of Sweet-marjoram; put it into tubs ready scalded, till the next day towards evening.  Then tun it up into your vessel, let it work for three days; after which hang a bag in the barrel with what quantity of Mace and sliced Nutmeg you please.  To make it stronger then this, 'tis but adding more hony, to make it bear an Egg the breadth of a six pence, or something more.  You may bottle it out after a month, when you please.  This is the way, which is used in Sussex by those who are accounted to make it best.  (*ibid.*)

# 76  TO MAKE MEATH – 1669

*This is two recipes in one.   The numbers in brackets have been added to help differentiate the recipes.*

[1]
4 to 6 parts water                                       1 part honey

Time to completion: 1 year.

If you will have it to keep a year or two, take six parts of water, and one of honey; But if you will have it to keep longer, take but four parts of water to one of honey. Dissolve the honey very well in the water, then boil it gently, skimming it all the while as the scum riseth, till no more scum riseth. Then pour it out of the Copper into a fit vessel or vessels to cool. Then Tun it up in a strong and sweet cask, and let it stand in some place, where there is some little warmth; (It will do as well without warmth, but be longer growing ripe) This will make it work. At first a course foul matter will work over; to which purpose it must be kept always full with fresh Liquor of the same, as it worketh over. When it begins to work more gently, and that which riseth at the top, is no more foul, but is a white froth; then fill and stop it up close, and set it in a cool cellar, where it is to stand continually.
       After half a year or a year, you may draw it off from the Lees into a clean vessel, or let it remain untouched.  It is not fit to be drunk for it's perfection till the sweetness be quite worn off, yet not to be sower, but vinous.  You may drink it at meals instead of wine, and is wholesomer and better then wine.


[2]
8 or 9 parts water                                       1 part honey
ginger root                                              yeast

Time to completion:  2 or 3 months.

       To small Meath, that is to be drunk presently, you may put a little Ginger to give it life, and work it with a little barm. If the Meath work not at all, it will nevertheless be good, and peradventure better than that which worketh; but it will be longer first, and the dregs will fall down to the bottom, though it work not.
       Small Meath of eight or nine parts of water to one of honey, will be very good, though it never work, but be barrell'd up as soon as it is cold, and stopped close: and after two or three months drunk from the barrel without botteling.  This is good for Meals. (*ibid.*)

# # 72  TO MAKE WHITE MEATH – 1669

*Note: every change of water in which the herbs have been boiled is to be <u>discarded</u> so long as it "looketh any thing green." (See his recipes # 29 and # 83, pp. 47 and 65.)*

water                                    1 quart honey per gallon liquor
1 spoonful yeast                         ash tree bark
eringo roots                             6 egg shells
8 egg whites                             cinnamon sticks
mace blades                              1 spoonful wheat flour
cloves                                   whole nutmegs

<u>Equal parts of</u>:  rosemary; thyme; sweetbrier; pennyroyal;[1] bay leaves; water cress; agrimony;[1] marsh mallow leaves and flowers; liverwort; wood betony; eyebright; scabious.
<u>1/16 handful each per each handful of the above herbs</u>:  wild angelica; ribwort; sanicle; Roman wormwood.[1]

Take Rose-mary, Thyme, Sweet-bryar, Peny-royal, and Bays, Water-cresses, Agrimony, Marsh-mallows, leaves and flowers: Liver-wort, Wood-betony, Eye-bright, Scabious, of each a like quantity; of the bark of Ash-tree, of Eringo-roots-green, of each a proportion to the herbs; of wild Angelica, Ribwort, Sanicle, Roman-worm-wood, of each a proportion, which is, to every handful of the Herbs above named, a sixteenth part of a handful of these latter; steep them a night and a day, in a woodden boul of water covered; the next day boil them very well in another water, till the colour be very high; Then take another quantity of water, and boil the herbs in it, till it look green, and so let it boil three or four times, or as long as the liquor looketh any thing green; then let it stand with these herbs in it a day and a night.
To every Gallon of this water, put a quart of pure clear honey, the Liquor being first strained from the herbs. Your Liquor if it be strong enough will bear an Egg, the breadth of a three pence above water. When you have put the honey into the Liquor, you must work and Labour it together a whole day, until the honey be consumed. Then let it stand a whole night again a clearing. Then put it into a kettle, and let it boil a quarter of an hour, with the whites and shells of six Eggs; Then strain it clean, and so let it stand a cooling. Then put it into a barrel, and take Cloves, Mace, Cinamon, Nutmegs, and beat them together: put them into a linnen bag, hang it with a thread into the barrel. If you would have it work, that you may drink of it presently, take the whites of two or three Eggs, a spoonful of barm, a spoonful of wheat-flower; beat all these together: Let it work, before you stop it up. Then afterwards stop it well with clay and salt tempered together, to keep it moist.
(From *The Closet ...Opened*, 1669.)

---

[1] CAUTION! (*See Appendix.*)

# #74 ANOTHER SORT OF MEATH – 1669

| | |
|---|---|
| 36 gallons water | 4 gallons fresh black currants |
| 12 gallons honey | |

Take thirty six Gallons of fountain water (first boiled, &c,) and dissolve twelve Gallons of Honey in it. Keep them boiling an hour and a half after they begin to boil, skimming well all the while. It will be an hour upon the fire before it boil. When it is clear and enough boiled, pour it out into woodden vessels to cool. When you are ready to Tun it, have four Gallons of Black-currants, bruise them in a stone mortar, that they may the more easily part with their juyce to the Liquor. Put them and their juyce to the Liquor. Put them and their juyce into the barrel, and pour the cool Liquor upon them, so as the vessel be quite full. Cover the bung with a plate of lead[1] lying loose on, that the working of the Liquor may lift it up, as it needeth to cast out the filth. And still as it worketh over, fill it up with fresh Liquor, made in the same proportion of honey and water. A moneth after it works no longer, stop up the bung very close.
(From *The Closet ...Opened*, 1669.)

# #82 TO MAKE MEATH – 1669

| | |
|---|---|
| 1 quart honey | thyme |
| 2 quarts ale | rosemary |
| 4 quarts water | agrimony[2] |
| parsley | other herbs to taste |
| fennel | cloves |
| cinnamon sticks | ginger root |
| licorice | mace blades |
| yeast | |

To every quart of honey put four quarts of Spring-water; temper the honey in the water, being a little warmed; then put it on the fire again, with Fennel, Rose-mary, Thyme, Agrimony, Parsley or the like. Let them boil half an hour, and upwards; and as it boileth, scum the froth; Then take it off, and strain it, and let it cool as you do your wort. Then put a little barm into it, then take off the froath again, and stir it well together. Then take two quarts of Ale, boiled with Cloves. Mace, Cinnamon, Ginger and Liquorice; and put it to the Meath and Tun it up. (*ibid.*)

---

[1] CAUTION! Do not use lead.

[2] CAUTION! (*See Appendix.*)

# # 77  TO MAKE WHITE MEATH – 1669

*Sweetbrier.*
From *The Herball or Generall Historie of Plants*,
by John Gerard.  London, 1597.

3 1/3 gallons honey
10 gallons water

*optional:* cinnamon sticks, mace blades, ginger root, whole nutmegs, cloves.

1 large handful total: thyme, sweet marjoram, winter savory, sweetbrier, and bay leaves, mixed.

Time to completion:  approx. 6 months.

Take to every three Gallons of water, one Gallon of honey and set the water over the fire, and let the honey melt, before the water be too hot; then put in a New-laid-egg, and feel with your hand; if it comes half way the water, it is strong enough; Then put into it these Herbs, Thyme, Sweet-marjoram, Winter-savoury, Sweet-bryar, and Bay-leaves, in all a good great handful; which a proportion for ten Gallons; Then with a quick-fire boil it very fast half an hour, and no longer; and then take it from the fire, and let it cool in two or three woodden vessels; and let it stand without stirring twenty four hours.  Then softly drain it out, leaving all the dregs behind.  Put the clear into your vessel; and if you like any spice, take Ginger, Nutmeg, Cinnamon, Mace and Cloves, and bruise them a little, and put them in a bag, and let them hang in your vessel. Before you put your Meath into the vessel, try if it will bear an Egg as broad as a peny; if it do, then it is very well; and if it be made with the best White-honey, it usually is just so.  But if it should prove too strong, that it bears the Egge broader; then boil a little more honey and water very small, and put to it, when it is cold:  and then put it into the vessel.  It is best to be made at Michaelmas, and not drunk of till Lent.
(From *The Closet ...Opened*, 1669.)

## #81 MEATH FROM THE MUSCOVIAN AMBASSADOUR'S STEWARD – 1669

3 parts water
whole nutmegs
ginger root
cardamom seeds
anise seeds

1 part honey
toast spread with yeast
cloves
orange peel

Take three times as much water as honey; then let the tubs, that the honey must be wrought in, be cleansed very clean with scalding water, so that it may not prove sowre; also when you mix them together, take half-warm-water, and half cold, and squeese them well together; Afterwards when you think the honey is well melted, then let it run through a sieve; and see your kettle of Copper or Iron[1] (but Copper is better than Iron) be very clean; then put in your spice, as, Nutmegs, Ginger, Cloves, Cardamome, Anisseeds, Orange peel; put these in according to the quantity you make, and let them all be bruised, except the Orange peel, which leave whole. The Meath must boil an hour by the Clock; after put it into Tubs to cool, and when it is cold, take three or four slices of White-bread, tost them very hard, and spread very good yest on both sides of the tosts; then put them into the Tubs. If it be warm weather, let the Tubs be uncovered; but if it be cold, cover them. This being done, you will find it worked enough by the black that cometh up by the sides of the Tubs; then take a sieve and take off the yest and bread. Afterwards draw it off at a tap in the Tub into the cask you intend to keep it in; then take a quantity of spice as before, well-bruised, and put it into a bag, and make it fast at the bung, with a string, and if it begins to work, after it is in the cask, be sure to give it vent, or else you will loose all. (*ibid.*)

*Moving an enormous cauldron.*
From *Il Cuoco Segreto di Papa Pio V*, by Bartolomeo Scappi, Venice, 1570.

---

[1] Although copper pots are traditionally used for brewing beer, you may find it preferable to use enamelled pots when making meads and wines. Iron, copper, and other metals may impart disagreeable flavors or colors to the brew, especially if the liquid has a high acid content. Many herbs can also produce colors when boiled in metal pots, especially in the presence of certain acids or bases, and may have been deliberately added to provide color. (*See Appendix for a list of dye plants.*)

# # 83 A RECEIPT TO MAKE WHITE MEATH – 1669

| | |
|---|---|
| 18+ gallons water | honey |
| 1 spoonful flour | 9 egg whites |
| 6 egg shells | whole nutmegs |
| cinnamon sticks | 1 spoonful yeast |
| cloves | mace blades |

<u>As much as you like of</u>: rosemary, thyme, sweetbrier, pennyroyal,[1] bay leaves, watercress, agrimony,[1] marsh mallow leaves and flowers, liverwort, maidenhair, betony, eyebright, scabious, Ash tree bark, Eringo roots, wild angelica, ribwort, sanicle, roman wormwood,[1] tamarisk, mother of thyme, saxifrage, philipendula

Time to completion: approx. 2 1/2 months.

Take Rose-mary, Thyme, Sweet-bryar, Peny-royal, Bays, Water-cresses, Agrimony, Marsh-mallow-leaves and flowers, Liver-wort, Maiden-hair, Betony, Eye-bright, Scabious, the bark of an Ash-tree, young Eringo-roots, Wild-Angelica, Ribwort, Sinacle, Roman-worm-wood, Tamarisk, Mother-thyme, Saxafrage, Philipendula, of each of these herbs a like proportion; or of as many as you please to put in. You must put in all but four handfuls of herbs, which you must steep a night and a day, in a little bowl of water, being close covered. The next day take another fresh quantity of water, and boil the same herbs in it, till the colour be very high; then take another quantity of water, and boil the same herbs in it, untill it look green; and so let them boil three or four times in several waters, as long as the Liquor looketh anything green.[2] Then let it stand with these herbs in it a day and a night. Remember the last water you boil it in, to this proportion of herbs, must be eighteen Gallons. And when it hath stood a day and a night with these herbs in it after the last boiling, then strain the Liquor from the herbs; and put as much of the finest and best honey into the Liquor, as will bear an Egg; you must work the honey and liquor together a whole day, until the honey be consumed; then let it stand one whole night; then let it be well laboured again, and set it a clearing; and so boil it again with the whites of six New-laid-eggs with the shells; skim it very clean; and let it stand a day a cooling; then put it into a barrel, and take Cloves, Mace, Cinnamon and Nutmegs as much as will please your taste, and beat them all together, and put them in a Linnen bag, and hang it with a thread into the barrel. Then take the whites of two or three New-laid-eggs, a spoonful of barm, a spoonful of Wheat-flower, and beat them all together, and put it into your Liquor in the barrel, and let it work before you stop it; then afterwards stop it well, and set it in a cold place, and when it hath been settled some six weeks: draw it into bottles, and stop it very close, and drink not of it in a month after.
(From *The Closet ...Opened*, 1669.)

---

[1] CAUTION! (*See Appendix.*)          [2] See note p. 61.

# # 87 TO MAKE MEATH – 1669

| | |
|---|---|
| 1 gallon water | 1 quart honey |
| 2 ounces ginger root | 3 or 4 spoonsful ale yeast |
| 1 ounce whole nutmegs | 1/2 ounce mace blades |

<u>2 handfuls each</u>:  sweet marjoram; rosemary; lemon balm; fennel roots; parsley roots; asparagus roots.

Take to every Gallon of water, a quart of honey, and set it over a clear fire, and when it is ready to boil, skim it very clear.  Then take two handfulls of Sweet-marjoram, as much Rose-mary, and as much Baulm:  and two handful of Fennel-roots, as much of Parsley-roots, and as many Esparages-roots:  slice them in the middle, and take out the pith, wash and scrape them very clean, and put them with your herbs into your Liquor.  Then take two Ounces of Ginger, one Ounce of Nutmegs, half an Ounce of Mace:  bruise them and put them in:  and let it boil till it be so strong that it will bear an Egg:  then let it cool:  and being cold, put in 3 or 4 spoon fulls of New-ale yest:  and so skim it well, and put it into a Runlet, and it will work like Ale:  and having done working, stop it up close, as you do New-beer:  and lay salt upon it.[1]
(From *The Closet ...Opened*, 1669.)

# # 89 ANOTHER MEATH – 1669

| | |
|---|---|
| 20 gallons water | honey |
| 1 spoonful flour | 6 scant handfuls rosemary |
| 20 egg shells | ale yeast |
| 1 1/2 lbs. ginger root | 22 egg whites |

Time to completion:  approx. 1 month.

Take twenty Gallons of fair Spring-water.  Boil it a quarter of an hour, then let it stand till the next day.  Then beat into it so much honey, as will make it so strong as to bear an Egg the breadth of a two pence above the water.  The next day boil it up with six small handfulls of Rosemary, a pound and a half of Ginger, (being scraped and bruised) and the whites of twenty Eggs together with their shells beaten together, and well mingled with the Liquor.  Clarifie it and skim it very clean, still as the scum riseth, leaving the Ginger and Rosemary in it.  Let it stand till the next day, then Tun it up, and take some New-ale-yest, the whites of two Eggs, a spoonful of flower, beat all these together, and put it on the top of the barrel, when the barrel is full.  Let it work, and when it hath done working, stop it up close for three weeks, or a month.  Then you may bottle it, and a few days after, you may drink it.  (*ibid.*)

---

[1] This was a means of stopping the bung with salt and clay; it does <u>not</u> mean to add salt to the liquor.

# #90 ANOTHER [*MEATH*] – 1669

| | |
|---|---|
| 3 gallons water | 1 gallon honey |
| ale yeast | 2 ounces ginger root |

1 handful each: rosemary flowers; cowslips;[1] sage flowers; agrimony;[1] betony; thyme.

Take three Gallons of water, and boil in it a handful of Rose-mary (or rather the flowers) Cowslips, Sage-flowers, Agrimony, Betony, and Thyme, *ana*, one handful. When it hath taken the strength of the herbs, strain it through a hair-sieve, and let it cool twenty hours. Then to three Gallons of the clear part of this decoction, put one Gallon of honey, and mingle it very well with your hand, till it bear an Egg the breadth of a groat. Then boil it and skim it as long as any scum will rise. Afterwards let it cool twenty four hours. Then put to it a small quantity of Ale-barm, and skim the thin-barm that doth rise on it, morning and evening, with a feather, during four days. And so put it up into your vessel, and hang in it a thin linnen bag with two Ounces of good White-ginger bruised therein: And stop it up close for a quarter of a year. Then you may drink it. (From *The Closet ...Opened*, 1669.)

# #102 MEATH WITH RAISINS – 1669

| | |
|---|---|
| 40 gallons water | 40 lbs. raisins (preferably with seeds) |
| 10 gallons honey | |

Put forty Gallons of water into your Caldron, and with a stick take the height of the water, making a notch, where the superficies of the water cometh. Then put to the water ten Gallons of Honey, which dissolve with much Laving it; then presently boil it gently, skimming it all the while, till it be free from scum. Then put into it a thin bag of boulter-cloth containing forty pound weight of the best blew Raisins of the Sun, well picked and washed and wiped dry; and let the bag be so large, that the Raisins may lie at ease and loosly in it. When you perceive that the Raisins are boiled enough to be very soft, that you may strain out all their substance, take out the bag, and strain out all the Liquor by a strong Press. Put it back to the Honey-liquor, and boil all together (having thrown away the husks of the Raisins with the bag) till your Liquor be sunk down to the notch of your stick, which is the sign of due strength. Then let it cool in a woodden vessel, and let it run through a strainer to sever it from the settlings, and put it into a strong vessel, that hath had Sack or Muscadine in it, not filling it to within three fingers breadth of the top (for otherwise it will break the vessel with working) and leave the bung open whiles it worketh, which will be six weeks very strongly, though it be put into a cold cellar. And after nine moneths, you may begin to drink it. (*ibid.*)

---

[1] CAUTION! (*See Appendix.*)

*Der Trincker*, by Johan Bader.
Stettin, 1614.

# 92  ANOTHER RECEIPT – 1669

3 gallons water
3 quarts honey
1 quart white wine *or* Sack
1 ounce whole nutmegs
1 ounce ginger root
1 ounce cinnamon sticks
yeast
<u>2 handfuls each</u>:  thyme; strawberry leaves.
<u>1 handful each</u>:  organy; fennel roots; parsley roots.

Time to completion:  2 or 3 weeks.

Take to every Gallon of Fountain-water a good quart of honey.  Set the water on the
fire, till it be pretty warm; then take it off, and put it in your honey, and stir it till it be
dissolved.  Then put into every three Gallons, two handfuls of Thyme:  two good
handfuls of Strawberry-leaves, one handful of Organ; one handful of Fennel-roots, the
heart being taken out, and one handful of Parsley-roots the heart taken out:  But as for
the herbs, it must be according to the constitution of them, for whom the Mead is
intended.  Then set the Herbs in it on the fire, to boil for half an hour, still skimming it,
as the scum riseth; it must boil but half an hour; then take it off the fire, and presently
strain it from the herbs, and let it stand till it be fully cold; then pour it softly off the
bottom, and put it in a vessel fit for it, and put a small quantity of barm in it, and
mingle it with it, and when it hath wrought up, which will be in three or four days,
skim off that barm, and set on fresh:  but the second barm must not be mingled with the
Meath, but onely poured on the top of it.  Take an Ounce of Nutmeg sliced:  one Ounce
of Ginger sliced:  one Ounce of Cinnamon cut in pieces, and boil them a pretty while in
a quart of White-wine or Sack:  when this is very cold, strain it, and put the spices in a
Canvas-bag to hang in your Meath, and pour in the Wine it was boiled in.

This Meath will be drinkable, when it is a fortnight or three weeks old.
(From *The Closet ...Opened*, 1669.)

# #96 TO MAKE MEATH – 1669

| | |
|---|---|
| 6 quarts water | ale yeast |
| 1+ quart honey | ginger root |
| rosemary | |

Time to completion: 10 days.

Take to six quarts of water, a quart of the best honey, and put it on the fire, and stir it, till the honey is melted: and boil it well as long as any scum riseth: and now and then put in a little cold water, for this will make the scum rise: keep your kettle up as full as you did put it on; when it is boiled enough, about half an hour before you take it off, then take a quantity of Ginger sliced and well scraped first, and a good quantity of Rosemary, and boil both together. Of the Rosemary and Ginger you may put in more or less, for to please your taste: And when you take it off the fire, strain it into your vessel, either a well seasoned-tub, or a great cream pot, and the next morning when it is cold, pour off softly the top from the settlings into another vessel; and then put some little quantity of the best Ale-barm to it and cover it with a thin cloth over it, if it be in summer, but in the winter it will be longer a ripening, and therefore must be the warmer covered in a close place, and when you go to bottle it, take with a feather all the barm off, and put it into your bottles, and stop it up close. In ten days you may drink it.

If you think six quarts of water be too much, and would have it stronger, then put in a greater quantity of honey. (*ibid.*)

# #107 TOO MAKE A PRITEY SORT OF MEDE TOO KEEP TOO MONTHS – c. 1674

| | |
|---|---|
| 10 quarts warm water | 1 quart honey |
| 1 lb. sugar | juice and peels of 4 lemons |
| 20 cloves | 2 ginger roots |
| 2 or 3 sprigs rosemary | toast spread with 2 spoonsful ale yeast |

Time to completion: 1 week.

Take 10 quarts of spring watter and Lett it bee hot then put in a quart of honey and a pound of Lofe suger Lett it boyle together till no scum Rises which as it dus must bee taken off it may boyle about 1/2 an houer, then pore it forth in too the vesell, or what you desire too keep it in, and wring into it the juce of 4 Lemons put in peell and all, 20 cloves 2 Rase of ginger 2 or 3 springs of Rosmary, and when it is allmost cold make sum tostes and spred one them 2 spunfulls of good ale yeist put them in warm, so Lett it stand 4 or 5 days then bottell it off, you may drinke it in a weeke after it is botteled, and it will keep 3 months in the winter, it must bee not stoped before it has dun workin-(From *Penn Family Recipes, etc.*, c. 1674.)

# # 127  TOO MAKE SMALL MEED – c. 1674

| | |
|---|---|
| 6 quarts warm water | 1 lemon |
| 1 quart honey | 1/4 lb. whole nutmegs |
| yeast | |

Time to completion:  3 or 4 weeks.

Take 6 quarts of watter and warme it one quart of the finest hony, stur very well, one Lemon and a qr of a pound of nuttmegs sett it one the fire and Lett it boyle till the scum is Black, then take it of the fire and Colle it, and when it is Luke warme, put yeist too it into a stand or spickett pot and at the 4 day draw it into bottells, Corke them Close keep it a fortnight or 3 weeks in sand before you Drinke it, this will keep good 3 months – (From *Penn Family Recipes, etc.*, c. 1674.)


# TO MAKE MEAD – 1723

| | |
|---|---|
| 3 gallons water | 3 lbs. honey per gallon of liquor |
| lemon balm | lemon |
| sugar | 30 cloves |
| sweet marjoram | rosemary |
| 5 or 6 handfuls borage | 5 or 6 handfuls bugloss |
| 2 ounces whole nutmegs | 6 ounces ginger |
| 1 1/2 pints ale yeast | thyme |

Set three gallons of water on the fire, put in Balm, Lemon, Thyme, Sweet Marjoram, and Rosemary, let them boil some time, then put in five or six handfuls of Borrage and Bugloss, and when they have boiled a little take them off, strain them and set the liquor by to settle for a Night.  Then to every gallon of liquor add three Pound of Honey; put on the Fire, boil and scum as long as any scum rises; then take thirty cloves, two ounces of Nutmegs, and six ounces of Ginger, beat them, put them in a Bag and boil them in the liquor, a little before you take it off the Fire.  Then empty it into a vessel, put to it a pint and a half of Ale yeast, lay a sheet over it and a Blanket upon that.  Let it work sufficiently, then tun it, hang the Bag of Spice in the Cask, and stop it up close for six or seven weeks; then bottle it off with some sugar.
(From *The Receipt Book of John Nott*, 1723.)

## TO MAKE WHITE MEAD – 1723

*It is uncertain how much water is to be used here, but judging by the quantity of herbs called for, about 5 gallons seems appropriate. Also, in this homeopathic approach to mead making, the water in which the herbs steep is to be <u>discarded</u> as long as it is tinted green by the herbs. (See note p. 61.)*

water

1 spoonful yeast

6 egg shells

whole nutmegs

mace blades

1+ lb. honey per 2 quarts of liquor

9 egg whites

cinnamon sticks

cloves

<u>1 handful each</u>: thyme; rosemary; sweetbrier; eyebright; wood betony; scabious; roman wormwood;[1] agrimony.[1]

Put a handful of Thyme, Rosemary, Sweet Briar, Eyebright, Wood Betony, Scabious, Roman Wormwood, Agrimony (of each a like quantity), and steep for twenty-four hours in a Wooden bowl, uncovered, then boil them in another water till it be very high coloured; then change the water and boil them till it is coloured green, and as long as any green mess remain, then set it by for twenty-four hours more. Then strain the liquor from the Herbs and put a Pound of Honey to every two Quarts of the liquor and when it will bear an egg to three pence breadth above the water work it together till the Honey is all dissolved; then let it settle for a Night; the next day boil it with the shells and whites of half a dozen eggs; then strain it, set it by to cool; then put it up into the Cask, then bruise cinnamon, nutmeg, cloves, mace, and put them in a Bag and hang them in the Cask and stop it up.

If you would have it fit to drink in a little time, beat together the whites of three or four eggs; add to them a spoonful of yeast, two spoonfuls of Honey, and put them into the Cask and then temper some Clay with Bay salt and stop it up close.[2]

*(ibid.)*

YEST.

To toot—to toot—too too—. East ! Here's East !''

*A Yeast Vendor*
selling liquid yeast door-to-door.
By Samuel Wood, 1814.

---

[1] CAUTION! *(See Appendix.)*

[2] This was a means of stopping the bung with salt and clay *"to keep it moist."*

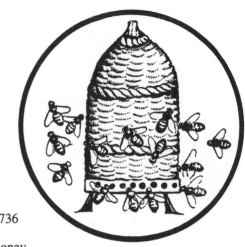

...Like many swarmes of
Bees assembled round,
After their hiues with
honny do abound...
From *The Faerie Queene*,
by Edmund Spenser.

TO MAKE MEAD, FROM LADY G. – 1736

8 gallons water                           honey
rind and juice of 6 lemons

Time to completion: 3 months.

Take eight Gallons of Water, and as much Honey as will make it bear an Egg; add to
this the Rind of ſix Lemmons, and boil it well, ſcumming it carefully as it riſes. When
'tis off the Fire, put to it the Juice of the ſix Lemmons, and pour it into a clean Tub, or
open earthen Veſſel, if you have one large enough, to work three Days; then ſcum it
well, and pour off the clear into the Cask, and let it ſtand open till it has done making a
hiſſing Noiſe; after which, ſtop it up cloſe, and in three Months time it will be fine, and
fit for bottling.
(From *The Country Housewife and Lady's Director*, by R. Bradley, 1736, p. 136.)

HOW TO MAKE MEAD – 1796

10 gallons water                  2 or 3 spoonsful yeast
2 gallons honey                   2 lemons
1 handful ginger root

Take ten gallons of water, and two gallons of honey, a handful of raced ginger; then
take two lemons, cut them in pieces, and put them into it, boil it very well, keep it
ſkimming; let it ſtand all night in the ſame veſſel you boil it in, the next morning barrel it
up, with two or three ſpoonfuls of good yeaſt. About three weeks or a month after, you
may bottle it.
(From *The Art of Cookery Made Plain and Easy*, v. 8, by Mrs. Glasse, 1796, p. 347.)

## TO MAKE WHITE MEAD – 1796

| | |
|---|---|
| 5 gallons water | 1 gallon honey |
| 2 or 3 ginger roots | cinnamon sticks |
| whole nutmegs | ale yeast |

Time to completion: 3 or 4 months.

Take five gallons of water, add to that one gallon of the beʃt honey; then ʃet it on the fire, boil it together well, and ʃkim it very clean; then take it off the fire, and ʃet it by; then take two or three races of ginger, the like quantity of cinnamon and nutmegs, bruiʃe all theʃe groʃly, and put them in a little Holland bag in the hot liquor, and ʃo let it ʃtand cloʃe covered till it be cold; then put as much ale-yeaʃt to it as will make it work. Keep it in a warm place, as they do ale; and when it hath wrought well, tun it up; at two months you may drink it, having been bottled a month. If you keep it four months, it will be the better. (*ibid.*, pp. 347-8.)

## 96th. MEAD – 1815

| | |
|---|---|
| 6 gallons water | 6 quarts honey |
| 1/4 ounce mace blades | 1/4 ounce ginger root |
| 1/2 ounce whole nutmegs | |

<u>1 handful total</u>: sweet marjoram, thyme, sweetbrier, mixed.

Take six gallons of water, and thereto put six quarts of honey, stirring it till the honey be thoroughly mixed; then set it over the fire, and when ready to boil, scum it very well: then put to it a quarter of an ounce of mace, and as much ginger, and half an ounce of nutmegs, some sweet marjoram thyme, and sweet briar, together a handful: then boil them in the liquid, then let it stand by till cold, and then barrel it up for use. (From *The Dyer's Companion*, by Elijah Bemiss, 1815, p. 302.)

## SASSAFRAS MEAD – 1925

*Note how the definition of mead has changed by 1925. This drink is not fermented with yeast, it is aerated with cream of tartar and bicarbonate of soda! Perhaps this, or a similar recipe, was responsible for mead falling into disfavor in the past century?*

| | |
|---|---|
| 6 cloves | 2 quarts water |
| 3 pints molasses | 1 1/2 pints honey |
| 5 bunches sassafras roots[1] | 1 heaping tablespoon cream of tartar |

1 pinch bicarbonate of soda per serving
1 teaspoon minced candied orange peel per serving
<u>1 pinch each</u>:  cinnamon powder; grated nutmeg.

Purchase from the druggist five bunches of sassafras roots, scrape and cover with two quarts of boiling water, adding a pinch each of powdered cinnamon and grated nutmeg; cover closely, and when of the desired strength, strain through cheesecloth, stirring in three pints of New Orleans molasses, a pint and a half of strained white honey and six whole cloves.  Place in a saucepan and bring slowly to the boiling point, allowing it to simmer for about ten minutes; again strain and add a heaping tablespoon of cream of tartar and seal in air-tight bottles.  Serve in tall slender glasses containing two tablespoons of shaved ice and a liberal pinch of bicarbonate of soda; fill quickly with the mead and stir vigorously with a long handled spoon, adding a teaspoon of minced candied orange peel.

(From *The Kitchen Guide*, by Catharine V. Ferns, 1925.)

---

[1] CAUTION!  The root cambium, or growth layer, of sassafras contains an aromatic oil which was used as a flavoring agent; it has since been found to be toxic, and commercial use of sassafras extract has been banned in the United States.  A commercial extract of birch mixed with sassafras (toxin removed), called "Sassy Frassy," is available at Hickory Farms outlets.  Additionally, "Pappy's Sassafras Concentrate" (toxin removed), is available from H & K Products, Columbus Grove, OH   45830.

"'During the day they place the water in the sun, and when night comes they strain the thick sediment and again expose the water to the air in earthen jars set on the highest part of the house, while throughout the entire night two slaves wet down jars with water. At dawn they take the jars downstairs, and again drawing off the sediment, they thus make the water clear and in every way healthful.'"[1]

✳✳✳

[HYDROMELI] – circa 77 A.D.

*This, the oldest of our mead/hydromel recipes, dates to circa 77 A.D. It uses the same proportion of water to honey as does our next recipe, dated 1669, but is very simple in that it calls for no other ingredients.*

*Many of these older recipes spend a great deal of time doing something we would not normally do: they clarify the water used to make the liquor. Most of us in the United States take unlimited supplies of clean, safe drinking water for granted, but our ancestors had to go to great pains to obtain clean water. They used egg whites and egg shells, sand or charcoal 'filters,' or prolonged boilings and settlings to rid their drinking water of the sediment and filth commonly found in it. This must be why springs of sparkling clear water are mentioned so often and in such glowing terms in the old romances.[2]*

3 parts rainwater                    one part honey

A wine is also made of only water and honey. For this it is recommended that rain-water should be stored for five years. Some who are more expert use rain-water as soon as it has fallen, boiling it down to a third of the quantity and adding one part of old honey to three parts of water, and then keeping the mixture in the sun for 40 days after the rising of the Dog-star. Others pour it off after nine days and then cork it up. This beverage is called in Greek 'water-honey' [*'hydromeli'*]; with age it attains the flavour of wine.
(From *Natural History*, by Pliny the Elder, Book XIV, section XX, p. 261.)

---

[1] Protagorides, quoted in Athenaeus, Book III, pp. 77-79.

[2] Read "*Privies Galore*," by Mollie Harris, Alan Sutton Publ., 1990. You will find it enlightening as to what went on upstream in olden times!

# # 12 (B) [HYDROMEL WITH CLOVE-GILLYFLOWERS] – 1669

*Many of Sir Kenelme's recipes are written in a chatty style, and tend to go off in several directions at once. This is one such recipe. It begins with instructions for Sack with clove gilliflowers (found on pp. 177-178), progresses to a recipe for hydromel flavored with clove gilliflowers, breaks in the middle for a note on hydromel flavored with juniper berries, rosemary, and bay leaves; digresses to discuss how to keep mead for a long time, and how to make various fruit-flavored meads; then returns to the secondary subject, only to tell us we need to add more flavoring to make it taste better!*

| | |
|---|---|
| 3 parts water | clove gilliflowers |
| 1 part honey | yeast |
| rosemary | bay leaves |
| sweet marjoram | thyme |
| broad thyme | angelica root |
| elecampane root | eringo root |
| raspberry juice | cherry juice |
| bilberry juice | *optional*: Sack wine. |

...Upon better consideration; I conceive the best way of making Hydromel with Clove-gillyflowers, is thus: Boil your simple Liquor to its full height (with three parts of water to one of Honey), take a small parcel out, to make a strong infusion of flowers, pouring it boyling hot upon the flowers in earthen vessels. If you have great quantity, as six to one, of Liquor, you will easily draw out the tincture in fourteen or sixteen hours infusion; otherwise you may quicken your liquor with a parcel of Sack. In the mean time make the great quantity of Liquor work with yest. When it hath almost done fermenting, but not quite, put the infusion to it warm, and let it ferment more if it will. When that is almost done, put to it a bag with flowers to hang in the bung.[1]

I conceive that Hydromel made with Juniper-berries (first broken and bruised) boiled in it, is very good. Adde also to it Rosemary and Bayleaves.

## [*MEAD FLAVORED WITH VARIOUS FRUITS:*]

| | |
|---|---|
| 1 quart fruit juice | 3 to 4 gallons mead |

Upon tryal of several ways, I conclude (as things yet appear to me) that to keep Meath long, it must not be fermented with yest (unless you put Hops to it) but put it in the barrel, and let it ferment of it self, keeping a thick plate of lead[2] upon the bung, to

---

[1] This recipe continues with "Since I conceive," etc., found on the next page.

[2] Use an airlock instead of a lead weight.

lie close upon it, yet so that the working of the Liquor may raise it, to purge out the foulness, and have always some new made plain Liquor, to fill it up as it sinks, warm whiles it works:  but cold during three or four month's after.  Then stop the bung exceeding close.  And when you will make your Mead with Cherries or Morello-Cherries, or Raspes, or Bilberries, or Black-cherries, put their juyce to the Liquor when you tun it, without ever boiling it therein; about one quart of juyce to every three or four gallons of Liquor.  You may squeese out the clear juyce, and mingle it with the Liquor, and hang the Magma in a bag in the bung.  I think it is best to break the stones of the Cherries,[1] before you put their Magma[2] into the bag.

Since I conceive, that Clove-gilly-flowers must never be boiled in the Liquor:  that evaporateth their Spirits, which are very volatile:  But make a strong infusion of them, and besides hang a Bag of them in the bung.  I conceive that it is good to make the Liquor pretty strong (not too much, but so as the taste may be gratefull) of some strong herbs, as Rosemary, Bayleaves, Sweet-marjoram, Thyme, Broad-thyme, and the like. For they preserve the drink, and make it better for the stomack and head.  Standing in the Sun is the best way of Fermentation, when the drink is strong.  The root of Angelica or Elecampane, or Eringo, or Orris,[3] may be good and pleasant, to be boiled in the Liquor.  Raspes and Cherries and Bilberies are never to be boiled, but their juyce put into the Liquor, when it is tunning.  Use onely Morello-Cherries (I think) for pleasure, and black ones for health.  I conceive it best to use very little spice of any kind in Meathes.  (From *The Closet ...Opened*, 1669.)

#3  SOME NOTES ABOUT HONEY – 1669

The Honey of dry open Countries, where there is much Wild-thyme, Rosemary, and Flowers, is best.  It is of three sorts, Virgin-honey, Life-honey, and Stock-honey.  The first is the best.  The Life-honey next.  The Virgin-honey is of Bees, that swarmed the Spring before, and are taken up in Autumn; and is made best by chusing the Whitest combs of the Hive, and then letting the Honey run out of them lying upon a Sieve without pressing it, or breaking of the Combs.  The Life-honey is of the same Combs broken after the Virgin-honey is run from it; The Merchants of Honey do use to mingle all the sorts together.  The first of a swarm is called Virgin-honey.  That of the next year, after the Swarm was hatched, is Life-honey.  And ever after, it is Honey of Old-stocks.  Honey that is forced out of the Combs, will always taste of Wax.  Hampshire Honey is most esteemed at London.  About Bisleter there is excellent good.  Some account Norfolk honey the best.  (*ibid.*)

BORAGE

---

[1] Breaking the cherry stones releases highly poisonous *hydrocyanic acid*.  Commercially available oil of bitter almond has had the poison removed and may be used for brewing and cooking in recipes which call for crushed pits or kernels.  (*See Appendix.*)

[2] Magma is the leftover cherry pulp.

[3] Orris roots are poisonous; <u>do not</u> use them!  (*See Appendix.*)

## # 25 HYDROMEL AS I MADE IT WEAK FOR THE QUEEN MOTHER – 1669

18 quarts water  
1 ginger root  
4 cloves

1 quart honey  
1 spoonful ale yeast  
1 sprig rosemary

Time to completion: 6 weeks to 2 months.

Take 18 quarts of spring-water, and one quart of honey; when the water is warm, put the honey into it. When it boileth up, skim it very well, and continue skimming it, as long as any scum will rise. Then put in one Race of Ginger (sliced in thin slices,) four Cloves, and a little sprig of green Rosemary. Let these boil in the Liquor so long, till in all it have boiled one hour. Then set it to cool, till it be blood-warm; and then put to it a spoonful of Ale-yest. When it is worked up, put it into a vessel of a fit size; and after two or three days, bottle it up. You may drink it after six weeks, or two moneths. Thus was the Hydromel made that I gave the Queen, which was exceedingly liked by everybody.  
(From *The Closet ...Opened*, 1669.)

## # 23 MY LORD HOLLIS HYDROMEL – 1669

4 parts water  
ginger root  

1 or more parts honey

*optional*: rosemary, sweetbrier leaves, and one slice of white toast spread with crushed mustard seeds.

Time to completion: 1 year.

In four parts of Springwater dissolve one part of honey, or so much as the Liquor will bear an Egge to the breadth of a Groat. Then boil it very well, and that all the scum be taken away. He addeth nothing to it but a small proportion of Ginger sliced: of which He putteth half to boil in the Liquor, after all the scum is gone; and the other half He putteth into a bag, and hangeth in the bung, when it is tunned. The Ginger must be very little, not so much as to make the Liquor taste strongly of it, but to quicken it. I should like to adde a little proportion of Rosemary, and a greater of Sweet-bryar leaves, in the boiling. As also, to put into the barrel a tost of white bread with mustard, to make it work. He puts nothing to it; but his own strength in time makes it work of it self. It is good to drink after a year. (*ibid.*)

# #85  TO MAKE HONEY DRINK – 1669

| | |
|---|---|
| 2 quarts water | 1 lb. honey |
| 4 or 5 cloves per bottle | 4 or 5 slices of ginger root per bottle |

Time to completion:  10 or 12 days.

To two quarts of water take one pound of Honey.  When it boileth, skim it clean as long as any scum ariseth; boil it a pretty while; then take it off the fire, and put it in an earthen pot, and let it stand till the next day; then put it into clean bottles, that are throughly dry, rinsing first every bottle with a little of the liquor; Fill them not too full, and put into every bottle four or five Cloves, and four or five slices of Ginger: and stop it very close, and set it in Sand; and within ten or twelve days it will be ready to drink.

  Some, when they take their Bees, put the honey-combs into fair-water, and make it so strong of the honey that it will bear an Egg; and then boil it with some Spice, and put it into a barrel:  but I think it not so good, as that which is made of pure honey.  (*ibid.*)

# #115  WEAK HONEY-DRINK – 1669

| | |
|---|---|
| 9 pints warm water | 1 pint honey |
| 1 spoonful ginger root | 1/2 spoonful orange rind |
| 1 spoonful ale yeast | |

Time to completion:  2 or 3 days.

Take nine pints of warm fountain water, and dissolve in it one pint of pure White-honey, by laving it therein, till it be dissolved.  Then boil it gently, skimming it all the while, till all the scum be perfectly scummed off; and after that boil it a little longer, peradventure a quarter of an hour.  In all it will require two or three hours boiling, so that at last one third part may be consumed.  About a quarter of an hour before you cease boiling, and take it from the fire, put to it a little spoonful of cleansed and sliced Ginger; and almost half as much of the thin yellow rinde of Orange, when you are even ready to take it from the fire, so as the Orange boil only one walm in it.  Then pour it into a well-glased strong deep great Gally-pot,[1] and let it stand so, till it be almost cold, that it be scarce Luke-warm.  Then put to it a little silver-spoonful of pure Ale-yest, and work it together with a Ladle to make it ferment:  as soon as it beginneth to do

---

[1] CAUTION!  Do not suddenly pour the boiling hot liquid into a ceramic or glass container – the container may shatter.  You must first bring it up to temperature by rinsing it with hot water.

so, cover it close with a fit cover, and put a thick dubbled woollen cloth about it. Cast all things so that this may be done when you are going to bed. Next morning when you rise, you will find the barm gathered all together in the middle; scum it clean off with a silver-spoon and a feather, and bottle up the Liquor, stopping it very close. It will be ready to drink in two or three days; but it will keep well a month or two. It will be from the first very quick and pleasant. (*ibid.*)

## TO MAKE HYDROMEL, OR MEAD – 1736

*This first paragraph is a recipe for hydromel, while the second is a recipe for mead made with ale, or braggot made without herbs and spices.*

| 8 gallons water | honey |
|---|---|
| 1/4 lb. whole cloves | |

Take eight Gallons of Water, and as much Honey as will make the Water bear an Egg; put to this a quarter of a pound of Cloves tied in three or four pieces of Muſlin or Linnen Cloth, and ſet it to boil till the Scum has done riſing, ſcumming it as it riſes; then take it off the Fire, and take out the Cloves, which may be waſh'd and dry'd for other Uſes, and pour your Mead into an open Tub to ferment for about three days, till the Violence of the Working is over; after which, ſcum it very well, and pour the clear into a Veſſel, leaving the Bung open till it has done hiſſing, which you may know by holding your Ear cloſe to it, for at a diſtance you can hardly diſcover it. When this hiſſing is over, ſtop it cloſe, and let it ſtand three Months till it is fine, before you bottle it; remember in bottling this, as well as all other Liquors, that the Bottles muſt be clean, and perfectly dry, and that every Bottle be well cork'd. This will keep good ſeveral Years.

| 8 gallons ale wort | honey |
|---|---|
| 1/4 lb. whole cloves | |

Beſides this way of making Mead, there is another which I have approved to be very good, which, in all particulars, except the Water, is the ſame with this; and inſtead of the Water, put the like Quantity of ſmall Ale-Wort, brew'd with pale Malt: but this will require leſs Honey than the former, and will require more time in the Veſſel before it is fine and fit to bottle; but it will laſt many Years good, and will drink like *Cyprus* Wine when it is a Year old. In this Liquor, take particular care that your Cloves are freſh and ſound, for elſe you muſt add a Quantity in proportion.
(From *The Country Housewife and Lady's Director*, by R. Bradley, 1736, pp. 136-7.)

# 262  TO MAKE METHEGLIN – c. 1550 to 1625

| | |
|---|---|
| 1 quart honey | yeast |
| 6 quarts water | lemon |
| 3 ginger roots | raisins |
| cinnamon sticks | |

Time to completion:  14 days.

Take a quart of honey & 6 quarts of wat[er].  let it boyle y^e third part away, & boyle [wth] it 3 races of ginger.  when it is cold, put it [in] a pot which hath a spicket, & put yeast into [it] & let it stand 3 dayes, then bottle it up & put into y^r bottles a little leamon & a stick of cinna[mon] & a few raysons of y^e sun.  & let it be a fortnig[ht] befor you drink it.

(From *Martha Washington's Booke of Cookery*, ed. by Karen Hess, 1981.  Letters in brackets were reconstructed by the editor.)


[21. METHEGLEN] – 1609

*The original manuscript of this recipe included margin notes; these have been incorporated into our text using brackets.  In some places the printer has used "vv" in place of "w."*

*Metheglen* is meth compouded with herbs:  ſo called *quaſi Meth e glen*, meth of the vallie, becauſe it is made in the vallies, where is abundance and variety of holſome herbes.  He that liſteth to knowe the many and ſundrie makings of this holſome drinke, muſt learne it of the ancient Britaines:  vvho therein do paſſe all other people.  One excellent receipte I will heere ſet downe: and it is of that, which our renowmed Queene of happie memory did ſo vvel like, that ſhee vvould every yeere haue a veſſel of it.

[22. The Queens metheglen.]

1 gallon honey per 6 gallons water
1 bushel sweetbrier leaves     1 bushel thyme
1/2 bushel rosemary     1 peck bay leaves
a large quantity working new ale or beer     water
<u>spice bag containing 1 ounce total</u>: mace blades and cloves.

Time to completion:  6 months.

Firſt gather a buſhell of ſvveete-bryar-leaues, and a buſhell of tyme, halfe a buſhell of roſemarie, and a pecke of bay-leaues.  Seeth al theſe being vvell vvaſhed in a furnace

*81*

of faire vvater: let them boile the ſpace of halfe an hovvre, or better; and then powre out al the water and herbes into a vate, and let it ſtand til it be cold. Then ſtraine the water fró the herbs, & take to every [If you maruaile that ſo great a quantitie of water is required; it is partly becauſe of the goodneſſe of the hony, which being pure and fine goeth further then ordinary: but chiefly that it may haue the longer time to be clarified in boiling, before it come to his ſtrength. And therfore ſome wil haue eight parts of water to one of hony: but then they boile it ſo much the longer.] ſix gallons of water one gallon of the fineſt hony, and put it into the water cold, and labour it together halfe an houre, and let it ſtand two daies, ſtirring it well twiſe or thriſe each day. Then take the liquor and boile it anew, and when it doth ſeeth, skim it as long as there remaineth any droſſe. When it is cleer [The third part at leaſt being waſted.] put it into the vate as before, & there let it be cooled. You muſt then haue in a readines a kiue[1] of new ale or beere: which as ſoone as you haue emptied, ſoddainly whelme it vpſide downe, and ſet it vp again, and preſently put in the metheglen, & let it ſtand three daies a working: and then tun it vp in barrels, tying at every tap-hole, by a packthread, a little bag of cloues and mace, to the valew of an ounce.

   It muſt ſtand halfe a yeer before it be drunk of.

(From *The Feminine Monarchie or A Treatise Concerning Bees, and the Dve Ordering of Them, etc.*, by Charles Butler, 1609.)

## #9 THE COUNTESS OF BULLINGBROOK'S WHITE METHEGLIN – 1669

| | |
|---|---|
| 8 gallons water | honey |
| 1 ounce ginger root | 4 egg whites |
| rosemary | yeast |

Take eight Gallons of Conduit-water, and boil it very well; then put as much Honey in it, as will bear an Egge, and stir it well together. Then set it upon the fire, and put in the whites of four Eggs to clarifie it; And as the scum riseth, take it off clean: Then put in a pretty quantity of Rose-mary, and let it boil, till it tasteth a little of it: Then with a scummer take out the Rosemary, as fast as you can, and let it boil half a quarter of an hour; put it into earthen pans to cool; next morning put it into a barrel, and put into it a little barm, and an Ounce of Ginger scraped and sliced; And let it stand a Month or six Weeks. Then bottle it up close; you must be sure not to let it stand at all in Brass.

(From *The Closet ...Opened*, 1669.)

---

[1] A 'kiue' or 'kiver' is a large vessel used to hold the working liquor. In this instance the kiver is emptied, leaving the lees behind. This is usually considered a desirable circumstance by those seeking clarity. However, our Mr. Butler, fearful perhaps that the ale or beer he is using has insufficient yeast suspended in it, wishes the lees to be stirred up and added to the metheglin.

# 1  A RECEIPT TO MAKE METHEGLIN AS IT IS MADE AT LIEGE, COMMUNICATED BY MR. MASILLON – 1669

| | |
|---|---|
| 1 measure honey | 1 lb. beer hops per 45 gallons liquor |
| 3 measures water | *optional*: cloves; ginger root; beer *or* bread yeast. |

Take one Measure of Honey, and three Measures of Water, and let it boil till one measure be boiled away, so that there be left three measures in all; as for Example, take to one Pot of Honey, three Pots of Water, and let it boil so long, till it come to three Pots. During which time you must Skim it very well as soon as any scum riseth; which you are to continue till there rise no scum more. You may, if you please, put to it some spice, to wit, Cloves and Ginger; the quantity of which is to be proportioned according as you will have your Meath, strong or weak. But this you do before it begin to boil. There are some that put either Yeast of Beer, or Leaven of bread into it, to make it work. But this is not necessary at all; and much less to set it into the Sun. Mr. Masillon doth neither the one nor the other. Afterwards for to Tun it, you must let it grow Luke-warm, for to advance it. And if you do intend to keep your Meath a long time, you may put into it some hopps on this fashion. Take to every Barrel of Meathe a Pound of Hops without leaves, that is, of Ordinary Hops used for Beer, but well cleansed, taking only the Flowers, without the Green-leaves and stalks. Boil this pound of Hops in a Pot and half of fair water, till it come to one Pot, and this quantity is sufficient for a Barrel of Meathe. A Barrel at Liege holdeth ninety Pots, and a Pot is as much as a Wine quart in England. (I have since been informed from Liege, that a Pot of that Countrey holdeth 48 Ounces of Apothecary's measure; which I judge to be a Pottle according to London measure, or two Wine-quarts.) When you Tun your Meath, you must not fill your Barrel by half a foot, that so it may have room to work. Then let it stand six weeks slightly stopped; which being expired, if the Meath do not work, stop it up very close. Yet must you not fill up the Barrel to the very brim. After six Months you draw off the clear into another Barrel, or strong Bottles, leaving the dregs, and filling up your new Barrel, or Bottels, and stopping it or them very close.

The Meath that is made this way, (*Viz.* In the Spring, in the Month of April or May, which is the proper time for making of it,) will keep many a year. (*ibid.*)

## #2 WHITE METHEGLIN OF MY LADY HUNGERFORD: WHICH IS EXCEEDINGLY PRAISED – 1669

*All the herbs mentioned in this recipe were used during this period to cure diseases of the liver. Read this recipe carefully before proceeding.*

| | |
|---|---|
| honey | 8 or 9 gallons water |
| 1/2 handful violet leaves | 1/4 handful wood sorrel |
| 12 sprigs rosemary | 4 or 5 sprigs lemon balm |
| thyme | red sage |
| 1/2 ounce cloves | 1/2 ounce whole nutmegs |
| 4 or 5 ginger roots | |

<u>1 handful each</u>: strawberry leaves; hart's-tongue; liverwort.[1]

Time to completion: 6 months to 1 year.

Take your Honey, and mix it with fair water, until the Honey be quite dissolved. If it will bear an Egge to be above the liquor, the breadth of a groat, it is strong enough; if not, put more Honey to it, till it be so strong; Then boil it, till it be clearly and well skimmed; Then put in one good handful of Strawberry-leaves, and half a handful of Violet leaves; and half as much Sorrel: a Douzen tops of Rosemary; four or five tops of Baulme-leaves: a handful of Harts-tongue, and a handful of Liver-worth; a little Thyme, and a little Red-sage; Let it boil about an hour; then put it into a Woodden Vessel, where let it stand, till it be quite cold; Then put it into the Barrel; Then take half an Ounce of Cloves, as much Nutmeg; four or five Races of Ginger; bruise it, and put it into a fine bag, with a stone to make it sink, that it may hang below the middle: Then stop it very close.

    The Herbs and Spices are in proportion for six Gallons.

    Since my Lady Hungerford sent me this Receipt, she sent me word, that she now useth (and liketh better) to make the Decoction of Herbs before you put the Honey to it,

---

[1] *Marchantia polymorpha* L. (*see Appendix*). The liverworts called for are very small non-vascular plants which are either aquatic or inhabit moist areas. Culpeper's Herbal (p. 174) mentions Liverworts: "bruised and boiled in small beer, and drunk, it cooleth the liver and kidneys and cures the running of the reins in men, and whites in women; stays the spreading of tetters, ringworms, and other running sores or scabs, and is a first-rate remedy for such whose livers are corrupted by surfeits, which cause their bodies to break out, for it fortifieth the liver exceedingly..."
A group of vascular plants, the Noble Liverworts (*Hepática*), share a similar name, but are not the plants being called for here. Noble Liverworts were grown in gardens during the Middle Ages, and a large woodcut of several species can be found in Parkinson's *Paradisi in Sole Paradiſus Terrestris* (p. 227). I can find no mention of the Noble Liverworts being used in cooking or brewing.

This Proportion of Herbs is to make six Gallons of Decoction, so that you may take eight or nine Gallons of water. When you have drawn out into your water, all the vertue of the Herbs, throw them away, and take the clear Decoction (leaving the settlings) and when it is Lukewarm, Dissolve your proportion of Honey in it. After it is well dissolved and laved with strong Arms or woodden Instruments, like Battle-doors or Scoops, boil it gently; till you have taken away all the scum; then make an end of well boyling it, about an hour in all. Then pour it into a wooden vessel, and let it stand till it be cold. Then pour the clear through a Sieve of hair, ceasing pouring when you come to the foul thick settling. Tun the clear into your vessel (without Barm) and stop it up close, with the Spices in it, till you perceive by the hissing that it begins to work. Then give it some little vent, else the Barrel would break. When it is at the end of the working, stop it up close. She useth to make it at the end of Summer, when she takes up her Honey and begins to drink it in Lent. But it will be better if you defer piercing it till next Winter. When part of the Barrel is drunk, she botteleth the rest, which maketh it quicker and better. You clear the Decoction from the Herbs by a Hair-sieve.
(From *The Closet ...Opened*, 1669.)

# 34  TO MAKE WHITE METHEGLIN – 1669

4 gallons water
1 gallon honey
ginger root
cloves
yeast
cinnamon sticks
*optional*: lemon peel

Time to completion: 1 month to 6 weeks.

*Liverwort.*
From Gerard's
*Herball*, 1597.

Take a Gallon of Honey; put to it four Gallons of water; stir them well together, and boil them in a Kettle, till a Gallon be wasted with boiling and scumming. Then put it into a vessel to cool. When it is almost as cold as Ale-wort, then clear it out into another vessel: Then put Barm upon it, as you do to your Ale, and so let it work. And then Tun it up into a vessel, and put into it a bag with Ginger, Cloves, and Cinamon bruised a little, and so hang the bag in the vessel, and stop it up very close; and when it hath stood a month or six weeks, bottle it up and so drink it. You may put in a little Limmon-peel into some of your Metheglin, for those that like that taste; which most persons do very much. (*ibid.*)

# # 8 A RECEIPT TO MAKE A TUN OF METHEGLIN – 1669

| | |
|---|---|
| water | honey and honeycombs |
| saxifrage | wild sage |
| blue buttons | agrimony[1] |
| scabious | betony |
| wild marjoram | 2 elecampane roots |
| 1 handful sage | 3 whole borage plants |
| 1 peck garden thyme | 1 peck mother of thyme, stems and roots |
| 3 handfuls sweet marjoram | <u>1 sieveful each</u>: avens; violet leaves. |

<u>2 handfuls each</u>:  dock; bay leaves; rosemary; parsley roots; fennel.

Take two handfuls of Dock (*alias* wild Carrot) a reasonable burthen of Saxifrage, Wild-sage, Blew-button, Scabious, Bettony, Agrimony, Wild-marjoram, of each a reasonable burthen; Wild-thyme a Peck, Roots and all.  All these are to be gathered in the fields, between the two Lady days in Harvest.[2]  The Garden-herbs are these; Bay-leaves, and Rosemary, of each two handfuls; a Sieveful of Avens, and as much Violet-leaves:  A handful of Sage:  three handfuls of Sweet-Marjoram, Three Roots of young Borrage, leaves and all, that hath not born seed; Two handfuls of Parsley-roots, and all that hath not born Seed.  Two Roots of Elecampane that have not seeded:  Two handfuls of Fennel that hath not seeded:  A peck of Thyme; wash and pick all your herbs from filth and grass:  Then put your field herbs first into the bottom of a clean Furnace, and lay all your Garden-herbs thereon; then fill your Furnace with clean water, letting your herbs seeth, till they be so tender, that you may easily slip off the skin of your Field-herbs, and that you may break the roots of your Garden-herbs between your Fingers. Then lade forth your Liquor, and set it a cooling.  Then fill your Furnace again with clear water to these Herbs, and let them boil a quarter of an hour.  Then put it to your first Liquor, filling the Furnace, until you have sufficient to fill your Tun.  Then as your Liquor begins to cool, and is almost cold, set your servants to temper Honey and wax in it, Combs and all, and let them temper it well together, breaking the Combes very small; let their hands and nails be very clean; and when you have tempered it very well together, cleanse it through a cleansing sieve into another clean vessel; The more Honey you have in your Liquor, the stronger it will be.  Therefore to know, when it is strong enough, take two New-laid eggs, when you begin to cleanse, and put them in whole into the bottome of your cleansed Liquor; And if it be strong enough, it will cause the Egge to ascend upward, and to be on the top as broad as sixpence; if they do not swim on the top; put more [*honey*].

(From *The Closet ...Opened*, 1669.)

---

[1] CAUTION!  (*See Appendix.*)

[2] August 15th to September 8th.

# 24  A RECEIPT FOR WHITE METHEGLIN – 1669

| | |
|---|---|
| 1 quart honey | 4, 5, or 6 quarts water |
| rosemary | ginger root |
| yeast | |

Take to every quart of honey, 4, 5, or 6, quarts of water; boil it on a good quick fire as long as any scum riseth; as it boils, put about half a pint of water at a time very often, and scum it very well as it riseth; and be sure to keep it up to the same height and quantity as at the first: Put into it a little Rosemary, according to the quantity that you make, and boil it half a quarter of an hour; scum it very well. You may put a little Ginger into it, onely to give it a taste thereof, and let it have a little walm of heat after it. Then take and put it into a Woodden vessel, (which must be well scalded, least it taste of any thing) let it stand all night, and the next morning strain it through a sieve of hair.

Then if you please, you may boil up your grounds that are in the bottome of the vessel with three or four quarts of water; and when it is cold, strain it, to the rest, and put to it a little good light barm. That which you make in the winter, you must let it stand three days and three nights covered up, before you bottle it up; and two nights in summer, and then bottle it up. But be sure, you scum off the barm before the bottling up.

(From *The Closet ...Opened*, 1669.)

# 48  TO MAKE METHEGLIN – 1669

| | |
|---|---|
| 8 gallons water | 16 lbs. honey |
| 2 whole nutmegs, quartered | 2 handfuls malt, ground |
| 1 wine pint ale yeast | |

Time to completion:  3 or 4 weeks.

Take eight Gallons of water, and set it over a clear fire in a Kettle; and when it is warm, put into it sixteen pounds of very good honey; stir it well together, till it be all mixed; and when it boileth, take off the scum, and put in two large Nutmegs cut into quarters, and so let it boil at least an hour. Then take it off, and put into it two good handfuls of grinded Malt, and with a white staff keep beating it together, till it be almost cold; then strain it through a hair sieve into a tub, and put to it a wine pint of Ale-yest, and stir it very well together; and when it it [*sic*] cold, you may, if you please, Tun it up presently in a vessel fit for it, or else let it stand, and work a day: And when it hath done working in your vessel, stop it up very close. It will be three weeks or a month, before it will be ready to drink. (*ibid.*)

# # 13  METHEGLIN COMPOSED BY MYSELF OUT OF SUNDRY RECEIPTS – 1669

*These two recipes were apparently written by Sir Kenelme as he was making the metheglin, which did not turn out to his liking. His end note states that he has added too much of each of the herbs, and that he would prefer to use less marjoram and thyme.*

| | |
|---|---|
| 60 gallons water | ale yeast |
| 1 gallon honey per 3 gallons liquor | 3 handfuls rosemary |
| 6 eringo roots | egg whites |
| 10 handfuls sweetbrier leaves | ginger root |
| cinnamon sticks | cloves |
| cardamom seeds | |

<u>2 handfuls each</u>:  mint; angelica; bay leaves; mother of thyme; sweet marjoram.
<u>4 handfuls each</u>:  eyebright; liverwort; agrimony; scabious; balm; wood betony; strawberry leaves; burnet.

In sixty Gallons of water, boil ten handfuls of Sweet-bryar-leaves; Eyebright, Liverwort, Agrimony, Scabious, Balme, Wood-bettony, Strawberry-leaves, Burnet, of each four handfuls; of Rosemary, three handfuls; of Minth, Angelica, Bayes and Wild-thyme, Sweet-Marjoram, of each two handfuls:  Six Eringo-roots.  When the water hath taken out the vertue of the herbs and roots, let it settle, and the next day pour off the clear, and in every three Gallons of it boil one of honey, scumming it well, and putting in a little cold water now and then to make the scum rise, as also some whites of Eggs. When it is clear scummed, take it off, and let it cool; then work it with Ale-yest; tun it up, and hang it in a bag [*sic*], with Ginger, Cinamom, Cloves and Cardamom.  And as it worketh over, put in some strong honey-drink warmed.  When it works no more, stop it up close.

| | |
|---|---|
| 20 gallons water | 1 gallon honey per 2 1/2 gallons liquor |
| 4 eringo roots | cloves |
| cardamom seeds | ginger roots |
| cinnamon sticks | 10 handfuls clove gilliflowers |

<u>5 handfuls each</u>:  sweetbrier leaves; eyebright; rosemary; bay leaves.

In twenty Gallons of water boil Sweet-bryar-leaves, Eye-bright, Rosemary, Bayes, Clove-gilly-flowers, of each five handfuls, and four Eringo-roots.  To every two gallons and a half of this decoction, put one gallon of honey; boil it, &c.  When it is tunned up, hang in it a bag containing five handfuls of Clove-gillyflowers, and sufficient quantity of the spices above.

In both these Receipts, the quantity of the herbs is too great.  The strong herbs preserve the drink, and make it nobler.  Use Marjoram and Thyme in little quantity in all.  (*ibid.*)

# # 15  SIR THOMAS GOWER'S METHEGLIN FOR HEALTH – 1669

| | |
|---|---|
| 12 gallons water | 6 handfuls sweetbrier leaves |
| 2 gallons honey | 1 ounce unspecified spices |
| 3 whole eggs | |

<u>1 handful each</u>:  sweet marjoram; rosemary; thyme.
<u>2 handfuls each</u>:  marigold flowers; borage; bugloss; sage.

First boil the water and scum it; Then to 12 Gallons put 6 handfuls of Sweet-bryar-leaves, of Sweet-marjoram, Rosemary, Thyme, of each one a handful:  Flowers of Marigold, Borrage, Bugloss, Sage, each two handfuls.  Boil all together very gently, till a third waste.  To eight Gallons of this put two Gallons of pure honey, and boil them till the Liquor bear an Egge, the breadth of threepence or a Groat, together with such spices as you like (bruised, but not beaten) an ounce of all is sufficient.

You must observe carefully.  1. Before you set the Liquor to boil, to cause a lusty Servant (his Arms well washed) to mix the honey and water together, labouring it with his hands at least an hour without intermission.  2. That when it begins to boil fast, you take away part of the fire, so as it may boil slowly, and the scum and dross go all to one side, the other remaining clear.  When you take it off, let none of the liquor go away with the dross.  3. When you take it from the fire, let it settle well, before it be tunned into the vessel, wherein you mean to keep it:  and when it comes near the bottom, let it be taken carefully from the sediment, with a thin Dish, so as nothing be put into the vessel, but what is clear.  4. Stop it very close (when it is set in the place, where it must remain) cover it with a cloth, upon which some handfuls of Bay-salt and Salpeter is laid, and over that lay clay, and a Turf.[1]  5. Put into it, when you stop it, some New-laid-eggs in number proportionable to the bigness of the vessel, Shell's unbroken.  Six Eggs to about sixteen Gallons.  The whole Egg-shell and all will be entirely consumed. (From *The Closet ...Opened*, 1669.)

---

[1] These are instructions for storing the cask.  In his recipe #72 we are told to "...stop it well with clay and salt tempered together, *to keep it moist*."

"The Conſerue or Syrupe made of the [*rasp*]berries, is effectuall to coole an hot ſtomacke, helping to refreſh and quicken vp thoſe that are ouercome with faintneſſe. The berries are eaten in the Summertime, as an afternoones diſh, to pleaſe the taſte of the ſicke as well as the ſound. The iuyce and the diſtilled water of the berries are verie comfortable and cordiall. It is generally held of many, but how true I know not, that the red wine that is vſually ſold at the Vintners, is made of the berries of Raſpis that grow in colder countries, which giueth it a kinde of harſhneſſe..."[1]

✳✳✳

## #16 METHEGLIN FOR TASTE AND COLOUR – 1669

*This is four recipes in one; the numbers in brackets have been added to differentiate the recipes.*

[1]
4, 5, or 6 gallons water
1 gallon honey
*optional*: raspberries *or* raspberry juice.
toast spread with spirit of barm (*see below*), *or* yeast mixed with 2 drops oil of cinnamon

Time to completion: 6 months.

Must be boiled as the other,[2] if you intend to keep it above half a year; but less according to the time, wherein you mean to use it. You must put in no Herbs, to avoid bitterness and discolouring; and the proportion of water and honey more or less, as you would drink it sooner or later; (as a Gallon of honey to 4, 5, or 6 of water.) If to be weak, and to be soon drunk, you must when it is tunned, put in a Tost of bread (hard tosted) upon which half a score drops of Spirit of yest or barm is dropped; for want of it, spread it with purest barm beaten with a few drops of Oyl of Cinnamon. If you intend to give it the taste of Raspes, then adde more barm, to make it work well, and during that time of working, put in your Raspes (or their Syrup) but the fruit gives a delicate Colour, and Syrup a duller Tincture. Drink not that made after the first manner, till six moneths, and it will endure drawing better then wine; but Bottleled, it is more spirited then any drink.

[2] The Spirit of Barm is made by putting store of water to the barm; then distill the Spirit, as you do other Spirits; At last an oyl will come, which is not for this use.

---

[1] Parkinson, pp. 557-8.
[2] *Sir Thomas Gower's Metheglin for Health*, #15.

[3]
8 gallons small ale                    1 gallon honey
yeast

Time to completion: 3 months.

Sir Thomas Gower maketh his ordinary drink thus: Make very small well Brewed Ale. To eight Gallons of this put one Gallon of honey; when it is well dissolved and clarified, tun up the Liquor, making it work in due manner with barm. When it hath done working, stop it up close, and in three months it will be fit to drink.

a *Caltha palustris minor.*
The small marsh Marigold.

[4]
<u>For each gallon of water take a decoction of</u>:
bay leaves
1 handful cowslip flowers[1]
1 handful sweetbrier leaves
scabious
1 pinch thyme
1 pinch sweet marjoram
rosemary
betony
1/3 to 1/6 part honey to each part clear liquor

He makes Metheglin thus. Make a good Decoct of Eglantine-leaves, Cowslip flowers, a little Sweet-marjoram, and some Rosemary and Bayleaves, Betony, and Scabious, and a little Thyme. After the sediment hath settled, put 1/3 or 1/4 or 1/5 or 1/6 part of honey, (according as you would have it strong, and soon ready) to the clear severed from the settlement, and stir it exceeding well with stripped arms 4 or 5 hours, till it be perfectly incorporated. Then boil and scum it; let it then cool and tun it up, &c. After it hath cooled, lade the clean from the settlement, so that it may not trouble it, and run up the clear thus severed from the settlings. Much of the perfection consisteth in stirring it long with stripped arms before you boil it. Then to boil it very leisurely till all the scum be off. And order your fire so, that the scum may rise and drive all to one side. This will be exceeding pale clear and pleasant Metheglin. He useth to every Gallon of water, a good handful of Eglantine-leaves, and as much Cowslip flowers; but onely a Pugil of Thyme or Marjoram.
(From *The Closet ...Opened*, 1669.)

---

[1] CAUTION! (*See Appendix.*)

## # 17  AN EXCELLENT WAY OF MAKING WHITE METHEGLIN – 1669

water                              honey
2 whole nutmegs                    flour
yeast                              2 egg whites
2 or 3 ginger roots                egg whites and egg shells
cinnamon sticks
1 handful each:  sweetbrier hips; rosemary; broad thyme.

Take of Sweet-bryar berries, of Rosemary, broad Thyme, of each a handful.  Boil them in a quantity of fair water for half an hour; then cleanse the water from the herbs, and let it stand 24 hours, or until it be thorough cold.  Then put your hony into it (hony which floweth from the Combs of it self in a warm place is best) make it so strong of the honey that it bear an egge (if you will have it strong) the breadth of a groat above the Liquor.  This being done, lave and bounce it very well and often, that the honey and water may incorporate and work well together.  After this boil it softly over a gentle fire, and scum it.  Then beat the whites of eggs with their shells, and put into it to clarifie it.  After this, put some of it into a vessel, and take the whites of two eggs, and a little barm, and a small quantity of fine flower; beat them well together, and put it into the vessel close covered, that it may work.  Then pour the rest into it by degrees, as you do Beer.  At last take a quantity of Cinamon, 2 or 3 races of Ginger, and two Nutmegs (for more will alter the colour of it.)  Hang these in a little bag in the vessel.  Thus made, it will be as white as any White-wine.
(From *The Closet ...Opened*, 1669.)


## # 66  TO MAKE METHEGLIN – 1669

5 gallons water                    yeast
1 gallon honey                     6 ounces ginger root
1 ounce whole nutmegs              2 ounces cinnamon sticks

Time to completion:  1 week.

Take five Gallons of water, and one Gallon of good White-honey; set it on the fire together, and boil it very well, and skim it very clean; Then take it off the fire, and set it by.  Take six ounces of good Ginger, and two ounces of Cinamon, one Ounce of Nutmegs; bruise all these grosly, and put them into your hot Liquor, and cover it close, and so let it stand, till it be cold.  Then put as much Ale-barm to it, as will make it work; then keep it in a warm place, as you do Ale; and when it hath wrought well, Tun it up, as you do Ale or Beer:  and when it is a week old, drink of it at your pleasure.
(*ibid.*)

## # 20  TO MAKE WHITE METHEGLIN – 1669

| | |
|---|---|
| 12 gallons water | 4 sprigs rosemary |
| 3 to 4 gallons honey | yellow wall flowers |
| 1 pint ale yeast | clove gilliflowers |
| 2 mace blades | 1 nutmeg |
| 1 ginger root | 3 grains musk |
| cinnamon sticks | 1 whole aril of mace |

<u>1/2 handful each</u>:  agrimony;[1] bugloss; borage.

<u>1 spoonful each</u>:  anise seeds; fennel seeds; caraway seeds.

<u>1 handful each</u>:  sweetbrier; violet flowers; violet leaves; sweet marjoram; strawberry leaves.

Take of Sweet-bryar a great handful:  of Violet-flowers, Sweet-marjoram, Strawberry-leaves, Violet-leaves, *ana*, one handful, Agrimony, Bugloss, Borrage, *ana*, half a handful.  Rosemary four branches, Gilly-flowers, No. 4 (the Yellow-wall-flowers, with great tops)[2] Anniseeds, Fennel, and Caraway, of each a spoonful, Two large Mace.  Boil all these in twelve Gallons of water for the Space of an hour; then strain it, and let it stand until it be Milk-warm:  Then put in as much honey, as will carry an Egge to the breadth of sixpence, at least.  Then boil it again, and scum it clean; then let it stand, until it be cold; then put a pint of Ale-barm into it, and ripen it as you do Beer, and tun it.  Then hang in the midst of the vessel a little bag with a Nutmeg quartered, a Race of Ginger sliced, a little Cinamon, and mace whole, and three grains of Musk in a cloth put into the bag amongst the rest of the Spices.  Put a stone in the bag, to keep it in the midst of the Liquor.  This quantity took up three Gallons of honey; therefore be sure to have four in readiness.

(From *The Closet ...Opened*, 1669.)

*A Feast Scene.*
From *Biblia Sacra Vulgatae Editionis...*,
Venice, 1686.

---

[1] CAUTION!  (*See Appendix*).

[2] Number 4?  Could our dear Sir Kenelme, or one of his uncredited correspondents, have been consulting a gardening manual?

# 26  SEVERAL WAYS OF MAKING METHEGLIN – 1669

*Here are four different recipes for making metheglin; the numbers in brackets have been added to help differentiate the recipes. All begin with the same clarified water which is made in the first paragraph.*

Take such quantity as you judge convenient of Spring, or pure rain water, and make it boil well half an hour. Then pour it out into a Woodden fat, and let it settle 74 hours. Then power [*pour*] off the clear, leaving the sediment in the bottome. Let such water be the Liquor for all the several Honey-drinks, you will make.

1 *Scabiosa maior vulgaris.*
Common Scabious.

[1]
16 gallons warm water
2 gallons honey
lemon peel
egg whites
mace blades
1 cinnamon stick
1 handful ginger root
cloves

Time to completion:  6 to 8 weeks.

*Scabious.*
From Gerard's
*Herball*, 1597.

1.  Warm sixteen Gallons of this water (lukewarm) and put two Gallons of Honey to it, in a half tub or other fit Woodden vessel. Lave it very well with a clean arm, or woodden battle-door for two or three hours, dissolving the honey very well in the water. Let it stand thus two or three days in wood, laving it thrice a day, a pretty while each time. Then put it back into your Copper and boil it gently, till you have scummed away all the foulness that will rise; and clarifie it with whites of Eggs: Then put into it a little handful of cleansed and sliced white Ginger, and a little mace; when they have boiled enough, put in a few Cloves bruised, and a stick of Cinamon, and a little Limmon-peel, and after a walm or two, pour the Liquor into a woodden half tub, with the spices in it. Cover it close with a Cloth and blanquet, and let it stand so two days. Then let the liquor run through a bolter, to sever the spice, stopping before any settlings come. Then pour this clear liquor into pottle-bottles of glass, not filling them by a fingers breadth or more. Stop them close with Cork tied in, and set them in a cool place for 6, 7 or 8 weeks. [*Continued on next two pages.*]

[2]
40 gallons water
ale yeast
2 ounces mustard seed

2 handfuls betony tops
1/2 lb. ginger root
egg whites and egg shells
1 gallon honey per 4 gallons strained liquid

<u>1 handful each</u>: thyme; sweet marjoram.

<u>4 handfuls each</u>: agrimony;[1] scabious.

<u>5 handfuls each flowers of</u>: cowslip;[1] primrose;[1] rosemary; sage; borage; bugloss; and sweetbrier tops.

<u>3 ounces each</u>: cinnamon sticks; coriander seeds; elder flowers; cloves.

2. In fourty Gallons of the first boiled and settled water, boil five handfuls of sweet-bryar tops, as much of Cowslip-flowers, as much of Primrose-flowers, as much of Rosemary-flowers, as much of Sage-flowers, as many of Borage-flowers, as many of Bugloss-flowers; two handfuls of the tops of Betony, four handfuls of Agrimony, and as many of Scabious, one handful of Thyme, as much of Sweet-marjoram, and two ounces of Mustard-seed bruised. When this hath boiled so long, that you judge the water hath drawn out all the vertue of the Herbs (which may be in half an hour) pour out all into a vatte to cool and settle. Scum away the herbs, and pour the clear from the sediment, and to every four gallons of liquor (luke-warm) put one gallon of honey, and lave it to dissolve the honey, letting it stand two or three days, laving it well thrice every day. Then boil it till it will bear an Egge high, then clarifie it with whites and shells of Eggs, and pour it into a vatte to cool, which it will do in a days space or better. Whilst it is yet luke-warm, put Ale-yest to it, (no more then is necessary) to make it work, and then tun it into a Rundlet of a fit Size, that hath been seasoned with Sack; and hang in it a boulter bag containing half a pound of white Ginger cleansed and sliced, three ounces of Cloves and as much of Cinamon bruised, as much Coriander seed prepared, and as much Elder-flowers. As it purgeth and consumeth by running over the bung, put in fresh honey-liquor warmed, that you keep or make on purpose for that end. When the working is even almost at an end, stop it up close with clay and sand, and have great care to keep it always close stopped. After a year draw in into [*sic*] pottle Glass-bottles stopped with ground stoppels of glass, and keep them in a cool place, till they are ready to drink, if they as yet be not so.

Have a care, that never any Liquor stay in Copper longer then whilst it is to boil.

---

[1] CAUTION! (*See Appendix.*)

[3]

| | |
|---|---|
| 20 gallons water | elder flowers |
| ale yeast | cloves |
| 1/2 handful mother of thyme | ginger root |
| cinnamon sticks | lemon peel |
| 1 part honey per 6 parts strained liquid | |
| toast spread with ground mustard seeds | |
| 6 handfuls each flowers of: sweetbrier; cowslip;[1] primrose;[1] rosemary. | |

3. In 20 Gallons of the first boiled and settled water, boil six handfuls of Sweet-bryar-leaves, as many of Cowslip flowers, as many of Primrose-flowers, and as many of Rosemary-flowers; and half a handful of Wild thyme, during the space of a quarter or half an hour. Then take the clear, and dissolve in it a sixth part of honey, doing as above for the boiling and clarifying it. But boil it not to bear an Egge, but onely till it be well scummed and clarified. Then pour it into a woodden Tub, and Tun it with Ale-yest, when it is in due temper of coolness, as you would do Ale-wort; and let it work (close covered) sufficiently. Then Tun it up into a seasoned firkin, and put into it a tost of white-bread spread with quick Mustard, and hang it in a boulter bag containing loosly some Ginger, Cloves and Cinamon bruised, and a little Limon-peel and Elder-flowers, with a Pebble-stone at the bottome, to make it sink towards the bottom, and fastned by a string coming out of the bung to hinder it from falling quite to the bottome. Stop the bung very close, and after six weeks or two moneths draw it into bottles.

[4]

| | |
|---|---|
| 20 gallons water | 1 gallon honey per 4 gallons strained liquid |
| lemon peels | cloves |
| yeast | ginger root |
| cinnamon sticks | egg whites and egg shells |
| | 10 handfuls each: sweetbrier leaves; cowslips.[1] |

4. In 20 Gallons of boiled and settled water, boil a quarter of an hour ten handfuls of sweet bryar-leaves, and as many of Cowslips. Then let it cool and settle in wood, and take the clear; and to every four Gallons of Liquor, put one of honey, dissolving it as the others formerly set down. Boil it, till no more scum rise, and that a fourth part be consumed. Then clarifie it with whites of Eggs and their shells, and make it work with yest. After sufficient working Tun it up, hanging it in a bag with Ginger, Cloves, Cinamon and Limon-peel. Stop it very close, and after two or three moneths, draw it into bottles. (*ibid.*)

---

[1] CAUTION! (*See Appendix.*)

# # 37 ANOTHER METHEGLIN – 1669

3 gallons water                    2 handfuls cowslips[1]
1 gallon honey                     1/2 ounce cinnamon sticks
1 pint ale yeast
1/2 handful each:  rosemary; liverwort; balm.
1 ounce each:  ginger root; whole nutmegs.
*optional*:  2 handfuls sweetbrier leaves, 1 handful betony.

In every three Gallons of water, boil Rosemary, Liverwort, Balm, *ana*, half a handful, and Cowslips two handfuls. When the water hath sufficiently drawn out the vertue of the herbs, pour all into a Tub, and let it stand all night. Then strain it. And to every three Gallons of the clear Liquor (or 2 1/2, if you will have your drink stronger) put one Gallon of honey, and boil it, till it bear an Egge, scuming it till no more scum will rise: which to make rise the better, put in now and then a Porrenger full of cold water. Then pour it into a Tub, and let it stand to cool, till it be blood warm, and then put by degrees a Pint of Ale-yest to it, to make it work. So let it stand three days very close covered. Then skim off the yest, and put it into a seasoned barrel; but stop it not up close, till it have done hissing. Then either stop it very close, if you will keep it in the barrel, or draw it into bottles. Put into this proportion, Ginger sliced, Nutmegs broken, *ana*, one ounce, Cinamon bruised half an ounce in a bag, which hang in the bung with a stone in it to make it sink. You may add, if you please, to this proportion of water, or one Gallon more, two handfuls of Sweet-bryar-leaves, and one of Betony. (From *The Closet ...Opened*, 1669.)

# # 79 A RECEIPT TO MAKE METHEGLIN – 1669

4 gallons water                    2 ounces ginger root
2 quarts honey                     2 ounces dried orange peel
1 ounce whole nutmegs              1 handful each: rosemary; bay leaves.
yeast

Take four Gallons of water, two quarts of Honey, two ounces of Ginger, one ounce of Nutmegs, a good handful of Rose-mary tops, and as much of Bay-leaves, two ounces of dried Orange-peel. Boil all these till it be so strong as will bear an Egg, and not sink; when it is milk warm, work it up with barm, during twenty four hours, and then barrel it up. And after three months you may bottle it up at your pleasure.

As you desire a greater quantity of the drink, you must augment the ingredients, according to the proportions above recited. (*ibid.*)

---

[1] CAUTION! (*See Appendix.*)

# # 38 MR. PIERCE'S EXCELLENT WHITE METHEGLIN – 1669

*This is a very thorough and detailed early recipe.*

| | |
|---|---|
| 3 hogsheads water | 1 handful broad thyme |
| 1 part honey to 4 parts water | 1 lb. ginger root |
| 2 quarts ale barm | 1 ounce cinnamon powder |
| 4 ounces clove powder | <u>4 handfuls each</u>: eyebright; sweetbrier. |
| | <u>2 handfuls each</u>: rosemary; sweet marjoram. |

Time to completion: 1 year.

In a Copper, that holdeth conveniently three hogsheads, or near so much, boil the best water, (as full as is fitting). As soon as it boileth well and high, put to it four handfuls of Sweet-bryar-leaves, as much of Eye-bright: two handfuls of Rosemary, as much of Sweet-Marjoram, and one of Broad-thyme. Let them boil a quarter of an hour (He letteth them boil no longer, to preserve the colour of the Metheglin pale) then scum away the herbs, scuming also the water clear. Then lade out the water, (letting it run through a Ranch-Sieve) into a wide open vessel, or large Vat to cool, leaving the settlement and dregs. (He often leaves out the Eye-bright and Thyme, when he provideth chiefly for the pure tast; though the Eye-bright hurts it but little.) When it is blood-warm, put the honey to it, about one part, to four of water; but because this doth not determine the proportions exactly (for some honey will make it stronger then other) you must do that by bearing up an Egge. But first, lave and scoop your mixture exceedingly, (at least an hour) that the honey be not onely perfectly dissolved, but uniformly mixed throughout the water. Then take out some of it in a great Woodden bowl or pail, and put a good number, (ten or twelve) New-laid-eggs into it, and as round ones as may be; For long ones will deceive you in the swiming; and stale ones, being lighter then new, will emerge out of the Liquor, the breadth of a sixpence, when new ones will not a groats-breadth. Therefore you take many, that you make a medium of their several emergings; unless you be certain, that they which you use, are immediately then laid and very round. The rule is, that a Groats-breadth (or rather but a threepence) of the Egg-shel must Swim above the Liquor; which then put again into your Copper to boil. It will be some while, before it boil, (peradventure a good quarter of an hour) but all that while scum will rise, which skim away still as it riseth; and it should be clear scummed by then it boileth: which as soon as it doth, turn up an hour Glass, and let it boil well a good hour. A good quarter before the hour is out, put to it a pound of White-Ginger beaten exceedingly small and searsed (which will sever all the skins and course parts from the fine) which having boiled a quarter of an hour, so to make up the whole hour of boiling, pour out the Liquor into wide open Vats to cool. When it is quite cold, put a pottle of New-ale-barm into a Pipe or Butt, standing endwise with his head out, and pour upon it a Pail-full of your cool Liquor out of one of the Vats; which falling from high upon it with force, will break and dissipate the barm into atoms, and mix it with the Liquor. Pour immediately another pail-ful to that, continuing to do so, till all the Liquor be in. Which by this time and this course will be uniformly mixed with the barm, and begin to work. Yet scoop and lade it well a while, to make the mixtion more perfect, and set the working well on foot. Then cover your But-head with a sheet onely in Summer, but blankets in Winter; and let your Liquor work about 24 hours or more. The measure of that is, till the barm (which is raised to a great head) beginneth a little to fall. Then presently scum of the thick head of the barm, but take not all away so scrupulously, but that there may remain a little white froth upon the face of the Liquor. Which scoop and lade strongly, mingling all to the bottom, that this little remaining barm may by this agitation be mixed a new with the whole. Then immediately Tun this Liquor into two hogsheads that have served for Spanish-wine (be sure to fill them quite full) and there let it work two or three days; that is to say, till you see that all the feculent substance is wrought out, and that what runneth out, beginneth to be clear, though a little whitish or frothy on the upperside of the stream that runs down along the outside of the hogshead. (If there should be a little more then to fill two hogsheads, put it in a Rundlet by it self.) Then take some very strong firm Paper, and wet it on one side with some of the barm that works out, and lay that side over the bung to cover it close. The barm will make it stick fast to the hogshead. This covering will serve for a moneth or two. Then stop it close with strong Cork fitted to the hole, with a linnen about it, to press it fast in: But let a little vent with a peg in it be made in hogshead, in some fit place above. This may be fit to broach in five or six moneths; but three weeks or a moneth before you do so, put into each hogshead half an ounce of Cinnamon; and two ounces of Cloves beaten into most subtile powder. (Sometimes he leaves out the Cloves) which will give it a most pleasant flavor; and they (as the Ginger did) sink down to the bottome and never trouble the Liquor. If they be put in long before (much more if they be boiled) they loose all their taste and Spirits entirely. This will last very well half a year drawing. But if you stay broaching it a year, and then draw it into bottles, it will keep admirable good three or four years, growing to be much better, then when broached at six months end. It will be purer, if you first boil the water by it self, then let it settle 24 hours; and pour the clear from the earthy sediment, which will be great, and dissolve your honey in that. You may Aromatise it with Ambergreece or Musk, or both (if you like them) by dissolving a very few Pastils in a Runlet of this Liquor, when you draw it into little vessels, (as He useth to do after five or six moneths) or with a few drops of the Extract of them. This Metheglin is a great Balsom and strengthener of the *Viscera*; is excellent in colds and coughs and consumptions. For which last they use to burn it (like wine) or rather onely heat it. Then dissolve the yolk of an Egge or two in a Pint of it, and some fresh Butter, and drink it warm in the morning fasting. As it comes from the Barrel or Bottle, it is used to be drunk a large draught (without any alteration or admixtion, with a toste early in the morning (eating the toste) when they intend to dine late. Consider of making Metheglin thus with purified rain water (of the *Œquinoxe*) or Dew.

The handfuls of Herbs, are natural large handfuls (as much as you can take up in your hand) not Apothecaries handfuls, which are much less.  If a pottle of Barm do not make work enough to your mind, you may put in a little more.  Discretion and Experience must regulate that.

You may make small Meathe the same way, putting but half the proportion of honey or less.  But then after three weeks or a months barrelling, you must bottle it. (From *The Closet ...Opened*, 1669.)

# 40  TO MAKE GOOD METHEGLIN – 1669

| | |
|---|---|
| 4 gallons honey | 2 or 3 egg whites |
| 12 gallons water | assorted spices |
| 2 or 3 spoonsful ale yeast | ginger root |

1 handful each:  sweetbrier; rosemary; bay leaves; thyme; marjoram; savory.

Take to every Gallon of Honey, three Gallons of water, and put them both together, and set them over so soft a fire, that you may endure to melt and break the honey with your hands.  When the honey is all melted, put in an Egge, and let it fall gently to the bottome, and if the Egge rise up to the top again of the Liquor, then is it strong enough of the honey; but if it lie at the bottome, you must put in more honey, stirring of it till it do rise.  If your honey be very good, it will bear half a Gallon of water more to a Gallon of Honey.  Then take Sweet-bryar, Rose-mary, Bayes, Thyme, Marjoram, Savory, of each a good handful, which must be tyed up all together in a bundle.  This Proportion of herbs will be sufficient for 12 Gallons of Metheglin; and according to the quantity you make of Metheglin, you must add of your herbs or take away.  When you have put these things together set it upon a quick fire, and let it boil as fast as you can for half an hour, or better, skiming of it very clean, which you must Clarifie with two or three whites of Eggs.  Then take it off from the fire, and put it presently into some clean covers, and let it stand till the next morning; then pour the clear from the bottom and tun it up; putting in a little bag of such spice as you like, whereof Ginger must be the most.  After it hath stood some three or four days, you may put in some two or three spoonfuls of good-ale-yest; it will make it ready the sooner to drink, if you let it work together, before you stop it up.

The older the honey is, the whiter coloured the Metheglin will be.  (*ibid.*)

# #39 AN EXCELLENT WAY TO MAKE METHEGLIN, CALLED THE LIQUOR OF LIFE, WITH THESE FOLLOWING INGREDIENTS – 1669

| | |
|---|---|
| 3 hogsheads water | 1 part honey to 4 parts water |
| 1/2 handful sanicle | 2 ounces coriander |
| 2 ounces sandalwood | 1/2 lb. ginger root |
| 1 ounce cloves | 3 quarts ale yeast |

2 handfuls each: agrimony;[1] balm; betony; bistort; blue-buttons; borage; bugle; bugloss; burnet; clowns-all-heal; coltsfoot; comfrey; cowslip;[1] fennel roots; french thyme; hart's-tongue; hyssop; licorice; liverwort; maiden-hair; meadssweet; mouse ear; organy; Paul's-betony; rosemary; Saint John's wort;[1] selfheal; spleenwort; sweet marjoram; sweet-oak; tormentil-roots; wall-rue spleenwort.

Time to completion: 1 year.

Take Bugloss, Borage, Hyssop, Organ, Sweet-marjoram, Rosemary, French-cowslip, Coltsfoot, Thyme, Burnet, Self-heal, Sanicle a little, Betony, Blew-buttons, Harts-tongue, Meadssweet, Liverwort, Coriander two ounces, Bistort, Saint John's wort, Liquorish, Two ounces of Carraways, Two ounces of Yellow-saunders, Balm, Bugle, Half a pound of Ginger, and one ounce of Cloves, Agrimony, Tormentil-roots, Cumfrey, Fennel-root's, Clowns-all-heal, Maiden-hair, Wall-rew, Spleen-wort, Sweet-oak, Pauls-betony, Mouse ear.

For two Hogsheads of Metheglin, you take two handfuls a piece of each herb, Excepting Sanicle; of which you take but half a handful. You make it in all things as the white Meathe of Mr. Pierce's is made, excepting as followeth. For in that you boil the herbs but a quarter of an hour, that the colour may be pale: But in this, where the deepness of the colour is not regarded, you boil them a good hour, that you may get all the vertue out of them. Next for the strength of it; whereas in that, an Egge is to emerge out of the Liquor but the breadth of a three pence; in This it is to emerge a large Groats-breadth. Then in this you take but half a pound of Ginger, and one ounce of Cloves. Whereas the white hath one pound of Ginger, and two ounces of Cloves. To this you use three quarts, or rather more of Ale-yest (fresh and new) and when all your Liquor is in a high slender tall pipe with the narrowest circumference that may be (which makes it work better then a broad one, where the Spirits loose themselves) you have the yest in a large Noggin with a handle, or pail, and put some of the Liquor to it, and make that work; then pour it from pretty high unto the whole quantity in the pipe, and lade it strongly with that Noggin five or six, or eight times, pouring it every time from high, and working it well together, that so every Atome of the yest may be mingled with every Atome of the Liquor. And this course (in this particular) you may also use in the white. It is best not to broach this, till a year be over after the making it. (From *The Closet ...Opened*, 1669.)

---

[1] CAUTION! (*See Appendix.*)

# # 41  TO MAKE WHITE METHEGLIN OF SIR JOHN FORTESCUE – 1669

| | |
|---|---|
| 12 gallons water | honey |
| ginger root | 6 egg whites |
| yeast | whole nutmegs |
| mace blades | cinnamon sticks |
| cloves | |

1 handful each:  sweetbrier; rosemary; parsley; strawberry leaves; mother of thyme; balm; liverwort; betony; scabious.

Take twelve Gallons of water, one handful of each of these herbs, Eglantine, Rosemary, Parsley, Strawberry-leaves, Wild-thyme, Balm, Liver-wort, Betony, Scabious; when your water begins to boil, cast in your herbs, and let them boil a quarter of an hour. Then strain it from the herbs.  When it is almost cold, then put in as much of the best honey, as will make it bear an Egge, to the breadth of two pence; and stir it till all the honey be melted.  Then boil it well half an hour at the least, and put into it the whites of six Eggs beaten to a froth to clarifie it; and when it hath drawn all the scum to the top, strain it into woodden vessels.  When it is almost cold, put barm to it, and when it worketh well, Tun it into a well-seasoned vessel, where neither Ale nor Beer hath been, for marring the colour; and when it hath done working, take a good quantity of Nutmegs, Mace, Cinnamon, Cloves and Ginger bruised, and put it into a boulter bag, and hang it in the barrel.

If you will have it taste much of the spice, let it boil 3 or 4 walms in it, after you have put in the honey.  But that will make it have a deep colour.
(From *The Closet ...Opened*, 1669.)


# # 84  TO MAKE METHEGLIN – 1669

| | |
|---|---|
| 8 gallons water | 2 whole nutmegs |
| 16 lbs. honey | 2 handfuls malt, ground |
| 1 wine pint ale yeast | |

Time to completion: 3 to 4 weeks.

Take eight Gallons of water, set it over a clear fire in a Kettle; and when it is warm, put it to sixteen pounds of very good honey, and stir it well together; take off the scum, and put two large Nutmegs cut in quarters, and so let it boil at least an hour; Then take it off the fire, and put to it two good handfulls of grinded Malt, and with a white staff keep beating it together till it be almost cold; then strain it through a hair-sieve into a Tub, and put to it a wine-pint of Ale-yest, and stir it very well together; and when it is cold, you may if you please, Tun it up presently into a vessel fit for it, or else let it stand, and work a day, and when it hath done working in your vessel, stop it up very close.  It will be three weeks or a month before it be ready to drink.  (*ibid.*)

# # 44 THE LADY VERNON'S WHITE METHEGLIN – 1669

*This is two recipes for white metheglin. The numbers in brackets have been added to help differentiate the recipes.*

[1]

| | |
|---|---|
| 3 gallons water | 1 quart honey |
| yeast | ginger root |
| cloves | orange and lemon peels |
| 1 whole nutmeg | cinnamon sticks |

<u>3 handfuls each</u>: broad thyme; rosemary; pennyroyal.[1]

Time to completion: 3 or 4 days.

Take three Gallons of water (rain water is best) boil in it broad Thyme, Rose-mary, Peny-royal, of each three handfuls. Then put it into a stone Pan to cool, and strain away the herbs; and when it is cold, put in one quart of honey, and mix it very well; then put to it one Nutmeg, a little Cinnamon; Cloves and Ginger; some Orange and Limon-peels. Then boil and scum it very well, while any scum will rise. Then put in your spices, and try with a New-laid-egg; and the stronger it is, the longer you may keep it; and if you will drink it presently, put it up in bottles, and rub the Corks with yest, that it may touch it, and it will be ready in three or four days to drink.

[2]

3 gallons water
1 quart honey
clove gilliflowers
marigolds
cinnamon sticks
cloves
cowslips[1]
orange peels
violets
lemon peels

*Picking Herbs.*
From *The Grete Herball*, 1526.

<u>3 handfuls each</u>: broad thyme; rosemary; pennyroyal.[1]

And if you make it in the spring put no spices, but Cloves and Cinnamon, and add Violets, Cowslips, Marigolds, and Gillyflowers; and be sure to stop your vessel close with Cork; and to this put no yest, for the Clove-gillyflowers will set it to work. (From *The Closet ...Opened*, 1669.)

---

[1] CAUTION! (*See Appendix.*)

# # 51  TO MAKE WHITE METHEGLIN – 1669

| | |
|---|---|
| 3 gallons water | unspecified spices and herbs |
| 1 gallon honey | cloves |
| ale yeast | lemon peel |
| eringo roots | |

Put to three Gallons of Spring-water, one of honey.  First let it gently melt; then boil for an hour, continually skiming it; then put it into an earthen or a woodden vessel, and when it is a little more than Blood-warm, set it with Ale-yest, and so let it stand twelve hours.  Then take off the yest, and bottle it up.  Put into it Limon-peel and Cloves, or what best pleaseth your taste of Spice or Herbs.  Eringo-roots put into it, when it is boiling, maketh it much better.

Note, That if you make Hydromel by fermentation in the hot Sun (which will last about fourty days, and requireth the greater heat) you must take it thence, before it be quite ended working; and stop it up very close, and set it in a cold Cellar, and not pierce it in two months, at the soonest.  It will be very good this way, if you make it so strong, as to bear an Egge very boyant.  It is best made by taking all the Canicular days[1] into your fermentation.

(From *The Closet ...Opened*, 1669.)

# # 95  TO MAKE A SMALL METHEGLIN – 1669

| | |
|---|---|
| 4 gallons water | 8 lbs. honey |
| 3 whole nutmegs | 3 or 4 ginger roots |
| 1 pint ale yeast | 2 handfuls malt, ground |

Time to completion:  3 weeks.

Take four Gallons of water, and set it over the fire.  Put into it, when it is warm, eight pounds of honey; as the scum riseth, take it clean off.  When it is clear, put into it three Nutmegs quartered; three or four Races of Ginger sliced; Then let it boil a whole hour, Then take it off the fire, and put to it two handfuls of ground Malt; stir it about with a round stick, till it be as cold as wort, when you put yest to it.  Then strain it out into a pot or Tub, that hath a spiggot and faucet, and put to it a pint of very good Ale-yest; so let it work for two days; Then cover it close for about four or five days, and so draw it out into bottles.  It will be ready to drink within three weeks.  (*ibid.*)

---

[1] The Dog Star Days, early July to early September.

"Make your Metheglin as soon as ever you take your Bees; for if you wash your combs in the water you boil your herbs in, when it is cold, it will sweeten much. But you must afterwards strain it through a cloth, or else there will be much wax."[1]

✳✳✳

# # 53 TO MAKE WHITE METHEGLIN – 1669

| | |
|---|---|
| honeycombs soaked in water | 2 or 3 egg whites |
| honey | mace blades |
| grains of paradise | ale barm |
| 4 handfuls angelica | ginger root |
| whole nutmegs | cloves |

<u>one ounce each</u>: marsh mallow root; parsley root; fennel root.

<u>1 handful each</u>: rosemary; borage; maidenhair; pennyroyal;[2] hart's-tongue; liverwort; watercress; scurvy grass.

*optional*: 2 grains ambergris, 2 grains musk.

Take the Honey-combs, that the Honey is run out from them, and lay them in water over night; next day strain them, and put the Liquor a boiling; Then take the whites of two or three Eggs, and clarifie the Liquor. When you have so done, skim it clean. Then take a handful of Peny-royal; four handfuls of Angelica; a handful of Rosemary; a handful of Borrage; a handful of Maidenhair, a handful of Harts-tongue; of Liverwort, of Water-cresses, of Scurvy-grass, *ana*, a handful; of the Roots of Marshmallows, Parsley, Fennel, *ana*, one Ounce. Let all these boil together in the Liquor, the space of a quarter of an hour. then strain the Liquor from them, and let it cool, till it be Blood-warm. Put in so much honey, until an Egge swim on it; and when your honey is melted, then put it into the Barrel. When it is almost cold, put a little Ale barm to it; And when it hath done working, put into your barrel a bag of Spice of Nutmegs, Ginger, Cloves and Mace, and grains good store; and if you will, put into a Lawn-bag[3] two grains of Amber-greece and two grains of Musk, and fasten it in the mouth of your barrel, and so let it hang in the Liquor. (*ibid.*)

---

[1] Digby, #75.

[2] CAUTION! (*See Appendix.*)

[3] From Middle English *laun*, a cotton or linen bag.

## # 54  A MOST EXCELLENT METHEGLIN – 1669

| | |
|---|---|
| 1 part honey | mustard seeds |
| 8 parts water | *optional*: 1 part hop juice per 30 parts liquid |

Take one part of honey, to eight parts of Rain or River-water; let it boil gently together, in a fit vessel, till a third part be wasted, skiming it very well.  The sign of being boiled enough is, when a New-laid-egg swims upon it.  Cleanse it afterwards by letting it run through a clean Linnen-cloth, and put it into a woodden Runlet, where there hath been wine in, and hang in it a bag with Mustard-seeds[1] by the bung, that so you may take it out, when you please.  This being done, put your Runlet into the hot Sun, especially during the Dog-days, (which is the onely time to prepare it) and your Metheglin will boil like Must; after which boiling take out your Mustard-seeds, and put your vessel well stopped into a Cellar.  If you will have it the taste of wine, put to thirty measures of Hydromel, one measure of the juyce of hops, and it will begin to boil without any heat.  Then fill up your vessel, and presently after this ebullition you will have a very strong Metheglin.

(From *The Closet ...Opened*, 1669.)

*1 Angelica sativa.*
Garden Angelica.

## # 80  TO MAKE METHEGLIN – 1669

| | |
|---|---|
| 4 gallons water | yeast |
| 1 gallon honey | liverwort |
| 1 parsley root | dock |
| 1 fennel root | hart's-tongue |
| yarrow[2] | rosemary |
| bay leaves | *optional*: spices to taste. |

Take four Gallons of water and one of Honey; boil and skim it:  then put into it, Liverwort, Harts-tongue, Wild-carrot,[3] and Yarrow, a little Rose-mary and Bays, one Parsly-root, and a Fennel-root; let them boil an hour altogether.  You may, if you please, hang a little bag of spice in it.  When it is cold, put a little barm to it, and let it work like Beer.  The roots must be scraped, and the Pith taken out.  (*ibid.*)

---

[1] Mustard seed was sometimes called for in place of yeast to start fermentation.  It is doubtful however that the mustard actually performed this function.  More likely, the unwashed runlet contained the necessary yeast, and the mustard merely provided a biting flavor.

[2] CAUTION!  (*See Appendix.*)

[3] He means dock.  (*See his recipe # 8, p. 86.*)

# # 55 TO MAKE WHITE METHEGLIN OF THE COUNTESS OF DORSET – 1669

| | |
|---|---|
| 12+ gallons water | honey |
| 9 egg whites | whole cloves |
| cinnamon sticks | mace blades |
| whole nutmegs | 1 spoonful flour |
| 1 spoonful yeast | |

<u>4 handfuls total:</u> agrimony,[1] angelica, ash tree bark, bay leaves, betony, eringo roots, eyebright, liverwort, marsh mallow leaves, maidenhair, mother of thyme, pennyroyal,[1] philipendula, ribwort, roman wormwood,[1] rosemary, sanicle, scabious, sassafras,[1] sweetbrier, tamarisk, thyme, watercress.

Take Rosemary, Thyme, Sweet-bryar, Peny-royal, Bays, Water-cresses, Agrimony, Marshmallow leaves, Liver-wort, Maiden-hair, Betony, Eyebright, Scabious, the bark of the Ash-tree, Eringo-roots, Green-wild-Angelica, Ribwort, Sanicle, Roman-wormwood, Tamarisk, Mother-thyme, Sassafras, Philipendula, of each of these herbs a like proportion; or of as many of them as you please to put in. But you must put in all but four handfuls of herbs, which you must steep one night, and one day, in a little bowl of water, being close covered; the next day take another quantity of fresh water, and boil the same herbs in it, till the colour be very high; then take another quantity of water, and boil the same herbs in it, until they look green; and so let it boil three or four times in several waters, as long as the Liquor looketh any thing green.[2] Then let it stand with these herbs in it a day and night. Remember the last water you boil it in to this proportion of herbs, must be twelve gallons of water, and when it hath stood a day and a night, with these herbs in it, after the last boiling, then strain the Liquor from the herbs, and put as much of the finest and best honey into the Liquor, as will make it bear an Egg. You must work and labour the honey and liquor together one whole day, until the honey be consumed. Then let it stand a whole night, and then let it be well laboured again, and let it stand again a clearing, and so boil it again a quarter of an hour, with the whites of six New-laid-eggs with the shells, the yolks being taken out; so scum it very clean, and let it stand a day a cooling. Then put it into a barrel, and take Cloves, Mace, Cinamon, and Nutmegs, as much as will please your taste, and beat them altogether; put them into a linnen bag, and hang it with a thread in the barrel. Take heed you put not too much spice in; a little will serve. Take the whites of two or three New-laid-eggs, a spoonful of barm, and a spoonful of Wheat-flower, and beat them altogether, and put it into your Liquor into the barrel, and let it work, before you stop it. Then afterwards stop it well, and close it well with clay and Salt tempered together,[3] and let it be set in a close place; and when it hath been settled some six weeks, draw it into bottles, and stop it very close, and drink it not a month after: but it will keep well half a year, and more. (*ibid.*)

---

[1] CAUTION! (*See Appendix.*)      [2] See note p. 61.      [3] See notes p. 66, 71.

# #56 ANOTHER WAY TO MAKE WHITE METHEGLIN – 1669

10 gallons water     3 handfuls broad thyme
2 gallons honey      6 ginger roots
30 egg whites       6 whole nutmegs
1/4 ounce cloves     1/2 ounce cinnamon sticks
<u>6 handfuls each</u>: sweetbrier; sweet marjoram; muscovy.
*optional*: 2 grains ambergris, 1 grain musk.

Time to completion: 9 or 10 weeks.

Take ten Gallons of water; then take six handfuls of Sweet-bryar; as much of Sweet-marjoram; and as much of Muscovy. Three handfuls of the best Broad-thyme. Boil these together half an hour; then strain them. Then take two Gallons of English-honey, and dissolve it in this hot Liquor, and brew it well together; then set it over the fire to boil again, and skim it very clean; then take the whites of thirty Eggs wel beaten, and put them into the Liquor, and let it boil an hour; then strain it through a jelly bag, and let it stand 24 hours cooling: then put it up in a vessel. Then take six Nutmegs, six fair Races of Ginger, a quarter of an Ounce of Cloves, half an ounce of Cinamon; bruise all these together, and put them into a Linnen-bag, with a little Pebble-stone to make it sink. Then hang it in the vessel. You may adde to it, if you please, two grains of Amber-greece, and one grain of Musk. Stop the vessel with a Cork, but not too close, for six days; then taste it: and if it taste enough of the Spice, then take out the bag; if not, let the bag hang in it, and stop it very close, and meddle with it no more. It will be ready to drink in nine or ten weeks. (*ibid.*)

# #97 METHEGLIN OR SWEET DRINK OF MY LADY STUART – 1669

water         honey
3 spoonsful yeast     6 egg whites and egg shells
<u>1 handful each</u>: rosemary; bay leaves; sweetbrier; broad thyme; sweet marjoram.

Time to completion: 3 months.

Take as much water as will fill your Firkin: of Rosemary, Bays, Sweet-bryar, Broad-thyme, Sweet-majoram, of each a handful; set it over the fire, until the herbs have a little coloured the water; then take it off, and when it is cold, put in as much honey, till it will bear an Egg; Then lave it three days morning and evening. After that boil it again, and skim it very clean, and in the boiling clarifie it with the whites of six Eggs, shells and all, well beaten together. Then take it off, and put it to cool; and when it is cold, put it into your vessel, and put to it three spoonfuls of yest; stop it close, and keep it, till it be old at least three months. (*ibid.*)

# #61 ANOTHER SORT OF METHEGLIN – 1669

1 part honey                          *optional*: 20 lbs. black currants.
3 parts water

Time to completion: 9 months to 1 year.

Take to one part of honey, three parts of water: and put them into clean vessels, mixing them very well together, and breaking the honey with stripped arms, till it be well dissolved. Then pour out your Liquor into a large Kettle, and let it boil for two hours and a half, over a good fire, skiming it all the while very carefully as long as any scum riseth. When it is boiled enough, pour out your Liquor into clean vessels, and set it to cool for 24 hours. Afterwards put it into some Runlets, and cover the bung with a piece of Lead[1]: have a care to fill it up always with the same boiled Liquor for three or four months and during the time of working. This Meath the older it is, the better it is. But if you will have your Meath red, then take twenty pound of black Currants, and put them into a vessel, and pour your Liquor on them. Of this honey-Liquor you cannot drink till after nine months, or a year.
(From *The Closet ...Opened*, 1669.)

# #100 ANOTHER [METHEGLIN] OF THE SAME LADY – 1669

*This recipe originally followed a metheglin recipe by Lady Windebanke.  (See p. 122.)*

4 1/4 gallons water                   1 gallon honey
1/2 pint ale yeast                    a few cloves
1/2 ounce ginger root                 mace blades
2 whole nutmegs
*optional*:  rosemary; bay leaves; sweet marjoram; sweetbrier.

To four Gallons of water put one Gallon of honey; warm the water Luke-warm before you put in your honey; when it is dissolved, set it over the fire, and let it boil half an hour with these Spices grosly beaten and put in a Canvass-bag: namely, half an Ounce of Ginger, two Nutmegs, a few Cloves and a little Mace; and in the boiling put in a quart of cold water to raise the scum, which you must take clean off in the boiling. If you love herbs, put in a little bundle of Rosemary, Bays, Sweet-marjoram and Eglantine. Let it stand till it is cold, then put into it half a pint of Ale-barm, and let it work twelve hours; then Tun it, but take out the bundle of herbs first. (*ibid.*)

---

[1] Do not use lead.

# # 60  TO MAKE METHEGLIN – 1669

*Judging from the sizable quantity of herbs called for, it is likely that this recipe is to make at least a hogshead, if not two, of metheglin.  Allow for one part of honey for each four to six parts of water.  See the recipes for Mr. Pierce's metheglin and Mr. Webbe's mead, pp. 37, 99.*

| | |
|---|---|
| water | honey |
| 3 handfuls rosemary | sweetbrier and roots |

<u>1 peck each</u>:  winter savory; organy; thyme; hart's tongue; liverwort.
<u>1 handful each</u>:  strawberry leaves; violet leaves; woodbine.
<u>1/2 peck each</u>:  salad burnet; ribwort.
<u>2 handfuls each</u>:  white wort;[1] hyssop; marigolds; borage; fennel; wormwood;[2] wood sorrel; betony and roots; blue bottles and roots; eyebright.

Take of Rosemary three handfuls, of Winter-savory a Peck by measure, Organ and Thyme, as much, White-wort two handfuls, Blood-wort half a peck, Hyssop two handfuls, Marygolds, Borage, Fennil, of each two handfuls; Straw-berries and Violet-leaves, of each one handful; Of Harts-tongue, Liverwort a peck; Ribwort half a peck, of Eglantine with the Roots, a good quantity; Wormwood as much as you can gripe in two hands; and of Sorrel, Mead-sutt Bettony with the Roots, Blew-bottles with the Roots, the like quantity; of Eyebright two handfuls, Wood-bind one handful.  Take all these herbs, and order them so, as that the hot herbs may be mastered with the cool.[3]  Then take the small herbs, and put them into the Furnace, and lay the long herbs upon them.  Then take a weight or stone of Lead, having a Ring, whereunto fasten a stick to keep down the Herbs into the furnace; then boil your water and herbs three or four hours, and as the water doth boil away, adde more.  Then take the water out of the Furnace seething hot, and strain it through a Range-sieve; then put in the honey, and Mash it well together: then take your Sweet-wort, and strain it through a Range.  Then try it with a New-laid-egg.  It must be so strong as to bear an Egg the breadth of a groat above the Liquor:  and if it doth not, then put in more honey, till it will bear the Egg.  Then take the Liquor, and boil it again; and as soon as it doth boil, skim the froth very clean from it:  Then set it a cooling, and when it is cold, then put it into a Kive, and put barm thereto, and let it work the Space of a Week; Then Tun it up:  But be careful when it is Tunned, that the vessels be not stopp'd up, till it hath done hissing.
(From *The Closet ...Opened*, 1669.)

---

[1] Many herbs have the prefix 'white-,' but I've found none called 'white wort.'

[2] CAUTION!  (*See Appendix.*)

[3] This is a reference to the pseudo-science of "humors" that was so popular during the Middle Ages. Plants, foodstuffs, etc. were considered to be hot, dry, cold, and moist, in the 1st, 2nd, 3rd or 4th degree; their 'temperaments' had to be balanced properly for a person to maintain good health. (*See note p. 264.*)

# 64  TO MAKE METHEGLIN – 1669

| | |
|---|---|
| 1 gallon water | whole nutmegs |
| 1 quart honey | cinnamon sticks |
| mace blades | ginger |
| cloves | herbs to taste |

1 or 2 sprigs each:  rosemary; thyme; sweet marjoram.

Take fair water, and the best honey; beat them well together, but not in a woodden vessel, for wood drinketh up the honey, put it together in a Kettle, and try it with a New-laid-egg, which will swim at top, if it be very strong; but if it bob up and sink again, it will be too weak.  Boil it an hour, and put into it a bundle of herbs, what sort you like best; and a little bag of Spice, Nutmegs, Ginger, Cloves, Mace and Cinamon; and skim it well all the while it boileth:  when it hath boiled an hour, take it off, and put it into earthen Pans, and so let it stand till next day.  Then pour off all the clear into a good vessel, that hath had Sack in it, or White-wine.  Hang the bag of Spice in it, and so let it stand very close stopp'd and well filled for a month, or longer.  Then if you desire to drink it quickly, you may bottle it up.  If it be strong of the honey, you may keep it a year or two.  If weak, drink it in two or three months.  One quart of honey, will make one Gallon of water very strong.  A sprig or two of Rose-mary, Thyme and Sweet-marjoram, are the Herbs that should go into it.
(From *The Closet ...Opened*, 1669.)


# 93  TO MAKE METHEGLIN THAT LOOKS LIKE WHITE-WINE – 1669

| | |
|---|---|
| 12 gallons water | honey |
| 6 egg whites | ale yeast |

1 handful each:  parsley; sweetbrier; rosemary; strawberry leaves; mother of thyme; balm; liverwort; betony; scabious.

*optional:*  cloves; whole nutmegs; mace blades; cinnamon sticks; ginger root.

Time to completion:  3 months or more.

Take to twelve gallons of water, a handful of each of these Herbs:  Parsley, Eglantine, Rosemary, Strawberry-leaves, Wild-thyme, Baulme, Liver-wort, Betony, Scabious:  when the water begins to boil, cast in the herbs:  let them boil a quarter of an hour:  then strain out the herbs; and when it is almost cold, then put in as much of the best honey, you can get, as will bear an Egg to the breadth of two pence; that is, till you can see no more of the Egge above the water, then a two pence will cover:  Lave it and stir it till you see all the honey be melted; then boil it well half an hour, at the least:  skim it

well, and put in the whites of six Eggs beaten, to clarifie it: Then strain it into some wooden vessels; and when it is almost cold, put some Ale-barm into it. And when it worketh well, Tun it into some well seasoned vessel, where neither Ale nor Beer hath been, for marring the colour of it. When it hath done working, if you like it, Take a quantity of Cloves, Nutmegs, Mace, Cinnamon, Ginger, or any of these that you like best, and bruise them, and put them in a boulter bag, and hang it in the vessel. Put not too much of the Spice, because many do not like the taste of much Spice. If you make it at Michaelmas [*Sept. 29*], you may tap it at Christmas [*Dec. 25*]: but if you keep it longer, it will be the better. It will look pure, and drink with as much spirit as can be, and very pleasant.
(From *The Closet ...Opened*, 1669.)

# 67  AN EXCELLENT METHEGLIN – 1669

| | |
|---|---|
| 1 gallon water | honey |
| 5 or 6 spoonsful ale yeast | 2 or 3 egg whites |

<u>1 handful total</u>: rosemary, sage, sweet marjoram, lemon balm, sassafras,[1] mixed.

<u>To each 6 gallons add</u>: 1/4 lb. ginger root; 1 pint grain alcohol *or* 1 quart Sack wine; peels of 2 or 3 lemons and oranges.

Take Spring-water, and boil it with Rose-mary, Sage, Sweet-Marjoram, Balm and Sassafras, until it hath boiled three or four hours: The quantity of the Herbs is a handful of them all, of each a like proportion, to a Gallon of water. And when it is boiled, set it to cool and to settle until the next day: Then strain your water, and mix it with honey, until it will bear an Egg the breadth of a Groat. Then set it over the fire to boil. Take the whites of twenty or thirty Eggs, and beat them mightily, and when it boileth, pour them in at twice; stir it well together, and then let it stand, until it boileth a pace before you scum it, and then scum it well. Then take it off the fire, and pour it in earthen things to cool: and when it is cold, put to it five or six spoonfuls of the best yest of Ale you can get: stir it together, and then every day scum it with a bundle of Feathers till it hath done working: Then Tun it up in a Sack-cask and to every six gallons of Metheglin put one pint of *Aquavitæ*, or a quart of Sack; and a quarter of a pound of Ginger sliced, with the Pills of two or three Limons and Orenges in a bag to hang in it.
    The Whites of Eggs above named, is a fit proportion for 10 or 12 Gallons of the Liquor. (*ibid.*)

---

[1] CAUTION! (*See Appendix.*) *See p. 74 for a 1925 "Sassafras Mead."*

> ...Her mouth was sweete as bragot or the meeth,
> Or hoord of apples leyd in hey or heeth...[1]

**\*\*\***

## # 65  TO MAKE SMALL METHEGLIN – 1669

| | |
|---|---|
| 6 quarts water | lemon peel |
| 1 quart honey | ginger root, sliced |
| about 1/2 cup ale yeast | sugar |
| raisins | *optional*: 1 handful rosemary. |

Take to every quart of White-honey, six quarts of fair-water. Let it boil, until a third part be boiled away; skiming it as it riseth: then put into it a small quantity of Ginger largely sliced; then put it out into earthen Pans, till it be Luke-warm, and so put it up into an earthen stand, with a tap in it. Then put to it about half a Porenger-ful of the best Ale-yest, so beat it well together; Then cover it with a cloth, and it will be twelve hours before it work; and afterwards let it stand two days, and then draw it out into stone bottles, and it will be ready to drink in five or six days after. This proportion of yest (which is about six good spoonfuls) is enough for three or four Gallons of Liquor. The yest must be of good Ale, and very new. You may mingle the yest first with a little of the Luke-warm-Liquor; then beat it, till it be well incorporated, and begins to work; Then adde a little more Liquor to it, and beat that. Continue so adding the Liquor by little and little, till a good deal of it be Incorporated with the yest; then put that to all the rest of the quantity, and beat it altogether very well; then cover it close, and keep it warm for two or three days. Before you bottle it, scum away all the barm and Ginger (whereof a spoonful or two is enough for three or four Gallons) then bottle up the clear, leaving the dregs. If you will, you may Tun it into a barrel, (if you make a greater quantity) when the barm is well Incorporated with the Liquor, in the same manner as you do Beer or Ale, and so let it work in the Barrel as long as it will; then stop it up close for a few days more, that so it may clear it self well, and separate and precipitate the dregs. Then draw the clear into bottles. This will make it less windy, but also a little less quick, though more wholesome. You may also boil a little handful of tops of Rosemary in the Liquor, which giveth it a fine taste: but all other herbs, and particularly Sweet-marjoram and Thyme, give it a Physical taste. A little Limon-peel giveth it a very fine taste. If you Tun it in a barrel, to work there, you may hang the Ginger and Limon-peel in it in a bag, till you bottle it, or till it have done working. Then you may put two or three stoned and sliced Raisins, and a lump of fine Sugar into every bottle to make it quick.
(From *The Closet ...Opened*, 1669.)

---

[1] Chaucer, "The Miller's Tale," lines 3261-2.

"...A full quart of old rum (French brandy is better,
But we ne'er in receipts, should stick close to the letter;)
And then, to your taste, you may add some perfume,
Goa-stone, or whatever you like in its room..."[1]
***

## # 71  TO MAKE WHITE METHEGLIN – 1669

*This recipe emphasizes how mead-making is dependent upon personal taste, rather than a fixed recipe.  All of the flavorings listed here are optional, so that, while strictly adhering to a period recipe, the modern brewer still has complete control over the outcome.  Some might argue that a historical re-creationist must conform to set notions of proportion and spice combinations, but there is no sound basis for this. Apart from using a sufficient proportion of honey to assure proper fermentation, you should take to heart the recurring phrase and use "what best pleaseth your taste."*

3 gallons water
1 gallon honey
ale yeast
clove gilliflowers
lemon peel
cloves
eringo roots
*optional*:  herbs and spices to taste.

From *Omnium Statuum Foeminei Sexus*,
by Anton Möller, 1601.

Take to three Gallons of Spring-water, one of Honey; first let it gently melt, then boil for an hour, continually skiming it; then put it into an earthen or woodden vessel, and when it is little more then Blood-warm, set it with Ale-yest, and so let it stand twelve hours; then take off the Yest, and Bottle it.  Put in it Limon-peel and Cloves, or what best pleaseth your taste of Herbs or Spices.  Eringo-roots put into it, when it is a boiling, maketh it much better.  So do Clove-gilly-flowers; a quantity of which make the Meath look like Claret-wine.  I observe that Meath requireth some strong Herbs to make it quick and smart upon the Palate; as Rose-mary, Bay-leaves, Sage, Thyme, Marjoram, Winter-savory, and such like, which would be too strong and bitter in Ale or Beer.
(From *The Closet ...Opened*, 1669.)

---

[1] Dods, 1829, pp. 459-60.

# # 73  TO MAKE METHEGLIN – 1669

| | |
|---|---|
| 6 gallons warm water | 1 gallon honey |
| cloves | mace blades |
| pepper | unspecified herbs and spices to taste |
| ginger root | |

If your honey be tryed, take six Gallons of Milk-warm-water, to one of honey, and stir it well together ever and anon, and so let it stand for a day and a night, or half a day may serve; then boil it with a gentle fire, for the space of half an hour or thereabouts, and skim it, still as the skum ariseth. After it is scummed once or twice, you may put in your herbs, and spice grosly beaten one half loose; the other in a bag, which afterwards may be fastned with a string to the tap-hole, as Pepper, Cloves, Mace, Ginger and the like; when it is thus boiled, let it stand in the vessel until it be cooled; then Tun it up into your barrel, and let it work two or three days, or more before you stop the bung-hole; but in putting up the boiled liquor into the barrel, reserve the thick grounds back, which will be settled in the pan or kettle.

If you would have it to drink within two or three months, let it be no stronger then to bear an Egg to the top of the water. If you would have it keep six months, or longer, before you drink it, let it bear up the Egg the breadth of two pence above the water. This is the surer way to proportion your honey then by measure. And the time of the tryal of the strength is, when you incorporate the honey and water together, before the boiling of it.

(From *The Closet ...Opened*, 1669.)

# # 75  TO MAKE VERY GOOD METHEGLIN – 1669

*This is two recipes in one; the numbers in brackets have been added to separate the recipes. A worked-out version of this recipe can be found in Lorwin (pp. 42-44).*[2]

[1]

| | |
|---|---|
| water | 1 gallon honey to 2 1/2 gallons liquid |
| cinnamon sticks | cloves |
| ale yeast | ginger root, sliced |

less than 1/2 handful each:  balm; mint; fennel; rosemary; angelica; mother of thyme; hyssop; agrimony;[1] burnet; and other herbs to taste.

Take of all sorts of herbs, that you think are good and wholesome, as Balm, Minth, Fennel, Rosemary, Angelica, Wild-thyme, Hyssop, Agrimony, Burnet, and such other

---

[1] CAUTION!  (*See Appendix.*)

[2] This recipe can also be found in *The Accomplisht Cook*, by Robert May, 1660.

as you may like; as also some field herbs; But you must not put in too many, especially Rose-mary or any strong herb. Less then half a handfull will serve of every sort. Boil your herbs, and strain them out, and let the Liquor stand till the morrow, and settle; Then take of the clearest of the Liquor two Gallons and a half to one Gallon of Honey; and in that proportion take as much of them as you will make, and let it boil an hour, and in the boiling scum it very clean. Then set it a cooling as you do Beer; and when it is cold, take some very good Ale-barm, and put it into the bottom of the Tub you mean the Metheglin shall work in, which pour into the Tub by little and little, as they do Beer, keeping back the thick settling, which lieth in the bottome of the vessels, wherein it is cooled. And when all is put together, cover it with a cloth, and let it work very near three days. And when you mean to put it up, scum off all the barm clean, and put it up into your Barrel or Firkin, which you must not stop very close in four or five days, but let it have a little vent, for it will work; and when it is close stopped, you must look to it very often, and have a peg in the top, to give it vent, when you hear it make a noise (as it will do) or else it will break the barrel.[1] You may also, if you please, make a bag, and put in good store of sliced Ginger, and some Cloves and Cinnamon, and boil it in, or put it into the barrel and never boil it. Both ways are good.

[2]

| | |
|---|---|
| 5 or 6 gallons water | 1 gallon honey and honeycombs |
| cinnamon sticks | cloves |

If you will make small Metheglin, you may put five or six Gallons of water to one of honey. Put in a little Cinnamon and Cloves and boil it well. And when it is cold, put it up in bottles very close stopped, and the stopples well tyed on. This will not keep above five or six weeks, but it is very fine drink.

Make your Metheglin as soon as ever you take your Bees; for if you wash your combs in the water you boil your herbs in, when it is cold, it will sweeten much. But you must afterwards strain it through a cloth, or else there will be much wax.

(From *The Closet ...Opened*, 1669.)

---

[1] He isn't kidding! Always give your working mead a "vent," either through an airlock or a loose bung. If your small mead is already bottled and the weather is warm, either refrigerate the bottles or check them daily and "burp" them to avoid popping corks or exploding bottles. Use champagne bottles for small mead because the glass is thicker and stronger than that used for wine bottles. (You will need 20 to 25 bottles per 5 gallons of liquor. They are available for the asking at most restaurants that offer champagne brunches.)

# #86 THE EARL OF DENBIGH'S METHEGLIN – 1669

| | |
|---|---|
| 20 gallons water | honey |
| 22 egg whites | 20 egg shells |
| ale yeast | 6 scant handfuls rosemary |
| 1 1/2 lbs. ginger root | 1 spoonful flour |

Time to completion: 4 or 5 weeks.

Take twenty Gallons of Spring-water; boil it a quarter of an hour, and let it stand, until it be all most cold; then beat in so much honey, as will make it so strong as to bear an Egg, so that on the Top, you may see the breadth of a hasel-nut swimming above; The next day boil it up with six small handfuls of Rosemary; a pound and a half of Ginger, being scraped and bruised; then take the whites of twenty Eggs shells and all; beat them very well, and put them in to clarifie it; skim it very clean, then take it off the fire and strain: But put the Rosemary and Ginger in again: then let it remain till it be all most cold: then Tun it up, and take some New-ale-yest; the whites of two Eggs, a spoonful of flower, and beat them well together, and put them into the barrel; when it hath wrought very well, stop it very close for three weeks or a month: then bottle it, and a week after you may drink it.
(From *The Closet ...Opened*, 1669.)

"...Supper was shortly dight and downe they sat,
Where they were served with all sumptuous fare,
Whiles fruitfull *Ceres*, and *Lyaeus* fat
Pourd out their plenty without spight or spare:
Nought wanted there, that dainty was and rare;
And aye the cups their bancks did ouerflow..."[1]

✳✳✳

## # 88  TO MAKE METHEGLIN – 1669

| | |
|---|---|
| 4 gallons water | 1 gallon honey |
| 2 ounces ginger root | 3 egg shells |
| rosemary leaves | 4 egg whites |
| flour | bran [*or* yeast?][2] |

Time to completion:  11 to 13 weeks.

Take four Gallons of running water, and boil it a quarter of an hour, and put it in an earthen vessel, and let it stand all night. The next day take only the water, and leave the settling at the bottom: so put the honey in a thin bag, and work it in the water, till all the honey is dissolved. Take to four Gallons of water, one Gallon of Honey: Then put in an Egg, if it be strong enough of the honey, the Egg will part of it appear on the top of the liquor: if it do not, put more honey to it, till it do. Then take out the Egg, and let the Liquor stand till next morning. Then take two Ounces of Ginger, and slice it and pare it: Some Rose-mary washed and stripped from the stalk: dry it very well. The next day put the Rose-mary and Ginger into the drink, and so set it on the fire: when it is all most ready to boil, take the whites of three Eggs well beaten with the shells, and put all into the Liquor: and stir it about, and skim it well till it be clear. Be sure you skim not off the Rose-mary and Ginger: then take it off the fire, and let it run through a hair sieve: and when you have strained it, pick out the Rose-mary and Ginger out of the strainer, and put it into the drink, and throw away the Eggshells, and so let it stand all night. The next day Tun it up in a barrel: Be sure the barrel be not too big: then take a little flower and a little bran[2], and the white of an Egg, and beat them well together, and put them into the barrel on the top of the Metheglin, after it is tunned up, and so let it stand till it hath done working; then stop it up as close as is possible: and so let it stand six or seven weeks: then draw it out and bottle it. You must tye down the Corks, and set the bottles in sand five or six weeks, and then drink it. (*ibid.*)

---

[1] Spenser, *The Faerie Queene*.
[2] Or perhaps he meant barm? (*See his recipe # 86, p. 117.*)

# # 94  TO MAKE WHITE METHEGLIN – 1669

8 gallons water
honey
1/2 pint ale yeast
1 grain musk
2 or 3 sprigs rosemary
1 cinnamon stick
3 or 4 mace blades
1 whole nutmeg
cloves

<u>2 spoonsful each seeds of</u>: caraway; coriander; fennel.

<u>1 handful each</u>: sweet marjoram; sweetbrier hips;
violet leaves and flowers; strawberry leaves.

<u>1/2 handful each</u>: broad thyme; borage; agrimony.[1]

Time to completion:  6 months.

FENNEL

Take Sweet-marjoram, Sweet-bryar-buds, Violet-leaves, Strawberry-leaves, of each one handful, and a good handful of Violet flowers (the dubble ones are the best) broad Thyme, Borrage, Agrimony, of each half a handful, and two or three branches of Rosemary, The seeds of Carvi, Coriander, and Fennel, of each two spoonfuls, and three or four blades of large-mace.  Boil all these in eight Gallons of running-water, three quarters of an hour.  Then strain it, and when it is but blood-warm, put in as much of the best honey, as will make the Liquor bear an Egg the breadth of six pence above the water.  Then boil it again as long as any scum will rise.  Then set it abroad a cooling; and when it is almost cold, put in half a pint of good Ale-barm; and when it hath wrought, till you perceive the barm to fall, then Tun it, and let it work in the barrel, till the barm leaveth rising, filling it up every day with some of the same Liquor.  When you stop it up, put in a bag with one Nutmeg sliced, a little whole Cloves and Mace, a stick of Cinnamon broken in pieces, and a grain of good Musk.  You may make this a little before Michaelmas, and it will be fit to drink at Lent.

This is Sir Edward Bainton's Receipt, Which my Lord of Portland (who gave it me) saith, was the best he ever drunk.
(From *The Closet ...Opened*, 1669.)

---

[1] CAUTION! (*See Appendix.*)

# # 98  A METHEGLIN FOR THE COLICK AND STONE OF THE SAME LADY – 1669

*This recipe originally followed one by Lady Stuart (see p. 108). It was intended as a medicinal drink – most of the ingredients have been used as diuretics or stomachics. Should you decide to make some, <u>omit the groundsel</u>.*

| | |
|---|---|
| 1 gallon honey | 7 gallons water |
| 4 whole nutmegs | 12 cloves |
| 1 1/2 ounces ginger root | 1/2 ounce cinnamon sticks |

<u>1 handful each</u>: pellitory of the wall; saxifrage; betony; parsley; groundsel.[1]
<u>2 ounces each seeds of</u>: parsley; nettle;[1] fennel; caraway; anise; gromwell.
<u>2 ounces each roots of</u>: parsley; alexander; fennel; mallow.

Take one Gallon of Honey to seven Gallons of water; boil it together, and skim it well; then take Pelitory of the Wall, Saxifrage, Betony, Parsley, Groundsel, of each a handful, of the seeds of Parsley, of Nettles, Fennel and Carraway-seeds, Anis-seeds and Grumelseeds,[2] of each two Ounces. The roots of Parsley, of Alexander, of Fennel and Mallows of each two Ounces, being small cut; let all boil, till near three Gallons of the Liquor is wasted: Then take it off the fire, and let it stand till it be cold; then cleanse it from the drugs [*dregs?*], and let it be put into a clean vessel well stopped, taking four Nutmegs, one Ounce and half of Ginger, half an Ounce of Cinnamon, twelve Cloves; cut all these small, and hang them in a bag into the vessel, when you stop it up. When it is a fortnight old, you may begin to drink of it; every morning a good draught. (*ibid.*)

---

[1] CAUTION! (*See Appendix.*)

[2] Although I can find no other mention of *Grumel* seeds, there is a mention of a plant called *Gromel* in Culpeper's Herbal (p. 142), as well as an illustration marked "Gromwell." ("Gromwell" comes from Middle English and Old French "Gromil.") The virtues he lists for this herb include curing the colic or stone, provoking urine, and bringing on faster labor. Of Gromell, Gerard (p. 487) also says "the ſeede of Gromell pound, and drunke in white wine, breaketh, diſſolueth, and driueth foorth the ſtone, and prouoketh vrine..."

Culpeper's illustration and description are fairly close to that of *Lithospermum officinale* L., called Gromwell or Puccoon, and related species, which are members of the Borage family.

| | |
|---|---|
| Latiné | CARYOPHILLI. |
| Gallicé | OEILLETS. |
| Anglicé | IELIFLOWERS. |

*Clove gilliflowers.*
From *La Clef des Champs*,
by J. le Moyne de Morgues, 1586.

# # 99  A RECEIPT FOR METHEGLIN OF MY LADY WINDEBANKE – 1669

| | |
|---|---|
| 4 gallons water | a few red nettle roots[1] |
| 1 gallon honey | hyssop |
| 6 spoonsful yeast | hart's-tongue |
| 5 or 6 eringo roots | 1 ounce whole nutmegs |
| 3 or 4 parsley roots | 1 fennel root |
| 2 ounces ginger root | lemon peel |

1/2 ounce each: cloves; mace blades; cinnamon sticks.
1/4 handful each: pellitory of the wall; sage; thyme; clove gilliflowers.
1/8 handful each: borage; bugloss flowers.

Take four Gallons of water; add to it, these Herbs and Spices following. Pellitory of the Wall, Sage, Thyme, of each a quarter of a handful, as much Clove gilly-flowers, with half as much Borage and Bugloss flowers, a little Hyssop, Five or six Eringo-roots, three or four Parsley-roots: one Fennel-root, the pith taken out, a few Red-nettle-roots, and a little Harts-tongue. Boil these Roots and Herbs half an hour; Then take out the Roots and Herbs, and put in the Spices grosly beaten in a Canvass-bag, *viz.* Cloves, Mace, of each half an Ounce, and as much Cinnamon, of Nutmeg an Ounce, with two Ounces of Ginger, and a Gallon of Honey: boil all these together half an hour longer, but do not skim it at all: let it boil in, and set it a cooling after you have taken it off the fire. When it is cold, put six spoonfuls of barm to it, and let it work twelve hours at least; then Tun it, and put a little Limon-peel into it: and then you may bottle it, if you please. (*ibid.*)

# # 101  TO MAKE METHEGLIN – 1669

| | |
|---|---|
| 12 gallons water | ginger root |
| 4 gallons honey | spices to taste |
| 2 or 3 egg whites | 2 or 4 spoonsful ale yeast |

1 handful each: sweetbrier; bay leaves; rosemary; thyme; marjoram; savory.

Take to every Gallon of Honey, three Gallons of water, and put them together and set them over so gentle a fire, as you might endure to break it in the water with your hand. When the Honey is all melted, put in an Egg, and let it fall gently to the bottom; and if your Egg rise up again to the top of the Liquor, then it is strong enough of the Honey.

---

[1] CAUTION! (*See Appendix.*)

But if it lie at the bottom, you must put in more honey, and stir it, till it doth rise. If your honey be very good, it will bear half a Gallon of water more to a Gallon of Honey. Then take Sweet-bryar, Bays, Rosemary, Thyme, Marjoram, Savoury, of each a good handfull, which you must tye up all together in a bundle. This Proportion of Herbs will be sufficient for twelve Gallons of Metheglin; and according to the quantity of Metheglin you make, you must add or diminish your Herbs. When you have put these things together, set it over a quick fire, and let it boil as fast as you can for half an hour or better, skiming of it very clean and clarifying it with the whites of two or three Eggs. Then take it from the fire, and put it into some clean vessel or other, and let it stand till the next morning; Then pour the Clear from the dregs, and Tun it up, putting in a little bag of such Spice as you like, whereof Ginger must be the most. After it hath stood three or four days, you may put in two or three spoon-fulls of good Ale-yest, it will make it the sooner ready to drink. It must work before you stop it up. The older your Honey is, the whiter your Metheglin will be.
(From *The Closet ...Opened*, 1669.)

METHEGLIN – 1846

*This recipe is atypical in that it calls for <u>powdered</u> spices, which not only are less flavorful than their whole counterparts, but tend to make the brew cloudy, so that additional rackings may be necessary.*

48 to 50 lbs. honey                    1/3 barrel water
1 spoonful yeast
<u>1 dessertspoonful each</u>:  ginger powder; clove powder; mace powder.

For a half a barrel of metheglin, allow forty-eight or fifty pounds of fresh honey. Boil it an hour in a third of a barrel of spring water. Skim it well. It should be so strong with honey that when cold an egg will not sink in it. Add a small dessert spoonful of ginger, and as much of powdered clove and mace; also a spoonful of yeast. Leave the bung of the cask loose till the fermentation has ceased; then stop it close. At the end of six months, draw off and bottle it. It improves until three or four years old, and has a fine color. It is a very healthful cordial.
(From *The Young Housekeeper's Friend, or A Guide to Domestic Economy and Comfort*, by Mrs. Cornelius, 1846.)

*A Medieval Skep*

Early peoples learned to "domesticate" bees by gathering wild swarms and keeping them close at hand in hollow logs, or in man-made hives of clay or straw. Hives made of sheets of mica are described by Pliny: "The best hive is made of bark; the next best material is fennel-giant, and the third is osier. Many too have made hives of transparent stone, so that they might look on the bees working inside."[1] Coiled straw hives, or skeps, are shown in many medieval woodcuts. All these early hives share the common drawback that the honey could not be harvested without damaging the hive or killing the bees. During the 1850s a new type of beehive was developed featuring stackable boxes containing removable wooden frames. This, and the invention of the centrifugal force honey extractor in the 1860s, led to a boom in honey production worldwide.

Today, rather than raising their own bees to pollinate their crops, farmers often *rent* bees, which are owned and cared for by independent beekeepers. The beekeepers truck their bees to farms all over the country. Surprisingly, the transportation of beehives from one spot to another is an ancient practice:

> ...when bee fodder fails in the neighborhood the natives place the hives on boats and carry them five miles upstream by night. At dawn the bees come out and feed, returning every day to the boats, which change their position until, when they have sunk low in the water under the mere weight, it is understood that the hives are full, and then they are taken back and the honey is extracted. In Spain too for a like reason they carry the hives about on mules.[2]

With the rise in organic farming, many people are starting to raise bees for fun and profit. Indeed, an avid mead-maker might find raising bees to be not only an enjoyable hobby, but also an economical alternative to buying honey at the store.

---

[1] Pliny the Elder, *Natural History*, c. 77 A. D., Book XXI, p. 219.     [2] *ibid.*, Book XXI, pp. 213-5.

# WINES

✳✳✳✳✳✳✳

"...an embracing vine,
Whose bounches hanging downe, seemed to entice
All passers by, to tast their lushious wine,
And did themselues into their hands incline,
As freely offering to be gathered:
Some deepe empurpled as the *Hyacint*,
Some as the Rubine, laughing sweetly red,
Some like faire Emeraudes, not yet well ripened..."
(*The Faerie Queene*, by Edmund Spenser.)

"Wine is also made from the Syrian carob, and from pears and all kinds of apples (one from pomegranates is called rhoites) as also from cornels, medlars, service berries, dried mulberries and fir-cones; the last are soaked in must before being pressed, but the juice of the preceding fruits is sweet of itself..."[1]

***

APPLE WINE – 1829

8 gallons apple cider
isinglass

16 lbs. sugar
yeast
1 cup grain alcohol *or* 1 pint French brandy

To every gallon of apple juice, immediately as it comes from the press, add 2 lbs. of common loaf sugar; boil it as long as any scum rises, then strain it through a sieve, and let it cool; add some good yeast, and stir it well; let it work in the tub for two or three weeks, or till the head begins to flatten, then skim off the head, draw it clear off, and turn it. When made a year, rack it off, and fine it with isinglass; then add 1/2 a pint of the best rectified spirit of wine, or a pint of French brandy, to every 8 gallons.
(From *Five Thousand Receipts, etc.*, by Mackenzie, 1829.)

TO MAKE APRICOT WINE FROM MRS. J. L.– 1736

*Many of the following recipes neglect to add yeast. This may have been a scribal oversight, or possibly the yeast was introduced inadvertently through poor sterilization techniques. (See note p. 58.)*

1 quart water
1 1/2 lbs. apricots

4 or 5+ ounces sugar

To every Quart of Water put a Pound and half of Apricots, that are not over-ripe, let them be wiped clean, and cut in pieces; boil thefe till the Liquor is ftrong of the Apricot Flavour; then ftrain the Liquor thro' a Sieve, and put to every Quart four or five Ounces of white Sugar, boil it again, and fcum it as it rifes, and when the Scum rifes no more, pour it into an Earthen Pot; the Day following bottle it, putting into every Bottle a lump of Loaf-sugar, as big as a Nutmeg. This will prefently be fit for drinking, is a very pleafant Liquor; but will not keep long.
(From *The Country Housewife and Lady's Director*, by R. Bradley, 1736, p. 127.)

---

[1] Pliny the Elder, *Natural History*, Book XIV, section XIX, pp. 255-257.

## APRICOT WINE – 1829

| | |
|---|---|
| 3 lbs. sugar | 3 quarts water |
| 6 lbs. apricots | 1 sprig clary |

Boil together three pounds of sugar, and three quarts of water; and skim it well. Put in six pounds of apricots pared and stoned, and let them boil till they become tender. Then take them up, and when the liquor is cold, bottle it. After taking out the apricots, let the liquor be boiled with a sprig of flowered clary. The apricots will make marmalade, and be very good for present use.

(From *Five Thousand Receipts, etc.*, by Mackenzie, 1829.)

✳✳✳

"The people of Cos mix in a rather large quantity of sea-water –a custom arising from the peculation of a slave who used this method to fill up the due measure, and this mixture is poured into white must, producing what is called in Greek 'white Coan.' In other countries a blend made in a similar way is called 'sea-flavoured wine,' and 'sea-treated' when the vessels containing the must have been thrown into the sea; this is a kind of wine that matures young."[1]

"...In Greece, on the other hand, they enliven the smoothness of their wines with potter's earth or marble dust or salt or sea-water..."[2]

✳✳✳

## [ASPARAGUS WINE] – c. 77 A. D.

*This recipe is for ten different herb-flavored wines, and is included in Pliny's discussion of Greek wines. The most curious feature of these early Greek wines is that they add sea-water or salt to improve the flavor!*

| | |
|---|---|
| 1 jar grape must | 1 pint concentrated grape juice |
| 2 handfuls asparagus roots | 1/2 pint sea water |

*optional*: substitute 2 handfuls savory, wild-marjoram, parsley-seed, southernwood, horse mint, rue,[3] catmint, mother of thyme *or* horehound for the asparagus.

...Among the plants grown in gardens, wine is made from the root of asparagus, and from savory, wild-marjoram, parsley-seed, southernwood, horse mint. [*sic*] rue, catmint, wild thyme and horehound; they put two handfuls of herb into a jar of must, together with a pint of boiled down grape-juice and half a pint of sea-water...

(From *Natural History*, by Pliny, Book XIV, section XIX, pp. 255-257.)

---

[1] Pliny the Elder, *Natural History*, Book XIV, section X, p. 239.

[2] *ibid.*, Book XIV, section XXIV, pp. 265-9.

[3] CAUTION! (*See Appendix.*)

## BALM WINE – 1788

| | |
|---|---|
| 20 lbs. sugar | 4 1/2 gallons water |
| yeast | 2 lbs. lemon balm tops |

Take twenty pounds of lump sugar and four gallons and a half of water, boil it gently for one hour, and put it into a tub to cool; take two pounds of the tops of green balm, and bruise them, put them into a barrel with a little new yeast, and when the liquor is nearly cold pour it on the balm; stir it well together; and let it stand twenty-four hours, stirring it often; then bung it tight, and the longer you keep it the better it will be.
(From *The Receipt Book of Richard Briggs*, 1788.)

## BALM WINE – 1829

| | |
|---|---|
| 40+ lbs. sugar | 9 gallons water |
| yeast | 2 1/2 lbs. lemon balm tops |

Take 40 pounds of sugar and 9 gallons of water, boil it gently for 2 hours, skim it well, and put it into a tub to cool. Take 2 pounds and a half of the tops of balm, bruise them, and put them into a barrel, with a little new yeast; and when the liquor is cold, pour it on the balm. Stir it well together and let it stand 24 hours, stirring it often. Then close it up, and let it stand 6 weeks. Then rack it off and put a lump of sugar into every bottle. Cork it well, and it will be better the second year than the first.
(From *Five Thousand Receipts, etc.*, by Mackenzie, 1829.)

## BALM WINE –1897

| | |
|---|---|
| 10+ lbs. sugar | 4 gallons water |
| toast spread with yeast | 1 1/4 lb. lemon balm tops |

Boil ten pounds of moist sugar in four gallons of water for over an hour, and skim it well. Pour into an earthenware vessel to cool. Bruise a pound and a quarter of balm tops and put them into a small cask with yeast spread on toast, and when the above liquor is cool, pour it on the balm. Stir them well together, and let the mixture stand for twenty-four hours, stirring it frequently; then close it up, lightly at first and more securely after fermentation has quite ceased. When it has stood for six or eight weeks bottle it off, putting a lump of sugar into each bottle. Cork the bottle well and keep it at least a year before putting it into use.
(From *Herbal Simples*, by Dr. Fernie, 1897.)

## BARLEY WINE – 1829

*The first two waters in which the barley is boiled are to be discarded.*

| | |
|---|---|
| 3/4 lb. sugar | 1/2 lb. barley |
| 3 pints barley water | 1 quart white wine |
| 1/2 pint borage water | 1/2 pint clary water |
| juice of 5 or 6 lemons | 1 lemon peel |
| rosewater | |

Boil half a pound of fresh barley in 3 waters, and save 3 pints of the last water. Mix it with a quart of white wine, half a pint of borage water, as much clary water, a little red rose-water, the juice of 5 or 6 lemons, 3 quarters of a pound of fine sugar, and the thin yellow rind of a lemon. Mix all these well together, run it through a strainer, and bottle it. It is pleasant in hot weather, and very good in fevers.
(From *Five Thousand Receipts, etc.*, by Mackenzie, 1829.)

## # 257  TO MAKE BIRCH WINE – c. 1550 to 1625

| | |
|---|---|
| 1 gallon birch sap | 1 lb. sugar |
| yeast | |

Time to completion: about 9 to 10 weeks.

First make an incission & an hole thorough ye bark of one of ye largest birch tree bows, & put a quill therein, & quickly you shall perceive ye Juice to distill. you may make incision into severall bowes at once, which water receive into whatever vessill you pleas. it will continew running 9 or 10 dayes, & if yr tree be large, it will afford you [many] gallons. boyle it well, as you doe bear, but first put to every gallon, one pound of white powdered sugar. when it is well boyled, take it of the fire, & put in A gilefate with yeast, as yu doe to ale or beere, & it will worke in the same mannor. after 4 or 5 dayes, bottle it up in the thickest bottles you can get, for fear of bursting. & then at 8 or 9 weeks end, you may drink it, but it is better if you keep it older. this drink is very pleasant and allsoe physicall, first for procuring an appetite, & allsoe it is an antydote against gravell and the stone. this liquor must be procurd & made up in march, which is ye onely time, and not at the latter end of march neyther, for then the trees will not run soe well & freely as at ye beginning of the moneth.
(From *Martha Washington's Booke of Cookery*, ed. by Karen Hess, 1981.)

"...the real duties of the butler are in the wine-cellar; there he should be competent to advise his master as to the price and quality of the wine to be laid in; "fine," bottle, cork, and seal it, and place it in the bins. Brewing, racking, and bottling malt liquors, belong to his office, as well as their distribution..."[1]

✳✳✳

### # 99  TOO MAKE BURTCH, BY A FREIND AT THE CLIFT IN LEWIS – c. 1674

| | |
|---|---|
| 1 gallon birch sap | 2 lbs. sugar |
| yeast | |

Bore a hole through a burtch tree and putt in a faset, and putt sumthing under, and when tis full boyle it of every 2 days with 2 pound of white sugger too a gallan, and when it is allmost Cold, worke it up with a Littell yeist, then put it up in Vesells observe that the time to sane it in is in March and at the begining of Aprill if it bee a forward spring it will scarse Run at all Aprill
(From *Penn Family Recipes, etc.*, c. 1674.)

### TO MAKE BIRCH-WINE.  FROM LADY W. – 1736

| | |
|---|---|
| 5 gallons birch sap | 5 lbs. granulated sugar |
| 1 lemon peel | 2 lbs. seedless raisins |
| 40 large cloves | |

When the Sap of the Birch-Tree will run, cut a large Notch in the Bark of the Trunk of the Tree, in such a place as one may conveniently place a Vessel to receive the Sap; which will flow at the Incision very plentifully, without doing any harm to the Tree. If the Trees are pretty large, you may expect about a Gallon of Liquor from each of them, which must be order'd in the following manner. Take five Gallons of the Liquor, to which put five Pounds of Powder-Sugar, and two Pounds of Raisins of the Sun stoned; to this, put the Peel of one large Lemon, and about forty large fresh Cloves: boil all these together, taking off the Scum carefully as it rises; then pour it off into some Vessel to cool, and as soon as it is cool enough to put Yeast to it, work it as you would do Ale for two days, and then tunn it, taking care not to stop the Vessel till it has done Working, and in a Month's time it will be ready to bottle...
(From *The Country Housewife and Lady's Director*, by Richard Bradley, 1736, p. 39.)

---

[1] Mrs. Beeton, 1861, p. 963.

*WINES*

## TO MAKE BIRCH WINE – 1796

| | |
|---|---|
| 1 gallon birch sap | 4 lbs. sugar |
| 1 lemon peel | toast spread with yeast |

The ſeaſon for procuring the liquor from the birch-trees is the beginning of March, while the ſap is riſing, and before the leaves ſhoot out; for when the ſap is come forward, and the leaves appear, the juice, by being long digeſted in the bark, grows thick and coloured, which before was thin and clear. The method of procuring the juice is, by boring holes in the body of the tree, and putting in foſſets, which are commonly made of the branches of elder, the pith being taken out. You may without hurting the tree, if large, tap it in ſeveral places, four or five at a time, and by that means ſave from a good many trees ſeveral gallons every day; if you have not enough in one day, the bottles in which it drops muſt be corked cloſe, and roſined or waxed; however, make uſe of it as ſoon as you can. Take the ſap and boil it as long as any ſcum riſes, ſkimming it all the time: to every gallon of liquor put four pounds of good ſugar, the thin peel of a lemon, boil it afterwards half an hour, ſkimming it very well, pour it into a clean tub, and when it is almoſt cold, ſet it to work with yeaſt ſpread upon a toaſt, let it ſtand five or ſix days, ſtirring it often; then take ſuch a caſk as will hold the liquor, fire a large match dipped in brimſtone, and throw it into the caſk, ſtop it cloſe till the match is extinguiſhed[1], tun your wine, lay the bung on light till you find it has done working; ſtop it cloſe and keep it three months, then bottle it off.
(From *The Art of Cookery Made Plain and Easy*, v. 8, by Mrs. Glasse, 1796, p. 346.)

## BIRCH WINE – 1829

*This recipe, dated 1829, appears to have been paraphrased either from the recipe above or from another, earlier, work (and is clearer than Mrs. Glasse's).*

| | |
|---|---|
| 1 gallon birch sap | 4 lbs. sugar |
| lemon peel | toast spread with yeast |

The season for obtaining the liquor from birchtrees, is in the latter end of February, or the beginning of March, before the leaves shoot out, and as the sap begins to rise. If the time is delayed, the juice will grow too thick to be drawn out. It should be as thin and clear as possible. The method of procuring the juice is by boring holes in the trunk of the tree, and fixing faucets of elder; but care should be taken not to tap it in too many places at once, for fear of injuring the tree. If the tree is large, it may be bored in five or six places at once, and bottles are to be placed under the aperture for the sap to flow

---

[1] This was an early method of sterilizing a cask.

into. When four or five gallons have been extracted from different trees, cork the bottles very close, and wax them till the wine is to be made, which should be as soon as possible after the sap has been obtained. Boil the sap, and put four pounds of loaf sugar to every gallon, also the peel of a lemon cut thin; then boil it again for nearly an hour, skimming it all the time. Now pour it into a tub, and as soon as it is almost cold, work it with a toast spread with yeast, and let it stand five or six days, stirring it twice or three times each day. Into a cask that will contain it, put a lighted brimstone match, stop it up till the match is burnt out, and then pour the wine into it, putting the bung lightly in, till it has done working. Bung it very close for about three months, and then bottle it. It will be good in a week after it is put into the bottles.
(From *Five Thousand Receipts, etc.*, by Mackenzie, 1829.)

ANOTHER [*BIRCH WINE*] – 1829

1 hogshead birch sap            400 [units?[1]] raisins
grape stems

Birch wine may be made with raisins, in the following manner: To a hogshead of birchwater, take four hundred of Malaga raisins: pick them clean from the stalks, and cut them small. Then boil the birch liquor for one hour at least, skim it well, and let it stand till it be no warmer than milk. Then put in the raisins, and let it stand close covered, stirring it well four or five times every day. Boil all the stalks in a gallon or two of birch liquor, which, when added to the other, when almost cold, will give it an agreeable roughness. Let it stand ten days, then put it in a cool cellar, and when it has done hissing in the vessel, stop it up close. It must stand at least nine months before it is bottled. (*ibid.*)

---

[1] The raisins in this recipe are included to provide sweetness as well as a little flavor, but we are not told how many to add. Using our most conservative measure of a hogshead (63 gallons), and our most conservative sugar measurement from the above birch wines (1 lb. per gallon), we need to use enough raisins to provide the sweetness found in roughly 63 lbs. of sugar. Granted that birch sap is sweeter than water and will therefore require less sweetening, just how many pounds of raisins will we need?
    • 400 [each] raisins equals 2 cups of raisins and is too little for a hogshead of wine.
    • 400 [bunches] of raisins sounds reasonable, and would also necessitate picking "them clean from the stalks."
    • 400 [cups] of raisins (at 2.5 cups per lb.) would be 25 gallons of raisins, or 160 lbs. per hogshead (2.5 lbs. per gallon); this is also a reasonable amount considering no sugar is being added.
    • 400 lbs. of raisins (6.4 lbs. per gallon) is only slightly more than what is called for to make Fronteniac Wine (p. 170), and, while quite sweet, is still within reason.
    • 400 [gallons], [hundredweight], or [hogsheads] of raisins are far too many.
    • 400 [bunches], [cups], or [pounds] seems to be the best guess.

## # 253 TO MAKE BLACKBERRIE WINE – c. 1550 to 1625

| | |
|---|---|
| 1/2 peck blackberries | 1 lb. raisins |
| 5 quarts water | 1 lb. sugar |
| 2 or 3 lemons, sliced | |

Take halfe a peck of black berries & stamp them in a stone morter, & strayne y$^e$ cleares[t] of y$^e$ Juice thorough A Jelley bagg. then take a pound of raysons of y$^e$ sun & beat them and put them into 5 quarts of water, & boyle it very well, then run it thorough A Jelley bagg, & mix y$^e$ Juice with it, & let it stand 2 or 3 days in y$^e$ po[t]. then put in about a pound of loaf sugar, & run it thorough y$^e$ Jelley bagg againe. when they are mixt together, boyle it over againe, & put in y$^e$ water you boyle y$^e$ raysons in, 2 or 3 leamons, slyced. boyle it with y$^e$ raysons & water, & it will make it brisk & give it a more pleasant taste. then bottle it.
(From *Martha Washington's Booke of Cookery*, ed. by Karen Hess, 1981.)

## HOW TO MAKE BLACKBERRY WINE – 1796

blackberries
water
1 pint white wine
4 ounces isinglass
1 lb. sugar per 10 quarts liquid

Take your berries when full ripe, put them into a large veſſel of wood or ſtone, with a ſpicket in it, and pour upon them as much boiling water as will juſt appear at the top of them; as ſoon as you can endure your hand in them, bruiſe them very well, till all the berries be broke: then let them ſtand cloſe covered till the berries be well wrought up to the top, which uſually is three or four days, then draw off the clear juice into another veſſel; and add to every ten quarts of this liquor one pound of ſugar, ſtir it well in, and let it ſtand to work in another veſſel like the firſt, a week or ten days; then draw it off at the ſpicket through a jelly-bag into a large veſſel; take four ounces of iſinglaſs, lay it in ſteep twelve hours in a pint of white wine; the next morning boil it till it be all diſſolved upon a ſlow fire; then take a gallon of your blackberry-juice, put in the diſſolved iſinglaſs, give it a boil together, and put it in hot.
(From *The Art of Cookery Made Plain and Easy*, v. 8, by Mrs. Glasse, 1796, p. 343.)

## BLACKBERRY WINE – 1866

1 part blackberry juice                    3 lbs. brown sugar per gallon liquid
2 parts water                              1/2 teacupful brandy per 6 gallons liquid

Take ripe blackberries; mash them well either with the hands or some broad wooden spoon; then strain the juice through a strong bag. Have your cask measured, and allow one-third of its contents to be pure juice. As soon as the juice is measured, put it into the cask, which must now be placed in a firm position in the cellar, with spigot provided, so that it may be drawn off without having to move the cask. For every gallon that the cask will hold allow three pounds of brown sugar, and dissolve it in a bucket of water, stirring well; then pour this into the cask, and add more water to the sugar remaining in the bucket until all of it is in the cask; then fill up with water to the bung, and leave it open for ten days to ferment. On the tenth day, remove from around the bung-hole all the froth that has collected, using the little finger to reach that inside; then add to a six-gallon cask a half-teacupful of good brandy, and immediately put in the bung pretty tightly. In a day or two, pound it in securely, and let the cask remain undisturbed until the first of January, when it may be quietly racked off, and will be found perfectly clear until the sediment in the bottom is reached. Like all other wine, it improves with age; and although when first drawn it is of a light-red color, it will soon acquire a rich wine tint...
(From *The Art of Confectionery*, 1866.)

## BLACKBERRY WINE – 1875

1 gallon blackberries                    1 quart boiling water
2 lbs. sugar

...Measure your berries and bruise them, to every gallon add one quart of boiling water. Let the mixture stand twenty-four hours, stirring occasionally, then strain off the liquor into a cask; to every gallon add two pounds of sugar; cork tight, and let stand till the following October.
(From *Domestic Receipt-Book*, by Mrs. Winslow, c. 1875. The same recipe appears in *Herbal Simples*, by Dr. Fernie, 1897.)

# # 250  TO MAKE CHERRY WINE – c. 1550 to 1625

| | |
|---|---|
| 12 quarts water | 4 lbs. raisins |
| 6 quarts cherry juice | cherry pulp and skins |

Take a good quantety of spring water & let it boy[le] halfe an houre. then beat 4 pound of raysons, clean pickt & washed, & beat them in a morter to pas[te]. then put them in an earthen pot, & pour on y^m 12 quarts of this water boyling hot, & put to it 6 quarts of y^e Juice of cheries, & put in the pulp & scins of y^e cheries after they are strayned. & let all these steep together, close covered, 3 days. then strayn all out & let it stand 3 or 4 hours to settle. take of y^e cleerest, & run y^e rest thorough a Jelley bagg. then put y^e Juice up into bottles & stop them up close, & set them in sand.[1]
(From *Martha Washington's Booke of Cookery*, ed. by Karen Hess, 1981.)


# # 117  THE COUNTESS OF NEWPORT'S CHERRY WINE – 1669

| | |
|---|---|
| cherries | 1+ lb. granulated sugar per gallon juice |

Pick the best Cherries free from rotten, and pick the stalk from them; put them into an earthen Pan. Bruise them, by griping and straining them in your hands, and let them stand all night; on the next day strain them out (through a Napkin; which if it be a course and thin one, let the juyce run through a Hippocras or gelly bag, upon a pound of fine pure Sugar in powder, to every Gallon of juyce) and to every gallon put a pound of Sugar, and put it into a vessel. Be sure your vessel be full, or your wine will be spoiled; you must let it stand a month before you bottle it; and in every bottle you must put a lump (a piece as big as a Nutmeg) of Sugar. The vessel must not be stopt until it hath done working.
(From *The Closet ...Opened*, 1669.)


# # 119  TO MAKE WINE OF CHERRIES ALONE – 1669

| | |
|---|---|
| cherries | sugar |

Take one hundred pounds weight, or what quantity you please, of ripe, but sound, pure, dry and well gathered Cherries. Bruise and mash them with your hands to press out all their juyce, which strain through a boulter cloth, into a deep narrow Woodden tub, and

---

[1] It seems to have been common practice to keep a pile of sand in one's cellar to hold bottles securely while at the same time keeping them at a constant temperature. Some colonial-era houses had streams running through the cellar, or even separate stream houses built for the purpose of refrigeration.

cover it close with clothes. It will begin to work and ferment within three or four hours, and a thick foul scum will rise to the top. Skim it off as it riseth to any good head, and presently cover it again. Do this till no more great quantity of scum arise, which will be four or five times, or more. And by this means the Liquor will become clear, all the gross muddy parts rising up in scum to the top. When you find that the height of the working is past, and that it begins to go less, tun it into a barrel, letting it run again through a boulter, to keep out all the gross feculent substance. If you should let it stay before you tun it up, till the working were too much deaded, the wine would prove dead. Let it remain in the barrel close stopped, a month or five weeks. Then draw it into bottles, into each of which put a lump of fine Sugar, before you draw the wine into it, and stop them very close, and set them in a cold Cellar. You may drink them after three or four months. This wine is exceeding pleasant, strong, spiritful and comfortable.

(From *The Closet ...Opened*, 1669.)


## #103 MORELLO [CHERRY] WINE – 1669

20 1/2 gallons white wine                    20 lbs. morello cherries
*optional*: 2 ounces cinnamon sticks

To half an Aume[1] of white wine, take twenty pounds of Morello Cherries, the stalks being first plucked off. Bruise the Cherries and break the stones.[2] Pour into the Wine the juyce that comes out from the Cherries; but put all the solid substance of them into a long bag of boulter-cloth, and hang it in the Wine at the bung, so that it lie not in the bottom, but only reach to touch it, and therefore nail it down at the mouth of the bung. Then stop it close. For variety, you may put some clear juyce of Cherries alone (but drawn from a larger proportion of Cherries) into another parcel of Wine. To either of them, if you will Aromatise the drink, take to this quantity two Ounces of Cinnamon grosly broken and bruised, and put it in a little bag at the spiggot, that all the wine you draw may run through the Cinnamon.

You must be careful in bruising the Cherries, and breaking the stones. For if you do all at once, the Liquor will sparkle about. But you must first bruise the Cherries gently in a mortar, and rub through a sieve all that will pass, and strain the Residue hard through your hands. Then beat the remaining hard so strongly, as may break all the stones. Then put all together, and strain the clean through a subtil strainer, and put the solider substance into the bag to hang in the Wine. (*ibid.*)

---

[1] An *aume* is a Dutch liquid measure approximately equal to 41 British gallons.

[2] CAUTION! (*See Appendix.*)

4 *Cerasu Gasconica.*
The Gascoine Cherrie tree.

"The Morello Cherrie is of a reasonable bignesse, of a darke red colour when they are full ripe, and hang long on, of a sweetish sower taste, the pulpe or substance is red, and somewhat firme: if they be dryed they will haue a fine sharpe or sower taste very delectable."[1]

## CHERRY WINE – 1719

1 gallon cherries
1 quart water
1/2+ lb. sugar
toast spread with yeast

Pick your cherryes from the Stalks break them very well but not to brake the Stone to every gallon of cherryes a quart of water. Set them over the fiare [*sic*] let them boyle a little. Straine them out to every gallon of wine put half a pound of Sugar. Spread some yeste upon a toste put it into low warme cover it up close let it Stand all night to worke then put it in your vessell and when it has don working Stope it close doune let it Stand a month then bottle it put some lose Sugar in each bottle corke it close and it will be ripe in a month.
(From *M.S. Book of Receipts*, by Thomas Newington, 1719.)

## MORELLO [CHERRY] WINE – 1723

24 lbs. morello cherries          9 or 10 gallons white wine
*optional*: spices.

Take twenty-four Pound of Morello Cherries pull off the stalkes, and bruise them so that the stones may be broken,[2] press out the juice and put it to nine or ten gallons of White-Wine. Put the skins and the stones in a Bag and let them be hung in a Cask so as not to touch the bottom of it and let it stand for a month or more. You may also put in spices if you please but the wine will be very pleasant without them.
(From *The Receipt Book of John Nott*, 1723.)

---

[1] Parkinson, p. 572.

[2] CAUTION! (*See Appendix.*)

"The late ripe Cherries which the French men keepe dried againſt winter, and are by them called *Morelle*, and we after the ſame name call them Morell Cherries, are dry, and do ſomwhat bind: theſe being dried are pleaſant to the taſte, and holeſome for the ſtomacke, like as Prunes be..."[1]

✳✳✳

CHERRY WINE – 1732

cherries                                    2+ lbs. sugar per gallon juice

Pick off the stalkes and stone your cherries, press out the juice, and to each gallon put two pounds of Sugar, put it in a Cask, set it a working, and when it has done, stop it up for two months, then bottle it off, putting a little Sugar, and after it has stood six weeks, it will be fit for use.
(From *The Receipt Book of Charles Carter,* Cook to the Duke of Argyll, 1732. *Another recipe for cherry wine, which uses only one pound of sugar per gallon of juice, may be found in "The Country Housewife and Lady's Director," by Richard Bradley, 1736, pp. 103-104.*)

TO MAKE CHERRY WINE – 1796

cherries                                    2 lbs. sugar per gallon juice

Pull your cherries when full ripe off the ſtalks, and preſs them through a hair ſieve; to every gallon of liquor put two pounds of lump ſugar beat fine, ſtir it together, and put it into a veſſel; it muſt be full: when it has done working and making any noiſe, ſtop it cloſe for three months, and bottle it off.
(From *The Art of Cookery Made Plain and Easy*, v. 8, by Mrs. Glasse, 1796, p. 345.)

94th. A SHORT WAY FOR CHERRY WINE – 1815

cherries                                    sugar

Time to completion: 1 month.

Squeeze the juice of the cherries into a cask, and thereto put a small quantity of sugar, corresponding to the quantity of juice; and when stood a month, it will be a pleasant liquor.
(From *The Dyer's Companion*, by Elijah Bemiss, 1815, p. 302.)

---

[1] Gerard, p. 1324.

> "'No man would prefer to drink wine hot;
> rather one likes it chilled in the well or mixed with snow.'"[1]

***

## CHERRY WINE – 1846

24 lbs. cherries          1 lb. sugar

Time to completion: 3 months.

Take twenty-four pounds of the finest ripe cherries, (the black English cherry is to be preferred), and after removing defective ones, bruise them in a cloth and press out the juice as dry as possible. Then take the skins and stones, and pound them with a mallet so as to crush the stones and kernels,[2] and put them into the juice again. When it has fermented twelve hours, strain it through a large flannel bag into a pan containing one pound of loaf sugar. Squeeze the bag with the hands, so as to extract as much juice as possible. When the sugar is dissolved, put the liquor into bottles, filling each within an inch of the cork; cork it loosely for a day or two, then cork it tight, and keep it three months before use, in a cool place, or buried in sand in the cellar.
(From *The Young Housekeeper's Friend, etc.*, by Mrs. Cornelius, 1846.)

## 88th. ARTIFICIAL CLARET – 1815

6 gallons water          2 gallons apple cider
8 lbs. raisins          1 pint black cherry juice
1 quart barberry juice      toast spread with mustard seed

Take six gallons of water, two gallons of the best cider, and thereto put eight pounds of the best Malaga raisins bruised; let them stand close covered in a warm place for two weeks, stirring them every two days well together; then press out the liquor into a vessel again, and add to it a quart of the juice of barberries, (which perhaps is best) to which put a pint of the juice of black cherries: work it up with mustard seed[3] covered with bread past for three or four days, by the fire side; after which, let it stand a week; then bottle it off, and it will become near as good, if not so as to exceed, common claret.
(From *The Dyer's Companion*, by Elijah Bemiss, 1815, p. 301.)

---

[1] Strattis, quoted in Athenaeus, Book III, p. 77.

[2] CAUTION! (*See Appendix.*)

[3] *See note p. 58.*

> Thus laboureth he til that the day gan dawe;
> And thanne he taketh a soppe in fyn clarree,
> And upright in his bed thanne sitteth he...[1]

***

## CLARY WINE – 1621

*This recipe seems to be calling for 130 pounds of sugar to make only 10 gallons of wine, or 13 pounds per gallon! This must have been a scribal error. Our 1807 recipe uses only 3 pounds of sugar per gallon of water, while the 1732 recipe uses 4 pounds of raisins per gallon.*

| | |
|---|---|
| 10 gallons water | 130 lbs. sugar |
| 16 egg whites | 1 pint ale yeast |
| 1 pint clary flowers | |

Ten gallons of water, thirteen pounds of sugar to the gallon, and the whites of sixteen eggs well beat. Boil it slowly one hour and skim it well. Then put it into a tub till it is almost cold. Take a pint of Clary flowers with the small leaves and stalks, put them into a barrel with a pint of ale yeast, then put in your liquor and stir it twice a day till it has done working. Make it up close and keep it four months, and then bottle it off.
(From *A Delightful Daily Exercise for Ladies and Gentlemen*, by John Murrell, 1621.)

## CLARY WINE – 1732

| | |
|---|---|
| 12 lbs. raisins, chopped | 12 quarts water |
| 1/4 peck clary tops and flowers | |

Time to completion: 3 or 4 months.

Take twelve pounds of Malaga Raisins, after they have been pick'd small and chop'd, put them into a Vessel, a quart of Water to each pound. Let them stand to steep for ten or twelve Days, being kept close covered all the while, stirring them twice every Day; afterwards strain it off, and put it up in a Cask, adding a quarter of a Peck of the Tops of Clary, when it is in Blossom; then stop it up close for six weeks, and afterwards you may bottle it off, and it will be fit to drink in two or three Months...
(From *The Receipt Book of Charles Carter*, Cook to the Duke of Argyll, 1732.)

---

[1] Chaucer, "The Merchant's Tale," lines 1842-44.

*WINES*

CLARY WINE – 1807

15 gallons water                1/4 pint yeast
45 lbs. sugar                   1 gallon brandy
12 quarts clary flowers

Boil fifteen gallons of water, with forty-five pounds of sugar, skim it, when cool put a little to a quarter of a pint of yeast, and so by degrees add a little more. In an hour pour the small quantity to the large, pour the liquor on claryflowers, picked in the dry; the quantity for the above is twelve quarts. Those who gather from their own garden may not have sufficient to put in at once, and may add as they can get them, keeping account of each quart. When it ceases to hiss, and the flowers are all in, stop it up for four months. Rack it off, empty the barrel of the dregs, and adding a gallon of the best brandy, stop it up, and let it stand six or eight weeks, then bottle it.
(From *A New System of Domestic Cookery, etc.*, 1807.)

[COW PARSNIP WINE] – 1597

"The people of Polonia, & Lituania, vſe to make drinke with the decoction of this herbe [cow parsnip], and leuen or ſome other thing made of meale, which is vſed in ſteed of beere, and other ordinarie drinke."
(From *The Herball or Generall Historie of Plants*, by John Gerard, 1597, p. 856.)

# 102   THE LADY OXENDONS TOO MAKE COUSLIP AND MARIGOLD WINE –
       c. 1674

2 gallons water               4 lbs. sugar
juice of 1 lemon             3 spoonsful yeast
1 peck cowslip or marigold (*Calendula*) flowers

Time to completion: 2 1/2 months.

Take 2 gallans of spring water too which put 4 pound of Lofe suger, and Lett them boyle gently one houer then take a peck of flours bruse them in a Morter, and when the Liquor is blood warm put the flouers into it with the Juce of a Lemon then take 3 spunfulls of yeist with 6 spunfulls of the Liquor and beat it well together, then put it to the other Liquor and Lett them stand five Days, then strain it out hard and put it out into a barrell, after it is done working stop it Close and Lett it stand a month or more then draw it into bottells, after 6 weeks boteling it will bee fitt to drinke, keep it a year or Longer, the larger the quantaty is made at a time the beter the wine will be
(From *Penn Family Recipes, etc.*, c. 1674.)

...Then came *October* full of merry glee:
For, yet his noule was totty of the must,
Which he was treading in the wine-fats see,
And of the ioyous oyle, whose gentle gust
Made him so frollick and so full of lust...[1]

\*\*\*

## # 120  TOO MAKE COUSLIP WINE – c. 1674

| | |
|---|---|
| 1 gallon water | 1/2 peck cowslip flowers |
| 2+ lbs. sugar | 2 ounces citron *or* lemon peel |
| 1 pint white wine | 1 or 2 lemons, halved |
| toast spread with yeast | |

Time to completion: 1 1/2 months.

Too every gallan of water add 2 pound of good whit shuger, boyle them together a Lest an houer, then taking of the scum, sett it too Colle till it bee hardly blood warme, then take too evry gallan 2 oz of Cittorn or Lemon, which must bee well beaten, with a quantaty of yeist fitt to sett it at worke, too 6 or 7 gallans I think wee use to put in 1/2 a pint, but of that more or Less too youre Discretion or acording as the yeist is new or stale make a great brown toast hot spred over with yeist – putt the toast with the syrrup and yeist, beaten as a fore said into the Liquor and so Lett it stand and work 2 days and a night or 2 According as you find it worke if you find it worke not kindly stur it about with a Ladell very well for a qr of an houer which will very much help it, after it hath stood the time to worke Take too 6 gallan 1/2 a peck of Couslip flouers put into a bagg fitt for the purpose made of Corse white Cloath Called bollster put it into a well sesoned vesell, if it hath had Latly wine in it the better, with a peece of Led[2] or waite a bout 3 or 4 pound in the bottom of the bagg too keep the flouers downe, then put in the Liquor, to which add to over a gallan a pint of white wine, then put to it a Lemon or 2 Cutt in 1/2 then bung up the Caske, Close, Leving only a Littell vent hole open one the top of the Caske nere the bung and so Lett it stand a month or 5 weeks then draw it out into bottells, and Lay it up in the sand, in bottelling of it wee use to put in a Lumpe of sugger about as bigg as a Large nuttmegg in to eatch bottell, this will keep good 9 or 12 months but it may bee drunke of in a weeke or tow –
(From *Penn Family Recipes, etc.*, c. 1674.)

---

[1] Edmund Spenser, *The Faerie Queene.*
[2] CAUTION! Do not use lead.

# 136 TOO MAK COUSLIP WINE – c. 1674

1 peck cowslip flowers    1 gallon water
4 lbs. raisins       sugar

Time to completion: 12 days.

take a peck of Couslips and a gallan of Runing water 4 pound of maligo Resons, put Couslips and Resons a stepe in the watter 9 days then strain it and put the Clerest in to bottells put a Lump of Lofe suger in to each bottell, stop them Close this will bee Redy to drinke in 3 days
(From *Penn Family Recipes, etc.*, c. 1674.)

## TO MAKE COWSLIP OR CLARY WINE – 1796

6 gallons water      6 ounces lemon *or* citron syrup
1 quart Rhenish wine    juice and peels of 6 lemons
12 lbs. sugar       toast spread with yeast
4 egg whites, beaten    1 peck cowslip flowers

Take ſix gallons of water, twelve pounds of ſugar, the juice of ſix lemons, the whites of four eggs beat very well, put all together in a kettle, let it boil half an hour, ſkim it very well: take a peck of cowſlips (if dry ones, half a peck), put them into a tub, with the thin peeling of ſix lemons, then pour on the boiling liquor, and ſtir them about; when almoſt cold, put in a thin toaſt baked dry and rubbed with yeaſt: let it ſtand two or three days to work. If you put in (before you tun it) ſix ounces of ſyrup of citron or lemons, with a quart of Rheniſh wine, it will be a great addition; the third day ſtrain it off, and ſqueeze the cowſlips through a coarſe cloth; then ſtrain it through a flannel bag, and tun it up; lay the bung looſe for two or three days to ſee if it works, and if it does not, bung it down tight; let it ſtand three months, then bottle it.
(From *The Art of Cookery Made Plain and Easy*, v. 8, by H. Glasse, 1796, pp. 346-7. *An undated recipe for cowslip wine can be found in "Martha Washington's Booke of Cookery," p. 389.*)

COWSLIP WINE – 1861

1817.  INGREDIENTS. – To every gallon of water allow 3 lbs. of lump sugar, the rind of 2 lemons, the juice of 1, the rind and juice of 1 Seville orange, 1 gallon of cowslip pips.  To every 4 1/2 gallons of wine allow 1 bottle of brandy.
*Mode*. – Boil the sugar and water together for 1/2 hour, carefully removing all the scum as it rises.  Pour this boiling liquor on the orange and lemon-rinds, and the juice, which should be strained; when milk-warm, add the cowslip pips or flowers, picked from the stalks and seeds; and to 9 gallons of wine 3 tablespoonfuls of good fresh brewers' yeast.  Let it ferment 3 or 4 days; then put all together in a cask with the brandy, and let it remain for 2 months, when bottle it off for use... Make this in April or May.
(From *Mrs. Beeton's Book of Household Management*, 1861.)


COWSLIP WINE – undated

| | |
|---|---|
| 9 pints water | 2 lbs. sugar |
| 1 quart cowslip flowers | 2 spoonsful yeast |

Nine pints of water, two pounds of Sugar.  Boil and skim well.  Pour it hot on one quart of picked cowslips.  Next day strain and add two spoonfuls of yeast.  Let it stand in an earthen pan a fortnight to work, covered close and stirred three times a day for the first three days.  Then drain into bottles and stop it tight.  It will keep for a year.
(From *Travels round our Village*, by E. G. Hayden.)

"...thoſe ſmall Raiſons which are commonly called Corans or Currans, or rather Raiſins of Corinth ... which come foorth cluſters of grapes, in forme like the other, but ſmaller, of a blewiſh colour; which being ripe are gathered and laid vpon hurdels, carpets, mats, and ſuch like, in the ſunne to drie: then are they caried to ſome houſe and laid vpon heapes, as we laie apples, or corne in a garner, vntil the marchants do buie them: then do they put them into Buttes or other wooden veſſels, and treade them downe with their bare feete, which they call Stiuing, and ſo are they brought into theſe parts for our vse."[1]

✳✳✳

## # 256   TO MAKE WINE OF CURRANS – c. 1550 to 1625

*This is two recipes for currant wine and a recipe for currant wine vinegar; the numbers in brackets have been added to separate the recipes.*

[1]

| 40 lbs. currants | 10 gallons water |
|---|---|

Take 40 pound of currans (or what quantety [you] pleas). infuse them in 10 gallons of water in a [tun] fit for yͤ purpose. cover it close with a cloth yͭ the vapours goe not forth. soe let it heat together 10, 12, or 14 dayes. then poure yͤ liquor from yͤ currans into a runlet, & give it time [to] clear & worke. after, stop it up close & broa[ch] it not till it be halfe a year old, & then [you] may bottle it up.

[2]

| 3 gallons water | 40 lbs. soaked currant grapes (from above) |
|---|---|

now to make a smaller win[e]. put into yͤ currans yͭ came from yͤ former wine, 3 gallons of water & stirr them very well, & let them infuse together as before. then stray[ne] out yͤ liquor into a convenient vessell, & after a moneth or 6 weeks, it will be fit to drink. [3] or you may set this vessell of smaller liquor in yͤ sun & it will make good vinegar. [1,2] you must observe to stir both yͤ stronger & smaller liquors every night & morning (with a spatula of wood) all yͤ time they are in yͤ infusion in [yͬ] tub. in warme weather, it will be quickly ready & sharp before yͤ vertue of yͤ currans be in yͤ water, so yͭ is not to be made when yͤ weather is very hot or very cold, for then it will not come to perfection at all. but spring or fall, you may make it in. when it beginneth to wax sharp, it is ripe enou[gh], & then you may put it up.[2]

(From *Martha Washington's Booke of Cookery*, ed. by Karen Hess, 1981.)

---

[1] Gerard, pp. 725-6.

[2] This recipe raises an important point concerning the temperature of the room in which fermentation

# # 104 CURRANTS WINE – 1669

1 lb. currants                                        6 pints hot water
3 spoonsful ale yeast

Take a pound of the best Currants clean picked, and pour upon them in a deep straight mouthed earthen vessel six pounds or pints of hot water, in which you have dissolved three spoonfuls of the purest and newest Ale-yest. Stop it very close till it ferment, then give such vent as is necessary, and keep it warm for about three days, it will work and ferment. Taste it after two days, to see if it be grown to your liking. As soon as you find it so, let it run through a strainer, to leave behind all the exhausted currants and the yest, and so bottle it up. It will be exceeding quick and pleasant, and is admirable good to cool the Liver, and cleanse the blood. It will be ready to drink in five or six days after it is bottled; And you may drink safely large draughts of it.
(From *The Closet ...Opened*, 1669.)


## TO MAKE CURRANT WINE – 1736

3 lbs. currants                                      1 quart water
1+ lb. granulated sugar

When your Currants are full ripe, gather them, and pick them from the Stalks and weigh them, in order to proportion your Water and Sugar to them. When this is done, bruiſe them to pieces with your Hands, and add to every three Pounds of Currants a Quart of Water, ſtirring all together, and letting it ſtand three Hours, at the end of which time, ſtrain it off gently thro' a Sieve, and put your Sugar into your Liquor, after the rate of a Pound to every three Pounds of Currants. This Sugar ſhould be powder Sugar, for Lisbon Sugar would give the Wine an ill Taſte. Stir this well together, and boil it till you have taken off all the Scum, which will riſe plentifully; ſet it then to cool, at leaſt ſixteen Hours, before you put it into the Veſſel. If you make the Quantity of twenty Gallons, it may ſtand in the Veſſel three Weeks before it will be fit for bottling; and if you make thirty Gallons, then it muſt ſtand a Month before it be bottled off,

---

takes place. If the room is too warm, the yeast will grow too quickly, using up all the available sugar and turning the brew sour. If the room is too cold, the yeast will not grow well and you will not have the wine you so heartily desired. A cool cellar where the temperature hovers around 68° F. is ideal for fermentation. In colder climates, or during the winter, a warm blanket, or even a carefully-monitored electric blanket, wrapped around the fermentation vessel should be enough to get the reaction going. (Once the reaction has started, the electric blanket may be replaced by a non-electric one, or turned off. If your house is particularly cold, you may choose to keep the electric blanket turned on, but check it daily to prevent overheating the mixture.)

obſerving then to put a ſmall Lump of Sugar into every Bottle; it muſt be kept in a cool place, to prevent its Fretting. By this Method it will keep good many Years, and be a very ſtrong and pleaſant Wine, at a very cheap rate.

It is neceſſary to obſerve, that the ſame ſort of Currant is not always of the ſame Sweetneſs when it is ripe, thoſe growing in the Shade will be leſs ſweet than thoſe that are more expoſed to the Sun. And when the Summer happens to be wet and cold, they will not be ſo ſweet as in a dry warm Seaſon; therefore tho' the Standard of the above Receipt be one Pound of Sugar to three Pounds of pick'd Currants, yet the Palate of the Perſon who makes the Wine ſhould be the Regulator, when the Sugar is put to the Juice, conſidering at the ſame time, that it is a Wine they are making, and not a Syrup. The Sugar is only put to ſoften and preſerve the Juice, and too much will make the Wine ropey.

(From *The Country Housewife and Lady's Director*, by Richard Bradley, 1736, pp. 101-102.)

\*\*\*

"The dryed grapes which we call great Rayſins, and the Currans which we call ſmall Rayſins, are much vſed both for meates, broths, and ſawces, in diuers manners, as this Countrey in generall aboue any other, wherin many thouſands of Frailesfull, Pipes, Hogs-heads, and Buts full are ſpent yearly, that it breedeth a wonder in them of thoſe parts where they growe and prouide them, how we could ſpend ſo many."[1]

\*\*\*

CURRANT WINE – 1788

currant grapes

2 1/2 lbs. sugar per gallon liquor
1 quart brandy per 6 gallons liquor

Gather your currants on a fine dry day, when the fruit is full ripe, strip them, put them in a large pan, and bruise them with a wooden pestle; let them stand in a pan or tub twenty-four hours to ferment; then run it through a hair sieve, and do not let your hand touch the liquor, to every gallon of this liquor put two pounds and a half of white sugar, stir it well together, and put it into your vessel; to every six gallons put in a quart of brandy, and let it stand six weeks; if it is fine, bottle it; if it is not, draw it off as clear as you can into another vessel, or large bottles, and in a fortnight bottle it in small bottles.

(From *The Receipt Book of Richard Briggs*, 1788. This can also be found in Glasse, v. 8, p. 345, and in Thornton.)

---

[1] Parkinson, p. 566.

## WHITE CURRANT WINE – 1796

| | |
|---|---|
| 1 gallon currant grape juice | 3 gallons water |
| 3 1/2 lbs. sugar | *optional*: 1 quart brandy; 1 handful clary. |

Squeeze your currants through a cullender, then wring them through a cloth; to each gallon of juice three gallons of water, three pounds and a half of ſugar; boil the ſugar and water together, take off the ſcum clear, put it to cool, put the juice to it, then put it in a barrel; let it ſtand a month or ſix weeks, then draw it off and put it in the ſame barrel again, with a quart of brandy; if you chooſe, you may add a handful of clary.
(From *The Art of Cookery Made Plain and Easy*, v. 8, by Mrs. Glasse, 1796, p. 345.)

## RED CURRANT WINE – 1810

| | |
|---|---|
| 4 gallons water | 4 gallons currant grapes |
| toast spread with yeast | |
| 3 1/2 lbs. brown *or* white sugar per gallon liquid | |

Four gallons of cold water to four of bruised currants, picked carefully from their stalks; let them stand together for four days, then strain them off, mix three pounds and a half of brown sugar or white sugar which is greatly to be preferred, to each gallon of diluted currant juice; stir it well, then put it into a Cask and add also a piece of toasted bread spread over with yeast which will ferment it; after this is over bring it up very light and it will be ready for bottling off in six months and for domestic use after six months keeping in the bottle...
(From *The Family Herbal*, by R. Thornton, 1810.)

## 87TH. CURRANT WINE – 1815

| | |
|---|---|
| 1 gallon currant grapes | 1 quart hot water |
| ale yeast | |

Pick the currants (when they are full ripe) clean from the stalks, then put them into an earthen vessel, and pour on them fair and clean hot water, that is, a quart of water to a gallon of currants; then bruise or marsh [*sic*] them together, and let them stand and ferment; then cover them for twelve hours, strain them through fine linen into a large earthen crock, (as they say in Sussex) and then put the liquor into a cask, and thereto put a little ale-yeast; and when worked and settled, bottle it off. This is exceeding pleasant, and very wholesome for cooling the blood. In a weak's time it will be fit for bottling.
(From *The Dyer's Companion*, by Elijah Bemiss, 1815, pp. 300-301.)

86th.   A METHOD OF MAKING CURRANT WINE, which had been practised by
many and found to be genuine. – 1815

1 part currant juice                                      3 lbs. sugar per gallon liquid
2 parts water

Gather your currants when full ripe; break them well in a tub or vat; press and measure
your juice; add two thirds water, and to each gallon of mixture, (juice add water) put
three pounds of muscovado sugar, the cleaner and drier the better; very coarse sugar,
first clarified, will do equally as well:  stir it well till the sugar is well dissolved, and
then bung it up.  Your juice should not stand over night if you can possibly help it, as it
should not ferment before mixture.  Observe that your cask be sweet and clean.  Do not
be prevailed on to add more than one third of juice, as above prescribed, for that would
render it infallibly hard and unpleasent:  nor yet a greater proportion of sugar, as it
will certainly deprive it of its pure vinous taste.
(From *The Dyer's Companion*, by Elijah Bemiss, 1815, p. 300.)


CURRANT WINE – 1832

*Currant wine must have been one of the most popular of homemade wines.  The
recipes presented here are merely a small sampling of all those which have survived;
many more recipes for currant wine can be found in Simon's collection and in period
cookbooks.*

1 part water                                             3 1/2 lbs. sugar per gallon liquid
1 part currant juice
*optional*:  use half currant and half raspberry juice.

Time to completion:  1 to 2 years.

Those who have more currants than they have money, will do well to use no wine but
of their own manufacture.  Break and squeeze the currants, put three pounds and a half
of sugar to two quarts of juice and two quarts of water.  Put n [*sic*] a keg or barrel.
Do not close the bung tight for three or four days, that the air may escape while it is
fermenting.  After it is done fermenting, close it up tight.  Where raspberries are
plenty, it is a great improvement to use half raspberry juice, and half currant juice.
Brandy is unnecessary when the above-mentioned proportions are observed.  It should
not be used under a year or two.  Age improves it.
(From *The American Frugal Housewife*, 1832, p. 82.)

"Strange that old wine should always be in favour among gay ladies,
but not an old man, rather the young one."[1]
✳✳✳

## CURRANT WINE – 1846

1 quart currant juice          2 quarts water
3 lbs. sugar          1 quart brandy per 15 gallons liquor

Strain the currants, which should be perfectly ripe.  To each quart of juice put a couple of quarts of water, and three pounds of sugar – stir the whole well together, and let it stand twenty-four hours, without stirring – then skim and set it in a cool place, where it will ferment slowly.  Let it remain three or four days – if, at the end of that time, it has ceased fermenting, add one quart of French brandy to every fifteen gallons of the liquor, and close up the barrel tight.  When it becomes clear, it is fit to bottle.  This will be good in the course of six months, but it is much improved by being kept several years.
(From *The Kitchen Directory, and American Housewife, etc.*, 1846.)


✳✳✳
"The great Damaske or Damſon Plummes are dryed in France in great quantities, and brought ouer vnto vs in Hogs-heads, and other great veſſels, and are thoſe Prunes that are vſually ſold at the Grocers..."[2]
✳✳✳


## 91st.  DAMSON [*PLUM*] WINE – 1815

1 quart damson plums          3 quarts water
sugar

Dry the damsons in an oven after you have taken out your bread,[3] then to every quart of damsons put three quarts of fair water, but first boil it very well; then put the water and damsons into a runlet with sugar; and having stood a time sufficient, bottle it of.
(From *The Dyer's Companion*, by Elijah Bemiss, 1815, p. 301.)

---

[1] Eubulus, quoted in Athenaeus, Book I, p. 113.

[2] Parkinson, p. 578.

[3] This was done to make the plums sweeter and more flavorful. (*See "To Make Fronteniac Wine," p. 170.*)

149

DANDELION WINE – c. 1922

| | |
|---|---|
| 4 pints dandelion flowers | 4 lbs. sugar |
| 1 gallon water | toast spread with 1/2 ounce yeast |
| 2 or 3 lemons | |

Four pints of dandelion bloom (in calyx), 4 lbs. Demarara sugar, 2 (or 3) lemons, gallon of water.

Boil bloom in water for 20 minutes. Strain boiling liquor on to the sugar. Halve lemons, peel and pip them: put remainder into liquor. Put 1/2 oz., or less, of yeast on a small piece of toast and lay it on the liquor when it has partly cooled, is warm but not hot. When it has fermented, probably at the end of two days, skim off yeast and toast and bottle, adding the lemon peel.

If you are putting the wine into sufficiently large vessels it is unnecessary to peel the lemons: after being pipped they can go in in halves or quarters with the peel on. (From *A Garden of Herbs* by E. S. Rohde, p. 66.)

1 *Sambucus.*
The common Elder tree.

DANDELION WINE – undated

9 gallons water
27 lbs. sugar
18 Seville oranges
27 quarts dandelion flowers
1 ounce hops
1/2 lb. brown ginger
12 lemons
orange and lemon peels to taste
yeast

*The Elder Tree.*
From Gerard's *Herball*, 1597.

To make nine gallons of wine. Boil twenty-seven quarts of pips in nine gallons of water for an hour. Strain and boil again with 13 1/2 lbs. best Demerara sugar, 1 oz. of hops, 1/2 lb. brown ginger, and sufficient orange and lemon peel to taste. Slice eighteen Seville oranges and twelve lemons, and put to them 13 1/2 lbs. sugar as above. Pour over them, and boiling beyond when blood warm, add a little brewer's yeast. Strain again before putting into a barrel. The wine should be allowed to work three or four days before being bunged tight. Bottle in six months. Like a sharp liqueur. (From *Travels round our Village*, by E. G. Hayden.)

"Walnuts, pomegranates, dates and other sweets, and little jars of date wine..."[1]

***

[DATE AND FIG WINES] – c. 77 A. D.

1 peck soft dates                    2 1/4 gallons water

...the wine made from date-palms, which is used by the Parthians and Indians and by the whole of the East, a peck of the rather soft dates called in Greek 'common dates' being soaked in two and a quarter gallons of water and then pressed.

1 peck figs                    2 1/4 gallons water or must

Also fig syrup is made from figs by a similar process, other names for it being pharnuprium and trochis; or if it is not wanted to be sweet, instead of water is added the same quantity of grape-skin juice...
(From *Natural History*, by Pliny, c. 77 A. D., Book XIV, section XIX, pp. 255-257.)

# 254 TO MAKE ELDERBERRY WINE – c. 1550 to 1625

3 1/2 gallons water
1 peck elderberries
1 pint honey *or* 1/2 lb. sugar per quart strained liquid
1 pint ale yeast per 2 quarts strained liquid

Take 3 gallons & a halfe of water & set it on ye fire, & when it is warme, put to it a peck of elderberries very rip[e]. bruise them well, & strayne them, & measure the liquor & set it on ye fire again, & let it boyle a quarter of an houre, & scum it very well. & to every quart of liquor, put a pinte of honey or halfe a pound of suga[r]. boyle & scim ym till it will bear an egg, then take it of, & when it is as cold as ale, put yeast to it & put to every 2 quarts, A pinte of ale yt is working.[2] & let it work a night together, yn tun it into a runlet. & after it is done working, stop it up, & at christmas, broach & bottl[e] [it, & it] will keep a year...
(From *Martha Washington's Booke of Cookery*, ed. by Karen Hess, 1981.)

---

[1] Ephippus, quoted in Athenaeus, Book I, p. 129.

[2] This can be interpreted in two ways. Either we are to add yeast *and* 1 pint of working ale per 2 quarts liquor, *or*, more likely, we are to add yeast *in the form of* working ale, commonly called barm.

"The pleasantest drink is that which has its share both of sweetness and of fragrance. Wherefore... certain people... prepare 'nectar' by mixing in the same potion wine, honey, and sweet-smelling flowers."[1]

✳✳✳

## TO MAKE RED ELDER WINE – 1736

20 lbs. raisins                    5 gallons water
6 pints elderberry juice

Take twenty Pounds of *Malaga* Raiſins pick'd and rubb'd clean, but not waſh'd; ſhred them ſmall, and ſteep them in five Gallons of Spring Water, putting the Water cold to them, and ſtirring them every day; then paſs the Liquor thro' a Hair Sieve, preſſing the Raiſins with your Hands, and have in readineſs ſix Pints of the Juice of Elder-Berries that have been firſt pick'd from the Stalks, and then drawn by boiling the Berries in a glaz'd Earthen Pot, ſet in a Pan of Water over the Fire. Put this Juice cold into the Liquor, ſtirring it well together, and then tunning it in a Veſſel that will juſt hold it, and let it ſtand ſix Weeks or two Months in a warm place; then bottle it, and it will keep a Year if the Bottles are well ſtopp'd...
(From *The Country Housewife and Lady's Director*, by Richard Bradley, 1736, p. 129. *Several other Elder Wine recipes can be found in his book.*)

## TO MAKE ALDER [ELDERBERRY] WINE – 1796

elderberries                    1 lb. sugar per quart of juice
1 gallon raisin wine

Pick the alder-berries when full ripe, put them into a ſtone-jar and ſet them in the oven, or a kettle of boiling water till the jar is hot through; then take them out and ſtrain them through a coarſe cloth, wringing the berries, and put the juice into a clean kettle: to every quart of juice put a pound of fine Liſbon ſugar, let it boil, and ſkim it well; when it is clear and fine, pour it into a jar; when cold, cover it cloſe, and keep it till you make raiſin wine; then when you tun your wine, to every gallon of wine put half a pint of the elder-ſyrup.
(From *The Art of Cookery Made Plain and Easy*, v. 8, by Glasse, 1796, pp. 343-4.)

---

[1] Ariston of Ceos, quoted in Athenaeus, Book II, p. 169.

## ELDER WINE – 1861

1818. INGREDIENTS. – To every 3 gallons of water allow 1 peck of elderberries; to every gallon of juice allow 3 lbs. of sugar, 1/2 oz. of ground ginger, 6 cloves, 1 lb. of good Turkey raisins; 1/4 pint of brandy to every gallon of wine. To every 9 gallons of wine 3 or 4 tablespoonfuls of fresh brewer's yeast.

*Mode.* – Pour the water, quite boiling, on the elderberries, which should be picked from the stalks, and let these stand covered for 24 hours; then strain the whole through a sieve or bag, breaking the fruit to express all the juice from it. Measure the liquor, and to every gallon allow the above proportion of sugar. Boil the juice and sugar with the ginger, cloves, and raisins for 1 hour, skimming the liquor the whole time; let it stand until milk-warm, then put it into a clean dry cask, with 3 or 4 tablespoonfuls of good fresh yeast to every 9 gallons of wine. Let it ferment for about a fortnight; then add the brandy, bung up the cask, and let it stand some months before it is bottled, when it will be found excellent. A bunch of hops suspended to a string from the bung, some persons say, will preserve the wine good for several years. Elder wine is usually mulled, and served with sippets of toasted bread and a little grated nutmeg... Make this in September.

(From *Mrs. Beeton's Book of Household Management*, 1861.)


## ELDER WINE – c. 1922

| | |
|---|---|
| 6 gallons water | 1/4 pint cognac per gallon of wine |
| 1/2 bushel elderberries | 1 ounce ginger root |
| 2 lbs. raisins | 4 tablespoons yeast per 9 gallons wine |
| 6 lbs. sugar | 8 cloves |

Pick the elderberries at midday on a hot sunny day. To half a bushel of berries allow 6 gallons of water, 6 pounds best Demerara Sugar, 2 pounds Valencia rasins [*sic*], 1 oz. finely ground ginger, 8 cloves. Pick the berries free of stalks and pour on them the boiling water and leave for 24 hours. Strain through muslin, breaking the berries to extract all the juice. Add the other ingredients and boil, removing the scum. Remove from the fire and leave the pot to stand until the contents are blood-heat. Strain through muslin into a cask and allow 4 tablespoons fresh brewer's yeast to each 9 gallons of wine. Leave to ferment a fortnight. Then to every gallon of wine allow quarter pint of old Cognac. Bung up tightly and leave for three or four months before bottling...

(From *A Garden of Herbs* by E. S. Rohde, pp. 72-73.)

## TO MAKE GILLYFLOWER WINE – 1655

| | |
|---|---|
| 1 bottle Sack wine | 2 ounces clove gilliflowers |
| 3 ounces sugar | ambergris |

Take two ounces of dryed Gillyflowers, and put them into a bottle of Sack, and beat three ounces of Sugar candy, or fine Sugar, and grinde some Ambergreese, and put it in the bottle and shake it oft, then run it through a gelly bag, and give it for a great Cordiall after a week's standing or more. You make Lavender wine as you doe this. (*The Queen's Closet Opened*, by W.M., Cook to Queen Henrietta Maria, 1655.)

GENGIOVO.

## TO MAKE CLOVE-GILLYFLOWER WINE – 1739

12+ lbs. sugar
6 1/2 gallons + 1 pint water
1 bushel clove gilliflowers
3 spoonsful ale yeast
6 ounces syrup of citron
8 egg whites
3 lemons, sliced

*Ginger.*
From *Tractado de las drogas y medicinas de las Indias Orientales con sus plantas*, by C. Acosta, 1578.

Take six Gallons and a half of Spring Water, and twelve Pounds of Sugar, and when it boils skim it, putting in the White of eight Eggs, and a Pint of Cold Water, to make the Scum rise; let it boil for an Hour and a half, skimming it well; then pour it into an Earthen Vessel, with three Spoonfuls of Baum; then put in a Bushel of Clove-Gillyflowers clip'd and beat, stir them well together, and the next Day put six Ounces of Syrup of Citron into it, the third Day put in three Lemons sliced, Peel and all, the fourth Day tun it up, stop it close for ten Days, then bottle it, and put a Piece of Sugar in each Bottle. (From *The Housekeeper's Pocket Book*, by Sarah Harrison, 1739.)

## 1105. GINGER-WINE, A PLEASANT CORDIAL WINE – 1829

| | |
|---|---|
| 10 gallons water | 15 lbs. sugar |
| 12 egg whites | 12 ounces ginger root |
| 1 glassful yeast | peels of 4 Seville oranges |
| peels of 6 lemons | |

*optional*: whole allspice, cloves, mace, cinnamon, and whole nutmegs infused in brandy.

To ten gallons of water, in which fifteen pounds of loaf-sugar have been dissolved, put the beat whites of a dozen eggs; whisk this well, and boil and skim it; then put to it twelve ounces of the best white ginger scraped and bruised. Boil the whole a half-hour in a covered boiler, to extract the flavour. When the liquor is nearly cold, put a glassful of fresh yeast into the tub. Let it ferment for three days at least, and on the second add the thin parings of four Seville oranges and six lemons. Cask it, and bottle off in six weeks or when bright. This wine may be aromatized, as it is called, by allspice, a few cloves, some mace, cinnamon, and nutmegs, bruised and infused in brandy: the strained infusion must be put to the wine just before it is bottled. *–Obs.* Ginger-wine, an insipid sort, is sometimes made without being fermented; and in the cheap wholesale way, allspice, and cayenne are used to flavour and give poignancy.
(From *The Cook and Housewife's Manual, etc.*, 1829, p. 471.)

## GINGER WINE – 1861

1819. INGREDIENTS. – To 9 gallons of water allow 27 lbs. of loaf sugar, 9 lemons, 12 oz. of bruised ginger, 3 tablespoonfuls of yeast, 2 lbs. of raisins stoned and chopped, 1 pint of brandy.
*Mode.* – Boil together for 1 hour in a copper (let it previously be well scoured and beautifully clean) the water, sugar, *lemon-rinds*, and bruised ginger; remove every particle of scum as it rises, and when the liquor is sufficiently boiled, put it into a large tub or pan, as it must not remain in the copper. When nearly cold, add the yeast, which must be thick and very fresh, and, the next day, put all in a dry cask with the strained lemon-juice and chopped raisins. Stir the wine every day for a fortnight; then add the brandy, stop the cask down by degrees, and in a few weeks it will be fit to bottle...
(From *Mrs. Beeton's Book of Household Management*, 1861.)

## GINGER WINE – c. 1922

| | |
|---|---|
| 10 gallons water | 6 egg whites |
| 5 lbs. raisins | peels of 7 lemons |
| 16 lbs. sugar | 1 1/2 lbs. ginger root |
| 2 ounces isinglass | 2 spoonsful yeast |

Time to completion: 3 months.

Ten gallons of water, sixteen pounds of lump sugar, five pounds raisins, the whites of six eggs well beaten, Mix cold and then boil skimming well. Add one and a half pounds bruised white ginger. Boil 20 minutes. Take the thinly peeled rinds of seven lemons and pour the liquor on to them. When cold tun with two spoonfuls of yeast. Take a quart of the liquor and put to it two ounces isinglass shavings, whisk when still warm and pour into the barrel. The next day stop it up and in three weeks bottle. It will be ready for use in three months. March is said to be the best month for making ginger wine.
(From *A Garden of Herbs*, by E. S. Rohde, p. 242-243.)

## # 252 TO MAKE GOOSBERRIE WINE – c. 1550 to 1625

| | |
|---|---|
| 3 quarts gooseberries | 2 gallons water |
| 1/2+ lb. sugar | *optional*: 2 quarts white wine. |

Take 3 quarts of ye ripest goosberries you can get. beat them to mash in a morter, then take 2 gallons of spring water & mix them well together. & when they have stood an houre or 2, let them run thorough a hare sive. then put to every gallon a quarter of a pound of loaf & sugar, & put it in a pot & cover it soe close yt noe aire can get in to it. make a little hole in ye top of yr cover, which stop up close with a corke. then let it stand 2 days soe close. & at two days end, give it a little vent, then let it stand 2 dayes longer and give it a little vent againe. after, let it stand 10 dayes, close covered, and give it noe more vent. after, take the corke out, & clear the wine into stone pans. If you dissern any thickness in it, run it thorough A Jelley bagg. then bottle it up and put into every bottle a lump of hard sugar. and to this you may put, If you pleas, two quarts of white wine, which will make it more quick and brisk and strong. this is a good way to make wine of rasberries, mulberries, blackberies, peaches, or any other fruit. but for peaches, which is a liquid fruit, you may make wine of their clear Juice without adding [any water] at all.
(From *Martha Washington's Booke of Cookery*, ed. by Karen Hess, 1981.)

# #139 TOO MAKE GOSBERY WINE OR OF ANY OTHER FRUIT – c. 1674

| | |
|---|---|
| 1 gallon gooseberries | 1 gallon water |
| 1 lb. sugar | |

Take to every gallan of gousberys A gallan of watter, bruse the gosberys and pore the water one them, Lett it stand a weeke straining it often, [add] as many pounds of suger as gallans of [gosberys] then Lett it Run through a gelly bagg: tunn it up you may boyle it in a furnis, in a fortnight or 3 weeks you may drinke it –
(From *Penn Family Recipes, etc.*, c. 1674.)


## TO MAKE RED GOOSBERRY WINE – 1736

| | |
|---|---|
| 1 peck red gooseberries | 8 lbs. granulated sugar |
| 4 gallons apple cider | toast spread with ale yeast |

When the Red Goosberries are well colour'd and not over-ripe, but grateful to the Taſte, gather them in a dry Day; take a Peck of theſe, and ſlit them a little more than half thro' the middle, putting them into a large glazed Earthen Pan, with eight Pounds of fine powder'd Sugar ſtrew'd over them; then boil four Gallons of Cyder, and pour it boiling hot upon the Sugar and Goosberries: this muſt ſtand eight or ten Days, ſtirring it once each Day, and at length ſtrain it thro' a Flannel in a Preſs, and put the Liquor into the Veſſel with a warm Toaſt of Wheat-bread, ſpread on both ſides with Ale-Yeaſt; this muſt ſtand two or three Months till it is fine, and then bottle it. This is a very ſtrong Wine, and of a bright red Colour.
(From *The Country Housewife and Lady's Director*, by R. Bradley, 1736, p. 116.)


## TO MAKE GOOſEBERRY WINE – 1796

| | |
|---|---|
| 1 gallon gooseberries | 3 lbs. sugar |

Gather your gooſeberries in dry weather, when they are half ripe, pick them, and bruiſe a peck in a tub, with a wooden mallet; then take a horſe-hair cloth and preſs them as much as poſſible, without breaking the ſeeds; when you have preſſed out all the juice, to every gallon of gooſeberries put three pounds of fine dry powder ſugar, ſtir it all together till the ſugar is diſſolved, then put it in a veſſel or caſk, which muſt be quite full: if ten or twelve gallons, let it ſtand a fortnight; if a twenty gallon caſk, five weeks. Set it in a cool place, then draw it off from the lees, clear the veſſel of the lees, and pour in the clear liquor again: if it be a ten gallon caſk, let it ſtand three months; if a twenty gallon, four months; then bottle it off.
(From *The Art of Cookery Made Plain and Easy*, v. 8, by Mrs. Glasse, 1796, p. 345.)

### 89th. GOOSEBERRY WINE – 1815

3 lbs. gooseberries                1 lb. sugar
1 quart water

Time to completion: 2 1/2 months.

The best way is to take for every three pounds of fruit, one pound of sugar, and a quart of fair water; boil the water very well, but you must put in the aforesaid quantity of sugar when it is boiled; bruise the fruit, and steep it twenty-four hours in the water; stir it some time, then strain it off, and put the sugar to it and let it stand in a runlet close stopped for a fortnight; then draw it off, and set it up in a cellar, and in two months, it will be fit to drink.
(From *The Dyer's Companion*, by Elijah Bemiss, 1815, p. 301.)


### GOOSEBERRY WINE – c. 1922

12 lbs. gooseberries               6 lbs. sugar
1 gallon water                     *optional*: isinglass.

Let your Gooseberries be gathered before they are too ripe, and to every twelve pounds of gooseberries take six pounds of Sugar and a gallon of Water. Stamp the Gooseberries and let them steep in the Water twenty-four Hours; then strain them and put the liquor into a Vessel, and let it stand close stopped up for two or three Weeks, and if it prove fine, draw it off, otherwise let it stand a Fortnight longer, and then bottle it; but rack it off, or use Isinglass if it be not sufficiently fine.
(From *A Garden of Herbs*, by E. S. Rohde, p. 234.)


### [AFTER-WINE] – c. 77 A.D.

The liquors made from grape-skins soaked in water, called by the Greeks seconds and by Cato and ourselves after-wine, cannot rightly be styled wines, but nevertheless are counted among the wines of the working classes. They are of three kinds: one is made by adding to the skins water to the amount of a tenth of the quantity of must that has been pressed out, and so leaving the skins to soak for twenty-four hours and then again putting them under the press; another, by a method of manufacture that has been commonly employed by the Greeks, *i.e.* by adding water to the amount of a third of the juice that has been pressed out, and after submitting the pulp to pressure, boiling it down to one-third of its original quantity; while the third kind is pressed out of the wine-lees —Cato's name for this is 'lees-wine.' None of these liquors is drinkable if kept more than a year.
(From *Natural History*, by Pliny the Elder, Book XIV, section XII, pp. 243-5.)

"...wine is sweet when sea water is poured into it."[1]

✳✳✳

[HONEY WINE] – c. 77 A. D.

30 pints grape must                    6 pints honey
1 cup salt

...Another wine of the sweet class is called honey-wine; it differs from mead because it is made from must, in the proportion of thirty pints of must of a dry quality to six pints of honey and a cup of salt, this mixture being brought just to the boil; this produces a dry-flavoured liquor.
(From *Natural History*, by Pliny, Book XIV, section XI, p. 243.)

[PROTROPUM] – c. 77 A. D.
But among these varieties ought also to be placed the liquor called in Greek *protropum*, the name given by some people to must that flows down of its own accord before the grapes are trodden. This as soon as it flows is put into special flagons and allowed to ferment, and afterwards left to dry for forty days of the summer that follows, just at the rise of the Dog-star. (*ibid.*)

92nd. WINE OF GRAPES – 1815

grapes

Time to completion: 4 days.

When they are full ripe, in a dry day, pick off those grapes that are ripest; and squeeze them in a vat or press made for that purpose, in which must be a fine canvass bag to contain the grapes, and when in the press do not squeeze them so hard as to break the seeds if you can help it; because the bruised seeds will give the wine a disagreeable taste: then strain it well, and let it settle on the lees in such a cask or vessel as you may draw it off without raising the bottom; then season a cask well with some scalding water, and dry it or sent it with a linen rag dipped in brimstone,[2] by fixing it at the bogue, by the bung or cork; then put the wine into it, and stop it close for forty-eight hours; then give it vent at the bogue, with a hole made with a gimblet; in which put a peg or fawcet, that may be easily moved with the fingers; then, in about two days time, it will be fit for drinking, and prove almost as good as French wine.
(From *The Dyer's Companion*, by Elijah Bemiss, 1815, p. 301.)

---

[1] Athenaeus, Book I, p. 113.

[2] This was a method of sterilizing the cask.

"And other certaine wines haue borrowed ſurnames of the plants that haue beene ſteeped, or infuſed in them: and yet all wines of the vine, as Wormwood wine, Mirtle wine, Hyſſope wine, and theſe are called artificiall wines."[1]

***

[HYSSOP WINE] – c. 77 A. D.

3 ounces hyssop                     3/4 to 1 1/2 gallons wine

...Similarly hyssop wine is made of Cilician hyssop by throwing three ounces of hyssop into a gallon and a half of wine, or, if the hyssop is first pounded, into three-quarters of a gallon...
(From *Natural History*, by Pliny the Elder, Book XIV, section XIX, p. 259.)

***

"He had us asked what we wanted to drink, wine or *terracina*, which is rice wine (*cervisia*), or *caracosmos*, which is clarified mare's milk, or *bal*, which is honey mead. For in winter they make use of these four kinds of drinks."[2]

***

KOUMISS, A VALUABLE WINE OF THE TARTARS – 1819

1 part mare's milk                  1/8 part cow's milk, soured
1/6 part water

Take of fresh mare's milk, of one day, any quantity; add to it a sixth-part water, and pour the mixture into a wooden vessel; use then, as a ferment, an eighth-part of the sourest cow's milk that can be got; but at any future preparation, a small portion of old koumiss will better answer the purpose of souring. Cover the vessel with a thick cloth, and set it in place of moderate warmth; leave it at rest twenty-four hours; at the end of which time the milk will have become sour, and a thick substance will be gathered on its top; then, with a stick, made at the lower end in the manner of churn staff, beat it till the thick substance above mentioned be blended intimately with the subjacent fluid. In this situation leave it again at rest for twenty-four hours more; after which, pour it into a higher and narrower vessel, resembling a churn, where the agitation must be repeated as before, till the liquor appear to be perfectly homogeneous; and in this state it is called koumiss: of which the taste ought to be a pleasant mixture of sweet and sour. Agitation must be employed every time before it is used...
(From *The American Economical Housekeeper and Family Receipt Book*, by Mrs. Esther Allen Howland, 1850.)

---

[1] Gerard, p. 730.
[2] From "A Mission to the Great Khan," by William of Rubruck, c. 1253-4, found in Ross, p. 469.

# 251  TO MAKE LEAMON WINE – c. 1550 to 1625

6 quarts water                          6 lemons, sliced
1 lb. raisins                           1 lemon peel
1+ lb. sugar

Take 6 quarts of spring water, then pare and slice 6 leamons into y$^e$ water, with a pound of y$^e$ best loaf sugar and A pound of raysons of y$^e$ sun, bruised small.  let them stand in steep 2 days, then boyle it pritty well, & let it stand after y$^t$ 8 dayes to settle in an earthen pipkin.  y$^n$ strayn it thorough a Jelley bagg & bottle it, adding a lump of loaf sugar to every bottle.  You must put in one leamon pill at first when you [put in your] leamons.
(From *Martha Washington's Booke of Cookery*, ed. by Karen Hess, 1981.)

LEMON WINE – 1732

2 quarts brandy
1 gallon water
1 quart white wine
sugar to taste
juice and peels of 24 large lemons

Time to completion:  approx. 4 1/2 months.

Take a dozen of large Malaga Lemons, pare off the Rind, cut the Lemons and squeeze out the Juice, put the Rind to steep, and add to it two quarts of Brandy; let it stand in an earthen Vessel for three Days close stopped, then squeeze another dozen of Lemons, and add a gallon of Spring water to them, and as much sugar as will sweeten the whole to your palate.  Boil the Water, the lemons and the Sugar together, and let it stand till it is cool; then add to it a quart of White Wine, and the other Lemon and Brandy, and having mixed them together, run it through a Flannel Bag into the Vessel you would keep it in, in which let it stand three months and bottle it off for use.  Let the Bottles be well cork'd and kept cool, and it will be fit to drink in a month or six weeks.
(From *The Receipt Book of Charles Carter*, Cook to the Duke of Argyll, 1732.)

## LEMON WINE – 1861

1823. INGREDIENTS. – To 4 1/2 gallons of water allow the pulp of 50 lemons, the rind of 25, 16 lbs. of loaf sugar, 1/2 oz. of isinglass, 1 bottle of brandy.
*Mode.* – Peel and slice the lemons, but use only the rind of 25 of them, and put them into the cold water. Let it stand 8 or 9 days, squeezing the lemons well every day; then strain the water off and put it into a cask with the sugar. Let it work some time, and when it has ceased working, put in the isinglass. Stop the cask down; in about six months put in the brandy and bottle the wine off...
(From *Mrs. Beeton's Book of Household Management*, 1861.)

## MARYGOLD WINE – 1732

1 gallon water
2 lbs. sugar
1 pint white *or* Rhenish wine
1 peck marigold flowers[1]
toast spread with yeast
1 1/2 ounces syrup of citron
2 lemons, sliced

*Marigold.*
From Gerard's
*Herball*, 1597.

To every gallon of water put two pounds of sugar, let it boil for an Hour, then set it by to cool; make a good brown Toast, spread it well on both sides with yeast; but before you put it in, put in an ounce and half of Syrup of Citron to each gallon of Liquor, and beat it well in, then put in the Toast while it is of a proper warmth for working, and let it work which it will do for two Days; during which time put in your marygold flowers a little bruised, but not much stamp'd, a Peck to each gallon, and two Lemons slic'd with the Rinds to each gallon; add a pint of White or Rhenish Wine to each gallon, and let it stand two Days, then tun it up in a sweet Cask.
(From *The Receipt Book of Charles Carter*, Cook to the Duke of Argyll, 1732.)

---

[1] This recipe calls for the English Marigold, *Calendula officinalis* L., and not the more familiar *Tagetes*, or "French Marigolds." (*See Appendix.*)

"...there was such an abundance of wine and strong drink, of pigment and claret, of new wine and mead and mulberry wine and all intoxicating liquors in so much abundance, that even ale which the English brew excellently (especially in Kent) found no place; but rather ale stood as low in this matter as the pot-herbs among other dishes"[1]

✳✳✳

WINE OF MULBERRIES – 1706

| | |
|---|---|
| 1 gallon mulberry juice | cinnamon |
| 1 gallon water | 6 ounces sugar |
| 1 pint white *or* Rhenish wine | |

Take mulberries when they are just changed from their redness to shining black, gather them in a dry day when the sun has taken off the dew, spread them thinly on a fine cloth on some floor or table for twenty-four hours, boil up a gallon of water to each gallon of juice you press out of these; scum the water well, and add a little cinnamon grossly bruised, put to every gallon six ounces of white sugar-candy finely beaten, scum and strain the water when it is taken off and settled, then put to it the juice of mulberries, and to every gallon of the mixture a pint of white or Rhenish wine; let them stand in a cask to purge and settle five or six days, then draw off the wine; and keep it cool.
(From *The Way to get Wealth*, 1706.)

*Making sugar.*
From Diderot's *L'encyclopédie.*
Paris, 1751.

---

[1] Giraldus Cambrensis, 12th Century.

[MYRTLE WINE] – circa 77 A.D.

*In the following quotations, Pliny the Elder tells us how to make three varieties of myrtle wine for general consumption. The <u>Myrtidanum</u> mentioned by Gerard was medicinal in nature.*

1 quart dried myrtle berries             1 1/2 pints wine

Cato taught how to make wine from the black myrtle, by drying it in the shade until no moisture remained and then putting it in must; he says that if the berries are not thoroughly dried, oil is produced. Afterwards a way was also discovered of making a white wine from the pale variety, by steeping a quart of pounded myrtle in a pint and a half of wine and then pressing out the liquor...
(From *Natural History*, by Pliny, c. 77 A.D., Book XV, section XXXVII, pp. 371-373.)

myrtle sprigs or berries            salted grape must
2 1/4 gallons grape must

...The Greeks...boil tender sprigs of myrtle with the leaves on in salted must, and after pounding them boil down one pound of the mixture in 2 1/4 gallons of must until only 1 1/2 gallons are left. The beverage made by the same process from the berries of the wild myrtle is called myrtle wine; this stains the hands...
(*ibid.*, Book XIV, section XIX, pp. 255-257.)

*Myrtle.*
From Parkinson's *Paradisi in Sole Paradiſus Terrestris.*
London, 1629.

"*Plinie* in his 14. booke 16. chapter ſaith, that the wine which is made of the wilde Myrtle tree is called *Myrtidanum*, if the copie be true. For *Dioicoridies* and likewiſe *Sotion* in his Geoponikes report, that wine is made of Myrtle berries when they be thorow ripe, but this is called *Vinum Myrteum*, or *Myrtites*, Myrtle wine." (Gerard, p. 1227.)

## TO MAKE ORANGE WINE WITH RAIſINS – 1796

1 lb. sugar
8 gallons water

juice and peels of 20 Seville oranges
30 lbs. raisins, chopped

Take thirty pounds of new Malaga raiſins picked clean, chop them ſmall, take twenty large Seville oranges, ten of them you muſt pare as thin as for preſerving; boil about eight gallons of ſoft water till a third be conſumed, let it cool a little; then put five gallons of it hot upon your raiſins and orange-peel, ſtill it well together, cover it up, and when it is cold let it ſtand five days, ſtirring it once or twice a day; then paſs it through a hair ſieve, and with a ſpoon preſs it as dry as you can, put it in a runlet fit for it, and put to it the rind of the other ten oranges, cut as thin as the firſt; then make a ſyrup of the juice of twenty oranges, with a pound of white ſugar. It muſt be made the day before you tun it up; ſtir it well together, and ſtop it cloſe; let it ſtand two months to clear, then bottle it up. It will keep three years, and is better for keeping.
(From *The Art of Cookery Made Plain and Easy*, v. 8, by Mrs. Glasse, 1796, p. 344.)

## TO MAKE ORANGE WINE – 1796

14 lbs. sugar
6+ gallons water
6 spoonsful yeast
8 or 10 egg whites

2 quarts Rhenish *or* white wine
juice and peels of 50 oranges
juice of 12 lemons

Take twelve pounds of the beſt powder ſugar, with the whites of eight or ten eggs well beaten, into ſix gallons of ſpring-water, and boil three quarters of an hour; when cold, put into it ſix ſpoonfuls of yeaſt, and the juice of twelve lemons, which, being pared, muſt ſtand with two pounds of white ſugar in a tankard, and in the morning ſkim off the top, and then put it into the water; then add the juice and rinds of fifty oranges, but not the white parts of the rinds, and ſo let it work all together two days and two nights; then add two quarts of Rheniſh or white wine, and put it into your veſſel. (*ibid.*, p. 344.)

1104. PARSNIP-WINE – 1829

| | |
|---|---|
| 4 lbs. parsnips | yeast |
| 1 gallon water | 1/2 ounce cream of tartar |
| 3 lbs. sugar | |

To every four pounds of parsnips, cleaned and quartered, put a gallon of water. Boil till they are quite soft, and strain the liquor clear off without crushing the parsnips. To every gallon of the liquor put three pounds of loaf-sugar, and a half-ounce of crude tartar. When nearly cold, put fresh yeast to it. Let it stand four days in a warm room, and then bung it up.

N.B. – Parsnip-wine is said to surpass all the other home-made wines as much as East-India Madeira does that of the Cape. So much is said for it, and on good authority, that it certainly deserves a trial. Horseradish-wine is made as above, and is recommended for gouty habits. In Ireland a pleasant table-beer is made from parsnips brewed with hops.

(From *The Cook and Housewife's Manual: a Practical System of Modern Domestic Cookery and Family Management*, by Mistress Margaret Dods, 1829, pp. 470-1.)


QUINCE WINE FROM MRS. E. B. – 1736

| | |
|---|---|
| 1 gallon water | 20 large ripe quinces, grated |
| 2 lbs. sugar | toast spread with yeast |
| juice and peel of 2 lemons | |

Gather the quinces when dry and full ripe. Take twenty large quinces, wipe them clean with a coarse cloth, and grate them with a large grater or rasp, as near the core as you can, but none of the core; boil a gallon of spring water throwing your quinces in, and let it boil softly a quarter of an hour, then strain them well into an earthen pan on two pounds of double-refined sugar; pare the peel of two large lemons, throw in and squeeze the juice through a sieve, and stir it about till it is very cool; then toast a little bit of bread, very thin and brown, rub a little yeast on it, let it stand close-covered twenty-four hours; then take out the toast and lemon, put it up in a keg, keep it three months and then bottle it. If you make a twenty gallon cask let it stand six months before you bottle it. When you strain your quinces you are to wring them hard in a coarse cloth.

(From *The Compleat Housewife*, by E. Smith, 1736. *This recipe can also be found in Glasse, v. 8, p. 346, and Bradley, p. 170.*)

***

There is moreover another kind of raisin-wine known in the Province of Narbonne, and there particularly to the Vocontii, under the name of 'sweet wine.' For the purpose of this they keep the grape hanging on the vine for an exceptional time, with the foot-stalk twisted. Some make an incision in the actual shoot as far as the pith and others leave the grapes to dry on tiled roofs, the grapes in all cases being those from the helvennaca vine. To these some add a wine called in Greek 'strained wine,' to make which the grapes are dried in the sun for seven days raised seven feet from the ground on hurdles, in an enclosed place where at night they are protected from damp; on the eighth day they are trodden out, and this process produces a wine of extremely good bouquet and flavour...[1]

***

*Stepony, Nectour, and Persencia are raisin wines.*

#263  TO MAKE STEPONY – c. 1599 to 1625

5 quarts water
2 lbs. raisins
1/2+ lb. sugar
1 lemon peel
juice and pulp of 2 lemons

Time to completion:  3 weeks.

*Quinces.*
From Gerard's *Herball*, 1597.

Put 5 quarts of spring water, boyled, into [an] earthen pot, & put therein 2 pound of rayson[s] of $y^e$ sun, stonned, 2 leamons, $y^e$ one with [$y^e$] pill & $y^e$ other squeesed but not $y^e$ pill & [$y^t$] which remains after $y^e$ leamon be strayned, cast into $y^e$ pipkin allsoe, & one penny worth of the best sugar, & cover $y^r$ pot very well. let it stand 4 or 5 dayes, stiring it once or twice A day, then let it run thorough a thin cloth, [$y^n$] bottle it up & put into every bottle a lump of hard sugar as bigg as a wallnut. stop it up clo[se] & set it in a chamber window where $y^e$ sun comes 5 or 6 dayes. & after that in a close roome for A fortnight. and then you may drink [it]. in stead of one penny worth of sugar prementioned, you must put in halfe a pound.
(From *Martha Washington's Booke of Cookery*, c. 1550 to 1625, ed. by Karen Hess. *Letters in brackets were reconstructed by the editor.*)

---

[1] Pliny the Elder, *Natural History*, Book XIV, section XI, p. 243.

# 264  TO MAKE NECTOUR – c. 1550 to 1625

| | |
|---|---|
| 2 lbs. raisins | 2 lemons, sliced |
| 2 gallons water | 1 lemon peel |
| 1 lb. sugar | |

Time to completion: about 3 weeks.

Take 2 pound of raysons of $y^e$ sunn and shread them, & a pound of powder sugar, & 2 leamons sliced, one leamon pill. put these into an earthen pot. take 2 gallons of water & let it boyle halfe an hour, then take if of $y^e$ fire, & put it into $y^e$ pot, stiring it very well. let it stand 3 or 4 dayes, & stir it twice a day. soe strayne it and bottle it. in a fortnights time, it will be ready to drink.
(From *Martha Washington's Booke of Cookery*, ed. by Karen Hess.)

# 266  TO MAKE PERSENCIA – c. 1550 to 1625

| | |
|---|---|
| 14 lbs. raisins | 1 lemon peel |
| 1 gallon milk | 1 or 2 lemons, sliced |
| 10 gallons water | *optional*: sugar; cloves. |

Take a stone of maligo raysons, pick, wash, & stomp $y^m$. then boyle 10 gallons of spring water, & put in $y^r$ raysons. let it stand 2 hours, then boyle it. $y^n$ after it hath stood an houre, strayne it into a tub. $y^e$ next day, clear it into a runlet, & put to it 4 quarts of new milk from $y^e$ cow, $y^n$ shake it well for halfe an houre. $y^n$ put in a leamon or 2, sliced, & $y^e$ rinde of one. stop up $y^e$ runlet & at 14 days end, bottle it. & put a bit of s[ugar into e]very bottle & a [few] cloves, if you like them. (*ibid.*)

# 114  TO MAKE STEPPONI – 1669

| | |
|---|---|
| 1 gallon water | 1 lb. raisins |
| 1/2 lb. sugar | juice and peels of 2 lemons |

Take a Gallon of Conduit-water, one pound of blew Raisins of the Sun stoned, and half a pound of Sugar. Squeese the juyce of two Limons upon the Raisins and Sugar, and slice the rindes upon them. Boil the water, and pour it so hot upon the ingredients in an earthen pot, and stir them well together. So let it stand twenty four hours. Then put it into bottles (having first let it run through a strainer) and set them in a Cellar or other cool place.
(From *The Closet ...Opened*, 1669.)

## RAISIN WINE – 1723

| | |
|---|---|
| 12 lbs. raisins | juice of 12 lemons |
| 6 lbs. sugar | 6 lemon peels |
| 12 gallons water | *optional*: cowslips *or* clove gilliflowers. |

Time to completion: 3 weeks.

Take twelve pounds of Raisins of the Sun and stone them, six pounds of White sugar, the juice of a dozen Lemons and the peels of six, put them into a pot with a cover with twelve gallons of water, let them boil for half an hour; then take them off the Fire, and let them stand close covered for three or four Days, stirring it twice a day, then strain it and bottle it up close for use, but do not fill the Bottles quite full, lest it should break them, set them in a cool place, and in a Fortnight's time you may drink it. If you make your wine when they are in season you may add cowslips or clove-gillyflowers.
(From *The Receipt Book of John Nott*, 1723.)

A farmer tending his vines. From *The Book of Trades*, by Jost Amman, 16th c.

## TO MAKE RAIſIN WINE – 1736

56 lbs. Malaga raisins
10 gallons water
toast spread with yeast

Time to completion: 4 months.

Take half a hundred weight of *Malaga* Raiſins, pick them clean from the Stalks, and chop the Raiſins ſmall, then put them into a large Tub, and boil ten Gallons of River Water, or ſuch Water as is ſoft, and pour it hot upon them; let this be ſtirr'd twice or thrice every Day for twelve Days ſucceſſively, and then pour the Liquor into a Cask and make a Toaſt of Bread, and while it is hot, ſpread it on both ſides with Yeaſt or Barm, and put it into the Veſſel to the Wine, and it will make it ferment gently, which you may know by its making a hiſſing Noiſe; during the time of working, the Bung of the Veſſel muſt be left open, and as ſoon as that is over, ſtop it up cloſe. This will be fine and fit for Drinking in about four Months time; but if you make twice the quantity, it ſhould ſtand five or ſix Months before you Broach it...
(From *The Country Housewife and Lady's Director*, by R. Bradley, 1736, pp. 66-67.)

## TO MAKE FRONTENIAC WINE – 1736

| | |
|---|---|
| 56 lbs. Malaga raisins | toast spread with yeast |
| 10 gallons water | 8 quarts Frontignac[1] grape syrup |

Time to completion: 4 months.

The foregoing Receipt [*see above*] muſt be followed in every particular, only when you put it into the Veſſel, add to it ſome of the Syrup of the white Fronteniac Grape, which we may make in *England*, tho' the Seaſon is not favourable enough to ripen that ſort of Grape; for in a bad Year, when the white Fronteniac, or the Muſcadella Grapes are hard and unripe, and without Flavour, yet if you bake them they will take the rich Flavour, which a good ſhare of Sun would have given them. You may either bake the Fronteniac Grapes with Sugar, or boil them to make a Syrup of their Juice, about a Quart of which Syrup will be enough to put to five Quarts of the Raiſin Wine... (*ibid.*, pp. 67-68.)


## TO MAKE RAIſIN WINE – 1796

| | |
|---|---|
| 200 [units?] raisins[2] | grape stems |
| water to fill a hogshead | |

Take two hundred of raiſins (ſtalks and all), and put them into a large hogſhead, fill it with water, let them ſteep a fortnight, ſtirring them every day; then pour off all the liquor and preſs the raiſins; put both liquors together in a nice clean veſſel that will juſt hold it, for it muſt be full; let it ſtand till it has done hiſſing, or making the leaſt noiſe, then ſtop it cloſe and let it ſtand ſix months; peg it, and if you find it quite clear, rack it off in another veſſel; ſtop it cloſe and let it ſtand three months longer; then bottle it, and when you uſe it, rack it off into a decanter.
(From *The Art of Cookery Made Plain and Easy*, v. 8, by Mrs. Glasse, 1796, p. 342.)

---

[1] "Fronteniac" grapes are probably *Frontignac* grapes, another name for the *Muscat blanc à petits* variety.

[2] No unit of measurement is given here or in the next recipe. (*See note p. 131.*)

## THE BEʃT WAY TO MAKE RAIʃIN WINE – 1796

*This is two recipes in one. The numbers in brackets and the break in the text have been added to differentiate the recipes.*

[1]
200 [units?] raisins[1]          water to fill a hogshead
grape stems                     2 quarts French brandy

Take a clean wine or brandy hogʃhead, take great care it is very ʃweet and clean, put in two hundred of raiʃins (ʃtalks and all), and then fill the veʃʃel with fine clear ʃpring-water; let it ʃtand till you think it has done hiʃʃing, then throw in two quarts of fine French brandy; put in the bung ʃlightly, and, in about three weeks or a month (if you are ʃure it has done fretting), ʃtop it down cloʃe; let it ʃtand ʃix months, peg it near the top, and if you find it very fine and good, fit for drinking, bottle it off, or elʃe ʃtop it up again, and let it ʃtand ʃix months longer: it ʃhould ʃtand ʃix months in the bottle. This is by much the beʃt way of making it, as I have ʃeen by experience, as the wine will be much ʃtronger, but leʃs of it: the different ʃorts of raiʃins make quite a different wine;

[2]
10 gallons water                soaked raisins from above
2 quarts brandy                 2 quarts elderberry syrup

and after you have drawn off all the wine, throw on ten gallons of ʃpring-water; take off the head of the barrel and ʃtir it well twice a day, preʃʃing the raiʃins as well as you can; let it ʃtand a fortnight or three weeks, then draw it off into a proper veʃʃel to hold it, and ʃqueeze the raiʃins well; add two quarts of brandy, and two quarts of ʃyrup of alder-berries, ʃtop it cloʃe when it has done working, and in about three months it will be fit for drinking. If you do not chooʃe to make this ʃecond wine, fill your hogʃhead with ʃpring-water, and ʃet it in the ʃun for three or four months, and it will make excellent vinegar.
(From *The Art of Cookery Made Plain and Easy*, v. 8, by H. Glasse, 1796, pp. 342-3.)

---

[1] *See note p. 131.*

# # 255 TO MAKE RASPIE WINE – c. 1550 to 1625

*This recipe is really several recipes in one: strong raisin wine; weak raisin wine; middle-strength raisin wine; and raisin wine flavored with raspberry, Angelica, clove-gilliflowers, balm, or wormwood. The numbers in brackets have been added to mark the beginning of another recipe.*

40 to 50 lbs. raisins                     40 to 50 quarts water

*optional*: 1 gallon raspberry juice, 6 spoonsful raspberry syrup, and 6 spoonsful sugar syrup; Angelica; clove gilliflowers; lemon balm; wormwood.[1]

[1] Take 40 or 50 pound of maligo raysons, pikt from y$^e$ stalks & stones. put them in a large vate, & put to every pound of them a quart of water. then cover them with a thick cloth & stir them once a day. steep them 6 or 7 dayes in y$^e$ winter & 5 dayes in y$^e$ sumer till y$^e$ water have soakt out y$^e$ strength of y$^e$ fruit. then strayne them & put y$^e$ liquor into a convenient vessell, & set it in y$^e$ sun or in y$^e$ chimney corner, that it may stand in some gentle heat to worke for 2 or 3 dayes, & purge away all y$^e$ dross. then bung it up close, & let it stand in y$^r$ seller, or where else you pleas, for halfe a year. y$^n$ draw it into bottles & corke it up close. & keep them for 5 or 6 weeks, & then it may be drunk. [2] you may put to y$^e$ raysons y$^e$ same proportion of water y$^e$ second time & order it just as you did y$^e$ first, but this will not keepe soe long, beeing much smaller then y$^e$ first. [3] but you may make a good middle wine, by mixing y$^e$ strong & smaller infusions together. [4] when you tun y$^r$ stongest liquor, put a gallon of y$^e$ Juice of raspas in it, or rather when you bottle it. put in 6 spoonfulls of y$^e$ sirrup of rasberies (into every bottle) made with y$^e$ Juice, & an equall weight of sugar, boyled a little & clarefyed. [5] thus you may make Jilliflower wine, [6] baume, [7] wormewood, or [8] Angelico wine, by hanging in y$^e$ barrell a convenient quantety of the herbs when you tun y$^e$ liquor up.
(From *Martha Washington's Booke of Cookery*, ed. by Karen Hess.)

---

[1] CAUTION! (*See Appendix.*)

## TO MAKE RASPBERRY WINE – 1655

raspberries                          1 gallon Rhenish wine
                                     2 ounces sugar per bottle of wine

Take a gallon of good Rhenish Wine, put into it as much Rasberries very ripe as will make it strong, put it in an earthen pot, and let it stand two days; then pour your Wine from the Rasberries, and put into every bottle two ounces of sugar. Stop it up and keep it by you.
(From *The Queen's Closet Opened*, by W.M., Cook to Queen Henrietta Maria, 1655.)

## # 176  TO MAKE RASBERY-WINE – 1669

4 gallons Deal wine[1]               12 gallons raspberries
sugar

Take four Gallons of Deal wine, put it into an earthen jugg; put to it four Gallons of Rasberries; let them stand so infusing seven days; then press it out gently; Then infuse as many more Rasberries seven days longer, and so three times if you please; put to it as much fine Sugar as will make it pleasant; Put it into a Runlet close stopped, let it stand till it is fine; and then draw it into bottles, and keep it till it be fine.
(From *The Closet ...Opened*, 1669.)

## TO MAKE RASBERY WINE – 1719

1 gallon Sack wine                   raspberries
toast spread with yeast              3/4 lb. sugar per quart liquid

Putt a gallon of Sack into an Earthen Vessell and fill it thick with rasberys cover it up close let it stand 3 or 4 Dayes then runn it through a Jelly bag to every quart 3 quarters of a pound of lose Sugar let it Stand till it has don working take off the Scum from the top to the bottom bottle it close and let it Stand.
    Spread yeast on both Sides of a Tost. Put in your wine cover it close to work – So you must doe by all your Wines.
(From *M.S. Book of Receipts*, by Thomas Newington, 1719.)

---

[1] According to the Oxford English Dictionary, 'Deal wine' refers to wine from the Low Countries.

## TO MAKE RASBERRY WINE – 1736

1 quart raspberry juice        1 pint water
1 lb. sugar per quart juice

To every Quart of the Juice of Rasberries, put a Pint of Water, and to every Quart of Liquor a Pound of fine Sugar; then ſet it on the Fire to boil half an hour, taking off the Scum as it riſes: then ſet it to cool, and when it is quite cold, put it in a Veſſel and let it ſtand ten Weeks or ſomething more if the Weather prove cold; when it is ſettled, bottle it, and it will keep two Years.
(From *The Country Housewife and Lady's Director*, by R. Bradley, 1736, p. 115.)

## TO MAKE RAſPBERRY WINE – 1796

1 quart raspberry juice        1 lb. sugar
2 quarts white wine

Time to completion: 1 week.

Take ſome fine raſpberries, bruiſe them with the back of a ſpoon, then ſtrain them through a flannel bag into a ſtone jar. to each quart of juice put a pound of double-refined ſugar, ſtir it well together, and cover it cloſe; let it ſtand three days, then pour it off clear. To a quart of juice put two quarts of white wine, bottle it off; it will be fit to drink in a week. Brandy made thus is a very fine dram, and a much better way than ſteeping the raſpberries.
(From *The Art of Cookery Made Plain and Easy*, v. 8, by Mrs. Glasse, 1796, p. 347.)

## 90th. RASPBERRY WINE – 1815

1 gallon raspberries        1 bottle + 1 cup white wine
mace blades        1/4 lb. sugar per gallon liquid
1 ounce cinnamon sticks

Take the raspberries clear from the stalks; to a gallon of which put a bottle of white-wine, and let them infuse in an earthen vessel two or three days close covered; then bruise the berries in the wine, and strain them through fine linen gently; then let it simmer over a moderate fire; skim off the froth, and then strain it again, and, with a quarter of a pound of loaf sugar to a gallon, let it settle; then, in a half a pint of white wine boil an ounce of well scented cinnamon, and a little mace, and put the wine, strained from the spice, into it, and bottle it up.
(From *The Dyer's Companion*, by Elijah Bemiss, 1815, p. 301.)

*...thou art the rose which ys
the floure of all good vertu,
and in color of fyre...*[1]

[ROSE WINE] – c. 77 A.D.

50 drams rose petals          2 1/2 gallons grape must

...wine is made from pounded rose-leaves [*petals*] wrapped in a linen napkin and
thrown into must with a small weight attached to make it sink, in the proportion of 50
drams of rose-leaves to 2 1/2 gallons of must –they say the jar must not be opened for
three months– and also wine is made from Gallic nard and another from wild nard.
(From *Natural History*, by Pliny the Elder, Book XIV, section XIX, pp. 255-257.)

ROSE WINE (ROSATUM)[2] – c. 100 B.C. to 300 A.D.

rose petals, trimmed          wine
honey to taste

Time to completion:  3 weeks.

Make rose wine in this manner:  rose petals, the lower white part removed, sewed into a
linen bag and immersed in wine for seven days.  Thereupon add a sack of new petals
which allow to draw for another seven days.  Again remove the old petals and replace
them by fresh ones for another week; then strain the wine through the colander.  Before
serving, add honey sweetening to taste.  Take care that only the best petals free from
dew be used for soaking.
(From *Apicius, Cookery and Dining in Imperial Rome*, c. 100 B.C. to 300 A.D., tr. by
J. D. Vehling, pp. 46-47.)

---

[1] Sir Thomas Malory, *Le Morte D'arthur.*

[2] Vehling cautions that this wine has a strong laxative effect.

## ROSE WINE WITHOUT ROSES (ROSATUM SINE ROSA) – c. 100 B.C. to 300 A.D.

wine                                             honey to taste
1 basketful fresh citrus leaves

Rose wine without roses is made in this fashion: a palm leaf basket full of fresh citrus leaves is immersed in the vat of new wine before fermentation has set in. After forty days retire the leaves, and, as occasion arises, sweeten the wine with honey, and pass it up for rose wine. (*ibid.*, p. 47.)

## ROSE WINE – c. 1790

3 gallons rosewater                      rose petals, trimmed
toast spread with yeast                  3 lbs. sugar per gallon of liquid
*optional*: wine and spices.

Take a well glazed earthen vessel and put into it three gallons of rose-water drawn with a cold still. Put into that a sufficient quantity of rose leaves [*petals*] cover it close, and set it for an hour in a kettle or copper of hot water, to take out the whole strength and tincture of the roses; and when it be cold press the rose leaves hard into the liquor, and steep fresh ones in it, repeating it till the liquor has got the full strength of the roses. To every gallon of liquor put three pounds of loaf sugar, and stir it well, that it may melt and disperse in every part. Then put it into a cask, or other convenient vessel, to ferment, and put into it a piece of bread toasted hard and covered with yeast. Let it stand about thirty days, when it will be ripe and have a fine flavour, having the whole strength and scent of the roses in it; and you may greatly improve it by adding to it wine and spices. By this method of infusion, wine of carnations, clove gilliflowers, violets, primroses, or any other flower, having a curious scent, may be made.
(From *The London Art of Cookery*, c. 1790. *This recipe can also be found in "The Way to get Wealth," 1706; it adds "fixed nitre and flour, and two or three whites of eggs...")*

## ROSEMARY WINE – c. 1922

rosemary tips                                    white wine

Infuse a bunch of rosemary tips (about six inches long) in sound white wine for a few days, when the wine will be fit to use.
(From *A Garden of Herbs*, by E. S. Rohde, p. 141.)

## RHUBARB WINE[1] – 1861

1829. INGREDIENTS.– To every 5 lbs. of rhubarb pulp allow 1 gallon of cold spring water; to every gallon of liquor allow 3 lbs. of loaf sugar, 1/2 oz. of isinglass, the rind of 1 lemon.

*Mode.* – Gather the rhubarb about the middle of May; wipe it with a wet cloth, and, with a mallet, bruise it in a large wooden tub or other convenient means. When reduced to a pulp, weigh it, and to every 5 lbs. add 1 gallon of cold spring water; let these remain for 3 days, stirring 3 or 4 times a day; and, on the fourth day, press the pulp through a hair sieve; put the liquor into a tub, and to every gallon put 3 lbs. of loaf sugar; stir in the sugar until it is quite dissolved, and add the lemon-rind; let the liquor remain, and, in 4, 5, or 6 days, the fermentation will begin to subside, and a crust or head will be formed, which should be skimmed off, or the liquor drawn from it, when the crust begins to crack or separate. Put the wine into a cask, and if, after that, it ferments, rack it off into another cask, and in a fortnight stop it down. If the wine should have lost any of its original sweetness, add a little more loaf sugar, taking care that the cask is full. Bottle it off in February or March, and in the summer it should be fit to drink. It will improve greatly by keeping; and, should a very brilliant colour be desired, add a little currant-juice... Make this about the middle of May.

(From *Mrs Beeton's Book of Household Management*, by Mrs. Isabella Beeton, 1861.)

✱✱✱
"Your best Sacks are of Seres in Spaine, your smaller of Galicia and Portugall, your strong Sacks are of the Ilands of the Canaries and Malligo."[2]
✱✱✱

## 12(A) SACK WITH CLOVE-GILLY FLOWERS – 1669

*Never leave flower petals infusing in the liquor for extended periods – the moist floating flowers are an excellent breeding ground for mold. See his recipe #11, p. 42, for his instructions on preparing gilliflowers for use.*

1 gallon Sack wine                    1/2 lb. or more clove gilliflowers

If you will make a Cordial Liquor of Sack with Clove-gillyflowers, you must do thus. Prepare your Gillyflowers, as is said before, and put them into great double glass-bottles, that hold two gallons a piece, or more; and put to every gallon of Sack, a good half pound of the wiped and cut flowers, putting in the flowers first, and then the Sack upon them. Stop the glasses exceeding close, and set them in a temperate Cellar.

---

[1] CAUTION! Use only the leaf stalk; the leaf blades of rhubarb are poisonous. (*See Appendix.*)
[2] Markham, 1623.

Let them stand so, till you see that the Sack hath drawn out all the principal tincture from them, and that the flowers begin to look palish; (with an eye of pale, or faint in Colour) Then pour the Sack from them, and throw away the exhausted flowers, or distil a spirit from them; For if you let them remain longer in the Sack, they will give an earthy tast to them. You may then put the tincted Sack into fit bottles for your use, stopping them very close. But if the season of the flowers be not yet past, your Sack will be better, if you put it upon new flowers, which I conceive will not be the worse, but peradventure the better, if they be a little dried in the shade. If you drink a Glass or two of this sack at a meal, you will find it a great Cordial...[1]
(From *The Closet ...Opened*, 1669.)

**✻✻✻**

"The Spanish Wine Vine, or the Vine of whoſe fruite the wine called Secke
is made, differeth woonderfully according to the place or countrie where it
groweth: for it is well knowen that wine of Madera, Canaria, Grecia, and ſuch
other countries where thoſe kindes of Vines do grow,
bring foorth wine differing very notably one from another in diuers reſpects,
and yet al and euery of them kindes of Secke..."[2]

**✻✻✻**

## TO MAKE SARAGOSSA WINE OR ENGLISH SACK – 1736

| | |
|---|---|
| 1 gallon water | 4 sprigs rue[3] |
| 3 lbs. honey | 1 handful fennel roots |

To every quart of water, put a sprig of Rue and to every gallon a handful of Fennel roots, boil these half an hour, then strain it out and to every gallon of this Liquor, put three pounds of Honey; boil it two hours and scum it well, and when it is cold pour it off and turn it into a Vessel, or such Cask as is fit for it; keep it a year in the Vessel and then Bottle it. 'Tis a very good sack.
(From *The Compleat Housewife*, by E. Smith, 1736. *This can also be found in Gelleroy, 1762.*)

---

[1] He continues this lengthy entry with a recipe for Hydromel with Clove gilliflowers. (*See p. 76.*)
[2] Gerard, pp. 724-725.
[3] CAUTION! (*See Appendix.*)

# 116  TOO MAKE SAIGE WINE – c. 1674

25 quarts water                               1 pint ale yeast
1/2 bushel red sage                        sugar
25 lbs. raisins                                1 quart Sack wine
*optional*: substitute 1 bushel cowslip flowers for the sage.

Time to completion:  1 1/2 to 2 months.

Take 25 quarts of spring water and boyle it and Lett it stand till it is a Littell more then blood warm take 25 pound Raisons, Clene picked and shred and 1/2 a bushall of the best Red saige and so shred it allso then put the fruite and saige into warme water, then take a pint of ale yeist and put ther too, and Cover it warme and Lett it stand 7 days sturing it once a day then strain it and put it into a Runlett, Lett it stand a weeke or more then putt too it a quart of malig sack, bottell it putting a Littell suger in eatch bottell, I think it the best way to put the sack in the bottells and so too fill them up with saige wine it may bee drunk in a month or 6 weeks but it will keep good a yeare in this manner, you may make Cowslipe wine only allow a bushall of Cowslips in sted of 1/2 a bushall of saige –
(From *Penn Family Recipes, etc.,* c. 1674.)

TO MAKE SAGE WINE – 1719

3 gallons water                               6+ lbs. sugar
1 gallon sage leaves                      ale yeast
juice of 6 lemons

Take three gallons of water and Six pound of Lose Sugar boyle the water and Sugar together and as the Scum rises take it of and when it is well boyled put it into a Clean Tubb have ready in the Tubb one gallon of Sage leaves free from Stalks. So let it then Stand till it be allmost cold then Put to it the Juice of 6 Lemmons beat them with a litle Ale yest brew it well together cover it very close that no Aire come in let it Stand 48 houers then Streyne it through a fine Sieve put it into a Small Runlet that it may be just full and when it hath don working Stop it very close and let it Stand three weeks or a month before you bottle it.  Putting into each bottle A litle lump of lose Sugar this wine is best kept a quarter of a year or longer before it is Drankt.
(From *M.S. Book of Receipts*, by Thomas Newington, 1719.)

## TO MAKE SAGE-WINE. FROM MRS. E. B. – 1736

3 gallons water
6+ lbs. sugar
ale yeast

1 gallon red sage leaves
juice of 4 large lemons

Time to completion:  approx. 4 months.

To three Gallons of Water put ſix Pounds of Sugar, boil theſe together, and as the Scum riſes take it off, and when it is well boiled put it in a Tub boiling hot, in which there is already a Gallon of red Sage Leaves clean pick'd and waſh'd; when the Liquor is near cold, put in the Juice of four large Lemons, beaten well with a little Ale Yeaſt, mix theſe all well together, and cover it very cloſe from the Air, and let it ſtand forty eight Hours; then ſtrain all thro' a fine Hair-Sieve, and put it into a Veſſel that will but just hold it, and when it has done working, ſtop it down cloſe, and let it ſtand three Weeks or a Month before you bottle it, putting a Lump of Loaf-Sugar into every Bottle. This Wine is beſt when it is three Months old. After this manner you may make Wine of any other Herb or Flower.
(From *The Country Housewife and Lady's Director*, by R. Bradley, 1736, p. 97.)

## SAGE WINE – c. 1922

30 lbs. raisins
1 bushel sage
5 gallons water

Time to completion:  7 months to 1 year.

Take thirty pounds of Malaga raisins picked clean and shred small, and one bushel of green sage shred small; then boil five gallons of water and let it stand till it is lukewarm.  Put into a tub the water, sage and raisins, let it stand five or six days, stirring it two or three times a day.  Then strain and press the liquor from the ingredients, put it in a cask and let it stand six months, then draw it clean off into another vessel. Bottle it in two days, and in a month or six weeks it will be fit to drink; but it is best when a year old. (From *A Garden of Herbs*, by E. S. Rohde, p. 151.)

1 *Fragaria & Fraga.*
Red Strawberries.

## TO MAKE SCURVY-GRASS WINE – 1759

6 handfuls scurvy grass                3 quarts Rhenish wine

Take fresh Scurvy-grass six Handfuls, powned it well in a Mortar, pour upon it three quarts of Rhenish Wine, set it in a cool place for three or four days; then strain it, and let it settle, then draw it off from the Dregs.
(From *The Receipt Book of Elizabeth Cleland*, 1759.)


## # 118  STRAWBERRY WINE – 1669

*The numbers in brackets and break in the text have been added to separate these two recipes.*

[1]  Bruise the Strawberries, and put them into a Linnen-bag which hath been a little used, that so the Liquor may run through more easily. You hang in the bag at the bung into the vessel, before you do put in your Strawberries. The quantity of the fruit is left to your discretion; for you will judge to be there enough of them, when the colour of the wine is high enough. During the working, you leave the bung open. The working being over, you stop your vessel.

[2]
cherries                        cinnamon
cloves

Cherry-wine is made after the same fashion. But it is a little more troublesome to break the Cherry-stones.[1] But it is necessary, that if your Cherries be of the black soure Cherries, you put to it a little Cinnamon, and a few Cloves.
(From *The Closet ...Opened*, 1669.)


## 93rd.  WINE OF STRAWBERRIES OR RASBERRIES – 1815

Mash the berries, and put them into a linnen bag, as aforesaid for the grapes and squeeze them into a cask, and then let it work as in the aforesaid grape receipt, &c. [*see p. 159.*]  In this manner may cherry wine be made; but then you must break the seeds,[1] contrary to what was said before concerning the grapes.
(From *The Dyer's Companion*, by Elijah Bemiss, 1815, pp. 301-302.)

---

[1] CAUTION! (*See Appendix.*)

## ROSA-SOLIS, [*SUNDEW WINE*] – 1597

| | |
|---|---|
| sundew leaves | grain alcohol |
| cinnamon sticks | ginger root |
| cloves | mace blades |
| whole nutmegs | sugar |
| a few grains of musk | |

It [Rosa-solis] ſtrengtheneth and nouriſheth the body, eſpecially if it be diſtilled with wine, and that liquor made thereof which the common people do call Roſa Solis.

If any be deſirous to haue the ſaide drinke effectuall for the purpoſes aforeſaid, let them lay the leaues of Roſa ſolis in the ſpirit of wine, adding thereto Cinnamom, Cloues, Maces, Ginger, Nutmegs, Sugar, and a fewe grains of Muske, ſuffering it ſo to ſtand in a glaſſe cloſe ſtopt from the aire, and ſet in the ſunne by the ſpace of ten daies more: then ſtraine the ſame, and keepe it for your vſe.

(From *The Herball or Generall Historie of Plants*, by John Gerard, 1597, p. 1367.)

"This Herb... grows in Bogs, and when we find it we may preſerve it artificially, by either planting it immediately in other boggy places, or elſe in artificial Bogs, made of Earth and Water in Tubs, or Earthen Pots, made without holes at the bottom."[1]

**Rosa-solis**, the Round-leaved Sundew, is a bog plant which traps insects for food with its sticky sweet "dew."
(Illus. from Gerard, p. 1356.)

*Rosa-solis.*
From Gerard's *Herball*, 1597.

---

[1] Bradley, p. 95.

"...in thoſe Cordial Waters where the Ros Solis, or Roſa Solis is uſed, which is an Herb not always to be found, and will not keep above a day or two after 'tis gather'd, this I ſay may be diſtilled by itſelf, and kept to uſe with other Waters at pleaſure; putting of this ſuch a proportion as would have been produced from the quantity directed, of the Plant, in the Receipt, if it had been diſtill'd with the other Herbs: and ſo of any other Herb that is hard to come by."[1]

✳✳✳

## 6. ROSA-SALIS [*SUNDEW WINE*] – 1609

*The costly gems and gold called for in this recipe were once believed to have medicinal properties.*

| | |
|---|---|
| 1 gallon sundew leaves | 1/2 lb. dates |
| 1 gallon Aqua composita | 1/2 ounce grains of paradise |
| 1 1/2 lbs. sugar | 2 or 3 grains each: ambergris; musk. |
| 4 handfuls rose petals | 1 ounce each: cinnamon sticks; ginger root; cloves. |

*optional:* gum amber, powdered coral, powdered pearls, leaf gold; pernambuco wood boiled in rosewater.

Take of the hearbe Rosa-solis,[2] gathered in Iulie, one gallon, pick out the black moates[3] from the leaues; Dates, halfe a pound; Cinamon, Ginger, Cloues, of each one ounce; grains, halfe an ounce; fine Sugar, a pound and a half; red Rose-leaues, green or dryed, foure handfuls; steep all these in a gallon of good Aqua Composita, in a glass close stopped with wax, during twenty daies: shake it well together once euery two daies. Your Sugar must be powdred, your spices bruised onely, or grossely beaten; your Dates cut in long slices, the stones taken away. If you adde two or three grains of Amber-greece, and as much Musk, in your glasse, among the rest of the Ingredients, it will haue a pleasant smell. Some adde the Gum Amber, with corall and pearle finely powdred, and fine leaf-gold. Some vse to boile Ferdinando buck in Rose-water, till they haue purchased a faire, deepe crimson colour: and when the same is cold, they colour their Rose-solis and Aqua Rubea therewith.
(From *Delightes for Ladies*, by Sir Hugh Plat, 1609.)

---

[1] Bradley, pp. 94-95.

[2] Rosa-solis is the Sun Dew, *Drosera rotundifolia* L., not a rose. (*See Appendix.*)

[3] Sir Hugh must have had poor eyesight. Those "black moates" were the remains of dead insects stuck to the sundew's leaves by its sticky sap.

[TURNIP WINE] – c. 77 A. D.

2 drams wild turnips                              1 quart grape must

A wine is made from the navew turnip by adding two drams' weight of navew to a quart of must...
(From *Natural History*, by Pliny the Elder, Book XIV, section XIX, pp. 255-257.)


## TO MAKE TURNIP DRINK – 1723

turnip juice                                      *optional*: yeast.

Pound your turnips and press them through a Hair-bag; then let it stand a Day or two in the open Tun, or only covered with a cloth or boards to keep it from the Dust, or in a Hogshead or other vessel not quite full, with an open Bung, till the more gross parts subside; then draw it off, and put it into the Vessels you design to keep it in longer, leaving them about an eighth part empty. Let the Vessels stand in a Cellar, with the Bung open, or covered only with a loose Cover, that there may be a free evaporation of the volatile particles of the Liquor. If you make this drink in very cold Weather, it will be requisite to treat the Liquor in a Copper, something more than Blood-warm to make it ferment; or you may put the yeast to it for the same purpose.
(From *The Receipt Book of John Nott*, Cook to the Duke of Bolton, 1723.)

TURNIP WINE – c. 1788

1 gallon turnip juice
3 lbs. sugar
1/2 pint brandy

Take a good many turnips, pare, slice, and put them in a cyder-press, and press out all the juice very well; to every gallon of juice put three pounds of lump sugar; have a vessel ready, just big enough to hold the juice; put your sugar into a vessel; and also to every gallon of juice half a pint of brandy; pour in the juice, and lay something over the bung for a week, to see if it works; if it does, you must not bung it down till it has done working; then stop it close for three months, and draw it off in another vessel; when it is fine, bottle it off.
(From *The New Art of Cookery*, by Richard Briggs, c. 1788. *The same recipe can also be found in Glasse, v. 8, p. 347, and "The British Jewel," 1872.*)

## VIOLET WINE (VIOLATIUM) – c. 100 B.C. to 300 A.D.

violet flowers                                    white wine
honey to taste

In a similar way as above[1] like the rose wine violet wine is made of fresh violets, and tempered with honey as directed.
(From *Apicius, Cookery and Dining in Imperial Rome*, tr. by J. D. Vehling, p. 47.)


## [WORMWOOD WINE] – c. 77 A. D.

1 pound wormwood[2]                               5 gallons grape must

...wormwood wine is made by boiling down a pound of Pontic wormwood in five gallons of must to one-third of its amount, or else by putting shoots of wormwood into wine.
(From *Natural History*, by Pliny, c. 77 A. D., Book XIV, section XIX, p. 259.)


## 33. HOW TO MAKE WORMEWOOD WINE VERY SPEEDILY AND IN GREAT QUANTITY – 1609

a few drops wormwood oil[2]                       Rochelle or Consake wine

Take small Rochelle or Consake wine, put a few drops of the extracted oyle of wormwood therein: brew it together (as before is set downe in bottle-ale)[3] out of one pot into another, and you shall haue a more neat and wholesome wine for your body, than that which is sold at the Stillyard for right wormwood wine.
(From *Delightes for Ladies*, by Sir Hugh Plat, 1609.)


## TO MAKE WORMWOOD-WINE – 1655

2 lbs. dried wormwood[2]                           2 gallons Rhenish wine

Take two Pounds of dry'd Wormwood, two gallons of Rhenish Wine, let the Wormwood lye in it to digest for three or four Months, shaking the Vessel often; when it is settled, decant the clear Tincture for use.
(From *The Queen's Closet Opened*, by W.M., Cook to Queen Henrietta Maria, 1655.)

---

[1] *See Rose Wine, p. 175.*                                      [3] *See p. 4.*
[2] CAUTION! (*See Appendix.*)

# CAUDLES,

# POSSETS,
## &

# SYLLABUBS

*and other warmful drinks of bygone days*

✳✳✳✳✳✳✳

The styward bit the spices for to hye,
And eek the wyn, in al this melodye.
The usshers and the squiers been ygoon,
The spices and the wyn is come anoon.
(*The Canterbury Tales*, by Geoffrey Chaucer.)

# # 89 FLEMISH CAUDLE – c. 1375

*A caudle was a warm spiced drink of wine or ale, similar to egg nog, that was typically thickened with egg yolks. When thickening with eggs, it is important to cool the hot liquid until it is lukewarm, then add some of this lukewarm liquid to the beaten eggs. Stir, and then add the egg mixture to the rest of the lukewarm liquid. You must stir it and heat it gently until it is thickened. Do not boil or overheat the mixture or it will curdle and have lumps. Dishes and beverages thickened with eggs are best served immediately.*

| water | egg yolks |
|---|---|
| white wine | salt |
| *optional*: verjuice | |

Put a bit of water to boil. Take egg yolks beaten without the white, temper with white wine, thread into your water, and stir very well so that it does not curdle. Add some salt [and move it to] the back of the fire. Some add just a bit of verjuice.
(*Le Viandier de Taillevent*, c. 1375, tr. by J. Prescott, 1989, p. 33.)

# # 127. CAUDLE – c. 1450

| egg yolks | ale *or* wine |
|---|---|
| saffron | salt |
| sugar | |

127 Caudle. Take fair picked yolks of eggs, and cast in a pot; and take good ale, or else good wine, a quantity, and set it over the fire/ And when it is at boiling, take it from the fire, and cast thereto saffron, salt, Sugar; and season it up, and serve it forth hot.
(From Harleian MS. 4016, c. 1450, tr. by C. Renfrow, 1990.)

# # 9 CAUDLE – c. 1450

| eggs | ale |
|---|---|
| wheat flour | saffron |
| sugar *or* honey | |

9. Caudle. Take eggs, & mix well together/ heat ale & put thereto/ mix it with wheat flour, put thereto a portion of sugar, or a part of honey, & a part of saffron; boil it, & give it forth.
(From Laud MS. 553, c. 1450., tr. by C. Renfrow, 1990.)

# # 47 CAUDLE *FERRY* – c. 1420

| | |
|---|---|
| egg yolks | wine |
| sugar | saffron |
| salt | mace blades |
| clove gilliflowers | cinnamon powder |
| galingale | |
| white powder (a spice mixture of ginger, cinnamon, and nutmeg)[1] | |

47. Caudle *Ferry*. Take yolks of eggs Raw, separated from the white; then take good wine, and warm it in the pot on a fair Fire, and cast thereon yolks, and stir it well, but let it not boil till it is thick; and cast thereto Sugar, Saffron, & Salt, Maces, Gilliflowers, and Galingale ground small, & flour of Cinnamon; & when thou dress in, cast white powder thereon.
(From Harleian MS. 279, c. 1420, tr. by C. Renfrow, 1990.)

# #107 CAUDLE FFERY – c. 1420

| | |
|---|---|
| egg yolks | wine |
| sugar | salt |

107 *Caudell ffery*. Take raw yolks of eggs and pick them, and bake them;[2] and take good wine, and warm it over the fire in a pot, And cast thereto the yolks, and stir it well, but let it not boil till it thickens; and then cast thereto sugar and salt, and serve it forth as *mortrews*. (*ibid.*)

# # 51 ALMOND CAUDLE – c. 1420

*This almond caudle was more than likely a Lenten dish. It is thickened with ground almonds in place of the egg yolks traditionally forbidden during Lent.*

| | |
|---|---|
| salt | saffron |
| sugar | almond milk made with ale and water |

51. Caudel of Almonds. Take Raw Almonds, & grind them, and mix them up with good ale, and a little Water, and draw it through a strainer into a fair pot, & let it boil a while: & cast thereto Saffron, Sugar, and Salt, & then serve it forth all hot in manner of pottage. (*ibid.*)

---

[1] Frere, p. 56.

[2] The phrase *and bake them* is probably a mistake. *Raw* yolks are typically used to thicken caudles.

# # 129 CAUDLE OF ALMONDS – c. 1450

salt                                    saffron
sugar                                   almond milk[1] made with ale and water

129. <u>Caudle of Almonds</u>. Take raw almonds, and grind them, And mix them with good ale and a little water; and draw them through a strainer into a fair pot, and let it boil awhile; And cast thereto saffron, Sugar and salt, and serve it forth hot.
(From Harleian MS. 4016, c. 1450, tr. by C. Renfrow, 1990.)

*Alkanet.*
From Gerard's *Herball*, 1597.

1 *Anchusa Alcibiadion*
Red Alkanet.

# # 150 CAUDLE OUT OF LENT – c. 1420

egg yolks                               sugar
salt                                    alkanet[2]
almond milk made with red *or* white wine
*optional*: saffron; rice flour *or* wheat flour;
sugar and mixed spices for garnish.

150. <u>Caudel out of Lent</u>. Take & make a good milk of Almonds drawn up with wine of Red, white is better; if it shall be white, then strain yolks of Eggs thereto a few. Put thereto Sugar & Salt, but Sugar enough; then when it begins to boil, set it out, & almost flat; serve it then forth, & ever keep it as white as thou may, & at the dresser drop Alkanet thereon, & serve forth; & if thou wilt have him thick, bind him up with flour [*of*] Rice, or with wheat flour, it is no matter. And if thou will, color him with Saffron, & strew on powder enough, & Sugar enough, & serve forth.
(From Harleian MS. 279, c. 1420, tr. by C. Renfrow, 1990.)

---

[1] To make almond milk, take 1 part ground blanched almonds, add 2 parts boiling water, wine, or broth. Add brown sugar or white sugar, and salt to taste. Let the mixture sit for 10 to 15 minutes, or until cloudy. Strain through cheesecloth. Save the liquid, discard the almonds.

[2] CAUTION! (*See Appendix.*)

# 312   A FLOMERY-CAUDLE – 1669

flummery[1]                          ale
white wine                           sugar to taste

When Flomery is made and cold, you may make a pleasant and wholesome caudle of it, by taking some lumps and spoonfuls of it, and boil it with Ale and White wine, then sweeten it to your taste with Sugar. There will remain in the Caudle some lumps of the congealed flomery, which are not ungrateful.
(From *The Closet ...Opened*, 1669.)


## TO MAKE WHITE CAUDLE – 1736

2 quarts water                       1/2 pint wine per quart strained liquid
4 spoonsful oatmeal                  2 mace blades
1 piece lemon peel                   1/4 ounce cloves
grated nutmeg and sugar to taste     1/4 ounce ginger

Take four spoonfuls of oatmeal, two blades of mace, a piece of lemon-peel, cloves and ginger, of each a quarter of an ounce; put these into two quarts of water, and let it boil about an hour, stirring it often; then strain it out, and add to every quart half a pint of wine, some grated nutmeg and sugar.
(From *The Compleat Housewife*, by E. Smith, 1736.)


## SEED WATER – 1788

1 pint water                         1 egg yolk
sugar to taste                       1 spoonful coriander seed
Sack wine                            1/2 spoonful caraway seed

Take a spoonful of Coriander seed, half a spoonful of carraway seed, bruised and boiled in a pint of water, then strain it, and bruise it with the yolk of an egg; mix it with sack and double refined sugar, according to your palate.
(From *The New Art of Cookery*, 1788.)

---

[1] Sir Kenelme's flummery is a wheat flour pudding or jelly flavored with sugar and rosewater or orange-flower water: "#152 WHEATEN FLOMMERY... Take half, or a quarter of a bushel of good Bran of the best wheat (which containeth the purest flower of it, though little, and is used to make starch,) and in a great woodden bowl or pail, let it soak with cold water upon it three or four days. Then strain out the milky water from it, and boil it up to a gelly or like starch. Which you may season with Sugar and Rose or Orange-flower-water, and let it stand till it be cold, and gellied..."

## TO MAKE WHITE CAUDLE – 1796

| | |
|---|---|
| 2 quarts water | 4 spoonsful oatmeal |
| 1 or 2 mace blades | sugar to taste |
| lemon peel | juice of 1 lemon |
| grated nutmeg | wine |

You muſt take two quarts of water, mix in four ſpoonfuls of oatmeal, a blade or two of mace, a piece of lemon-peel, let it boil, and keep ſtirring it often: let it boil about a quarter of an hour, and take care it does not boil over; then ſtrain it through a coarſe ſieve: when you uſe it, ſweeten it to your palate, grate in a little nutmeg, and what wine is proper; and if it is not for a ſick perſon, ſqueeze in the juice of a lemon.
(From *The Art of Cookery Made Plain and Easy*, v. 7, by Mrs. Glasse, 1796, p. 267.)

## TO MAKE BROWN CAUDLE – 1796

| | |
|---|---|
| 2 quarts water | 6 spoonsful oatmeal |
| 1 quart ale | sugar to taste |
| 1/2 pint white wine | |

Boil the gruel as above, with ſix ſpoonfuls of oatmeal, and ſtrain it; then add a quart of good ale, not bitter; boil it, then ſweeten it to your palate, and add half a pint of white wine: when you do not put in white wine, let it be half ale. (*ibid.*, pp. 267-268.)

## EGG WINE – 1861

*Egg wine was considered to be a nourishing drink for invalids.*

1867. INGREDIENTS. – 1 egg, 1 tablespoonful and 1/2 glass of cold water, 1 glass of sherry, sugar and grated nutmeg to taste.
*Mode.* – Beat the egg, mixing with it a tablespoonful of cold water; make the wine-and-water hot, but not boiling; pour it on the egg, stirring all the time. Add sufficient lump sugar to sweeten the mixture, and a little grated nutmeg; put all into a very clean saucepan, set it on a gentle fire, and stir the contents one way until they thicken, *but do not allow them to boil.* Serve in a glass with sippets of toasted bread or plain crisp biscuits. When the egg is not warmed, the mixture will be found easier of digestion, but it is not so pleasant a drink.
(From *Mrs. Beeton's Book of Household Management*, 1861.)

*191*

"...wine is made from Gallic nard and another from wild nard."[1]

✳✳✳

About the leaf, which is that of the nard, it is proper to speak at greater length, as it holds a foremost place among perfumes. The nard is a shrub, the root of which is heavy and thick but short and black, and although oily, brittle; it has a musty smell like the gladiolus, and an acrid taste; the leaves are small, and grow in clusters. ...Nard is also adulterated with a plant called bastard nard, which grows everywhere, and has a thicker and broader leaf and a sickly colour inclining to white; and also by being mixed with its own root to increase the weight, and with gum and silver-spume or antimony and gladiolus or husk of gladiolus...[2]

✳✳✳

## CONDITUM PARADOXUM – c. 100 B.C. to 300 A.D.

6 sextarii honey
4 ounces crushed pepper
3 scruples mastic[4]
20+ sextarii[5] wine

1 dram spikenard *or* bay laurel leaves[3]
1 dram saffron
crushed charcoal for filtering
5 drams roasted date stones

The composition of [this] excellent spiced wine [is as follows]. Into a copper bowl put 6 sextarii of honey and 2 sextarii of wine; heat on a slow fire, constantly stirring the mixture with a whip. At the boiling point add a dash of cold wine, retire from stove and skim. Repeat this twice or three times, let it rest till the next day, and skim again. Then add 4 ozs. of crushed pepper, 3 scruples of mastich, a drachm each of [nard or laurel] leaves and saffron, 5 drachms of roasted date stones crushed and previously soaked in wine to soften them. When this is properly done add 18 sextarii of light wine. To clarify it perfectly, add [crushed] charcoal twice or as often as necessary which will draw [the residue] together [and carefully strain or filter through the charcoal].

(From *Apicius, Cookery and Dining in Imperial Rome*, c. 100 B.C. to 300 A.D., tr. by Vehling, p. 45. *Words in brackets were added by the translator.*)

---

[1] Pliny the Elder, *Natural History*, Book XIV, section XIX, pp. 255-257.

[2] *ibid.*, Book XII, section XXVI, p. 31.

[3] Nard is Spikenard, *Nardostachys jatamansi*. (*See Appendix.*)

[4] Mastic is a tree resin, (*see Appendix*).

[5] One sextarius = approx. 1 1/2 English pints.

## WINE FOR THE GODS – 1682

| | |
|---|---|
| 2 large lemons | 3/4 lb. granulated sugar |
| 2 pippin apples | 1 pint burgundy wine |
| 6 cloves | orange-flower water |

Take two great lemons, peel them and cut them in slices with two Pippens pared and sliced like your lemons, put all this into a dish with three quarters of a pound of sugar in powder, a pint of Burgundy Wine, six cloves, a little orange-flower water. Cover this up and let it steep two or three hours then pass it through a bag as you do Hypocras and it will be most excellent.

(From *A Perfect School of Instructions for the Officers of the Mouth*, by Giles Rose, one of the Master Cooks to Charles II, 1682.)

## 1069. BISHOP HOT OR ICED – 1829

| | |
|---|---|
| 3 bitter oranges | 1 1/4 lb. sugar |

1 bottle Bordeaux *or* Madeira, *or* Rhine wine, *or* imperial Tokay
Note: if Madeira is used, add nutmeg, cloves, and mace to taste.

A delftware "Cardinal Bellarmine" beer jug.

The day before the liqueur is wanted, grill on a wire-grill, over a clear slow fire, three smooth-skinned large bitter oranges. Grill them of a pale brown. They may be done in an oven, or under a furnace. Place them in a small punch-bowl, that will about hold them, and pour over them a full half-pint from a bottle of old Bourdeaux wine, in which a pound and a quarter of loaf sugar is dissolved. Cover with a plate. When it is to be served next day, (though it may lie over two or three days,) cut and squeeze the oranges into a small sieve placed above a jug, containing the remainder of the bottle of wine previously made very hot. Add more syrup if it is wanted. Serve hot in large glasses; or in summer it may be iced. Bishop is often made of Madeira in England, and is perfumed with nutmegs, bruised cloves, and mace. It ought, however, to be made of old generous Bourdeaux wine, or it fails of its purpose as a tonic liqueur...

...When this compound is made of Bourdeaux wine, it is called simply *Bishop*; but according to a German amateur, it receives the name of *Cardinal* when old Rhine wine is used; and even rises to the dignity of *Pope* when imperial Tokay is employed.

(From *The Cook and Housewife's Manual: a Practical System of Modern Domestic Cookery and Family Management*, by Mistress Margaret Dods, 1829, pp. 460-462.)

## WINE A DELICIOUS SORT – 1723

| | |
|---|---|
| 2 pippin apples | 2 lemons |
| 1 quart red Port wine | orange-flower water |
| 1/2 lb. sugar | musk *or* ambergris |
| 6 cloves | cinnamon powder |

Cut a couple of Pippens and a couple of Lemons into slices into a Dish, with half a pound of fine Sugar; a quart of good red Port Wine, half a dozen Cloves, some Cinnamon powdered, and Orange-Flower water; cover these and let them infuse for three or four hours; then strain it through a bag, and give it a flavour with Musk or Amber, as you please.
(From *The Receipt Book of John Nott*, Cook to the Duke of Bolton, 1723.)

## 1082. ATHOLE BROSE – 1829

| | |
|---|---|
| 1 cup heather honey | *optional*: brandy; rum; 1 egg yolk. |
| 2 cups whisky | |

Mix with a cupful of heather-honey, two cupfuls of whisky, alias mountain-dew, or in this proportion; brandy and rum are also used, though the combination they form with honey cannot be called Athole brose. The yolk of an egg is sometimes beat up with the brose.
(From *The Cook and Housewife's Manual: a Practical System of Modern Domestic Cookery and Family Management,* by Mistress Margaret Dods, 1829, p. 464.)

## ATHOL BROSE – 1860

1 egg
2 wineglassesful scotch whisky
1 wineglassful heather honey

Add two wine-glassfuls of Scotch Whisky to a wine-glassful of heather-honey; mix well, and then stir in a well-beaten new-laid egg.
(From *The Practical Housewife: A Complete Encyclopedia of Domestic Economy and Family Medical Guide,* 1860.)

✱✱✱

"'Alcman ...speaks of "wine that knows no heat, redolent of its bouquet"...
By "no heat" he meant wine which has not been boiled;
for they used to drink mulled wine."'[1]

✱✱✱

MULLED CLARET – c. 1922

| | |
|---|---|
| 1 pint water | 1/2 cup sugar |
| 1 bottle claret wine | 1 pinch grated nutmeg |
| 1 handful borage | 12 cloves |
| 1 bay leaf | 1 teaspoon mixed spices |

Put into a double saucepan half a pint of water and when nearly boiling add a small handful of borage, 6 cloves, a pinch of nutmeg and a bay leaf and a teaspoon of mixed spice. Bring to the boil, stir in until dissolved three tablespoons of sugar and then remove from the fire. In another pan boil half a pint of water with 6 cloves, a little spice and two dessert spoons of sugar. Pour a bottle of claret into the first pan and bring to the boil again, stirring occasionally but do not lift the lid too often.[2] If not spicy enough add a very little from the second saucepan until the flavour is to your liking.
(From *A Garden of Herbs* by E. S. Rohde, pp. 213-214.)


ALE, MULLED – 1860

| | |
|---|---|
| 1+ pint ale | sugar |
| 3 eggs | 1 tablespoon brandy |
| grated nutmeg | toast sippets |

Boil a pint of good sound ale with a little grated nutmeg and sugar. Beat up three eggs, and mix them with a little cold ale; then add the hot ale to it gradually, and pour backwards and forwards from one vessel to the other several times, to prevent its curdling. Warm, and stir till it thickens, then add a table-spoonful of brandy, and serve hot with toast.
(From *The Practical Housewife: A Complete Encyclopedia of Domestic Economy and Family Medical Guide*, 1860.)

---

[1] Athenaeus, Book I, pp. 137-139.

[2] Lifting the lid allows the alcohol to escape (and the cook to get drunk).

*195*

"'For them Hecamedê of the beautiful tresses prepared a posset [*kykeôn*]. ...She it was that had first set in front of them a table fair, with black legs, well polished, and upon it had placed a bronze basket; then, as a relish for their drink, she had brought an onion, and yellow honey, and the fruit of sacred barley besides, and a cup of exceeding beauty which the aged man had brought from home. ...In it, then, the woman fair as a goddess made a mixture for him with Pramnian wine, and in it she grated goat's milk cheese with a bronze grater, and sprinkled white barley meal over it; then she bade him drink, for that she had prepared the posset.'"[1]

✳✳✳

## # 120  TO MAKE A SACK POSSET – 1669

| | |
|---|---|
| 2 quarts sweet cream | 3 or 4 cinnamon sticks |
| 9 or 10 egg yolks | 3 or 4 whole nutmegs, quartered |
| 4 egg whites | 1/2 pint of Sack wine *or* white muscadine |
| 3/4 lb. sugar | ambergris, ambered sugar *or* pastils |
| | *optional:* cinnamon powder and sugar for garnish. |

Boil two wine-quarts of Sweet-cream in a Possnet; when it hath boiled a little, take it from the fire, and beat the yolks of nine or ten fresh Eggs, and the whites of four with it, beginning with two or three spoonfuls, and adding more till all be incorporated; then set it over the fire, to recover a good degree of heat, but not so much as to boil; and always stir it one way, least you break the consistence. In the mean time, let half a pint of Sack or White muscadin boil a very little in a bason, upon a Chafing-dish of Coals, with three quarters of a pound of Sugar, and three or four quartered Nutmegs, and as many pretty big pieces of sticks of Cinnamon. When this is well scummed, and still very hot, take it from the fire, and immediately pour into it the cream, beginning to pour near it, but raising by degrees your hand so that it may fall down from a good height; and without anymore to be done, it will then be fit to eat. It is very good kept cold as well as eaten hot. It doth very well with it, to put into the Sack (immediately before you put in the cream) some Ambergreece, or Ambered-sugar, or Pastils. When it is made, you may put powder of Cinnamon and Sugar upon it, if you like it.
(From *The Closet ...Opened*, 1669.)

---

[1] Homer, quoted in Athenaeus, Book XI, pp. 193-195.

# # 121  ANOTHER [SACK POSSET] – 1669

2 quarts cream

2 to 7 egg yolks

ambergris *or* pastils

1/3 pint Sack wine *or* white muscadine

3/4 lb. sugar

To two quarts of Cream, if it be in the Summer, when the Cream is thick and best, take but two or three yolks of Eggs. But in the Winter when it is thin and hungry, take six or seven; but never no whites. And of Sack or Muscadin, take a good third (scarce half) of a pint; and three quarters of a pound of fine Sugar. Let the Sugar and Sack boil well together, that it be almost like a Syrup; and just as you take it from the fire, put in your ground Amber or Pastils, and constantly pour in the Cream with which the Eggs are incorporated; and do all the rest as is said in the foregoing Process.

Ambered-sugar is made by grinding very well, four grains of Ambergreece, and one of Musk, with a little fine Sugar; or grinding two or three Spanish Pastils very small.

(From *The Closet ...Opened*, 1669.)

# # 122  A PLAIN ORDINARY POSSET – 1669

1 pint milk

4 spoonsful ale

2 spoonsful Sack wine

sugar to taste

Put a pint of good Milk to boil; as soon as it doth so, take it from the fire, to let the great heat of it cool a little; for doing so, the curd will be the tenderer, and the whole of a more uniform consistence. When it is prettily cooled, pour it into your pot, wherein is about two spoonfuls of Sack, and about four of Ale, with sufficient Sugar dissolved in them. So let it stand a while near the fire, till you eat it. (*ibid.*)

# # 123  A SACK POSSET – 1669

3 pints cream

12 egg yolks, beaten

sugar to taste

cinnamon

1/2 pint plus 1 spoonful Sack wine

6 spoonsful ale

1 whole nutmeg, quartered

2 spoonfuls breadcrumbs

*optional*: ambergris; ambered sugar, *or* cinnamon sugar for garnish.

Take three pints of Cream; boil in it a little Cinnamon, a Nutmeg quartered, and two spoonfuls of grated bread; then beat the yolks of twelve Eggs very well with a little cold Cream, and a spoonful of Sack. When your Cream hath boiled about a quarter of an hour, thicken it up with the Eggs, and sweeten it with Sugar; and take half a pint of Sack and six spoonfuls of Ale, and put into the basin or dish, you intend to make it in, with a little Ambergreece, if you please. Then pour your Cream and Eggs into it, holding your hand as high as conveniently you can, gently stirring in the basin with the spoon as you pour it; so serve it up. If you please you may strew Sugar upon it.

You may strew Ambred sugar upon it, as you eat it; or Sugar-beaten with Cinnamon, if you like it.
(From *The Closet ...Opened*, 1669.)


# 199  TO MAKE A FRENCH BARLEY POSSET – 1669

| | |
|---|---|
| 2 quarts milk | 3 pints cream |
| 1/2 lb. French barley | mace |
| cinnamon | sugar to taste |

1 pint white wine, *or* 1 cup Sack wine mixed with 1 cup white wine

Take two quarts of Milk to half a pound of French-barley; boil it, until it is enough; when the Milk is almost boiled away, put to it three Pintes of good Cream. Let it boil together a quarter of an hour; then sweeten it; and put in Mace, Cinnamon in the beginning, when you first put in your Cream. When you have done so, take White-wine a Pint, or Sack and White-wine together, of each half a Pint; sweeten it, as you love it, with Sugar; pour in all the Cream, but leave your Barley behind in the Skillet. This will make an Excellent Posset; nothing else but a tender Curd to the bottom; let it stand on the Coals half a quarter of an hour. (*ibid.*)


# 124  A BARLEY SACK POSSET – 1669

| | |
|---|---|
| 1+ cup Rhenish wine | boiling water |
| 1+ cup Sack wine | 1/2 lb. French barley (not pearl barley) |
| 3 pints milk | verjuice *or* cider vinegar *or* orange juice |
| 3 pints cream | 1/2 lb. sugar *or* to taste |

*optional:* cinnamon sticks.

garnish with: cinnamon powder and sugar, *or* ambergris and sugar.

Take half a pound or more of French barley, (not Perle-barley) and pour scalding water upon it, and wash it well therein, and strain it from the water, & put it into the Corner of a Linnen-cloth and tie it up fast there, and strike it a dozen or twenty blows against a firm table or block, to make it tender by such bruising it, as in the Countrey is used with wheat to make frumenty. Then put it into a large skillet with three pints of

good milk. Boil this till at least half be consumed, and that it become as thick as hasty pudding, which will require at least two hours; and it must be carefully stirred all the while, least it burn too: which if by some little inadvertence it should do, and that some black burned substance sticketh to the bottom of the skillet, pour all the good matter from it into a fresh skillet (or into a basin whiles you scoure this) and renew boiling till it be very thick; All which is to make the barley very tender and pulpy, and will at least require two or near three hours. Then pour to it three pints of good Cream, and boil them together a little while, stirring them always. It will be sometime before the cold Cream boil, which when it doth, a little will suffice. Then take it from the fire, and season it well with Sugar. Then take a quarter of a pint of Sack, and as much Rhenish-wine (or more of each) and a little Verjuyce, or sharp Cider, or juyce of Orange, and season it well with Sugar (at least half a pound to both) and set it over Coals to boil. Which when it doth, and the Sugar is well melted, pour the Cream into it; in which Cream the barley will be settled to the bottom by standing still unmoved, after the Sugar is well stirred and melted in it, or pour it through a hair-sieve; and you may boil it again, that it be very hot, when you mingle them together; else it may chance not curdle. Some of the barley (but little) will go over with it, and will do no hurt. After you have thus made your Posset, let it stand warm a while that the curd may thicken: but take heed it boil not, for that would dissolve it again into the consistence of Cream. When you serve it up, strew it over with Powder of Cinnamon and Sugar. It will be much the better, if you strew upon it some Ambergreece ground with Sugar. You may boil bruised sticks of Cinnamon in the Cream, and in the Sack, before you mingle them. You must use clear Char-coal-fire under your vessels.[1] The remaining barley will make good barley Cream, being boiled with fresh Cream and a little Cinnamon and Mace; to which you may add a little Rosemary and Sugar, when it is taken from the fire: or butter it as you do wheat. Or make a pudding of it, putting to it a Pint of Cream, which boil; then add four or five yolks, and two whites of Eggs, and the Marrow of two bones cut small, and of one in lumps: sufficient Sugar, and one Nutmeg grated. Put this either to bake raw, or with puff-past beneath and above it in the dish. A pretty smart heat, as for white Manchet [*about 400° F.*], and three quarters of an hour in the Oven. You may make the like with great Oat-meal scalded (not boiled) in Cream, and soaked a night; then made up as the other.
(From *The Closet ...Opened*, 1669.)

---

[1] What follow are several suggestions for 'spoonmeats' which frugally use up the leftover soaked barley.

## # 125 MY LORD OF CARLILE'S SACK-POSSET – 1669

| | |
|---|---|
| 2 quarts cream | 18 egg yolks |
| 1 pint Sack wine | 8 egg whites |
| 3/4 lb. sugar | cinnamon sticks |
| 3 or 4 mace blades | 1 whole nutmeg, grated |
| 3 grains ambergris | 1 grain musk |
| cinnamon powder to taste | |

Take a Pottle of Cream, and boil in it a little whole Cinnamon, and three or four flakes of Mace. To this proportion of Cream put in eighteen yolks of Eggs, and eight of the whites; a pint of Sack; beat your Eggs very well, and then mingle them with your Sack. Put in three quarters of a pound of Sugar into the Wine and Eggs with a Nutmeg grated, and a little beaten Cinnamon; set the basin on the fire with the wine and Eggs, and let it be hot. Then put in the Cream boyling from the fire, pour it on high, but stir it not; cover it with a dish, and when it is settled, strew on the top a little fine Sugar mingled with three grains of Ambergreece, and one grain of Musk, and serve it up. (From *The Closet ...Opened*, 1669.)

## # 167 AN EXCELLENT POSSET – 1669

| | |
|---|---|
| 1/2 pint Sack wine | 10 egg yolks, add sugar to taste |
| 1/2 pint Rhenish wine | 1 or 2 cinnamon sticks |
| 8 egg whites | sugar to taste |
| juice of 1/4 lemon | |
| 3 pints cream, sweetened with cinnamon and sugar to taste | |
| *optional*: garnish with cinnamon powder and sugar, *or* ambergris. | |

Take half a pint of Sack, and as much Rhenish wine, sweeten them to your taste with Sugar. Beat ten yolks of Eggs, and eight of whites exceeding well, first taking out the Cocks-tread [*the blood spot found in fertilized eggs*], and if you will the skins of the yolks [*yolk membrane*]; sweeten these [*yolks & whites*] also, and pour them to the wine, add a stick or two of Cinnamon bruised, set this upon a Chafing-dish to heat strongly, but not to boil; but it must begin to thicken. In the mean time boil for a quarter of an hour three pints of Cream seasoned duly with Sugar and some Cinnamon in it. Then take it off from boiling, but let it stand near the fire, that it may continue scalding-hot whiles the wine is heating. When both are as scalding-hot as they can be without boiling, pour the Cream into the wine from as high as you can. When all is in, set it upon the fire to stew for 1/8 of an hour. Then sprinkle all about the top of it the juyce of a 1/4 part of a Limon; and if you will, you may strew Powder of Cinnamon and Sugar, or Ambergreece upon it. (*ibid.*)

## SACK-POSSET – 1744

1/2 lb. sugar
1 quart milk
1 pint Sack wine
20 eggs
nutmeg

From famed Barbadoes on the Western Main
Fetch sugar half a pound; fetch sack from Spain
A pint; and from the Eastern Indian Coast
Nutmeg, the glory of our Northern toast.
O'er flaming coals together let them heat
Till the all-conquering sack dissolves the sweet.
O'er such another fire set eggs, twice ten,
New born from crowing cock and speckled hen;
Stir them with steady hand, and conscience pricking
To see the untimely fate of twenty chicken.
From shining shelf take down your brazen skillet,
A quart of milk from gentle cow will fill it.
When boiled and cooked, put milk and sack to egg,
Unite them firmly like the triple League.
Then covered close, together let them dwell
Till Miss twice sings:  You must not kiss and tell.
Each lad and lass snatch up their murdering spoon,
And fall on fiercely like a starved dragoon.
(From *The New York Gazette*, February 13, 1744.)

## POSSET, SACK – 1860

1 quart milk
1/2 pint Sack wine

sugar to taste
grated nutmeg to taste
4 Damascus biscuits *or* a French roll

Put a quart of new milk into a saucepan, and place it over a slow clear fire.  When it boils, crumble four Damascus biscuits into it; give it one boil, remove from the fire, add grated nutmeg and sugar to taste, stir in half a pint of sack (canary wine), and serve.  French roll will answer instead of the biscuits.
(From *The Practical Housewife:  A Complete Encyclopedia of Domestic Economy and Family Medical Guide*, 1860.)

# # 126  A SYLLABUB – 1669

3 pints sweet cream                   3/4 lb. sugar
1/2 cup of Sack wine                   1 pint white *or* Rhenish wine
*optional:*  flavor with rosemary; lemon peel; ambered sugar; mace; cloves; cinnamon
essence; cassia bark (cinnamon sticks); *or* nutmeg.

My Lady Middlesex makes Syllabubs for little Glasses with spouts, thus.  Take 3 pints
of sweet Cream, one of quick white wine (or Rhenish), and a good wine glassful (better
the 1/4 of a pint) of Sack:  mingle with them about three quarters of a pound of fine
Sugar in Powder.  Beat all these together with a whisk, till all appeareth converted into
froth.  Then pour it into your little Syllabub-glasses, and let them stand all night.  The
next day the Curd will be thick and firm above, and the drink clear under it.  I conceive
it may do well, to put into each glass (when you pour the liquor into it) a sprig of
Rosemary a little bruised, or a little Limon-peel, or some such thing to quicken the
taste; or use Amber-sugar, or spirit of Cinnamon, or of Lignum-cassiæ; or Nutmegs, or
Mace, or Cloves, a very little.
(From *The Closet ...Opened*, 1669.)

# # 133  TO MAKE A WHIP SYLLABUB
– 1669

6 spoonfuls Sack wine
2 egg whites
1 pint cream
sugar to taste

Take the whites of two Eggs, and a pint
of Cream, six spoonfuls of Sack, as
much Sugar as will sweeten it; then take
a Birchen rod and whip it; as it riseth
with froth, skim it, and put it into the
Syllabub pot; so continue it with
whipping and skimming, till your
Syllabub pot be full.  (*ibid.*)

# # 134  TO MAKE A PLAIN SYLLABUB – 1669

*In these next few recipes we are quite literally being instructed to milk the cow directly into the syllabub! This produced a frothy head on the syllabub, and must have amused the guests no end.*

1 pint verjuice      sweet cream
Sack wine        milk
sugar

Take a pint of Verjuyce in a bowl; milk the Cow to the Verjuyce; take off the Curd; and take sweet-cream and beat them together with a little Sack and Sugar; put it into your Syllabub pot; then strew Sugar on it, and so send it to the Table.
(From *The Closet ...Opened*, 1669.)

## SYLLABUB – 1796

1 quart apple cider     1/2+ pint sweet cream
milk          grated nutmeg
sugar to taste

*To make a fine Syllabub from the Cow.* Sweeten a quart of cyder with double refined ſugar, grate nutmeg into it, then milk your cow into your liquor, when you have thus added what quantity of milk you think proper, pour half a pint or more, in proportion to the quantity of ſyllabub you make, of the ſweeteſt cream you can get all over it.
(From *The First American Cookbook, etc.*, by A. Simmons, 1796, p. 31.)

## A WHIPT SYLLABUB – 1796

2 porringersful cream    1 lemon rind
sugar to taste       1 porringerful white wine
3 egg whites

Take two porringers of cream and one of white wine, grate in the ſkin of a lemon, take the whites of three eggs, ſweeten to your taſte, then whip it with a whiſk, take off the froth as it riſes and put it into your ſyllabub glaſſes or pots, and they are fit for uſe.
(*ibid.*, p. 32.)

✳✳✳
Here we come a wassailing, Among the leaves so green,
Here we come a wandering, So fair to be seen.

(Chorus)
Love and joy come to you,
And to your wassel too,
And God send you a happy New Year,
A New Year,
And God send you a happy New Year!

Our wassel cup is made of rosemary-tree,
So is your beer of the best barley...
(Folksong.)
✳✳✳

RECEIPT FOR MAKING THE WASSAILBOWL – c. 1863

2, 4, or 6 bottles Port, Sherry, or Madeira wine

| | |
|---|---|
| 12 egg yolks | 1 teacupful water |
| 6 egg whites | 1 1/2 lbs. granulated sugar per 4 bottles wine |
| 12 roasted apples | |

For Each bottle of wine used, take the following whole spices:
10 grains mace; 46 grains cloves; 37 grains cardamom seeds; 28 grains cinnamon; 12 grains nutmeg; 48 grains ginger; 49 grains coriander seeds.

Simmer a small quantity of the following spices in a teacupful of water, viz.: –
Cardamums, cloves, nutmeg, mace, ginger, cinnamon, and coriander. When done, put the spice to two, four, or six bottles of port, sherry, or madeira, with one pound and a half of fine loaf sugar (pounded) to four bottles, and set all on the fire in a clean bright saucepan; meanwhile, have yolks of 12 and the whites of 6 eggs well whisked up in it. Then, when the spiced and sugared wine is a little warm, take out one teacupful; and so on for three or four cups; after which, when it boils, add the whole of the remainder, pouring it in gradually, and stirring it briskly all the time, so as to froth it. The moment a fine froth is obtained, toss in 12 fine soft roasted apples, and send it up hot. Spices for each bottle of wine: –10 grains of mace, 46 grains of cloves, 37 grains of cardamums, 28 grains of cinnamon, 12 grains of nutmeg, 48 grains of ginger, 49 grains of coriander seeds.
(From *The Book of Days, etc.*, ed. by R. Chambers, 1863, p. 28.)

# BRANDIES,

# LIQUEURS,
## &
# DISTILLED WATERS

✸✸✸✸✸✸✸

"There is drawne out of Wine a liquor,
which the Latines commonly call *Aqua vitae*,
or water of life, and alſo *Aqua ardens*,
or burning water,
which as diſtilled waters are drawne out of herbes and
other things, is after the ſame manner diſtilled out of
ſtrong wine, that is to ſay, by certaine inſtruments
made for this purpoſe,
which are commonly called Lembickes."
(Gerard, p. 734.)

## BRANDIES, LIQUEURS, & DISTILLED WATERS

### 1. HOW TO MAKE TRUE SPIRIT OF WINE – 1609

*Note:* *Distillation must properly be done* <u>*twice*</u> *– once to concentrate the alcohol, and again, skillfully, to remove toxic impurities that have also been concentrated by the first distillation. (See McGee, pp. 484-485.)*

Take the finest paper you can get, or else some Virgin parchment; straine it very tight and stiffe ouer the glasse body, wherein you put your Sack, Malmesie or Muskadine; oyle the paper or Virgin parchment with a pensill, moistened in the oyle of Ben, and distill it in Balneo with a gentle fire, and by this meanes you shall purchase only the true spirit of Wine. You shall not haue aboue two or three ounces at the most out of a gallon of Wine, which ascendeth in the forme of a cloud, without any dew or veines in the helme: lute all the joints well in this distillation. This Spirit will vanish in the ayre, if the glasse stand open.
(From *Delights For Ladies*, by Sir Hugh Plat, 1609.)

### 2. HOW TO MAKE THE ORDINARY SPIRIT OF WINE THAT IS SOULD FOR FIVE SHILLINGS AND A NOBLE A PINT – 1609

Put Sacke, Malmesie, or Muskadine into a glasse body, leauing one third or more of your glasse empty, set it in balneo, or in a pan of ashes, keeping a soft and gentle fire: draw no longer than till all or most part will burne away, which you may proue now and then, by setting a spoonefull thereof on fire with a paper, as it droppeth from the nose or pipe of the helme: & if your spirit thus drawne haue any phlegme therein, then rectifie or redistil that spirit againe in a lesser body, or in a bolt receiuer insted of another body, luting a small head on the top of the steele thereof, & so you shall haue a very strong spirit: or else for more expedition, distill 5 or 6 gallons of wine by Lymbecke; and that spirit, which ascendeth afterward, redistill in glasse, as before. (*ibid.*)

### 3. SPIRITS OF SPICES – 1609

*"Delights For Ladies" contains several recipes for distilled 'waters' or 'spirits' in the chapter entitled "Secrets in Distillation." Indeed, Sir Hugh's distillation apparatus seems to have been his favorite toy.*

Distil with a gentle heat either in Balneo, or ashes, the strong and sweete water, wherewith you haue drawne oyle of cloues, mace, nutmegs, Iuniper, Rosemary, &c. after it hath stood one moneth close stopt, and so you shall purchase a most delicate Spirit of each of the said aromaticall bodies. (*ibid.*)

## 13. SPIRIT OF HONEY – 1609

*This recipe for 'spirit of honey' is for a distilled alcohol made from mead.*

1 part honey                         5 parts water
yeast

Put one part of Honey to 5 parts of water: when the water boyleth, dissolue your Honey therein, skimme it, and hauing sodden an houre or two, put it into a woodden vessell, and when it is but bloudwarme, set it on worke with yeast after the vsuall manner of Beere and Ale: runne it, and when it hath lyen some time, it wil yeeld his Spirit by distillation, as Wine, Beere and Ale will doe.
(From *Delightes for Ladies*, by Sir Hugh Plat, 1609.)

✳✳✳

"the Portingale women that dwell in the Eaſt Indies, drawe from the Cloues when they be yet greene, a certaine liquor by diſtillation, of a moſt fragrant ſmell, which comforteth the hart; and of all cordials is the moſt effectuall."[1]

✳✳✳

## ANNISEED CORDIAL – 1839

2 quarts white brandy                1 lb. sugar
2 quarts water
*optional:* powdered cochineal dissolved in brandy.
1 tablespoon oil of anise seed (*or* clove oil *or* cinnamon oil)

Melt a pound of loaf-sugar in two quarts of water. Mix it with two quarts of white brandy, and add a tablespoonful of oil of annissed. Let it stand a week; then filter it through white blotting paper, and bottle it for use.

Clove or Cinnamon Cordial may be made in the same manner, by mixing sugar, water and brandy, and adding oil of cinnamon or oil of cloves. You may colour any of these cordials red by stirring in a little powdered cochineal that has been dissolved in a small quantity of brandy.
(From *Seventy-five Receipts for Pastry, Cakes, and Sweetmeats*, by Miss Leslie, 1838.)

---

[1] Gerard, p. 1353.

## ANISETTE DE BOURDEAUX – 1866

3 1/2 gallons grain alcohol
10 lbs. sugar
7 pints water
10 ounces green anise seed
1 ounce fennel
1 ounce coriander
4 ounces star anise seed
2 ounces hyson tea (a type of Chinese green tea)

*Musk melon.*
From Parkinson's Herbal, 1629.

Green anise-seed, ten ounces; hyson tea, two ounces; star anise-seed, four ounces; coriander, one ounce; fennel, one ounce. Macerate for fifteen days in three and a half gallons of alcohol; distil in the water-bath; then make a syrup with ten pounds of sugar and seven pints of water; mix well, and filter.
(From *The Art of Confectionery*, 1866.)


## ANOTHER ANISETTE DE BOURDEAUX – 1866

2 1/2 gallons water
3 1/2 gallons grain alcohol
1 quart orange-flower water
1 quart water
4 ounces fennel
4 ounces coriander

28 lbs. sugar
8 ounces green anise seed
4 ounces sassafras[1]
1 lb. dill [seed?]
4 ounces pearl gunpowder tea
1 ounce musk melon seed[2]

Dill, one pound; green aniseseed, eight ounces; fennel, four ounces; coriander, four ounces; sassafras-wood cut fine, four ounces; pearl gunpowder tea, four ounces; muskseed, one ounce. Macerate all these substances in three and a half gallons of alcohol for six days; then distil in the waterbath; add a syrup made with twenty-eight pounds of fine sugar, two and a half gallons of distilled water, one quart of double-distilled orange-flower water, and one quart of pure water. (*ibid.*)

---

[1] CAUTION! (*See Appendix.*)

[2] "The ſeede [of cucumbers] is vſed phyſically in many medicines that ſerue to coole, and a little to make the paſſages of vrine ſlippery, and to giue eaſe to hot diſeaſes...The ſeed of theſe Melons [musk melons] are vſed as Cowcumbers phyſically, and together with them moſt vſually." (Parkinson, p. 525.)

## 84TH. METHOD OF MAKING APPLE BRANDY – 1815

...Put the cider, previous to distilling, into vessels free from must or smell, and keep it till in the state which is commonly called good, sound cider; but not till sour, as that lessens the quantity and injures the quality of the spirit. In the distillation, let it run perfectly cool from the worm,[1] and in the first time of distilling, not longer than it will flash when cast on the still head and a lighted candle applied under it. In the second distillation, shift the vessel as soon as the spirit runs below proof, or has a disagreeable smell or taste, and put what runs after with the low wines. By this method, the spirit, if distilled from good cider, will take nearly or quite one third of its quantity to bring it to proof; for which purpose, take the last running from a cheese[2] of good water cider, direct from the press, unfermented, and in forty-eight hours the spirit will be milder and better flavoured than in several years standing if manufactured in the common way. When the spirit is drawn off, which may be done in five or six days, there will be a jelly, at the bottom, which may be distilled again, or put into the best cider or used for making cider royal, it being better for the purpose that the clear spirit, as it will greatly facilitate in refining the liquor.

(From *The Dyer's Companion*, by Elijah Bemiss, 1815, pp. 299-300.)

"BRANDY is the alcoholic or spirituous portion of wine, separated from the aqueous part, the colouring matter, &c., by distillation. The word is of German origin, and in its German form, *brantwein*, signifies burnt wine, or wine that has undergone the action of fire; brandies, so called, however, have been made from potatoes, carrots, beetroot, pears, and other vegetable substances; but they are all inferior to true brandy. Brandy is prepared in most wine countries, but that of France is the most esteemed. It is procured not only by distilling the wine itself, but also by fermenting and distilling the *marc*, or residue of the pressings of the grape..."[3]

---

[1] A "worm," in this usage, means the spiral-shaped condenser of the still.

[2] "Cheese" here refers to the mass of apple pulp which has been wrapped in cheesecloth and pressed in the cider press until it resembles a large cheese.

[3] Mrs. Beeton, p. 668.

## 5. HOW TO MAKE THE WATER WHICH IS VSUALLY CALLED BALME-WATER. – 1609

1 gallon claret wine                               1 lb. lemon balm

To euery gallon of Claret wine put one pound of green balme. Keep that which commeth first, and is clearest, by it selfe: and the second & whiter sort, which is weakest and commeth last, by it selfe: distill in a pewter Lymbeck luted with paste to a brasse pot. Draw this in May or Iune, when the herb is in his prime.
(From *Delightes for Ladies*, by Sir Hugh Plat, 1609.)

## A RECEIPT FOR BALME – 1682

1 quart brandy                               6 or 7 handfuls lemon balm
4 quarts strong ale                          1/2 ounce mace blades
sugar to taste                               saffron
                                             1 handful cowslip flowers, fresh or dried

Take 6 or 7 handfulls of balme, cut it a little, put it in an Earthen pott wth a handfull of cowslip flowers, green or dry, half an ounce of Mace, a little bruised pow[d]er in ym, 4 quarts of strong ale, let ym stand a night to infuse: in ye morning put it into your still, poure upon it a quart of brandy. Past up your Still; you may draw about 2 quarts of water. Sweeten it with Sugar to your Tast and tye up too pennyworth of Saffron in a ragg, put it into ye water and let it lye till it be colored. Squeeze it out and bottle it for your use.
(From *Mary Doggett: Her Book of Receipts*, 1682.)

## BLACKBERRY CORDIAL – 1838

1 quart blackberry juice                     1 quart brandy
1 lb. sugar

Take the ripest blackberries. Mash them, put them in a linen bag and squeeze out the juice. To every quart of juice allow a pound of beaten loaf-sugar. Put the sugar into a large preserving kettle, and pour the juice on it. When it is all melted, set it on the fire, and boil it to a thin jelly. When cold, to every quart of juice allow a quart of brandy. Stir them well together, and bottle it for use. It will be ready at once.
(From *Seventy-five Receipts for Pastry, Cakes, and Sweetmeats*, by Miss Leslie, 1838.)

# # 265  TO MAKE SHRUB – c. 1706

1 quart brandy
1 quart water
3 lemons

1 quart white wine
1 lb. sugar

Take one quart of brandy & a quart of white wine, & a quart of spring water. mix them together then slice 3 leamons, & put in with a pound of sugar. stir these very well, cover yʳ pot close, & let it stand 3 dayes, stiring it every day. then strayne it, & bottle it, & crush yᵉ leamons very well inside it.
(From *Martha Washington's Booke of Cookery*, ed. by Karen Hess, 1981. *This was dated before 1706 by Hess, based on etymological evidence.*)


# BRANDY SHRUB – 1829

7 gallons brandy
3 gallons raisin wine
1 gallon porter ale

5 gallons water
2 quarts orange-flower water
8 ounces citric acid

Time to completion:  7 to 10 days.

Take 8 oz. of citric acid, – 1 gallon of porter, – 3 gallons of raisin wine, – 2 quarts of orange flower water, – 7 gallons of good brandy, 5 ditto of water.  This will produce 16 gallons.  First, dissolve the citric acid in the water, then add to it the brandy:  next, mix the raisin wine, porter, and orange flower water together; and lastly, mix the whole:  and in a week or ten days, it will be ready for drinking, and of a very mellow flavour.
(From *Five Thousand Receipts, etc.*, by Mackenzie, 1829.)


# LEMON BRANDY – 1861

460.  INGREDIENTS. – 1 pint of brandy, the rind of two small lemons, 2 oz. of loaf-sugar, 1/4 pint of water.
*Mode.* – Peel the lemons rather thin, taking care to have none of the white pith. Put the rinds into a bottle with the brandy, and let them infuse for 24 hours, when they should be strained.  Now boil the sugar with the water for a few minutes, skim it, and, when cold, add it to the brandy.  A dessertspoonful of this will be found an excellent flavouring for boiled custards.
(From *Mrs. Beeton's Book of Household Management*, 1861.)

## 1062. CHERRY BRANDY OR WHISKY – 1829

*The method employed here can be used to produce brandies flavored with all sorts of fruits and sweet-scented flowers. The soused fruit left over in making these flavored wines and brandies may be used to make jams, jellies, mincemeat, cherries jubilee, etc.*

brandy
sugar syrup to taste
morello or black cherries

1/2 ounce cinnamon
1 dram cloves

Pick morello, or black cherries, from the stalks, and drop them into bottles, till the bottles are three-quarters full; fill up with brandy or whisky. In three weeks strain off the spirits, and season with cinnamon and clove mixture... adding syrup to taste... A second weaker decoction may be obtained by pouring more spirits on the fruit.
(From *The Cook and Housewife's Manual*, by Mistress Margaret Dods, 1829, p. 458.)

## CHERRY BRANDY – 1856

2 gallons water
5 gallons black cherries
5 gallons morello cherries
brandy
1 lb. brown sugar per gallon liquor

Get equal quantities of morello and common black cherries; fill your cask and pour on (to a ten gallon cask) one gallon of boiling water; in two or three hours, fill it up with brandy – let it stand a week, then draw off all, and put another gallon of boiling water, and fill it again with brandy – at the end of the week, draw the whole off, empty the cask of the cherries, and pour in your brandy with water, to reduce the strength; first dissolving one pound of brown sugar in each gallon of your mixture. If the brandy be very strong, it will bear water enough to make the cask full.
(From *The Virginia Housewife, etc.*, by Mrs. Mary Randolph, 1856.)

# # 289  TO MAKE CINNAMON WATER – c. 1550 to 1625

1 lb. cinnamon sticks                    1 gallon muscadine, malmsey *or* Sack wine

Take a gallon of muskadine, malmsey, or sack & put it in A vessill yt may be close covered, & put to it into ye vessell a pound of bruised cinnamon. let it stand 3 dayes, & every day stir 2 or 3 times. then put it in a limbeck of glass, stoped fast. set it in a brass pot full of water,[1] & put hay in ye bottome & about ye sydes. then make ye pot seeth, & let it distill in to a glass kept as close as may be. shift ye glass every houre after ye first time, for ye first will be ye strongest, & ye last will be very weak.

# # 290
3 quarts rose water                    1 quart white wine
2 lbs. cinnamon sticks

Put 3 quarts of red rose water & one quart of white wine into a limbeck of glass. yn bruise 2 pound of cinnamon & put therein, & let it stand 12 hours in luke warme water close stopt. then still it in water on a gentle fire, but it may not be taken out of ye glass reserve, the first comeing of, for it will be much ye better.

# # 291

1 gallon Sack wine                    1 lb. cinnamon sticks

Take a pound of ye best cinnamon you can get, & bruise it well. then put it into a gallon of ye best sack & infuse it 3 dayes and three nights, and then you must distill it as you doe your Aquecelestis.
(From *Martha Washington's Booke of Cookery*, ed. by Karen Hess.)


# # 292  TO MAKE CINNAMON WATER WITHOUT DISTILLING IT – c. 1550 to 1625

1 quart brandy                    1/2 dram cinnamon oil
1 pint water                      1/2 lb. sugar

Take one quart of brandy, & halfe a dram of oyle of cinnamon, & a pinte of water, & half[e] a pound of white sugar. boyle ye water & sugar together, & mix ye oyle & sugar together, yt is with a little of ye sugar before you put it to ye rest. then mix them alltogether, & set it by till it be cold. & then bottle it up. (*ibid.*)

---

[1] *i.e.*, place the alembic in a hot water bath, or 'balneo,' to heat it gently. The hay served as padding.

"The diſtilled water [of cinnamon]...comforteth the weake, colde, and feeble ſtomacke, eaſeth the paines and frettings of the guts... maketh ſweete breth, and giueth a moſt pleaſant taſte vnto diuers ſorts of meates..."[1]

*✳✳✳*

## 10. CINAMON WATER – 1609

6 gallons water                6 lbs. cinnamon sticks
2 gallons grain alcohol

Hauing a Copper bodie or Brasse pot that will hold xii gallons, you may well make ii or iii gallons of cinamon water at once.  Put into your body ouernight vi gallons of conduit water, and two gallons of Spirit of wine, or, to saue charge, two gallons of Spirit drawne from Wine lees, Ale, or lowe Wine, six pound of the best and largest Cinamon you can get, or else eight pound of the second sort well bruised, but not beaten into powder:  lute your Lymbeck,[2] and begin with a good fire of wood and coales, til the vessel begin to distill; then moderate your fire, so as your pype may drop apace, and runne trickling into the Receiuer, but blow not at any time.  It helpeth much heerin to keepe the water in the Bucket not too hote, by often change thereof:  it must neuer be so hot, but that you may well endure your finger therein.  Then diuide into quart glasses the Spirit which first ascendeth, and wherein you finde eyther no taste, or verie small taste of the Cinamon, then may you boldly after the Spirit once beginneth to come strong of the Cinamon, draw vntill you haue gotten at the least a gallon in the Receiuer, and then diuide often by halfe pintes and quarters of pints, lest you draw too long: which you shall know by the faint taste and milkie colour, which distilleth to the end: this you must now and then taste in a spoon.  Now when you haue drawne so much as you finde good, you may adde thereunto so much of your Spirit that came before your Cinamon water, as the same will well beare, which you must finde by your taste.  But if your Spirit and your Cinamon be both good, you may of the aforesaid proportion will make vp two gallons, or two gallons and a quart of good Cinamon water.  Heere note, that it is not amisse to obserue which glasse was first filled with the Spirit that ascended, and so of the second, third and fourth:  and when you mixe, begin with the last glasse first, and so with the next, because those haue more taste of the Cinamon than that which came first, and therefore more fit to bee mixed with your Cinamon water.  And if you meane to make but 8 or 9 pintes at once, then begin but with the halfe of this proportion.  Also that spirit which remaineth vnmixed doth serue to make Cinamon water the second time...

(From *Delightes for Ladies*, by Sir Hugh Plat, 1609.)

---

[1] Gerard, p. 1349.

[2] To "lute your Lymbeck" means to seal the connecting joints of the alembic with clay. (ME *lute* from OF *lut* and Latin *lutum*, meaning *potter's clay*.)

1051. *CURAÇOA* – 1829

*The numbers in brackets have been added to separate these two recipes.*

[1]
3 drams orange oil
1 pint grain alcohol
1 lb. sugar syrup

[2]
5 oz. dried bitter orange peel
sugar
1 quart grain alcohol
1 lb. sugar

[1] Infuse three drachms of sweet oil of orange-peel with a pint of rectified spirits and a pound of clarified syrup. [2] *Another way.*– Infuse five ounces of the dry peel of bitter oranges, beat to a paste with a little sugar, in a quart of pure spirit and a pound of clarified sugar. Let the mixture stand for a week in a warm place, and strain it off, first through a jelly-bag, and then patiently through filtering paper.
(From *The Cook and Housewife's Manual: a Practical System of Modern Domestic Cookery and Family Management*, by Mistress Margaret Dods, 1829, p. 456.)

TO MAKE CITRON-WATER,
FROM *BARBADOES* – 1736

1 gallon grain alcohol *or* French brandy
2 lbs. sugar
4 ounces lemon peels
4 ounces lemon *or* orange flowers
*optional:* 1/2 dram musk per 6 gallons liquid

*Distillation.*
From *The Queen's Royal Cookery.*
London, 1713.

...the word Citron in *French* ſignifies Lemon; though we generally in *England* eſteem the large Lemons to be Citrons, and the middle-ſiz'd we call Lemons, and the ſmalleſt of that race is call'd the Lime.
...We muſt take, either of Citron, Lemon, or Orange-Flowers, four Ounces to a Gallon of clean Spirit, or *French*-Brandy; put theſe in the Spirits, with two Pounds of white Sugar-Candy, beaten fine: then take of the beſt Citron-Peels, or Lemon-Peels, ſix Ounces, and let them ſteep in the Spirits till the Liquor is ſtrong enough of every Ingredient; and when that is done, pour it off, through a Sieve. And in ſome places they put about half a Drachm of Musk to ſix Gallons of Liquor...
(From *The Country Housewife and Lady's Director*, by R. Bradley, 1736, pp. 10-11.)

## BRANDIES, LIQUEURS, & DISTILLED WATERS

### L'EAU DE LA VIE – 1829

7 large oranges
1 quart rum *or* French brandy
6 ounces sugar
1/2 pint water
1/4 pint milk
lemon rind
*optional:* perfume, such as musk or ambergris, to taste.

*A Drinking Party,*
1489.

"'...Your mandates obeying, he sends with much glee,
The genuine receipt to make *l'Eau de la Vie.*
Take seven large oranges, and pare them as thin
As a wafer, or, what is much thinner, your skin:
Six ounces of sugar next take, and bear mind,
That the sugar be of the best double-refined.
Clear the sugar in near half a pint of spring-water,
In the neat silver sauce-pan you bought for your daughter.
Then the fourth of a pint, you must fully allow,
Of new milk, made as warm as it comes from the cow.
Put the rinds of the lemons, the milk, and the syrup,
In a jar, with the rum, and give them a stir up.
A full quart of old rum (French brandy is better,
But we ne'er in receipts, should stick close to the letter;)
And then, to your taste, you may add some perfume,
Goa-stone, or whatever you like in its room.
Let it stand thus ten days, but remember to shake it;
And the closer you stop it, the richer you make it.
Then filter through paper, 'twill sparkle and rise,
Be as soft as your lips, and as bright as your eyes.
Last, bottle it up, and believe me, the Vicar
Of E— himself never drank better liquor.
In a word, it excels, by a million of odds,
The nectar your sister presents to the gods!'"
(From *The Cook and Housewife's Manual: a Practical
System of Modern Domestic Cookery and Family Management,*
by Mistress Margaret Dods, 1829, pp. 459-460.)

## 1052. NOYAU – 1829

| | |
|---|---|
| 1 quart brandy *or* grain alcohol | 2 ounces peach, nectarine *or* apricot kernels[1] |
| 1 ounce unpitted French prunes | 2 grains celery seed |
| 1/2 pint water | lemon or bitter orange essence |
| 6 ounces sugar syrup | |

To a quart of pure brandy, or aquavitae, put six ounces of clarified syrup, one ounce of French prunes, with the kernels broken, two ounces of sound peach, nectarine, or, what is better, apricot kernels bruised; a few grains of celery-seed, and a *flavour* of essence of lemon or bitter orange. Infuse for ten days or more, and filter, adding a half-pint of water. (*ibid.*, pp. 456-457.)


## A CORDIAL MINT WATER – 1732

| | |
|---|---|
| 2 lbs. mint leaves | sugar |
| 2 gallons claret wine | saffron |
| 2 lbs. raisins | 2 ounces anise seeds |
| 1/2 lb. licorice root | 2 ounces caraway seeds |

Strip Mint from the stalks, weigh two pounds of the leaves and tops, add two pounds of Raisins of the Sun stoned, of Carraway seeds, and anniseeds of each two ounces and half a pound of Liquorice sliced thin; infuse these in two gallons of good Claret, and distil it in an Alembick or cold Still; let it drop on some fine Sugar through a Bag of Saffron. (From *The Receipt Book of Charles Carter*, 1732.)


## TO MAKE ORANGE-FLOWER BRANDY – 1736

| | |
|---|---|
| 1 gallon French brandy | 1 lb. orange flowers |
| sugar syrup | |

Take a gallon of French Brandy, boil a pound of orange flowers a little while, and put them in, save the water and with that make a syrup to sweeten it. (From *The Compleat Housewife*, by E. Smith, 1736.)

---

[1] CAUTION! (*See Appendix.*)

## [ORANGE FLOWER BRANDY] – 1736

| | |
|---|---|
| 1/2 lb. orange flowers | 1/2 lb. sugar |
| 1 gallon brandy | 1/4 lb. orange peel |

...about half a Pound of them [*orange-flowers*] put into a Gallon of Brandy, with a quarter Pound of Orange-Peel, and half a Pound of double refin'd Loaf-Sugar, makes a very agreeable Cordial; We may let theſe Ingredients infuſe in the Brandy nine or ten days before we pour the Brandy from them. Some chuſe rather to put the Sugar to the Brandy after it is pour'd from the Orange-Flowers.
(From *The Country Housewife and Lady's Director*, by Richard Bradley, 1736, p. 94.)

## BENJAMIN FRANKLIN'S ORANGE SHRUB – c. 1750

| | |
|---|---|
| 1 gallon rum | 2 quarts orange juice |
| 2 lbs. sugar | *optional*: orange peel. |

To a Gallon of Rum two Quarts of Orange Juice and two pound of Sugar – dissolve the Sugar in the Juice before you mix it with the Rum – put all together in a Cask & shake it well – let it stand 3– or 4–Weeks & it will be very fine & fit for Bottling – when you have Bottled off the fine pass the thick thro' a Philtring paper put into a Funnell – that not a drop may be lost. To obtain the flavour of the Orange Peel paire a few Oranges & put it in Rum for twelve hours – & put that Rum into the Cask with the other – For Punch thought better without the Peel.
(From *The Franklin Papers*, c. 1750.)

## ORANGE SHRUB – c. 1788

| | |
|---|---|
| 100 lbs. sugar | 6 egg whites |
| 30 gallons Jamaica rum | 15 gallons strained orange juice |
| 20 gallons water | |

Break a hundred pounds of loaf sugar in small pieces, put it into twenty gallons of water, boil it till the sugar is melted, skim it well, and put it in a tub to cool; when cold, put it into a cask, with thirty gallons of good Jamaica Rum, and fifteen gallons of orange juice (mind to strain all the seeds out of the juice), mix them well together, then beat up the whites of six eggs very well, stir them well in, let it stand a week to fine, and then draw it off for use. By the same rules you may make any quantity you want.
(From *The New Art of Cookery*, c. 1788.)

## RASPBERRY BRANDY – 1807

| | |
|---|---|
| 1 pint raspberry juice | 1/2 lb. sugar |
| 1 pint brandy | |

Pick fine dry fruit, put into a stone jar, and the jar into a kettle of water, or on a hot hearth, till the juice will run; strain, and to every pint add half a pound of sugar, give one boil, and skim it; when cold, put equal quantities of juice and brandy, shake well, and bottle. Some people prefer it stronger of the brandy.
(From *A New System of Domestic Cookery, etc.*, 1807.)

## ROSE BRANDY – 1856

| | |
|---|---|
| French brandy | 2+ pitchersful trimmed rose petals |

Gather leaves from fragrant roses without bruising, fill a pitcher with them, and cover them with French Brandy; next day, pour off the brandy, take out the leaves, and fill the pitcher with fresh ones, and return the brandy; do this till it is strongly impregnated, then bottle it; keep the pitcher closely covered during the process. It is better than distilled rose water for cakes, & c.
(From *The Virginia Housewife: or, Methodical Cook*, by Mrs. Randolph, 1856.)

## # 281  A CORDIALL WATER – c. 1550 to 1625

| | |
|---|---|
| borage flowers | bugloss flowers |
| Sack wine | 1 grain ambergris |
| claret wine | 2 ounces sugar per 1 pint liquid |

Take burrage & buglos flowers, as many as will [gap in MS] a still, & put thereto as much sack & clare[t] as will wet them well. & to every pinte of [*cordial*] water, you must put 2 ounces of white sugar candie & one grayne of ambergreece, finely beaten. ye sugar candy must be put into ye glass bottles & let ye water distill upon it very gently.
(From *Martha Washington's Booke of Cookery*, ed. by Karen Hess.)

## A RECEIPT FROM *BARBADOES*, TO MAKE RUM; WHICH PROVES VERY GOOD – 1736

| | |
|---|---|
| 2 to 2 1/4 gallons molasses | fennel seeds |
| 15 3/4 to 16 gallons water | *optional*: musk; substitute anise seeds for the fennel. |

In *Barbadoes* the Rum is made of the Scum and Offal of the Sugar, of which they put one ninth part, or eighth part, to common Water, about eighteen Gallons, all together, in a wooden open Veſſel or Tub; cover this with dry Leaves of Palm, or for want of them, with the Leaves of *Platanus* or the Leaves of Fern in *England*, or the Parts or Leaves which Flagg-Brooms are made of.[1] Let this remain for nine Days, till it changes of a clean yellow Colour, and it will be then fit to diſtil; then put it into an Alembic, and you will have what we call the Low-Wines. A Day or two after diſtil it again, and in the Cap of the Still, hang a ſmall muſlin Bag of ſweet Fennel-Seeds, and the Spirit will be of a fine Flavour. Some will uſe Anniſeed in the Bag, and ſome uſe a little Musk with the ſweet Fennel-Seeds, or elſe diſtil the Spirit twice, *viz*. once with the ſweet Fennel-Seeds, and the next with a little Musk.
(From *The Country Housewife and Lady's Director*, by R. Bradley, 1736, II, p. 9.)


## 9. AQUA BATH OR IRISH AQUA VITAE – 1609

| | |
|---|---|
| 1 gallon Aqua composita[2] | 2 ounces licorice root |
| 2 ounces anise seeds | 5 or 6 spoonsful molasses |
| *optional*: dates and raisins. | |

To euery gallon of good Aqua composita, put two ounces of chosen liquorice bruised, and cut into small peeces, but first cleansed from all his filth, and two ounces of Annisseeds that are cleane and bruised: let them macerate five or sixe daies in a woodden vessell, stopping the same close, and then draw off as much as will runne cleere, dissoluing in that cleere Aqua vitae five or sixe spoonefuls of the best Malassoes you can get (Spanish Cute, if you can get it, is thought better than Malassoes) then put this into another vessell: and after three or foure daies (the more the better) when the liquor hath fined it selfe, you may vse the same, some adde Dates and Raisins of the Sun to this receipt; those grounds which remaine you may redistil, and make more Aqua composita of them, and of that Aqua composita you may make more Vsque-bath.
(From *Delightes for Ladies*, by Sir Hugh Plat, 1609.)

---

[1] The palm and plantain leaves, bracken fronds, and broom leaves are merely used to cover the liquid loosely. A cheesecloth or muslin will serve as well.

[2] *See p. 223.*

# # 282 TO MAKE THE LORD VERNEYS VSQUEBATH – c. 1550 to 1625

| | |
|---|---|
| 2 quarts grain alcohol | licorice root |
| 1 lb. raisins | 6 dates |
| 10 figs | 2 ounces cinnamon sticks |

To a pottle of aquevity, take a pound of raysons of yᵉ sun; & a pritty quantety of licorish, scraped & slyced; 6 dates, & 10 figgs slyced; two ounces of cinnamon, A little bruised. let all these lie in yᵉ Aquavite 10 dayes, stir it every day 2 or 3 times, and then strayne it & bottle it for your use.
(From *Martha Washington's Booke of Cookery*, ed. by Karen Hess.)

# # 283 TO MAKE VSQUEBATH – c. 1550 to 1625

| | |
|---|---|
| 1 quart grain alcohol | caraway seeds |
| 1 ounce licorice root | 1 ounce cinnamon sticks |
| 4 dates | 4 figs |
| 1 lb. raisins | |

Put in A pound of raysons of yᵉ sun, stoned & slyced, into a quart of aquavite. & slyce in an ounce of licorish, & an ounce of cinnamon, 4 dates, as many figgs slyced, A few carraway seeds bruised; all these must ly in steep 10 dayes, & be stired 3 or 4 times a day. then strayne it & put it into glasses for yʳ use. (*ibid.*)

# TO MAKE GREEN *UʃQUEBAUGH* – 1736

| | |
|---|---|
| 1 gallon French brandy | 1 ounce anise seeds |
| 1 lb. raisins | 1 ounce fennel seeds |
| 1 quart white wine | 2 drams coriander seeds |
| licorice root soaked in grain alcohol | 1 dram spirit of saffron |
| spinach juice for color | 1 lb. sugar per gallon liquid |

To every Gallon of *French*-Brandy put one Ounce of Anniʃeeds, and another of ʃweet Fennel-Seeds, two Drachms of Coriander-Seeds. Let theʃe infuʃe nine Days, then take of the Spirit of Saffron one Drachm, diʃtil'd from Spirit of Wine, mix with the reʃt; infuʃe during this time ʃome Liquorice ʃliced in Spirits, one Pound of Raiʃins of the Sun, and filter it; put then a Quart of pure White-Wine to a Gallon of the Liquor, and when all is mix'd together, take the Juice of Spinach boil'd, enough to colour it; but do not put the Spinach Juice into the Liquor till it is cold. To this put one Pound of white Sugar candied, finely powder'd, to a Gallon of Liquor.
(From *The Country Housewife and Lady's Director*, by R. Bradley, 1736, II, p. 13.)

TO MAKE *IRISH UſQUEBAUGH*; from Lord Capell's Receipt, when he was Lord Lieutenant of *Ireland* – 1736

| | |
|---|---|
| 1+ gallon French brandy | 1 ounce licorice root |
| 1 lb. seedless raisins | 1 ounce fennel seeds |
| 1/4 lb. figs | 1 ounce anise seeds |
| 1/2 ounce saffron | 2 drams coriander seed |
| 1 dram musk | |

To every Gallon of *French*-Brandy, put one Ounce of Liquorice ſliced, one Ounce of ſweet Fennel-Seeds, one Ounce of Anniſeeds, one Pound of Raiſins of the Sun ſplit and ſtoned, a quarter of a Pound of Figs ſplit, two Drachms of Coriander-Seeds; let theſe infuſe about eight or nine Days, and pour the Liquor clear off, then add half an Ounce of Saffron, in a Bag, for a Day or two, and when that is out, put in a Drachm of Musk. If when this Compoſition is made, it ſeems to be too high a Cordial for the Stomach, put to it more Brandy, till you reduce it to the Temper you like. This is the ſame Receipt King *William* had when he was in *Ireland*.
(From *The Country Housewife and Lady's Director*, by R. Bradley, 1736, II, p. 12.)

## 1065. USQUEBAUGH, THE IRISH CORDIAL – 1829

*The spinach has been included here, and in Bradley's recipe, to serve as green food coloring. If you wish to make the Aqua bath yellow instead, substitute saffron for the spinach.*

| | |
|---|---|
| 2 quarts brandy or whisky | sugar lumps |
| 1/2 ounce whole nutmegs | 1/4 ounce cloves |
| 1/4 ounce cardamom | peel of 1 Seville orange |
| 1 lb. raisins | saffron *or* spinach juice |
| 1/2 lb. brown sugar | |

To two quarts of the best brandy, or whisky without a smoky taste, put a pound of stoned raisins, a half-ounce of nutmegs, a quarter-ounce of cloves, the same quantity of cardamoms, all bruised in a mortar; the rind of a Seville orange, rubbed off on lumps of sugar, a little tincture of saffron, and a half-pound of brown candy-sugar. Shake the infusion every day for a fortnight, and filter it for use. –*Obs.* Not a drop of water must be put to Irish cordial. It is sometimes tinged of a fine green with the juice of spinage, instead of the saffron tint, from which it takes the name (as we conjecture) of usquebeæ or *yellow-water*.
(From *The Cook and Housewife's Manual*, by Mistress Margaret Dods, 1829, p. 459.)

## 8. D. STEUENS  AQUA COMPOSITA – 1609

*The recipe for Doctor Steven's Cordial Water, or Aqua composita, was very popular and was reprinted many times with many variations. Aqua composita was originally intended to be a health tonic – most of the medicinal herbs and seeds are, or have been, used as digestive aids.*

1 gallon Gascony wine

<u>1 dram each</u>:  anise seeds; caraway seeds; cinnamon sticks; fennel seeds; galingale; ginger root; grains of paradise; whole nutmegs.

<u>1 handful each</u>:  chamomile; lavender; mint; pellitory; red rose petals; rosemary; sage; thyme; mother of thyme.

Take a gallon of Gascoin wine of Ginger, Galingale, Cinamon, Nutmegs and graines, Anniseeds, Fennell seeds, and Carroway seeds, of each a dram; of Sage, Mints, red Roses, Thyme, Pellitory, Rosmary, wild Thyme, Camomil, Lauender, of each a handfull:  bray the spices small, and bruise the herbs, letting them macerate 12 houres, stirring it now & then, then distil by a Limbecke of pewter, keeping the first cleare water that commeth, by it selfe, and so likewise the second. You shall draw much about a pint of the better sort from euery gallon of wine.
(From *Delightes for Ladies*, by Sir Hugh Plat, 1609.)

## #275  TO MAKE DOCTOR STEEPHENS HIS CORDIALL WATER – c. 1550 to 1625

1 gallon Gascony wine

<u>1 dram each</u>:  anise seeds; caraway seeds; cinnamon sticks; cloves; fennel seeds; galingale; ginger root; grains of paradise; whole nutmegs.

<u>1 handful each</u>:  hyssop; lavender; mint; pellitory of the wall; red rose petals; rosemary; sage; thyme; mother of thyme.

Take a gallon of y$^e$ best gascoyne wine; then take cloves, ginger, gallinggall, cinnamon, & nutmeggs, graynes, anny seeds, fennell seeds, carraway seeds, of each a dram.  then take wild time, lavender, sage, mints, hysope, red roses, garden time, pellitory of y$^e$ wall, & rosemary, of each one handfull.  bray the hearbs small, & stamp y$^e$ spices alltogether very small & put all into your wine & cover it close for 12 hours, except when you stir it, which must be often.  distill it in A limbeck, & keep y$^e$ first water by it selfe, it beeing y$^e$ strongest.  but of y$^e$ second sort, you may drink A greater quantety.
(From *Martha Washington's Booke of Cookery*, ed. by Karen Hess.)

## 7. AQUA RUBEA – 1609

| | |
|---|---|
| 1 gallon Aqua composita[1] | 6 grains musk |
| 1 lb. granulated sugar | 1 dram turnsole[2] |
| 1 ounce cinnamon sticks | 1 ounce ginger root |

Take of Musk six grains: of Cinamon and Ginger, of each one ounce; white sugar-candy, one pound: powder the Sugar, & bruise the spices grossly: binde them vp in a clean linnen cloth, and put them to infuse in a gallon of Aqua composita, in a glasse close stopt twenty foure hours, shaking them together diuers times: then put thereto of Turnsole one dramme: suffer it to stand one houre, and then shake all together: then, if the colour like you after it is settled, poure the cleerest forth into another glasse: but if you will haue it deeper coloured, suffer it to worke longer vpon the Turnsole.
(From *Delightes for Ladies*, by Sir Hugh Plat, 1609.)

✳✳✳

"...the Carmani, ...'eager to prove their friendship in their drinking bouts, open the veins of the forehead, and mixing the blood which streams down in their wine, they imbibe it, in the belief that to taste each other's blood is the highest proof of friendship. After this peculiar mode of drinking the wine, they smear the head with perfume, preferably of rose, but failing that, of quince, in order to repel the effects of the draught and not be injured by the fumes from the wine; if quince perfume is not at hand, they use orris or nard.'"[3]

✳✳✳

## ROMAN VERMOUTH (ABSINTHIUM ROMANUM) – c. 100 B.C. to 300 A.D.

| | |
|---|---|
| 18 quarts wine | 1 Theban ounce wormwood[2] |
| 3 scruples saffron | 6 scruples mastic |
| 3 scruples spikenard leaves[4] | 3 scruples costmary leaves |

Roman vermouth [or Absinth] is made thus: according to the recipe of Camerinum you need wormwood from Santo for Roman vermouth or, as a substitute, wormwood from the Pontus cleaned and crushed, 1 Theban ounce of it, 6 scruples of mastich, 3 each of [nard] leaves, costmary and saffron and 18 quarts of any kind of mild wine. [Filter cold] charcoal is not required because of the bitterness.
(From *Apicius, Cookery and Dining in Imperial Rome*, tr. by J. D. Vehling, p. 46.)

---

[1] (*See p. 223.*)
[2] CAUTION! (*See Appendix.*)
[3] Poseidonius, quoted in Athenaeus, Book II, p. 199.
[4] Nard = Spikenard, *Nardostachys jatamansi*. (*See Appendix.*)

## WORMWOOD BRANDY – 1772

| | |
|---|---|
| 1 pint brandy | 1 ounce wormwood flowers[1] |

Put an ounce of these flowers with a pint of Brandy and let it stand six weeks. There will be a tincture produced of which a tablespoon should be taken in half a gill of water. (From *The British Herbal*, by Sir John Hill, 1772.)

## CREME d'ABSINTHE, BY M. BEAUVILLIERS' RECEIPT – 1829

| | |
|---|---|
| 12 pints French brandy | 1/4 ounce cinnamon |
| 7 pints water | 1 dram mace |
| 1 lb. sugar | 1 handful fresh *or* 1/2 ounce dried wormwood[1] |

Take in the proportions of twelve pints (old measure) of French brandy and two of water; a small handful of fresh wormwood, or a large half-ounce of the dried herb, a quarter-ounce of cinnamon, and a drachm of mace. Infuse for some days, and, if convenient, distil the compound. If not, infuse in a warm place for a fortnight, strain the liquor, and add a pound of sugar made into clear syrup, with five pints of water... (From *The Cook and Housewife's Manual*, by M. Dods, 1829, p. 458.)

*Danse Macabre.*
From the *Liber chronicorum*,
by Hartmann Schedel.

---

[1] CAUTION! Wormwood was formerly used to make the licorice-flavored liqueur *absinthe*. Wormwood contains *thujone*, which can cause brain damage; it is addictive, with habitual use also causing vomiting, tremors, vertigo, hallucinations, violent behavior and convulsions. *Absinthe* was responsible for many deaths and has been banned in several countries since the turn of the century. A wormwood-free version of *absinthe*, called *pastis*, is now popular in France.

# CIDER & PERRY

\*\*\*\*\*\*\*

Wine made of the iuice of Peares
called in Engliſh Perry,
is ſoluble, purgeth thoſe that are not accuſtomed to drinke thereof;
notwithſtanding it is as wholeſome a drinke being taken in ſmall
quantitie as wine; it comforteth and warmeth the ſtomacke, and
cauſeth good digeſtion.

(Gerard, p. 1270.)

An apple mill and cider press, 1780.

Some ſorts are beſt to make Cider of, as in the Weſt Countrey of England in great quantities, yea many Hogſheads and Tunnes full are made, eſpecially to bee carried to the Sea in long voyages, and is found by experience of excellent vſe, to mix with water for beuerage. It is vſually ſeene that thoſe fruits that are neither fit to eate raw, roaſted, nor baked, are fitteſt for Cider, and make the beſt.[1]

✷✷✷

# # 109  SIR PAUL NEALE'S WAY OF MAKING CIDER – 1669

*These first three recipes are for sweet, unfermented cider. Although Sir Paul, Mrs. Glass, and Mr. Bemiss were quite determined that their cider not 'work,' thereby staying 'sweet,' all cider will work, given the slightest opportunity. This is due to the presence of naturally occurring yeast on the apples themselves. When the apples are pressed for cider, the yeast washes into the liquid and happily sets to work. The only way to stop the process is by pasteurization (chilling will slow it somewhat, but cider yeast seems to like colder temperatures than mead yeast). You may use these recipes as the basis for the following fermented cider recipes.*

The best Apples make the best Cider, as Pear-mains, Pippins, Golden-pippins, and the like. Codlings make the finest Cider of all. They must be ripe, when you make Cider of them: and is in prime in the Summer season, when no other Cider is good. But lasteth not long, not beyond Autumn. The foundation of making perfect Cyder consisteth in not having it work much, scarce ever at all; but at least, no second time; which Ordinary Cider doth often, upon change of weather, and upon motion: and upon every working it grows harder. Do then thus:

Choose good Apples. Red streaks are the best for Cider to keep; Ginet-moils the next, then Pippins. Let them lie about three weeks, after they are gathered; Then stamp and strain them in the Ordinary way, into a woodden fat *[vat]* that hath a spigot three or four fingers breadth above the bottom. Cover the fat with some hair or sackcloth, to secure it from any thing to fall in, and to keep in some of the Spirits, so to preserve it from dying; but not so much as to make it ferment. When the juyce hath been there twelve hours, draw it by the spigot (the fat inclining that way, as if it were a little tilted) into a barrel; which must not be full by about two fingers. Leave the bung open for the Air to come in, upon a superficies, all along the barrel, to hinder it from fermenting; but not so large a superficies as to endanger dying, by the airs depredating too many spirits from it.

The drift in both these settlings is, that the grosser parts consisting of the substance of the Apple, may settle to the bottom, and be severed from the Liquor; for it is that, which maketh it work again (upon motion or change of weather) and spoils it. After twenty four hours draw of it, to see if it be clear, by the settling of all dregs, above

---

[1] Parkinson, p. 589.

which your spigot must be. If it be not clear enough, draw it from the thick dregs into another vessel, and let it settle there twenty four hours. This vessel must be less then the first, because you draw not all out of the first. If then it should not be clear enough, draw it into a third, yet lesser than the second; but usually it is at the first. When it is clear enough draw it into bottles, filling them within two fingers, which stop close. After two or three days visit them; that if there be a danger of their working (which would break the bottles) you may take out the stopples, and let them stand open for half a quarter of an hour. Then stop them close, and they are secure for ever after. In cold freesing weather, set them upon Hay, and cover them over with Hay or Straw. In open weather in Winter transpose them to another part of the Cellar to stand upon the bare ground or pavement. In hot weather set them in sand. The Cider of the Apples of the last season, as Pippins, not Peermains, nor codlings, will last till the Summer grow hot. Though this never work, 'tis not of the Nature of Strummed Wine; because the naughty dregs are not left in it.
(From *The Closet ...Opened*, 1669.)

HOW TO MAKE CYDER – 1796

apples                                        1 ounce isinglass per quart cider

After all your apples are bruiſed, take half of your quantity and ſqueeze them; and the juice you preſs from them, pour upon the others half bruiſed, but not ſqueezed, in a tub for the purpoſe, having a tap at the bottom; let the juice remain upon the apples three or four days; then pull out your tap, and let your juice run into ſome other veſſel ſet under the tub to receive it; and if it runs thick, as at the firſt it will, pour it upon the apples again, till you ſee it run clear; and as you have a quantity, put it into your veſſel, but do not force the cyder, but let it drop as long as it will of its own accord; having done this, after you perceive that the ſides begin to work, take a quantity of iſinglaſs (an ounce will ſerve forty gallons), infuſe this in ſome of the cyder till it be diſſolved; put to an ounce of iſinglaſs a quart of cyder, and when it is ſo diſſolved, pour it into the veſſel, and ſtop it cloſe for two days, or ſomething more; then draw off the cyder into another veſſel: this do ſo often till you perceive your cyder to be free from all manner of ſediment that may make it ferment and fret itſelf: after Chriſtmas you may boil it. You may, by pouring water on the apples and preſſing them, make a pretty ſmall cyder: if it be thick and muddy, by uſing iſinglaſs, you may make it as clear as the reſt; you muſt diſſolve the iſinglaſs over the fire till it be jelly.
(From *The Art of Cookery Made Plain and Easy*, v. 8, by Mrs. Glasse, 1796, p. 350.)

## 83th. GOOD CIDER AS EASILY MADE AS BAD. – 1815

To make cider of early or late fruit, that will keep a length of time, without the trouble of frequent drawing off – Take the largest cask you have on your farm, from a barrel upwards; put a few sticks in the bottom, in the manner that house-wives set a lye cask, so as to raise a vacancy of two or three inches from the bottom of the cask; then lay over these sticks either a clean old blanket, or if that be not at hand, a quantity of swindling flax, so as to make a coat of about a quarter of an inch thick, then put in so much cleaned washed sand, from a beach or road, as will cover about six or eight inches in depth of your vessel; pass all your cider from the press through a table cloth, suspended by the corners, which will take out the pummice; and pour the liquor gently upon the sand, through which it must be suffered to filter gradually, and as it runs off by a tap inserted in your vessel, in the vacancy made by the sticks at the bottom, it will be found by this easy method, as clear cider can be expected by the most laborious process of refining; and all the mucilaginous matter, which causes the fermentation and souring of cider, will be separated so as to prevent that disagreeable consequence.
(From *The Dyer's Companion*, by Elijah Bemiss, 1815, p. 299.)

## # 267 TO MAKE SYDER – c. 1550 to 1625

apples                                            unspecified spices

Beat & squeese your apples, & let them sta[nd] 4 dayes at y$^e$ least to settle. then tun y$^e$ liquor up into a clean vessell, but close it not up [till] it hath done working, & then hang A little ha[*gap in MS*] bagg full of spices in ye midst of ye vessill. then stop it up very close, & at 6 months end, draw it out, & bottle some of it, & drink y$^e$ rest at y$^r$ pleasure.
(From *Martha Washington's Booke of Cookery*, ed. by Karen Hess, 1981.)

## # 107 TO MAKE CIDER – 1669

1 peck plus 3 measures [?] apples          1 barrel water

Take a Peck of Apples, and slice them, and boil them in a barrel of water, till the third part be wasted; Then cool your water as you do for wort, and when it is cold, you must pour the water upon three measures of grown Apples. Then draw forth the water at a tap three or four times a day, for three days together. Then press out the Liquor, and Tun it up; when it hath done working, then stop it up close.
(From *The Closet ...Opened*, 1669.)

# # 108  A VERY PLEASANT DRINK OF APPLES – 1669

*It may be necessary to add yeast to this and several of the following recipes. This is because we are instructed to boil the apples, thereby killing off all the naturally occurring yeast.*

50 pippin apples                              3 gallons water
1 1/2 lbs. sugar

Take about fifty Pippins; quarter and core them, without paring them: for the paring is the Cordialest part of them. Therefore onely wipe or wash them well, and pick away the black excrescence at the top; and be sure to leave out all the seeds, which are hot. You may cut them (after all the superfluities are taken away) into thinner slices, if you please. Put three Gallons of Fountain water to them in a great Pipkin, and let them boil, till the Apples become clear and transparent; which is a sign, they are perfectly tender, and will be in a good half hour, or a little more. Then with your Ladle break them into Mash and Pulpe, incorporated with the water; letting all boil half an hour longer, that the water may draw into it self all the vertue of the Apples. Then put to them a pound and a half of pure dubble refined Sugar in powder, which will soon dissolve in that hot Liquor. Then pour it into an Hippocras bag, and let it run through it two or three times, to be very clear. Then put it up into bottles; and after a little time, it will be a most pleasant, quick, cooling, smoothing drink...
(From *The Closet ...Opened*, 1669.)

# # 110  DOCTOR HARVEY'S PLEASANT WATER-CIDER, WHEREOF HE USED TO DRINK MUCH, MAKING IT HIS ORDINARY DRINK – 1669

1 bushel pippin apples                        12 gallons water
5 lbs. brown sugar                            1 pint ale yeast

Take one Bushel of Pippins, cut them into slices with the Parings and Cores; boil them in twelve Gallons of water, till the goodness of them be in the water; and that consumed about three Gallons. Then put it into an Hypocras-bag, made of Cotton; and when it is clear run out, and almost cold, sweeten it with five pound of Brown-sugar, and put a pint of Ale-yest to it, and set it a working two nights and days: Then skim off the yest clean, and put it into bottles, and let it stand two or three days, till the yest fall dead at the top: Then take it off clean with a knife, and fill it up a little within the neck (that is to say, that a little about a fingers breadth of the neck be empty, between the superficies of the Liquor, and the bottom of the stopple) and then stop them up and tye them, or else it will drive out the Corks. Within a fortnight you may drink of it. It will keep five or six weeks. (*ibid.*)

# #113 APPLE DRINK WITH SUGAR, HONEY, &c – 1669

apples, sliced        water
sugar                 lemon peel
rosemary

A very pleasant drink is made of Apples, thus; Boil sliced Apples in water, to make the water strong of Apples, as when you make to drink it for coolness and pleasure. Sweeten it with Sugar to your tast, such a quantity of sliced Apples, as would make so much water strong enough of Apples; and then bottle it up close for three or four months. There will come a thick mother at the top, which being taken off, all the rest will be very clear, and quick and pleasant to the taste, beyond any Cider. It will be the better to most taste, if you put a very little Rosemary into the liquor, when you boil it, and a little Limon-peel into each bottle, when you bottle it up. (*ibid.*)

# #92 A WAY TOO MAKE CYDOR – c. 1674

1 barrel apple cider
1 quart hulled wheat
4 lbs. raisins
1/2 ounce cinnamon
1/2 ounce mace
1/4 ounce whole nutmegs
2 ounces sulfur[1]

Take Brimston 2 oz malego Resone 4 pound mace Cinomon of each 1/2 an oz: of nutmegs a 1/4 of an oz: with a quart of wheat only the huske beat of as for furmaty all these hang in a barell of cydor –
(From *Penn Family Recipes, etc.*, c. 1674.)

*An Apple Grinder and a Cider Press.*
From *A Treatise of Cider*.
London, 1691.

---

[1] CAUTION! Sulfur may cause allergic reactions.

## 85TH. A RECEIPT TO MAKE AN EXCELLENT AMERICAN WINE – 1815

*The sand mixed with egg whites is being used here to fine the cider.*

| | |
|---|---|
| 1 barrel apple cider | honeycomb |
| 1 pint clean sand | honey |
| 8 egg whites | 1 gallon distilled alcohol made from cider |

...I put a quantity of the comb, from which the honey had been drained, into a tub to which I added a barrel of cider immediately from the press: This mixture was well stirred, and left to soak for one night. It was then strained, before a fermentation had taken place; and honey was added until the strength of the liquor was sufficient to bear an egg. It was then put into a barrel; and after the fermentation commenced, the cask was filled every day, for three or four days, that the filth might work out the bung hole. When the fermentation moderated, I put the bung in loosely, lest stopping it tight might cause the cask to burst. At the end of five or six weeks the liquor was drawn off into a tub, and the white of eight eggs, well beat up, with a pint of clean sand, were put into it. – I then added a gallon of cider spirit; and after mixing the whole together, I returned it into the cask, which was well cleansed, bunged it tight and placed it in a proper situation for racking off when fine. In the month of April following, I drew it off into kegs, for use; and found it equal, in my opinion, to almost any foreign wine... I am persuaded, that by using the clean honey, instead of the comb, ...an improvement might be made...
(From *The Dyer's Companion*, by Elijah Bemiss, 1815, p. 300.)

## [*APPLE*] CIDER WINE – 1838

| | |
|---|---|
| cider | honey |

Take sweet cider immediately from the press. Strain it through a flannel bag into a tub, and stir into it as much honey as will make it strong enough to bear up an egg. Then boil and skim it, and when the scum ceases to rise, strain it again. When cool, put it into a cask, and set it in a cool cellar till spring. Then bottle it off; and when ripe, it will be found a very pleasant beverage. The cider must be of the very best quality, made entirely from good sound apples.
(From *Seventy-five Receipts for Pastry, Cakes, and Sweetmeats*, by Miss Leslie, 1838.)

"Perry is made after the same manner as cider, only from pears, which must be quite dry. The best pears for this purpose are such as are least fit for eating, and the redder they are the better."[1]

*A Cider Press.*
Detail from *Systima Agriculturae, or the Mistery of Husbandry, etc.*, 1694.

## OF MAKING PERRY OR CYDER - 1615

*The second paragraph of this recipe includes frugal directions to make a weaker perry or cider using the leftover pressings from the first batch.*

As for the making Perrie and Cider which are drinks much vſed in the weſt parts, and other Countries well ſtored with fruit in this kingdome; you ſhal know that your Perry is made of Peares only, and your Cider of Apples; and for the manner of making therof it is done after one faſhion, that is to ſay after your Peares or Apples are well pickt from ſtalkes, rottenneſſe and all manner of other filth, you ſhall put them in the preſſe mill which is made with a mil-ſtone running round in a circle, vnder which you ſhall cruſh your Peares or Apples, and then ſtraining them through a bagge of haire cloth, tunne vp the ſame after it hath beene a little ſetled into Hogſ-heads, Barrels and other cloſe veſſels.

Now after you haue preſt all you ſhall ſaue that which is within the haire cloth bagge, and putting it into ſeuerall veſſels, put a pretty quantitie of water thereunto, and after it hath ſtood a day or two, and hath been well ſtirred together, preſſe it ouer alſo againe, for this will make a ſmall perrie or cider, and muſt be ſpent firſt Now of your beſt ſider that which you make of your ſummer or ſweet fruite, you ſhall call ſummer or ſweet cider or perrie, and that you ſhall ſpende firſt alſo; and that which you make of the winter and hard fruite, you ſhall call winter and ſowre cider, or perry; and that you ſhall ſpend laſt for it will endure the longeſt.

(From *The English Huſ-wife, etc.*, by Gervase Markham, 1615, pp. 124-125.)

---

[1] Mackenzie, 1829.

# HYPOCRAS

**\*\*\*\*\*\*\***

...Soone after that, this hastif Januarie
Wolde go to bedde, he wolde no lenger tarye.
He drynketh ypocras, clarree, and vernage
Of spices hoote, t'encreessen his corage...
("The Merchant's Tale," by Geoffrey Chaucer.)

# 217.  HIPPOCRAS – c. 1375

*The following recipes for hippocras (or hypocras, ypocras, ipocras, etc.), a spiced wine drink named after Hippocrates, can be divided into three types, although this has not been done here. These are: red wine and spices; white wine and spices; and those which call for milk or cream in addition to wine and spices.*

8 ounces sugar
1 quart wine
1/2 ounce spice mixture

Spice mixture:
4 ounces cinnamon
1 ounce Mecca ginger
1/12 ounce nutmeg
1 ounce grains of paradise
2 ounces cassia flowers[1]
1/12 ounce galingale

Take four ounces of very fine cinnamon, 2 ounces of fine cassia flowers, an ounce of selected Mecca ginger, an ounce of grains of paradise, and a sixth [of an ounce] of nutmeg and galingale combined. Crush them all together. Take a good half ounce of this powder and eight ounces of sugar [(which thus makes Sweet Powder)], and mix it with a quart of wine.
(From *Le Viandier de Taillevent*, c. 1375, tr. by J. Prescott, 1989, p. 68.)

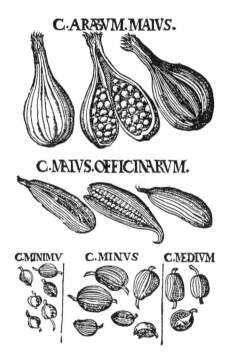

*Cardomomi genera.*
The kindes, or forts of Graines.

C. ARÆVM. MAIVS.

C. MAIVS. OFFICINARVM.

C.MINIMV    C.MINVS    C.MEDIVM

*Grains of Paradise.*
From Gerard's *Herball*, 1597.

---

[1] Perhaps this should read 'flour,' i.e. 'powder,' of cassia?

PUR FAIT YPOCRAS [*Id eſt, Pour faire Ypocras*] – 1390

*The 1780 typeface reprint of the 1390 manuscript contains a great many smudges, shorthand marks, and editorial notes, which have been added here in brackets. The marks [–], ['], and [~], appear above the final letter of each word so noted. [–] appears to be a pronunciation note, rather than a letter; it appears elsewhere above the final 'n' in 'saffron,' 'venison,' 'capon,' 'ayren,' etc. ['] and [~] should probably be read as 'e' and 'r,' respectively. As this recipe is so difficult to read, a 'best guess' translation has been appended. The wine has been taken for granted in this recipe.*

3 ounces cinnamon sticks
3 ounces ginger
long pepper
marjoram
cloves
2 ounces cinnamon powder

1 denier's worth spikenard
galingale
whole nutmegs
5 pennyweights cardamom
clove gilliflowers
2 ounces grains of paradise

**Treys Unces de canell.** [dot, smudge] **iij unces de gyngen**['], **ſpykenard de Spayn le pays dun dener**['][*le poys d'un Denier*]. **garyngale. clowes, gylofre. pocur**['] **long** [*poivre long*], **noiez mugadez** [*muguette, nutmegs*]. **maziozame** [*marjoram*] **cardemonij** [*cardamones*] **de cheſcun**[–] **i. qrt'**['] **douce** [*d'once, 5 penny weights*] **grayne** [smudge][*dele*] **de paradys flo**[~] **de queynel** [*canell?*] **de cheſcun**[–] **dí** [*dj*] **unce de tout**[']. **ſoit fait powdo**[~] [smudge]**c.**
(From *The Forme of Cury*, 1390, reprinted 1780.)

'Best Guess' Translation:
Three ounces of cinnamon. 3 ounces of ginger. A denier's worth of spikenard of Spain. Galingale. Cloves. Gilliflowers. Long pepper. Nutmegs. Marjoram. Cardamom of chescun, 5 pennyweights. Grains of paradise, [and] flour of cinnamon of chescun two ounces of each, whether or not, in fact, they are powdered. Etc.

*Pressing Sugarcanes.*
From *Historia Naturalis Brasiliae.*
Leyden, 1648.

## HIPPOCRAS – c. 1395

*The numbers in brackets have been added to differentiate these two recipes.*

[1]
<u>Spice mixture</u>:

| | |
|---|---|
| 1 ounce ginger root | 1/8 measure cinnamon powder |
| 1 ounce grains of paradise | 1/12 measure nutmeg powder |
| 1/12 measure galingale powder | 1/4 measure cinnamon sticks |

<u>Hippocras</u>:

| | |
|---|---|
| 1/2 ounce spice mixture | 1/2 measure sugar |
| 1 quart wine | |

To make powdered hippocras, take a quarter of very fine cinnamon selected by tasting it, and a half a quarter of fine flour of cinnamon, an ounce of selected string ginger (*gingembre de mesche*), fine and white, and an ounce of grain [of Paradise,] a sixth of nutmegs and galingale together, and bray them all together. And when you would make your hippocras, take a good half ounce of this powder and two quarters of sugar and mix them with a quart of wine, by Paris measure. And *note* that the powder and the sugar mixed together is [hight] *the Duke's powder.*[1]

[2]

| | |
|---|---|
| 5 drams cinnamon sticks | 3 drams ginger root, pared |
| 1 1/8 lb. sugar | red wine |

<u>1 1/4 drams of a mixture made of the following (*see text*)</u>:  clove powder, cardamom powder, mace powder, galingale powder, nutmeg powder, spikenard powder.

For a quart or a quarter of hippocras by the measure of Béziers, Carcassonne or Montpellier, take five drams of fine cinnamon, selected and peeled; white ginger selected and pared 3 drams; of cloves, cardamom, mace, galingale, nutmegs, nard, altogether a dram and a quarter, most of the first and less of each of the others in order. Let a powder be made thereof, and with it put a pound and a half a quarter (by the heavy weight) of lump sugar, brayed and mingled with the aforesaid spices; and let wine and sugar be set and melted on a dish on the fire, and mixed therewith; then put it in the strainer, and strain it until it runs clear red. *Note*, that the sugar and the cinnamon ought to predominate.
(From *Le Menagier de Paris*, c. 1395.)

---
[1] "is [called] the Duke's powder."

237

*HYPOCRAS*

...He sente hire pyment, meeth, and spiced ale,
And wafres, pipyng hoot out of the gleede...[1]

✳✳✳

HYPOCRAS – undated

*This elaborate recipe for Hypocras is attributed to a manuscript belonging to Thomas Astle, esq.; judging from the wording, it probably dates to circa 1450.*

1 or 2 gallons red wine

use spice mixture 1 (for lords):  ginger root, cinnamon sticks, grains of paradise, sugar, turnsole.[2]

*or* spice mixture 2 (for the commoners):  ginger root, cinnamon sticks, long pepper, clarified honey.

To make Ypocraſſe for lords with gynger, ſynamon, and graynes ſugour, and tureſoll: and for comyn pepull gynger canell, longe peper, and claryffyed hony.  Loke ye have feyre pewter baſens to kepe in your pouders and your ypocraſſe to ren ynne.  and to vi baſens ye muſte have vi renners on a perche as ye may here ſee.  and loke your poudurs and your gynger be redy and well paryd or hit be beton into poudr.  Gynger colombyne is the beſt gynger, mayken and balandyne be not ſo good nor holſom... now thou knowiſt the propertees of Ypocras.  Your poudurs muſt be made everyche by themſelfe, and leid in a bledder in ſtore, hange ſure your perche with baggs, and that no bagge twoyche other, but baſen twoyche baſen.  The fyrst bagge of a galon, every on of the other a potell.  Fyrſt do in to a baſen a galon or ij of red wyne, then put in your pouders, and do it in to the renners, and ſo in to the ſeconde bagge, then take a pece and aſſay it.  And yef hit be eny thyng to ſtronge of gynger alay it withe ſynamon, and yef it be ſtrong of ſynamon alay it withe ſugour cute.  And thus ſchall ye make perfyte Ypocras.  And loke your bagges be of boltell clothe, and the mouthes opyn, and let it ren in v or vi bagges on a perche, and under every bagge a clene baſen.  The draftes of the ſpies is good for ſewies.[3]  Put your Ypocraſe in to a ſtanche weſſell, and bynde opon the mouthe a bleddur ſtrongly, then ſerve forthe waffers and Ypocraſſe.
(Found in the Addenda to the Ancient Cookery (1381) section of *The Forme of Cury*, 1390, reprinted 1780.)

---

[1] Chaucer, "The Miller's Tale," lines 3378-9.

[2] CAUTION!  (*See Appendix.*)

[3] Perhaps this should be read: "the leftover spices are good to use for stews." *See the next recipe.*

# # 258 TO MAKE HIPPOCRIS – c. 1550 to 1625

| | |
|---|---|
| 4 gallons French wine | 1 ounce whole nutmegs |
| 2 gallons Sack wine | 1 ounce coriander seeds |
| 9 lbs. granulated sugar | 12 ounces cinnamon sticks |
| 2 quarts milk | 1/2 ounce cloves |
| 9 ounces ginger root | *optional:* red wine. |

Take 4 gallons of french wine, & 2 gallons [of] sack, & 9 pound of powder sugar, & 12 ounces of cinnamon, 9 ounces of ginger, one ounce of nutm[egg], one ounce of corriander seeds, halfe an ounce of cloves, & 2 quarts of new milk. put ye wine & 2 pound of sugar into a clean tub, & bruis[e] all ye spices, but not small, & strow them on [the] top of ye wine. & let stand close covered [24] hours, then put in ye rest of ye sugar & ye mil[k], & stir them well together. then put into a cle[an] coten bagg, & let it run twice thorough it into a clean pot. & when it is clear, bottle it up for yr [use]. these spices will make ye same quantety againe.[1] [If] you would have it red, culler it with red wine.

(From *Martha Washington's Booke of Cookery*, ed. by Karen Hess, 1981. *Letters in brackets were reconstructed by the editor.*)

# # 259 TO MAKE HYPPOCRIS – c. 1550 to 1625

| | |
|---|---|
| 3 quarts sweet wine | 4 whole nutmegs |
| 1 quart Sack wine | 1/2 ounce ginger root |
| 1 pint milk | 1/2 ounce coriander seeds |
| 2 lbs. granulated sugar | 2 ounces cinnamon sticks |

Take 3 quarts of sweet wine & one quart of swee[t] sack, 2 pound of lofe sugar, 2 ounces of cinnamon, halfe an ounce of ginger, halfe an ounce of corriander seeds, 4 numeggs, beat yr sugar ve[ry] well, but ye othes spices must be onely crusht. yn put [in] ye other halfe of ye sugar & a pinte of new milke. stir them [well] together, yn put them in a bagg yt is small at one end, [&] put a whalebone on ye top yt may hang even.[2] when it [is thoroough (?)], bottle it close. it will keep a quarter of a ye[ar]. (*ibid.*)

---

[1] Whole spices were often removed and reused by thrifty housewives.

[2] The whalebone serves to hold open the mouth of the hypocras bag. The spices are put into the bag (as we put coffee into a drip coffee pot), and the sweetened wine is poured through the spices to gather their flavor.

## TO MAKE WHITE IPOCRAS – 1594

| | |
|---|---|
| 1 gallon wine | 1 ounce cinnamon sticks |
| 1 lb. sugar | 2 ounces ginger root |
| 20 whole cloves | 20 peppercorns, crushed |

Take a gallon of wine, an ounce of Synamon, two ounces of Ginger, one pound of Sugar, twentie Cloves bruised, and twentie cornes of pepper big beaten, let all these soake together one night, and let it run through a bag, and it will be good Ipocras.

(From *The good Huswifes Handmaide for the Kitchin*, by John Partridge, 1594. *A modernized version of this recipe can be found in Lorwin, pp. 409-410.*)

## TO MAKE HYPOCRAS – 1655

| | |
|---|---|
| 4 gallons claret wine | whole cloves |
| 6 lbs. sugar | 8 ounces cinnamon sticks |
| ginger root | whole nutmegs |
| 1 quart milk | 3 sprigs rosemary |
| oranges | |

Take four gallons of Claret Wine, eight ounces of Cinamon, and Oranges, of Ginger, Cloves, and Nutmegs a small quantity, Sugar six pound, three sprigs of Rosemary, bruise all the spices somewhat small, and so put them into the Wine, and keep them close stopped, and often shaked together a day or two, then let it run through a jelly bagge twice or thrice with a quart of new milk.

(From *The Queen's Closet Opened*, by W.M., Cook to Queen Henrietta Maria, 1655.)

## TO MAKE IPOCRAS WITH RED WINE – 1660

| | |
|---|---|
| 1 gallon wine | 2 ounces ginger root |
| 2 quarts cream | 1/4 ounce whole cloves |
| 3 lbs. sugar | 20 peppercorns |
| 1 ounce whole nutmegs | 1 ounce mace blades |
| 3 ounces cinnamon sticks | |

Take a gallon of wine, three ounces of cinamon, two ounces of slic't ginger, a quarter of an ounce of cloves, an ounce of mace, twenty corns of pepper, an ounce of nutmegs, three pound of sugar, and two quarts of cream.

(From *The Accomplisht Cook*, by Robert May, 1660. *A modernized version can be found in Lorwin, pp. 47-48.*)

## TO MAKE HYPOCRAS PRESENTLY – 1669

| 1 quart wine | sugar to taste |
|---|---|

Spice mixture (a flavored sugar paste, use it to season to taste):

| 12 drops clove oil | 8 drops nutmeg oil |
|---|---|
| 5 drops cinnamon oil | 2 ounces sugar |
| 20 drops rosewater | ambergris |
| musk | |

Take twelve drops of Oyl of Cloves, eight of Oyl of Nutmegs, and five of Oyl of Cinamon. Put them into a large strong drinking glass, and mingle well with them two ounces of the purest double refined sugar in powder. Then take twenty drops of Rosewater in a spoon, and in it a little Ambergris, and a little Musk, and then pour that to your former Composition and work all well together; and if you find the matter too moist, knead some more sugar amongst it. If you put a little of this Composition into a quart of Wine, and make it sweet with sugar besides, it will taste like excellent Hypocras.

(Found in *A Garden of Herbs* by E. S. Rohde, p. 219, and credited to *The Closet ...Opened,* 1669, however, this recipe is missing from my copy of Digby.)

## HYPOCRAS OF WHITE WINE – 1682

| 3 quarts white wine *or* claret | 1 grain musk |
|---|---|
| 1 1/2 lb. sugar | 2 or 3 lemon slices |
| 1 ounce cinnamon sticks | 2 or 3 sprigs sweet marjoram |
| 2 grains peppercorns | |

Take about three quarts of the best white wine, a pound and a half of sugar, an ounce of cinamon, two or three leaves of sweet margerum, two grains of whole pepper, let all this pass through your bag with a grain of Musk, two or three slices of lemon when it hath stood and infused altogether the space of three or four hours. That of Claret may be made the same way.

(From *A Perfect School of Instructions for the Officers of the Mouth*, by Giles Rose, 1682.)

# #2 TOO MAKE WHITE HIPOCHRISTS – c. 1674

*The last sentence of this recipe contains directions to make a strong spiced beer using the leftover hypocras spices.*

| | |
|---|---|
| 1 gallon Sack wine | 1/8 ounce long pepper |
| 1/2 pint milk | 6 whole nutmegs |
| 2 lbs. granulated sugar | 2 ounces coriander seeds |
| 1 ounce cinnamon sticks | 1 or 2 ginger roots |

Take a gallan of sack: and putt in too tow puter pots on oz of very good Cinomon well brused 6 nutmegs 2 oz of Colleandr seed and 1/2 a qt of an oz of long peper all peal but not too small, severally 2 pounds of the best Refined shugger and a Rase or 2 of ginger thin shred, put all these things in to the sacke, sum into one pot sum in the other and so Lett them steepe together sturing of it now and then, with that which may ketch to the botom, for an houre or too, then put into it 1/2 a pint of new milke sum into one pot and sum into an other, and Lett it Steep with sturing of it as before a Litell time, then hang youre hepoikrist bagg upon a stafe with sum stick at the uper end of the bagg, and then put in to it youre hipochrists and Lett it Run softly throu the bagg, thus don twise or thris, Leting it Run softly till it bee Cleare the oftener you Run it the Clerer it will bee, so put it into a botell, and stop it very Close, you may Lett strong bere Run through 2 or 3 times, and it will make a very plesant Drinke –
(From *Penn Family Recipes, Cooking Recipes of Wm. Penn's Wife, etc.*, c. 1674.)

# #55 TOO MAKE HIPOCHRISTS – c. 1674

| | |
|---|---|
| 6 quarts Sack wine | 1 ounce cinnamon powder |
| 2 1/2 lbs. granulated sugar | 1 ounce clove powder |
| 1 pint milk | 2 or 3 grains musk *or* ambergris |

Take 6 quarts of the best sacke and put into it one oz of the best Cinomen in pouder one oz of Cloves beaten in pouder, in to it 2 1/2 pound of suger beten to pouder, and brue it in 2 flagons well all together, and then put in a bagg 2 or 3 grains of muske or Ambergrece, then put all youre Liquor in and when youre Liquor hath once Run quite throw it, put into the bagg a pint of milke and put over in to the bagg youre Liquor again, and so as many times till it com to bee Clere – (*ibid.*)

RED HIPPOCRAS – 1732

| | |
|---|---|
| 1 gallon claret | 1 mace blade |
| 2 lbs. granulated sugar | 12 sweet almonds |
| 1 glassful brandy | coriander seed |
| 1 glassful milk | 4 grains white pepper |
| 1 dram cinnamon sticks | long pepper |

Put a gallon of Claret into an earthen vessel, put to it two pounds of sugar beaten in a mortar, a dozen of sweet almonds stampt with a glass of brandy;[1] add to the infusion a dram of cinnamon, a little long pepper, four grains of white pepper, a blade of Mace, and some Coriander seeds, all these bruised. Cover the vessel close and let all these infuse for an hour, stirring it often with a spoon, that the sugar may dissolve and incorporate. Then add a glass of milk, and pass all through the straining bag.
(From *The Receipt Book of Charles Carter*, Cook to the Duke of Argyll, 1732.)

*Harvesting Cinnamon.*

---

[1] Steep the crushed almonds in the brandy to make a type of almond milk before proceeding.

# *METHODS*
## *&*
## *CURES*

✱✱✱✱✱✱✱

*A hodgepodge of miscellaneous "quick fixes,"*
*presented for your amusement.*

[ON THE ADULTERATION OF WINES] – c. 77 A. D.
The importance of the wine of Beziers does not extend outside the Gallic provinces; and about the rest of the wines grown in the Province of Narbonne no positive statement can be made, inasmuch as the dealers have set up a regular factory for the purpose and colour them by means of smoke, and I regret to say also by employing noxious herbs and drugs– inasmuch as a dealer actually uses aloe for adulterating the flavour and the colour of his wines...[1]
...But it may also be proper to give an account of the method of preparing wine, as Greek authors have written special treatises on this subject and have made a scientific system for it –for instance Euphronius, Aristomachus, Commiades and Hicesius. The practice in Africa is to soften any roughness with gypsum, and also in some parts of the country with lime. In Greece, on the other hand, they enliven the smoothness of their wines with potter's earth or marble dust or salt or sea-water, while in some parts of Italy they use resinous pitch for this purpose, and it is the general practice both there and in the neighbouring provinces to season must with resin; in some places they use the lees of older wine or else vinegar for seasoning... In some places they boil the must down into what is called sapa, and pour this into their wines to overcome their harshness. Still both in the case of this kind of wine and in all others they supply the vessels themselves with coatings of pitch... The method of seasoning wine is to sprinkle the must with pitch during its first fermentation, which is completed in nine days at most, so that the wine may be given the scent of pitch and some touches of its piquant flavour...[2]
...parsley enclosed in bags is also employed by butlers to rid the wine of disagreeable odour."[3]

---

[1] Pliny , *Natural History*, Book XIV, section VII, p. 233.

[2] *ibid.*, Book XIV, section XXIV, pp. 265-269.

[3] *ibid.*, Book XIX, p. 541.

TO CLARIFY MUDDY WINE (VINUM EX ATRO CANDIDUM FACIES) – c. 100 B.C. to 300 A.D.
Put bean meal and the whites of three eggs in a mixing bowl. Mix thoroughly with a whip and add to the wine, stirring for a long time. The next day the wine will be clear. Ashes of vines have the same effect.
(From *Apicius, Cookery and Dining in Imperial Rome*, c. 100 B.C. to 300 A.D., tr. by J. D. Vehling, pp. 47-8.)


# 161 TO IMPROVE AND REDDEN MUST OR NEW WINE FOR EARLY SALE – c. 1375
For a hogshead of wine of Paris measure, take 3 deniers weight of milled saffron soaked in the same must. Take a potful of honey which holds 2 deniers, 16 deniers of wine, boil in a pan, stir very well, and let cool. This done, take a bowlful of wheat flour, soak these three things together, [and put them in the barrel]. It will soon be fine and good for drinking and selling.
(From *Le Viandier de Taillevent*, c. 1375, tr. by J. Prescott, 1989, p. 49.)


# 162 TO KEEP WINE FROM BECOMING ROPY AND BEING TROUBLED – c. 1375
To a hogshead of wine, add a bowlful of red wine pips dried and then boiled. Take white wine dregs, dry them, burn them to ashes, and put a bowlful of ashes in the barrel without stirring anything. (*ibid.*, p. 49.)


# 163 TO CURE ROPINESS IN ALL WINES – c. 1375
Take a bowlful of red wine pips (dried and milled only), a bowlful of fat of the appearance or colour of the wine, a denier of pastry leaven, a half pound of alum, two bells of ginger and a bit of gritty ashes. Put all these 6 things, well ground and beaten, in the barrel. Stir well with a short stick (split at the end into four) so that the scum gushes out. The stick should be only a foot inside the barrel. Tap the bung in. (*ibid.*, p. 50.)


# 164 TO CURE WINE TURNED ROPY – c. 1375
For a Paris hogshead, boil a potful of wheat until it has burst, drain it, and put it to cool. Take some well beaten egg whites, skim them, and put everything in the barrel. Stir with a short stick (split into 4 at the end) which does not reach the dregs, so that they are not disturbed. Hang a pound of ground bastard lovage in a cloth sachet by a thread in the bunghole of the barrel. (*ibid.*, p. 50.)

# 165  TO CURE WINE TURNED ROPY OR WHICH SMELLS FUSTY, MUSKY OR SPOILED – c. 1375
Beat two denier's worth of ginger and two denier's worth of turmeric together well, boil this powder in 2 quarts of wine, skim it well, put it hot into the barrel, and stir it well right to the bottom.  Stopper it well and let it rest until it has settled.
(From *Le Viandier de Taillevent*, c. 1375, tr. by J. Prescott, 1989, p. 50.)

# 166  TO CURE WINE TURNED SOUR – c. 1375
For a hogshead of wine, boil a pint of the same wine, soak half an ounce of the milled berry [bay? juniper?[1]] in the hot wine, put it in the barrel without stirring it a little or a lot, and tap the bung in.
(*ibid.*, p. 50. *Words in brackets were added by the translator.*)

# 167  TO CURE WINE TURNED FUSTY – c. 1375
For a hogshead, take [some wine], ten ounces of sugar and half an ounce of milled berry [bay? juniper?], soak everything together, and put it in the barrel without stirring. Alternatively, put live coals in the tun, stopper it very well, and leave it for three days in this state.  (*ibid.*, p. 51.)

# THE BEST THING FOR ROPE – 1796
Mix two handfuls of bean flour and one handful of falt, throw this into a kilderkin [*18 gallons*] of beer, do not ftop it clofe till it has done fermenting, then let it ftand a month, and draw it off; but fometimes nothing will do with it.
(From *The Art of Cookery Made Plain and Easy*, v. 8, by Mrs. Glasse, 1796, p. 350.)

# 168  FOR WINE WHICH HAS THE VIGOUR BROKEN – c. 1375
Mix a bowlful of tannin and a fistful of peas together, put them in the barrel, and tap the bung in without stirring.
(From *Le Viandier de Taillevent*, c. 1375, tr. by J. Prescott, 1989, p. 51.)

# 169  TO CLARIFY RED WINE IN WINTER – c. 1375
For a hogshead, take half a pound of new almonds, soak them in the same wine, and put them in the barrel without stirring.  To remove redness from red wine in summer, take two fistfuls of wild mulberry leaves per hogshead, put them in the barrel without stirring, and tap the bung in.  (*ibid.*, p. 51.)

---

[1] Bay laurel berries or Juniper berries.

# # 170  TO CLARIFY RED WINE – c. 1375
Put into the tun 40 egg whites beaten and well skimmed, plus a fistful of salt and two ounces of milled pepper soaked together in the same wine. Stir everything together, dregs and all, tap the bung in, and let it rest. (*ibid.*, p. 51.)

### *[TO FINE WINE] – 1861*
2166. There are various modes of fining wine: isinglass, gelatine, and gum Arabic are all used for the purpose. Whichever of these articles is used, the process is always the same. Supposing eggs (the cheapest) to be used, – Draw a gallon or so of the wine, and mix one quart of it with the whites of four eggs, by stirring it with a whisk; afterwards, when thoroughly mixed, pour it back into the cask through the bunghole, and stir up the whole cask, in a rotatory direction, with a clean split stick inserted through the bunghole. Having stirred it sufficiently, pour in the remainder of the wine drawn off, until the cask is full; then stir again, skimming off the bubbles that rise to the surface. When thoroughly mixed by stirring, close the bunghole, and leave it to stand for three or four days. This quantity of clarified wine will fine thirteen dozen of port or sherry. The other clearing ingredients are applied in the same manner, the material being cut into small pieces, and dissolved in the quart of wine, and the cask stirred in the same manner.
(From *Mrs. Beeton's Book of Household Management*, 1861.)

### RULES FOR BREWING – 1796
Care muſt be taken, in the firſt place, to have the malt clean; and after it is ground, it ought to ſtand four or five days.

For ſtrong October, five quarters of malt to three hogſheads, and twenty-four pounds of hops. This will afterwards make two hogſheads of good keeping ſmall beer, allowing five pounds of hops to it.

For middling beer, a quarter of malt makes a hogſhead of ale, and one of ſmall beer; or it will make three hogſheads of good ſmall beer, allowing eight pounds of hops. This will keep all the year. Or it will make twenty gallons of ſtrong ale, and two hogſheads of ſmall beer that will keep all the year.

If you intend your ale to keep a great while, allow a pound of hops to every buſhel; if to keep ſix months, five pounds to a hogſhead; if for preſent drinking, three pounds to a hogſhead, and the ſofteſt and cleareſt water you can get.

Obſerve the day before to have all your veſſels very clean, and never uſe your tubs for any other uſe except to make wines.

Let your caſk be very clean the day before with boiling water; and if your bung is big enough, ſcrub them well with a little birch-broom or bruſh; but if they be very bad, take out the heads, and let them be ſcrubbed clean with a hand-bruſh, ſand, and fullers-earth. Put on the head again, and ſcald them well, throw into the barrel a piece of unſlacked lime, and ſtop the bung cloſe.

The firſt copper of water, when it boils, pour into your maſh-tub, and let it be cool enough to ſee your face in; then put in your malt, and let it be well maſhed; have a copper of water boiling in the mean time, and when your malt is well maſhed, fill your maſhing-tub, ſtir it well again, and cover it over with the ſacks. Let it ſtand three hours, ſet a broad ſhallow tub under the cock, let it run very ſoftly; and if it is thick, throw it up again till it runs fine, then throw a handful of hops in the under tub, let the maſh run into it, and fill your tubs till all is run off. Have water boiling in the copper, and lay as much more as you have occaſion for, allowing one third for boiling and waſte. Let that ſtand an hour, boiling more water to fill the maſh-tub for ſmall beer; let the fire down a little, and put it into tubs enough to fill your maſh. Let the ſecond maſh be run off, and fill your copper with the firſt wort; put in part of your hops, and make it boil quick. About an hour is long enough; when it has half boiled, throw in a handful of ſalt. Have a clean white wand, and dip it into the copper; and if the wort feels clammy, it is boiled enough; then ſlacken your fire, and take off your wort. Have ready a large tub, put two ſticks acroſs, and ſet your ſtraining baſket over the tub on the ſticks, and ſtrain your wort through it. Put other wort on to boil with the reſt of the hops; let your maſh be covered again with water, and thin your wort that is cooled in as many things as you can; for the thinner it lies, and the quicker it cools, the better. When quite cool, put it into the tunning-tub. Throw a handful of ſalt into every boil. When the maſh has ſtood an hour, draw it off; then fill your maſh with cold water, take off the wort in the copper, and order it as before. When cool, add to it the firſt in the tub; ſo ſoon as you empty one copper, fill the other, ſo boil your ſmall beer well. Let the laſt maſh run off, and when both are boiled with freſh hops, order them as the two firſt boilings; when cool, empty the maſh-tub, and put the ſmall beer to work there. When cool enough, work it; ſet a wooden bowl of yeaſt in the beer, and it will work over with a little of the beer in the boil [sic]. Stir your tun up every twelve hours, let it ſtand two days, then tun it, taking off the yeaſt. Fill your veſſels full, and ſave ſome to fill your barrels; let it ſtand till it has done working; then lay your bung lightly for a fortnight, after that ſtop it as cloſe as you can. Mind you have a vent-peg at the top of the veſſel; in warm weather open it; and if your drink hiſſes, as it often will, looſen it till it has done, then ſtop it cloſe again. If you can boil your ale in one boiling it is beſt, if your copper will allow of it; if not, boil it as conveniency ſerves.

When you come to draw your beer, and find it is not fine, draw off a gallon, and ſet it on the fire, with two ounces of iſinglaſs cut ſmall and beat; diſſolve it in the beer over the fire: when it is all melted, let it ſtand till it is cold, and pour it in at the bung, which muſt lay looſe on till it has done fermenting, then ſtop it cloſe for a month. Take great care your caſks are not muſty, or have any ill taſte; if they have, it is a hard thing to ſweeten them. You are to waſh your caſks with cold water before you ſcald them, and they ſhould lie a day or two ſoaking, and clean them well, then ſcald them.

(From *The Art of Cookery Made Plain and Easy*, vol. 8, by Mrs. Glaſſe, 1796, pp. 348-350.)

## WHEN A BARREL OF BEER HAS TURNED SOUR – 1796
To a kilderkin [*18 gallons*] of beer throw in at the bung a quart of oatmeal, lay the bung on looſe two or three days, then ſtop it down cloſe, and let it ſtand a month. Some throw in a piece of chalk as big as a turkey's egg, and when it has done working, ſtop it cloſe for a month, then tap it. (*ibid.*, p. 350.)

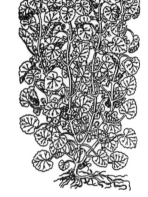

*Hedera terreſtrk.*
*Alehoofe.*

## [ON ALEHOOF]
"The women of our Northerne parts, especially about Wales and Cheshire, do turne the herbe Ale-hoof into their Ale; but the reason thereof I know not..."[1]

"It [*Ale-hoof*] is good to tun up with new drink, for it will clarify it in a night, that it will be the fitter to be drank the next morning; or if any drink be thick with removing or any other accident, it will do the like in a few hours."[2]

## # 106  TO MAKE ALE DRINK QUICK – 1669
When small Ale hath wrought sufficiently, draw into bottles; but first put into every bottle twelve good raisins of the Sun split and stoned; Then stop up the bottle close, and set it in sand (gravel) or a cold dry Cellar. After a while this will drink exceeding quick and pleasant. Likewise take six Wheat-corns, and bruise them, and put into a bottle of Ale; it will make it exceeding quick and stronger.
(From *The Closet ...Opened*, 1669.)

## 27. THE TRUE BOTTLING OF BEER – 1609
When your Beer is 10 or 12 dayes olde, whereby it is growne reasonable cleare, then bottle it, making your corkes very fit for the bottle, and stoppe them close: but drinke not of this beer, till they begin to work againe, and mantle, and then you shall find the same most excellent and spritely drinke: and this is the reason why bottle ale is both so windy and muddy, thundering and smoking vpon the opening of the bottle, because it is commonly bottled the same day that it is laid into the cellar; whereby his yeast, being an exceeding windy substance, being also drawn with the Ale not yet fined, doth incorporate with the drinke, and maketh it also very windy: and this is all the lime and gunpowder wherewith bottle ale hath beene a long time so wrongfully charged.
(From *Delightes for Ladies*, by Sir Hugh Plat, 1609.)

---

[1] Woodward, p. 201.

[2] Culpeper, p. 16.

2167.  TO BOTTLE WINE – 1861

Having thoroughly washed and dried the bottles, supposing they have been before used for the same kind of wine, provide corks, which will be improved by being slightly boiled, or at least steeped in hot water, –a wooden hammer or mallet, a bottling-boot, and a squeezer for the corks.  Bore a hole in the lower part of the cask with a gimlet, receiving the liquid stream which follows in the bottle and filterer, which is placed in a tub or basin.  This operation is best performed by two persons, one to draw the wine, the other to cork the bottles.  The drawer is to see that the bottles are up to the mark, but not too full, the bottle being placed in a clean tub to prevent waste.  The corking-boot is buckled by a strap to the knee, the bottle placed in it, and the cork, after being squeezed in the press, driven in by a flat wooden mallet.

(From *Mrs. Beeton's Book of Household Management*, 1861.)

EMPTINS – 1796

*This is a recipe for making a liquid yeast, similar to a sourdough starter, which is to be made ahead and used as necessary.*

| | |
|---|---|
| 1 handful hops | thickening (flour, cornstarch, toasted bread, etc.) |
| 3 quarts water | yeast |

Take a handful of hops and about three quarts of water, let it boil about fifteen minutes, then make a thickening as you do for ſtarch, ſtrain the liquor, when cold put a little emptins to work them, they will keep well cork'd in a botttle [*sic*] five or ſix weeks.

(From *The First American Cookbook, A Facsimile of "American Cookery,"* by Amelia Simmons, 1796, p. 47.)

# 94  TOO CULLER CYDOR – c. 1674

*These next three recipes are for coloring and clarifying cider that has already been made.*

| | |
|---|---|
| elderberry juice | cider |

Take elder berys and strain them, and put the juce a mong the Cydor, it maketh it Loock Like Clarett and will Corectt the windiness

(From *Penn Family Recipes, etc.*, c. 1674.)

## FOR FINING CYDER – 1796

1 hogshead cider                                    4 ounces isinglass
2 quarts of skim milk

Take two quarts of ſkim-milk, four ounces of iſinglaſs, cut the iſinglaſs in pieces, and work it lukewarm in the milk over the fire; and when it is diſſolved, then put it cold into the hogſhead of cyder, and take a long ſtick and ſtir it well from top to bottom for half a quarter of an hour.
(From *The Art of Cookery Made Plain and Easy*, v. 8, by Mrs. Glasse, 1796, p. 350.)


## AFTER IT HAS FINED – 1796

1 hogshead cider                                    10 lbs. raisins
2 ounces turmeric                                   1/2 ounces ginger

Take ten pounds of raiſins of the ſun, two ounces of turmerick, half an ounce of ginger beaten; then take a quantity of raiſins, and grind them as you do muſtard-ſeed in a bowl, with a little cyder, and ſo the reſt of the raiſins; then ſprinkle the turmerick and ginger amongſt it; then put all into a fine canvaſs bag, and hang it in the middle of the hogſhead cloſe, and let it lie. After the cyder has ſtood thus a fortnight or a month, then you may bottle it at your pleaſure. (*ibid.*, p. 351.)


## TO MANAGE CIDER AND PERRY – 1829

1 hogshead cider *or* perry                         1 lb. alum
1 gallon French brandy                              1/2 ounce cochineal
3 lbs. sugar

To fine and improve the flavour of one hogs-head, take a gallon of good French brandy, with half an ounce of cochineal, one pound of alum, and three pounds of sugar-candy; bruise them all well in a mortar, and infuse them in the brandy for a day or two; then mix the whole with the cider and stop it close for five or six months. After which, if fine, bottle it off.

Cider or perry, when bottled in hot weather, should be left a day or two uncorked, that it may get flat; but if too flat in the cask, and soon wanted for use put into each bottle a small lump or two of sugarcandy, four or five raisins of the sun, or a small piece of raw beef;[1] any of which will much improve the liquor, and make it brisker.

Cider should be well corked and waxed, and packed upright in a cool place. A few bottles may always be kept in a warmer place to ripen and be ready for use.
(From *Five Thousand Receipts, etc.*, by Mackenzie, 1829.)

---

[1] Hartley (p. 547) says that one ingredient of Cornish Cider is sheep's blood!

252

# GLOSSARY

**Acetabulum**~~unit of measurement = 15 drachmae = 1/4 hemina.

**Allay it, alay it**~~<u>mix it</u> with whatever is specified in the recipe.

**Amber**~~fossilized resin; a semi-precious gem with static electrical properties, formerly used in medicine. Also sometimes refers to *ambergris.*

**Ambergris, Amber-greece**~~from Old French, *ambre gris*, a grayish, waxy substance obtained from the intestines of the sperm whale, occasionally found floating in the tropics; it was used formerly in perfume, and to retard evaporation. It is soluble in hot alcohol.

**Ambered-sugar**~~"Ambered-sugar is made by grinding very well, four grains of Ambergreece, and one of Musk, with a little fine Sugar; or grinding two or three Spanish Pastils very small." (Digby, # 121.)

**Amphora**~~a double-handled wine jug. A Greek amphora holds approximately 10.3 gallons. A Roman amphora holds approximately 6.84 gallons.

*Ana*~~from Medieval Latin meaning: "use equal quantities of each."

**Aqua bath**~~from the Gaelic, *uisce beatha*, "the water of life." The same as Usquebaugh, "The Irish Cordial."

**Aqua celestis** (heavenly water), **Aqua composita** (composed water), and **Aqua mirabilis** (miracle water), are medicinal concoctions. Several recipes for them may be found in *Martha Washington's Booke of Cookery*, and in Digby. [Please note that some of these recipes call for "Juice of Sellandine," or Celandine Poppy, *Chelidonium majus* L., Papaveraceae, (B&B, 2:141). <u>Celandine Poppy is poisonous, and may prove fatal if ingested</u>.]

**Aqua vitae**~~the water of life. Distilled or grain alcohol. In this case it means <u>ETHANOL</u> (ethyl alcohol), <u>not</u> isopropanol *(rubbing alcohol), denatured (poisoned) alcohol, or methanol (wood alcohol).* From the name *aqua vitae* comes the Scandinavian word *akavit*, or *aquavit*, a distilled liquor flavored with caraway seeds.

**Assay it**~~try it, taste it. An **assay** is also a unit of measurement equal to 4 drams plus 24 grains.

**Aume**~~a Dutch liquid measure approximately equal to 41 British gallons.

**Balneo**~~a water bath or bain marie, used to heat liquids gently during distillation.

**Barm**~~a yeast solution. (*See Yeast.*)

**Barrel**~~a cask holding 36 gallons British measure. "A Barrel at Liege holdeth ninety Pots, and a Pot is as much as a Wine quart in England. (I have since been informed from Liege, that a Pot of that Countrey holdeth 48 Ounces of Apothecary's measure; which I judge to be a Pottle according to London measure, or two Wine-quarts.)" (Digby, # 1.)

## GLOSSARY

**Battledore, Battle-door**~~from ME *batildore*, a flat wooden paddle.

**Bleddur**~~a piece of bladder, used as a stopper or lid to seal the container.

**Blink**~~a verb which means 'to alter the flavor by adding tannin.'

**Bogue**~~a word used by Bemiss: "sent it with a linen rag dipped in brimstone, by fixing it at the *bogue*, by the bung or cork; then put the wine into it, and stop it close for forty-eight hours; then give it vent at the *bogue*." Plat says "there is a lesser hole near the bung hole in beer Hogsheads," this may be what Bemiss means by "bogue."

**Boltell cloth**~~bolter cloth, used for straining or sifting.

**Boulter bag, bolter bag**~~a sifter made of bolter cloth.

**Braggot, Bragawd**~~a Welsh drink brewed from ale, honey, herbs, and spices.

**Bray**~~to crush or pound in a mortar with a pestle.

**Brimstone**~~sulfur, which was burned in order to sterilize bottles or casks. Sodium bisulfite solution, made from Campden tablets and boiled water, is a modern sterilizing agent used to prevent growth of unwanted organisms in wines and long mead. Sulfites can cause severe allergic reactions in sensitive individuals; a solution of common household bleach may be substituted (but may also cause allergic reactions), or simply scald the casks and bottles with boiling water.

**Bushel**~~a dry measure = 2 buckets = 4 pecks = 35.239 liters.

**But-head**~~as used by Digby's Mr. Pierce (p. 100): "Then cover your *But-head* with a sheet onely in Summer, but blankets in Winter...". The butt-head is the <u>unsealed</u> top of the butt, or cask. The cask has been left unsealed so that the scum may be easily skimmed off.

**Butt**~~(*See Cask.*)

**Cask**~~a wooden barrel, used for storage.

**Cast thereto**~~add.

**Caudle, caudel**~~a warm spiced drink of wine or ale, thickened with egg yolks. It was most often served to invalids or to friends enjoying a *reresoper*, or illicit late night meal (Henisch, p. 17). From "caudle" come our words "coddle" and "mollycoddle."

**Clout**~~cloth.

**Cochineal**~~a dried insect, *Coccus cacti* L., from Mexico and Central America, used for red and pink food coloring. Cochineal was used medicinally to treat whooping cough, and also has many manufacturing uses.

**Corall**~~ground red coral, the skeletons of certain marine animals, thought to have had medicinal properties. "Corall drunke in wine or water, preſerueth from the ſpleene ...[and] prouoketh ſleepe..." (Gerard, p. 1383.)

**Cordial**~~originally a heart medicine or tonic, but now the word refers to any liqueur.

254

**Cream of Tartar**~~Potassium Bitartrate, $KHC_4H_4O_6$, a compound made of potassium and tartaric acid, a naturally occurring acid found in grapes. Cream of tartar or pure tartaric acid may be added to wine, beer, etc., prior to fermentation to increase acidity. "The dryed Lees of wine called Argoll or Tartar, is put to the vʃe of the Goldsmith, Dyer, and Apothecary, ...Of it the Apothecaries make *cremor Tartari*, a fine medicine to bee vʃed, ...to purge humours by the ʃtoole" (Parkinson, p. 566).

**Cyathus**~~unit of measurement = 10 drachmae.

**Denier**~~a small French coin.

**Dessertspoonful**~~unit of measurement, between 1 teaspoonful and 1 tablespoonful.

**Distillation**~~a process whereby wine, mead, etc., is brought to the vapor point, and the vapors are then collected and cooled. This distillate has a much higher alcohol content than the original liquid. Note: distillation must properly be done twice – once to concentrate the alcohol, and then a second time to remove the toxic impurities that have also been concentrated by the first distillation. (*See McGee, pp. 484-485.*)

**Dog Days, Dog Star Days**~~the Canicular Days, early June to early September.

**Dram, Drachm, Drachma**~~unit of measurement equal to 1/16 ounce (U.S.), or 1/8 ounce (Apothecary measure):
> The Attic drachma... has the weight of a silver denarius, and the same makes six oboli, the obolus being ten chalci. The cyathus as a measure weighs ten drachmae; when the measure of an acetabulum is spoken of, it means the quarter of a hemina, that is fifteen drachmae. The mna, that our countrymen call the mina, weighs one hundred Attic drachmae. (Pliny, Book XXI, p. 291.)

**Droʃʃe, dross**~~(*See Scum.*)

**Ebullition**~~boiling or bubbling.

**Emptins**~~a yeast solution.

**Explosion**~~what happens when you tightly stopper a working jug of mead.

**Fahrenheit's thermometer**~~invented 1714. Freezing point of water = 32°F, Boiling point = 212°F. [°C = (°F – 32) ÷ 1.8].

**Fat**~~alternate spelling of 'vat.'

**Fine it**~~means to clarify the liquid.

**Fining**~~a substance (such as isinglass or egg whites) used to clarify wine, etc., by precipitating out the proteins and yeasts that cloud the liquid.

**Firkin**~~a small wooden barrel or covered bucket holding 1/4 barrel or 9 British gallons.

**Fixed nitre**~~possibly potassium nitrate, $KNO_3$.

**Frailesful**~~a frail was a large basket used for packing fruit. It typically held from 50 to 75 pounds.

**Fullers-earth**~~a type of kaolin clay which contains magnesium; it is used as a filter.

**Gallipot, Gally-pot**~~a small jar of glazed earthenware used formerly by apothecaries to store medicines.

**Gill**~~a unit of measurement = 1/2 cup = 4 ounces liquid. However, Monckton (p. 61) lists an English "gill" of circa 1382 which, by law, held 1 pint.

**Gimlet, Gimblet**~~a small tool used for boring holes.

**Goa stone**~~according to the dictionary, goa stone is the same thing as 'goa ball' – a drug mixture once used for fevers. However, this definition does not seem to fit Dods' usage (p. 216). The recipe refers to goa stone as a type of *perfume*. It is possible that the stone (testicle) of a goa (a type of Tibetan antelope) was meant by the author in a poetic circumlocution for the word *musk*.

**Godesgood**~~barm, yeast.

**Grain**~~unit of measurement = 64.799 milligrams.

**Groat**~~a silver English coin (issued 1279 to 1662) equal in value to 4 English pennies and weighing 1/8 ounce. Add so much honey "as the Liquor will bear an Egge to the breadth of a Groat" means to make a honey and water solution so strong that the portion of the egg floating above the solution has a diameter of a groat (or other coin). (*See Specific Gravity.*)

**Gruit**~~an herb mixture (mentioned by McGee, p. 467), consisting of yarrow, rosemary, bog myrtle, and other herbs; it was used instead of hops to flavor ale. Since bog myrtle contains an abortifacient, and yarrow an emmenagogue, I would recommend that women not consume ale flavored with gruit.

**Gyle**~~another term for the fermenting wort.

**Handful**~~"The handfuls of Herbs, are natural large handfuls (as much as you can take up in your hand) not Apothecaries handfuls, which are much less," (Digby, # 38). Note: the handfuls referred to by Sir Kenelme Digby are a man's handful, not a woman's.

**Hart's horn**~~shavings of the antlers of the male deer, used to make gelatine. Also the name of a chemical compound, ammonium carbonate, used in medicines and commercially in baking powder and many other substances. The name Hart's horn also applies to two plants. (*See Appendix, p. 276.*)

**Head**~~the foam that rises to the top of beer.

**Hemina**~~unit of measurement = 60 drachmae.

**Hippocras-bag**~~a cloth bag used for filtering hypocras and other drinks.

**Hogshead, Hoggeshead**~~a unit of liquid measure equal to 63 gallons. Also a large cask containing from 63 to 140 gallons.

**Holland Pints**~~"the Holland Pint is very little bigger then the English Wine-pint," (Digby, # 4).

**Hundredweight**~~unit of measurement = 100 pounds (45.36 kilograms) U.S. measure, or 112 pounds (50.8 kilograms) British measure.

**Isinglass**~~from Old Dutch *huizenblas*, meaning sturgeon's bladder. A clear gelatine made of the air bladders of the sturgeon, used here as a type of fining.

**Kilderkin**~~from Middle Dutch, *kindekijn*. An English unit of measurement equal to approximately 18 imperial gallons; also means a cask.

**Kiver, kiue**~~a large vessel used to hold the working liquor.

**Kumiss**~~fermented mare's milk.

**"Labour the honey with the Liquor," "Lade it... to dissolve the honey in the water"**~~these and similar phrases mean to mix and stir together the honey and water using your clean hands and arms, or a wooden paddle, until the honey is completely dissolved in the water. It is a time-consuming step, since *cold* water is usually called for, meaning that the honey dissolves *very* slowly. It is possible that this was done in the belief that more scum would rise to the surface, thereby rendering the final product less bitter. Some of the recipes containing these phrases also include the instructions to "now and then pour to it a ladle full of cold water, which will make the scum rise more."

**Lady Days**~~or Days of Our Lady, of which there are five: *Purification*, February 2; *Annunciation* or *Lady Day*, March 25 (formerly April 6); *Visitation*, July 2; *Assumption*, August 15; and *Nativity*, September 8.

**Lamb's Wool**~~spiced ale, traditionally drunk on New Year's Day in Scotland.

**Lead**~~many of the recipes in this book call for lead to be used either to seal the bungs of casks, or as a weight to weigh down bags of herbs and spices in the wort. Lead has been shown to be poisonous; please do not use it even if some commercial winemakers still do so. Parafilm or plastic wrap may be used to achieve a tighter seal on a bung; and a clean pebble may be used as a weight.

**Lees**~~the dregs or sediment.

**Lent**~~The Christian holiday which extends from Ash Wednesday until Easter. It has no fixed dates, but varies with matters astronomical.

**Lignum-cassia**~~probably the bark of *Cinnamomum cassia*, a type of cinnamon. The word *lignum* is Latin for *wood*.

**Limbecke**~~an alembic, a distillation apparatus.

**Lime, Unslaked**~~Unslaked lime (calcium oxide, $CaO$) becomes slaked to form calcium hydroxide, $Ca(OH)_2$, upon exposure to air and water. The reaction gives off heat and may start a fire.

**List, listeth**~~To like. "He that liʃteth to knowe" means "He who would like to know."

**Loaf sugar, lump sugar**~~sugar used to come in the form of large solid cones which had to be scraped, chipped, and pounded to produce granules. Since we are dissolving it anyway, granulated sugar may be substituted.

**Lute**~~ME *lute* from OF *lut* and Latin *lutum*, meaning *potter's clay*. "Lute your Lymbeck" means to seal the connecting joints of the alembic with clay.

**Magma**~~dregs or leavings.

**Maibowle**~~a German drink of Rhine wine flavored with Sweet Woodruff.

**Malmsey, Malvasia**~~a strong, flavorful, sweet white wine.

**Malt**~~typically barley or other grain that has been sprouted to produce amylases, starch-digesting enzymes that convert starch into sugars. The sprouted grain is dried and roasted for flavor and color, and is then ground, mixed with water, and heated to produce a *wort*. The word 'malt' also refers to beverages brewed from malted grain.

**Measurements**:
U.S. Liquid Measures:

| | | |
|---|---|---|
| 1 pint | = | 0.5506 liter |
| 1 quart | = | 1.1012 liters |
| 1 gallon | = | 3.7853 liters |
| 1 wine barrel | = | 31.5 gallons |
| 1 beer barrel | = | 36 gallons |
| 1 hogshead | = | 2 barrels |
| | = | 63 gallons U.S. (Others range from 63 to 140 gallons.) |
| 1 pipe | = | 2 hogsheads |

British Liquid Measures:

| | | | | |
|---|---|---|---|---|
| 1 gill | = | 4 ounces | = | 0.1183 liters |
| 1 pint | = | 0.5683 liter | = | 4 gills |
| 1 quart | = | 1.137 liters | = | 2 pints |
| 1 gallon | = | 4.546 liters | = | 32 gills |
| 1 barrel | = | 36 gallons | | |

Comparison Chart:

| | | | | |
|---|---|---|---|---|
| 1 US gallon | = | 0.8331 British Imperial gallons | = | 3.785 liters |
| 1 US quart | = | 0.8331 British Imperial quarts | = | 946.33 mL |
| 1 US pint | = | 0.8331 British Imperial pints | = | 473.16 mL |
| 1 British Imperial gallon | = | 1.2003 US gallons | = | 4.5435 liters |
| 1 British Imperial quart | = | 1.2003 US quarts | = | 1.136 liters |
| 1 British Imperial pint | = | 1.2003 US pints | = | 567.94 mL |

**Michaelmas**~~the Feast of St. Michael, Sept. 29; formerly Oct. 11 (Old Michaelmas).

**Mina, mna**~~a unit of measurement = 100 drachmae.

**Muscadine**~~muscatel, a sweet rich wine made from muscat grapes.

**Musk**~~a very smelly substance secreted by certain animals, most notably the male musk deer. Musk has been used in medicine for coughs, as a nerve stimulant, an antispasmodic, etc. Synthetic musk is available for use in perfumes, but it has no medicinal value.

**Must**~~the expressed juice of grapes, used to make wine. For red wine the skins and seeds remain in the must, for white wines the skins and seeds are removed. The longer the must remains in contact with the skins and seeds, the deeper the color of the wine, and the more astringent the flavor of the wine will be.

**Noggin**~~a unit of measurement = 1/4 pint = 1/2 cup.

**Obol**~~Ancient Greek unit of measurement = 1/6 drachma.

**Ounce**~~unit of measurement = 437.5 grains = 28.35 grams.

**Oyle of Ben**~~unknown oil used by Plat (#1, p. 206) to seal the connection around his filtration paper.

**Parel**~~a verb meaning to fine the wine, etc., using egg whites and other substances. 'Parel' also refers to the fining mixture itself.

**Parelling Staffe**~~a long stick, "one cubit in length," which was stuck through the bung hole, and used for mixing the liquid inside the cask.

**Pastil, Pastille**~~small scented tablets or lozenges; some were medicated, others were burned for their scents.

**Pearl, Pearle**~~the gem produced by oysters from a grain of sand and calcium carbonate, formerly thought to have medicinal properties, and still hyped today in rejuvenating lotions.

**Pearl ash**~~anhydrous potassium carbonate, $K_2CO_3$.

**Peck**~~unit of dry measure = 8 quarts = 0.25 bushels = 8.8098 liters.

**Penny(weight)**~~unit of dry measure = 8 carats = 32 grains (British) or 24 grains (French & Venetian).

**Physical**~~medicinally beneficial.

**Pipe**~~a cask holding from 100 to 140 gallons.

**Pomace, Pummice**~~the pulp left over after the fruit has been pressed for juice.

**Porringers**~~small round dishes used for eating porridge. Porringers varied in size, and typically had one or two triangular handles. Approximate volume = 1/2 to 1 1/2 cups.

**Porter**~~or Porter's ale; a dark ale made with toasted malt, invented c. 1720. (*See Monckton, p. 144.*)

**Posset, poshet, possot**~~a warm drink of spiced sweetened milk, curdled with wine or ale.

**Possnet**~~presumably a small saucepan used for making possets.

**Poteen**~~from the Gaelic *poitín*, Irish hootch; illegal whisky.

**Pottle**~~a unit of measurement = 2 quarts; also refers to a pitcher holding that amount.

**Pound**~~a unit of measurement = 16 ounces.

**Pugil**~~a unit of measurement = a pinch; as much as can be picked up between the thumb and first two fingers.

**Quarter**~~a unit of dry measure = 8 bushels; also means 3 months.

**Quarterne**~~one-fourth of a unit of measurement.

**Quibbibs**~~Cubebs. (*See Appendix, p. 273.*)

**Quintal**~~(*See Hundredweight, British measure.*)

**Querne**~~a hand mill used for grinding grain.

**Race**~~from MF *rais* – root, and from Latin *radix*, a root of ginger.

## GLOSSARY

**Rack**~~a verb meaning to draw off the clear liquid from the dregs.

**Ranch-Sieve**~~a type of sieve or strainer.

**Receipt**~~a recipe.

**Rectified spirit of wine**~~alcohol purified by distillation. (*See Aqua vitae and Distillation.*) "Alſo diſtilled of it ſelfe, is called Spirit of wine, which ſerueth to diſſolve, and to draw out the tincture of diuers things, and for many other purpoſes," (Parkinson, p. 566).

**Rope**~~a disease of wine caused by a bacterial infection in the yeast which causes the liquid to appear thick and **ropy**. To correct this, beat the wine or shake it vigorously and then add campden tablets. Or, throw the wine away and start over using fresh yeast. (*See Tritton, pp. 124-125.*)

**Rose-water**~~water to which essential oil of rose has been added. Rosewater is readily available in herb stores, gourmet shops, and some pharmacies.

**Runlet, Rundlet**~~from OF *rondelle*, a cask of varying capacity, but smaller than a hogshead. Identified by Mendelsohn (p. 288) as holding 15 imperial gallons or 18 1/2 wine gallons or 18 1/2 U.S. gallons. Harrison (p. 459) confirms it holds "18 gallons and a pottle."

**Sack**~~a strong, light colored wine from Spain.

**Sack Cask**~~a wooden cask which had contained Sack wine. The cask absorbed the wine's flavor and imparted that flavor to liquids subsequently stored in the cask. To simulate this flavor, add a small amount of Sack to your brew.

**Salpeter, Saltpeter**~~Potassium nitrate, $KNO_3$.

**Saltspoonful**~~1/4 teaspoonful.

**Scotch pint**~~"The Scotch pint is two quarts" (Dods, p. 469).

**Scruple**~~a unit of measurement = 1.3 grams = 20 grains.

**Scum**~~the froth that rises to the surface of the boiling liquid; it must be removed by skimming or the end product will be bitter.

**Searce**~~to sieve.

**Sextarius**~~a Roman unit of measurement = approx. 1 1/2 English pints or 0.853 liters.

**Shilling**~~a small British coin used to determine the Specific Gravity of the wort. (*See note under Groat.*)

**Short or Small Mead**~~the terms "small" and "short" refer to both the time it takes to make the mead and the time it will keep once it is made. This type of mead uses far less honey than "longer" meads; the proportion is one part honey to four, five, or six parts water, depending on the recipe.

**Specific Gravity, (SG)**~~Specific gravity is the ratio of the mass of a solid or liquid to that of an equal volume of distilled water at 4°C (39°F). Confused? Basically, SG tells us the density of the wort, compared to the density of distilled water; this in turn tells us the proportion of sugar or honey present in the wort. SG is a modern measurement used by brewers who don't like surprises, and is also used by those attempting to reconstruct old recipes given very limited data. The earlier equivalent of an SG measurement was to float a newly-laid egg in the wort; if a groat-sized portion of the eggshell could be seen floating above the wort, then enough honey had been added:

"put a good number, (ten or twelve) New-laid-eggs into it, and as round ones as may be; For long ones will deceive you in the swiming; and stale ones, being lighter then new, will emerge out of the Liquor, the breadth of a sixpence, when new ones will not a groats-breadth."

The SG of the wort is first measured using a hydrometer prior to fermentation to determine the initial sugar content of the wort, and is then measured again after fermentation (the yeast has eaten much of the sugar), in order to determine the alcohol content.

**Speck**~~1/4 saltspoonful = 1/16 teaspoonful.

**"Spread yeast on both Sides of a Tost"** or **"work it with a toast spread with yeast"**~~means to spread your semi-liquid yeast onto a piece of toasted bread; the bread then floats on top of the wort and, when left undisturbed, keeps the yeast from sinking to the bottom.

**Spoonful**~~a unit of measurement = 1 dram plus 6 grains.

**Stone**~~a unit of measurement = 14 pounds.

**Stopple**~~ a stopper or bung.

**Strom**~~according to the OED, a "strom" is "an oblong basket of wickerwork placed over the bung-hole within the wash-tub to prevent the grain and hops passing through when the liquor is drawn off."

**Superficies**~~the surface of the liquid in the cask or bottle.

**"Sweet and clean"**~~when used of a cask, or other container, it means one which is sterilized, clean, and ready to use.

**Syllabub**~~a drink made of milk or cream that is sweetened and curdled with wine, verjuice, cider, etc. A curd (or froth) forms on the top while the clear liquid settles to the bottom. Syllabub is traditionally passed around and drunk out of a special spouted jug or cup.

**Tannin**~~tannic acid.

## GLOSSARY

**Teacupful**~~a unit of measurement = 3 ounces.

**Teaspoonful**~~a unit of measurement = 1 dram.

**Temper**~~to mix.

**Theban Ounce**~~an unknown unit of measurement.

**Treacle**~~molasses.

**Verjuice**~~a sour juice made from unripe fruits such as grapes or crabapples. It has also been defined as crabapple vinegar. Substitute a mixture of apple cider vinegar and grape juice. I recently made some verjuice from doubly sour unripe wild grapes; it turned out muddy brown in color, surprisingly viscous, and extremely sour.

**Walm**~~dialect for a bubble or boil.

**Wash the fruit, herbs, etc.**~~means to rinse the ingredients in one or more changes of clean water, but for heaven's sake don't use soap!

**White powder**~~a spice mixture of ginger, cinnamon, and nutmeg.

**Wineglassful**~~a unit of measurement = 2 ounces = 1/2 gill.

**Woodden-fat**~~a wooden vat.

**Working**~~fermenting.

**Work up highly**~~ferment well.

**Wort, Woort**~~from ME or OE *wyrt*, a plant, *or* unfermented or fermenting beer.

**Yeast**~~(*Saccharomyces* spp.), many cultivated varieties of this tiny plant can be found dried and sold in small foil-lined packets in beer and wine-making supply stores. Please note: when most of these early recipes call for a pint or more of yeast, they are talking about a *solution* of active yeast, commonly referred to as "barm," and *not* a pint of dry yeast granules. You don't need to add enormous quantities of yeast to work the wort, as the yeast will grow and happily consume all the available sugars until it starves or poisons itself with its own alcohol waste (at about 15% alcohol). Make your own "barm" by dissolving the dried yeast (use one packet per 5 gallons liquor) in 1 pint of warm water (which has been sterilized by boiling and cooled to 89° – 95°F), or in 1 pint of warm wort. The liquid must be warm, not hot, or the yeast will die. The yeast should foam slightly. This "proving" step is the same as in baking bread. Once the yeast has been added to the wort, you may mix it well once to incorporate the yeast and then allow the fermentation to proceed undisturbed; shaking the jug slows the fermentation. You may notice a diurnal cycle of yeast activity – this is normal. When the fermentation slows sufficiently, the liquid is racked to filter off the clear and leave behind the yeast and sediment. The clear liquid is bottled and aged according to the recipe.

# APPENDIX OF HERBS AND FRUITS

*An Herb Garden.*
From *Liber de Arte Distillandi*, by Brunschwig.
Strassburg, Grüninger, 1500.

In presenting the following list I hope to give you some familiarity with the herbs called for in the preceding recipes, and to caution you, where appropriate, against using those that may cause harm. It is not my intention to frighten you away from trying these recipes, but merely to teach you caution when dealing with older recipes that call for unfamiliar ingredients.

I have done my best to identify these herbs, given that most are identified only by common or dialectical names, which are oftentimes shared by a number of different species. Choices have been given where uncertainty exists, and preference has been given to plants currently under, or escaped from, cultivation. The Latin nomenclature used generally follows that in Britton & Brown (B&B), except where a species is absent from that enormous work. The numbers following the letters B&B refer to volume and page number, respectively.

You will find the descriptions of plants listed here are far from comprehensive; should you require more information, I suggest you consult an up-to-date herbal, Mrs. Grieve's *A Modern Herbal*, and also the *AMA Handbook of Poisonous and Injurious Plants*. If you are using an older herbal for guidance, please be aware that the toxicity data are likely to be out of date and inaccurate; many plants have been moved to the "toxic" list in recent years due to improvements in testing methods. *Above all, please do not equate the word "herb" with the words "good" and "safe," as many of the world's most toxic poisons are derived from plants.* A great many herbs may cause uterine contractions, and, consequently, may cause miscarriages — *if you are pregnant, consult your doctor before taking any herbal concoction.* Some toxic plants may be used safely if properly prepared; see the following pages for more information.

It is important to realize that far too many medieval writers of herbals got their information from the works of ancient "Authorities." Too often they cited these works without question (and in many cases without attribution). They did not always know *which* herbs the Ancients were describing (they held debates on the subject), but this did not stop them from writing –with utter certainty– that this plant cures such-and-such diseases. Without a shred of empirical evidence, medicinal, and in some instances almost miraculous virtues were ascribed to a plant, many times simply due to the shape of the leaves, the color of the sap, or the plant's "temperament":

Doctrine of Signatures: Typically, the physical appearance of the plant (lobed leaves, red sap or root, etc.), was thought to indicate the use of the plant. This "Doctrine of Signatures" can be clearly seen in the virtues ascribed to Bistort and Tormentil, plants with reddish roots, which were used for small-pox, measles, and sores (red spots), bleeding, miscarriage, and wounds (red blood). Similarly Lungwort, with its spotted leaves, was used for lung diseases.

Humors and Temperaments: A person's health was thought to be controlled by the four humors: blood, phlegm, choler, and black bile. Plants, foodstuffs, and certain activities were considered to be hot, dry, cold, or moist, in the first, second, third, or fourth degree; these "temperaments" had to be balanced properly for a person to maintain good health. Each plant was also under the dominion of a certain planet or constellation, and was thought to help the parts of the body which were similarly influenced. It is very complicated nonsense, which, for the most part, I have deliberately ignored in the interests of clarity and brevity. *Culpeper's Herbal* (pp. 332-335) and *The Four Seasons of the House of Cerruti* (pp. 139-141) have Tables of Temperaments if you are curious. Although a few period "cures" have been cited here, these have been added only to demonstrate briefly how the herbs may have been used by our authors.

I find it curious that so many of the herbs called for in our recipes for wines, beers, etc., have also been used as sources of *dye* for cloth. A table of dye herbs has been appended to this list of plants so that you may draw your own conclusions as to whether a particular herb was included in the recipe for its taste, its medicinal properties, and/or its color.

**A SHORT LIST OF POISONOUS**
**OR HARMFUL PLANTS TO BE AVOIDED:**

BITTERSWEET
BOG MYRTLE (SWEET GALE)
CELANDINE POPPY
CHINA ROOT
FLORENCE IRIS
GROUNDSEL
KILL LAMB
LILY-OF-THE-VALLEY
ORRIS ROOTS
PENNYROYAL
RHUBARB LEAVES
SASSAFRAS
TURNSOLE
WORMWOOD

SEEDS AND PITS OF:
  Apple
  Apricot
  Cherry
  Citrus Fruit
  Peach
  Pear
  Plum

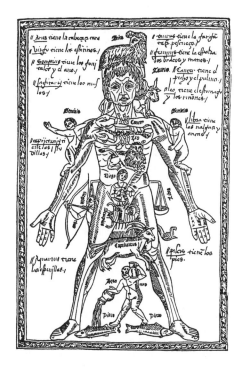

From *Epiligo en medicina y cirurgia*,
by Juan de Burgos, 1495.

## APPENDIX OF HERBS & FRUITS

(* = CAUTION.)

**\*Agrimony.** *Agrimonia Eupatoria* L., and related species, Rosaceae, (B&B, 2: 266-8). "The liver is the former of blood, and blood the nourisher of the body, and Agrimony a strengthener of the liver."[1] Agrimony is astringent and was used for binding cuts and wounds; a syrup of agrimony was used for coughs. Agrimony contains *psoralens* that can cause photodermatitis if the plant is rubbed on the skin. Water aids the absorption of the psoralens and causes hypersensitivity to sunlight; a mild burn or blisters may result.[2] Wear gloves when picking agrimony.

**Alecost.** (*See Costmary.*)

**Alehoof.** *Glechoma hederacea* L., (*Nepeta hederacea* B.S.P.), Labiatae, (B&B, 3: 114). Gill-over-the-ground, Ground Ivy, Tunhoof, Field-Balm. "It is good to tun up with new drink, for it will clarify it in a night, that it will be the fitter to be drank the next morning; or if any drink be thick with removing or any other accident, it will do the like in a few hours."[3] It is also used as a tonic, stimulant, astringent, and diuretic, and to make Gill Tea, a cough remedy.[4] Alehoof can be fatal to horses, if eaten, but it is not poisonous to humans.[5]

**Alexander, Alisander.**
1- *Zizia aurea* (L.) Koch., Umbelliferae, (B&B, 2: 641). Golden Alexanders, Wild Parsley.
2-*Angelica atropurpurea* L., Umbelliferae, (B&B, 2: 637). Angelica. Use like *A. Archangelica*. According to Culpeper, Alexander was a common garden herb needing no description. "...it warmeth a cold stomach, and openeth a stoppage to the liver and spleen; it is good to move women's courses, to expel the after-birth..."[6] Parkinson, says that the seeds are used more often in medicine, while the root is used to make broth "by reaſon of the aromaticall or ſpicie taſte, warming and comforting the ſtomack..."[7]

**\*Alkanet.** *Alkanna tinctoria* (Tausch.) or *Anchusa tinctoria*, Boraginaceae. Orchanet, Spanish Bugloss, Enchusa,[8] Bugloss of Languedoc, Alkanea, Orcanette or Orcanéte.[9] The root of alkanet yields a red dye which is used in medicines, chemistry, and the leather industry. Alkanet was sometimes used in medieval times as a red food dye. Mrs. Grieve[10] says that it is "perfectly harmless" when used as a coloring/adulterant in wine, and indeed the small amount consumed in such a diluted solution should cause no harm.
Nevertheless, Alkanet is closely related to the poisonous *Echium vulgare* L., or Vipers Bugloss, (B&B, 3: 94), and may be confused for it, even in the old herbals. The *AMA Handbook* cautions that toxicity data have not been completed for all plants, and that one should assume the worst for closely related plants. *Echium* has this listing: "The whole plant is poisonous. Toxin: Pyrrolizidine alkaloids. Symptoms: Toxicity is associated with use of the plant in herbal teas for folk medicine. The chronic consumption of these teas may cause veno-occlusive disease of the liver (Budd-Chiari syndrome) with hepatic vein thrombosis leading to cirrhosis. The symptoms are abdominal pain with ascites [accumulation of fluid in the peritoneum], hepatomegaly and splenomegaly [enlargement of the liver & spleen], anorexia with nausea, vomiting and diarrhea..."[11] Why take the risk ?

**\*Aloe.** *Aloe vera* L., and related species, <u>Liliaceae</u>.
Medicinally, aloe is used internally as a cathartic and emmenagogue; it is also used externally in folk medicine to soothe burns.

**Angelica.** *Angelica Archangelica* L., <u>Umbelliferae</u>, (B&B, 2: 636).
Angelica is an aromatic plant. Its stems are candied in sugar syrup as a confection; the leaves are used to make hop bitters. Oil of Angelica is used in the manufacture of liqueurs, especially *Vermouth*, *Chartreuse*, and *Benedictine*. Angelica is a truly useful plant, supplying medicines, flavorings, candies, a green vegetable, bread from the roots, beverages, etc.

**Anise, Annys.** *Pimpinella anisum* L., <u>Umbelliferae</u>.
Anise seeds are used medicinally as carminatives, and to relieve colic and coughs. They are also used for flavoring, especially in the liqueur *Anisette*. An oil of anise is available.

**\*Apple.** *Malus malus* (L.) Britton, (*Pyrus malus* L.), <u>Malaceae</u>, (B&B, 2: 290).
The cultivated varieties called for include Pippins, Golden-pippins, Peermains or Pear-mains, Codlings, Red Streaks, and Ginet-moils. (*See Peach for cautionary note.*)

**\*Apricot.** *Prunus armeniaca* L., <u>Amygdalaceae</u>.
Apricots were originally cultivated in China four thousand years ago, and were introduced to Persia in the first century A.D. (*See Peach for cautionary note.*)

**Arras** is a city in Northern France. Perhaps the pot herb **Arrach**, or **Orache**, or the fragrant Orris root (*which see*), was meant by Harrison. Culpeper[12] lists two arrachs:

**1-***Atriplex hortensis* L., and related species, <u>Chenopodiaceae</u>, (B&B, 2: 17). Orache.
Culpeper uses it for "swellings in the throat" and to cure yellow jaundice. This and other species of *Atriplex* are edible.

**2-***Chenopodium Vulvaria* L., <u>Chenopodiaceae</u>, (B&B, 2: 11). Stinking Mother Wort.
Culpeper uses it to cure all diseases of the womb, while Gerard[13] denies it has any medicinal virtue. Both report few plants smell worse. It is not what is being called for here.

**Ash tree.** *Fraxinus* species, <u>Oleaceae</u>, (B&B, 2: 724-7).
"The decoction of the leaves in white wine helpeth to break the stone and expel it, and cure the jaundice."[14]

**Asparagus.** *Asparagus officinalis* L.,
and related species, <u>Convallariaceae</u>, (B&B, 1: 513-4).
Sperage.
The roots were used as a diuretic, and as a remedy for gout and dropsy, but are no longer so used.[15]

*Orache.*

**Avens.**                               *Geum urbanum* L., and related species, <u>Rosaceae</u>, (B&B, 2: 269-72).
Herb Bennet.
"The root in the spring-time, steeped in wine, gives it a delicate savour and taste, ...it promoteth diges-tion, warmeth a cold stomach, and openeth obstructions of the liver and spleen."[16] The dried root has a clove-like flavor and is used to flavor Augsburg Ale.[17]

**Balm, Balme, Baulme, etc.**          *Melissa officinalis* L., <u>Labiatae</u>, (B&B, 3: 137).
Lemon Balm, Balm of Gilead.
Used as a flavoring in liqueurs. Gerard says "Bawme drunke in wine, is good again∫t the bitings of venemous bea∫ts, comforteth the hart, and driueth away all melancholie and ∫adne∫∫e."[18] Parkinson says "it is al∫o v∫ed by diuers to be ∫tilled, being ∫teeped in Ale, to make a Baulme water..."[19] An Oil of Balm is available and is used as a flavoring agent.

**\*Barberry.**                          *Berberis vulgaris* L., <u>Berberidaceae</u>, (B&B, 2: 127).
Red, elongated, acid fruit, much used for jams and pies. The root bark is used in medicines as a bitter tonic, astringent, and febrifuge. The roots are also the source of an alkaloid, *oxyacanthine*, which can cause stomach pains, salivation, and can adversely affect respiration.

**Barley.**                              *Hordeum vulgare* L., <u>Gramineae</u>, (B&B, 1: 286).
**Barley, Pearl.**                       *H. vulgare* var. *trifurcatum* (Schlect.) Alef.
The source of barley malt, barley was also much used in folk medicine to make nourishing drinks for invalids, and poultices for swellings, leprosy, gout, etc.

**Bayberry.**                            *Myrica cerifera* L., and related species, <u>Myricaceae</u>, (B&B, 1: 584-5).
A shrub, found primarily in North America, whose berries are naturally coated with sweet-smelling wax, formerly much prized for candles. The leaves and seeds may be used for seasoning. The flowers of *M. rubra* are edible and are used for making a beverage. (*See Sweet-oak and Sweet Fern.*)

**Bay.**                                               *Laurus nobilis* L., <u>Lauraceae</u>.
Sweet Bay, Bay Laurel.
The leaves and berries of bay are used for flavoring. Also, according to Culpeper, bay is another plant that cures just about everything, and it will keep you safe from witchcraft and lightning.[20]

**Beans.**                               probably *Phaseolus* species, <u>Fabaceae</u>, (B&B, 2: 341-425).
The Pea Family, of which beans are members, has over 5000 species, many of which are edible.

**Betony.**                              *Betonica officinalis* L, (*Stachys Betonica* L.), <u>Labiatae</u>, (B&B, 3: 128).
Herb christopher, Wild Hop, Wood Betony.
Gerard claims betony to be a cure for epilepsy, headaches, cramps and convulsions, rabies and poison. He also says "it maketh a man to have a good stomacke and appetite to his meate."[21]

**Bilberry.** Many plants produce edible fruits called 'bilberries':

> **1-***Amelianchier canadensis* (L.) Medic., and related species, <u>Malaceae</u>, (B&B, 2: 292). June-berry, Service-berry. Eaten raw, cooked, or in pemmican.

2- *Vaccinium* spp., Vacciniaceae, (B&B, 2: 698-703). Blueberry, Huckleberry.

3- *Gaylussacia* spp., Vacciniaceae, (B&B, 2: 695-6). Tangleberry, Huckleberry.

*4- *Viburnum* species, Caprifoliaceae, (B&B, 3: 269-74). Highbush Cranberry, Black Haw. The sour fruit is used for cooking and wine. *V. opulus* bark is used in folk medicine for uterine disorders. *V. Prunifolium* root bark is also used in folk medicine to bring on menstruation.

5- *Uva-Ursi Uva-Ursi* (L.) Britton, Ericaceae, (B&B, 2: 693). (*Arctostaphylos Uva-Ursi* Spreng.), Bearberry, Bear's-grape, Kinnikinic. This bilberry has mealy edible berries; its leaves are a tobacco substitute, and it is used medicinally as a diuretic and astringent.

6- *Vitis-Idaea Vitis-Idaea* (L.) Britton, Vacciniaceae, (B&B, 2: 697). Mountain Cranberry, Wine Berry, Red Whortleberry.

**Birch**.                                            *Betula lenta* L., Betulaceae, (B&B, 1: 609).
                                                            Cherry, Black, or Sweet Birch.
The bark of Sweet Birch contains *methyl salicylate*, as does wintergreen, and has been used to make oil of wintergreen and birch beer. The sap is used like that of sugar maples.

**Bistort**.                                        *Bistorta* species, Polygonaceae, (B&B, 1: 671).
Culpeper says "the decoction of the root in wine being drank, prevents abortion or miscarriage in child-bearing."[22] He also credits it with curing plague, poison, small-pox, measles, all infectious diseases, wounds, worms, etc.

**\*Bittersweet**.                                  *Solanum Dulcamara* L., Solanaceae, (B&B, 3: 167).
                                    Climbing or Bitter Nightshade, Poison-berry, European Bittersweet.
A medicine was prepared from the dried stems to treat dropsy, skin diseases, etc., but it is no longer so used. The berries are poisonous.

**Blackberry**.                                         *Rubus* species, Rosaceae, (B&B, 2: 278-281).
Wild and cultivated blackberry species bear delicious juicy fruits on thorny stems. The dried leaves are used for tea, and the young shoots for greens. The root bark of *R. nigrobaccus* Bailey, (*R. Alleghaniensis* Porter), is used medicinally as an astringent, and for diarrhea and dysentery.

**\*Blessed Thistle**.                               *Cnicus benedictus* L., Compositae, (B&B, 3: 560).
                                                                        Our Lady's Thistle.
Culpeper claims it is good for diseases of the liver, spleen, and kidneys.[23] It is an emetic, expectorant, and tonic.

**Bloodwort**. (*See Burnet.*)

**Blue bottle**.

**1-** *Centaurea cyanus* L., and related species, Compositae, (B&B, 3: 557). Corn-flower, Hurt-sickle. Used by Parkinson "as a cooling Cordiall."[24] Culpeper uses blue bottles for bruises, internal bleeding, poison, plague, sore eyes, etc., and says that "if you transplant them into your garden, especially towards the full moon, they will grow more double [*blossoms*], and many times change colour."[25]

**2-** *Muscari botryoides* (L.) Mill., Liliaceae, (B&B, 1: 510-11). Grape Hyacinth. (*See Muscovy.*)

**Blue-buttons**.                          *Scabiosa arvensis* L., and related species, Dipsaceae, (B&B, 3: 289-290).
                                                                        Scabious, Gypsy Rose, Pincushion.
Culpeper claims blue-buttons cure everything from ringworm to leprosy.[26] Its chief use seems to have been as a cough medicine when prepared with wine.

**\*Bog Myrtle**. (*See Sweet Gale.*)

**Borage**.                                    *Borago officinalis* L., Boraginaceae, (B&B, 3: 93).
Gerard says "the leaves and floures of Borrage put into wine make men and women glad and merry, driving away all sadnesse, dulnesse, and melancholy..."[27] He also claims borage is good for heart disease, epilepsy, fainting and lunacy. Borage is a very attractive plant with blue star-shaped flowers; it is useful as a potherb, garnish, confection, and drink flavoring.

**Box-berry**. (*See Winter Evergreen.*)

**Broad Thyme**. (*See Thyme.*)

**Bugle**.                                    *Ajuga réptans* L., Labiatae, (B&B, 3: 101).
                                          Carpenter's herb, Sickle-wort, Brown Bugle.
Bugle is an aromatic, astringent herb. Gerard says it is good for wounds.[28]

**Bugloss** is a name given to members of the Boraginaceae. (*See also Alkanet and Borage.*)

**Burnet**.                                    *Poterium Sanguisorba* L., Rosaceae, (B&B, 2: 266).
                          Salad Burnet, Toper's-plant, Pimpernelle, Bloodwort, Bibernel, Garden-burnet.
"Two or three of the stalks with leaves put into a cup of wine, especially claret, are known to quicken the spirits, refresh and clear the heart, and drive away melancholy."[29] The plant is astringent, and has been used in tonics, and for stanching bleeding.

**Caraway**.                                    *Carum Carui* L., Umbelliferae, (B&B, 2: 659).
The seeds are a common spice and flavoring, especially in German cookery, and are used medicinally as a tonic. The roots and leaves are also eaten. Oil of caraway is used to flavor soaps, perfumes, and liqueurs such as *Kummel*.

**Cardamom.** *Elettaria cardamomum* Maton, Zingiberaceae.
An expensive spice, cardamom is also used as a stomachic and carminative, especially in combination with caraway, cinnamon, and cochineal. It is sold powdered, as whole seeds, or as white seed pods.

**Carnation.** (*See Clove Gilliflowers.*)

**Carob.** *Ceratonia siliqua*, Fabaceae.
Large dark brown seed pods, which are often used to make an unconvincing substitute for chocolate.

**Cassia.**
  **1-***Cinnamomum cassia*, Lauraceae. This cassia is a type of cinnamon.

  **\*2-***Cassia* species, Caesalpinaceae, (B&B, 2: 335-336). Senna, Coffee-weed. These cassias are used as laxatives, cathartics, and purgatives, and may be fatal to animals.[31]

**\*Catmint.** *Nepeta Cataria* L., Labiatae, (B&B, 3: 113).
Catnip, Nep.
Culpeper (p. 203) uses it to cure 'pains of the mother,' cramps, bruises, and to bring on menstruation, etc.; it has been used medically as a carminative, for colic, and to cure dysmenorrhea. The leaves are used to make tea.

**\*Celandine Poppy.** *Chelidonium majus* L., Papaveraceae, (B&B, 2: 141).
Celandine poppy is poisonous, and may prove fatal if ingested.

**\*Chamomile.** *Anthemis nobilis* L., Compositae, (B&B, 3: 517).
Garden Camomile, Maythen, Manzanilla.
Chamomile has long been used in folk medicine as an aid to digestion, and to cure colds, fevers, worms and diarrhea; it is also an emetic. "The flowers boiled in posset-drink provoke sweat, and help to expel all colds, aches and pains, and promotes women's courses. Syrup made of the juice of camomile, with the flowers in white wine, is a remedy against jaundice and dropsy..."[32] It is an aromatic plant with a faint apple scent, used to flavor some sherries.

**Checkerberry.** (*See Winter evergreen.*)

**\*Cherry.** *Prunus cerasus* L., and related species, Amygdalaceae, (B&B, 2: 327-328).
Morello, Black English, and Black Cherries are called for here. (*See Peach for cautionary note.*)

**\*China Root.** possibly *Smilax* species, Smilaceae (B&B, 1: 528-529).
Sarsaparilla, Catbrier.
(*S. Pseudo-China* L. is False China Root.) Sarsaparilla was a common flavoring and was also used in medicine for rheumatism, skin diseases, and syphilis. According to Merck (p. 413), *S. medica* Cham. is the source of a hemolytic poison called *parillin* which is poisonous even at 1 part per 100,000. Other species of *Smilax* are edible as salads and potherbs.

**Cinnamon.** *Cinnamomum* species, Lauraceae.
A common spice; also used medicinally as a stomachic, carminative, and astringent.

**Citron.**                                            *Citrus medica*, <u>Aurantiodeae</u>.
The green rind of this fruit is candied and is most readily found at Christmastime. It is possible that some of our earlier recipes, while calling for 'citron,' were actually referring to large lemons. (*See "To Make Citron-Water...," p. 215.*)

**Clary.**                                   *Salvia sclarea* L., <u>Labiatae</u>, (B&B, 3: 131).
                                                                            Clear Eyes.
B&B contains the note that "the mucilage of the seeds [is] used to clear specks from the eye," which is almost exactly what Culpeper says on the subject. Culpeper adds "the seeds or leaves taken in wine, provoketh to venery... the juice of the herb in ale or beer, and drank, promotes the courses."[33]

**Clove.**                  *Eugenia aromatica*, (*Syzygium aromaticum*), <u>Myrtaceae</u>.[34]
The name is sometimes used of the clove pink or gilliflowers. Cloves are the unopened flower buds of the clove plant. Oil of cloves is available in pharmacies; it is anesthetic and antiseptic. Cloves are used for flavorings, and medicinally as stomachics, to relieve colic and flatulence.

**Clove Gilliflowers.**     *Dianthus caryophyllus* L., and related species, <u>Caryophyllaceae</u>, (B&B, 2: 73).
"They are great strengtheners... of the brain and heart, and will... do either for cordials..."[30] Use only cultivated edible varieties, as some members of the Pink Family are poisonous.

**Clown's-all-heal.**                     *Stachys palustris* L., <u>Labiatae</u>, (B&B, 3: 125).
                                                                     Clown's woundwort.
"A syrup made of the juice of it is inferior to no remedy for inward wounds, ruptures of the veins, bloody flux, vessels broken, spitting, voiding, or vomiting blood..."[35] *S. palustris* is also used as a potherb.

**Coltsfoot.**                          *Tussilago Farfara* L., <u>Compositae</u>, (B&B, 3: 531).
The leaves have long been used as a remedy for coughs.

**Comfrey.**                          *Symphytum officinale* L., <u>Boraginaceae</u>, (B&B, 3: 92).
                                           Healing-herb, Knit-back, Boneset, Bruisewort.
"The root boiled in water or wine, and the decoction drank, heals inward hurts, bruises, wounds, and ulcers of the lungs, and causes the phlegm that oppresses him to be easily spit forth."[36] Comfrey has been used to cure sores, gout, sprains, etc. "The ſlimie ſubſtance of the roote made in a poſſet of ale, and giuen to drinke againſt the paine in the backe, gotten by any violent motion, as wraſtling, or ouermuch vſe of women [!], doth in fower or fiue daies perfectly cure the ſame: although the inuoluntarie flowing of the ſeed in men be gotten thereby."[37]

**Cornel.**                                  *Cornus Mas*, <u>Cornaceae</u>, (B&B, 2: 660).
The fruits of this flowering dogwood, called Cornel Plums, are edible, and are used to make wines and liqueurs.

**Costmary, Coursemary.**          *Chrysanthemum Balsamita* L., <u>Compositae</u>, (B&B, 3: 519).
                                                                 Mint Geranium, Alecost.
"It is astringent to the stomach, and strengtheneth the liver and other vicera."[38] Costmary is very hard

to find, and is usually propagated by root division rather than by seed. "Coſtmary is vſed among thoſe herbes that are put in[t]o ale to cauſe it haue a good relliſh, and to be ſomewhat phyſicall in the moneth of May.[39] Costmary was used to flavor ale, to scent rooms, and also as a vegetable, an antiseptic, an astringent, a stomachic, and a vermifuge.

**\*Cow Parsnip.** *Heracleum Sphondylium* L., and related species, <u>Umbelliferae</u>, (B&B, 2: 635). *Heracleum* species can cause dermatitis. The cooked stems, leaf stalks, and roots may be eaten, as may the dried seeds. Be careful not to mistake the poisonous Water Hemlock for Cow Parsnip.

**Cowslip.**

    **\*1-***Primula veris* L., <u>Primulaceae</u>, (B&B, 2: 708). The English Primrose is probably what is being called for here – Leggatt uses them in several recipes. Parkinson devotes several pages to *P. veris* and related plants; he says they are used "to eaſe paines in the head...for the Palſie, and paines of the ioynts..."[40] Wine made of cowslip flowers is sedative in nature. (*See Primrose for cautionary note.*)

    **\*2-***Caltha palustris* L., <u>Ranunculaceae</u>, (B&B, 2: 85). The American Cowslip, or Marsh Marigold. The young leaves and flower buds of *C. palustris* may be eaten if cooked first to destroy the toxic *protoanemonin* contained in the whole plant.[41] Ingestion of the raw plant results in inflamation of the mouth and throat, gastroenteritis, bloody discharge and diarrhea.[42]

**Cubebs.** *Piper Cubeba* L., (*Cubeba officinalis* Raf.), <u>Piperaceae</u>. A spice sold as small dried black berries; the flavor is a cross between black pepper and allspice.

**Currants.** *Ribes* species, <u>Grossulariaceae</u>, (B&B, 2: 236-239). Currants are increasingly available fresh, and are sold as small red currant grapes.

**Dandelion.** *Taraxacum officinale* Weber, (*Leontodon Taraxacum* L.), <u>Compositae</u>, (B&B, 3: 315). The dandelion is a common weed and a truly useful plant. The flowers are used for wine, the leaves for greens and herb beers, the seed heads for toys, and the roasted root for a coffee substitute. Dandelions have been used medicinally for complaints of the liver and kidneys, and as diuretics and stimulants.

**Date.** *Phoenix dactylifera.* The sweet fruits of date palm trees.

**Dill.** *Anethum graveolens* L., <u>Umbelliferae</u>, (B&B, 2: 634). A common garden herb much used in Scandinavian cookery. The seeds and their oil are aromatic and carminative, and have been used as stomachics, and as flavorings in soups, sauces, vinegars, pickles, etc.

**\*Dock.** probably *Rumex Acetosa* L., and 15 related edible species, <u>Polygonaceae</u>, (B&B, 1: 654).
Green Sauce, Green Sorrel, Sour Dock, Sharp Dock.
*Rumex* species contain *oxalic acid*, a poisonous substance once used in medicine but since discarded as unreliable. The oxalic acid is destroyed by cooking; the cooked greens are safe to eat.

*APPENDIX OF HERBS & FRUITS*

**Eglantine.** (*See Sweetbrier.*)

**\*Elder**                    *Sambucus canadensis* L., and related species, Caprifoliaceae, (B&B, 3: 268).
According to the *AMA Handbook*, the whole plants of most *Sambucus* species are poisonous; ingestion of the bark, roots, or uncooked fruit may cause severe diarrhea and nausea. The fruit is rendered harmless when cooked, the flowers are "probably nontoxic." The Elder has been the subject of a great deal of superstition in many cultures.[43] Wines and cough medicines are made from the juice of the berries; lotions, tonics, and cold remedies are prepared from the flowers, which also flavor wine and ale.

**Elecampane.**                    *Inula helenium* L., Compositae, (B&B, 3: 457).
                    Horse-heal, Elfwort, Wild sunflower.
The dried rhizomes and roots of elecampane are used in medicines as expectorants, diuretics, astringents, and tonics; they were used formerly to cure bronchitis, coughs, psoriasis, and other ailments. Elecampane has been used to make *absinthe*, cordials, and candy.

**Eringo.**                    *Eryngium maritimum* L., Umbelliferae, (B&B, 2: 621).
                    Sea Holly.
A "venereal" plant, "hot and moist" in character. "The decoction of the root hereof in wine, is very effectual to open obstructions of the spleen and liver, and helpeth yellow jaundice, dropsy, pains of the loins and colic; provoketh urine, expelleth the stone, and procureth women's courses."[44] Eringo root has been used as a diuretic, a stimulant, and an expectorant; the young shoots and roots can be eaten as vegetables. The roots are also candied and have been sold as an aphrodisiac. Gerard[45] gives a long recipe for candying Eringo roots.

**Eyebright.**                    *Euphrasia officinalis* L., and related species, Scrophulariaceae, (B&B, 3: 217-8).
"[Eyebright] tunned with strong beer..., and drunk, ..., hath the same powerful effect to help and restore the sight decayed through age..."[46] An astringent and tonic, it was used for eye diseases and coughs.

**Fennel.**                    *Foeniculum* species, Umbelliferae, (B&B, 2: 643).
Parkinson says "there are three ſorts of Fenell, whereof two are ſweete... the ordinary ſweete Fenell...[and]... Cardus Fenell... out of Italy... [and]... common Fennel, whereof there is greene and red... The rootes are vſed with Parſley rootes, to be boyled in broths and drinkes to open obſtructions..."[47] Fennel is used medicinally with purgatives, and to cure flatulence and coughs; it is used in the kitchen for salads, sauces, flavoring sausages, etc.

**Ferdinando Buck.**                    probably *Cæsalpinia echinata* Lam., Cæsalpiniaceae.
                    Fernambuco wood.
Ferdinando buck is a dyestuff used by Plat (#6, p. 183) to produce a crimson color; the name may be a corruption of *pernambuco* or *fernambuco*, a type of brazilwood, which is the source of a red dye.

**Fever-bush**.
**1-***Benzoin aestivale* (L.) Nees., <u>Lauraceae</u>, (B&B, 2: 135). Spice-bush, Wild Allspice.

***2-****Ilex verticillata* (L.) A. Gray., <u>Ilicaceae</u>, (B&B, 2: 489). Fever-bush, Black Alder, Winterberry. *Ilex* <u>berries</u> are poisonous, but the dried leaves of several species are used for tea. *I. paraguariensis* is the source of *yerba maté*.

**Figs**.                 *Ficus carica* L., and related species, <u>Moraceae</u>, (B&B: 1: 632).
Figs have been cultivated since ancient times.

***Fir**.                 *Abies balsamea* (L.) Mill., <u>Pinaceae</u>, (B&B, 1: 63).
                                                                       Balsam Fir.
The inner bark and branch tips are used for flavoring. The plant can cause contact dermatitis; wear gloves when harvesting fir. It is the source of Balsam Canada, an aromatic resinous substance used in medicines for respiratory and urogenital ailments, and in industry for lacquers, etc. (*See Spruce*.)

***Florence iris**.                 *Iris florentina* L., <u>Iridaceae</u>, (B&B, 1: 536-541).
"*Iris alba Florentina*, The white Flowerdeluce... [it] is accounted of all to be the ſweeteſt root, fit to be vſed to make ſweet powders, &c. calling it by the name of *Orris* rootes."[48] It was used formerly for coughs. (<u>TOXIC</u> – *see Orris Root*.)

***French-cowslip**. (*See Cowslip*.)

**Galingale**.                 *Alpinia officinarum*, Hance, <u>Zingiberaceae</u>.
The dried rhizomes are used as a spice; the flavor is a cross between ginger and pepper. Galingale is also used medicinally as a stomachic and carminative.

**Gentian**.                 *Gentiana acuta* Michx., and related species, <u>Gentianaceae</u>, (B&B, 3: 9).
                                         Felwort, Bastard-gentian, Bald-money.
Culpeper (pp. 137-9) uses gentian to cure poison, rabies, snake bite, and to help digestion, kidney stones, etc. *G. lutea* L. is used in the manufacture of liqueurs, and to stimulate the appetite.

**Gillyflowers**. (*See Clove Gillyflowers*.)

**Ginger**.

**1-***Zingiber officinale*, Roscoe, <u>Zingiberaceae</u>. A common spice, readily available fresh or dried.

**2-***Asarum canadense* L., <u>Aristolochiaceae</u>, (B&B, 1: 642). Native to the United States, *A. canadense* has been used as a substitute for *Z. officinale*; both have been used as stomachics and stimulants, as well as for flavorings in food and drink.

**Gooseberry**.                 *Grossularia reclinata* (L.) Mill., <u>Grossulariaceae</u>, (B&B, 2: 241).
                         (*Ribes grossularia* L.), Garden Gooseberry, Wine-berry, Honey-blobs.
Gooseberries are small fruits, much used in British cooking.

**Grains of Paradise.**        *Amomum* (or *Aframomum*) *meleguetta*, Zingiberaceae.
The seeds of Grains of Paradise are a rare spice; cardamom may be substituted.

**Grape.**        *Vitis vinifera* L., and related species, Vitaceae, (B&B, 2: 505-509).
"Wine is vſually taken both for drinke and medicine, and is often put into ſawces, broths, cawdles, and gellies that are given to the ſicke. As alſo into diuers Phyſicall drinkes, to be as a *vehiculum* for the properties of the ingredients" (Parkinson, p. 565). When harvesting wild grapes, be careful not to mistake them for the poisonous Canada Moonseed, *Menispermum canadense*. Grapes have 1 to 4 pear-shaped seeds; Moonseed has a single crescent-shaped seed per fruit, and the vine has no tendrils.

**Gromwell.**        *Lithospermum officinale* L., Boraginaceae, (B&B, 3: 88).
       Puccoon.
"The ſeede of Gromell pound, and drunke in white wine, breaketh, diſſolueth, and driueth foorth the ſtone, and prouoketh vrine..."[49] (*See note p. 120.*)

**Ground Ivy.** (*See Alehoof.*)

**\*Groundsel.**        *Senecio* species., Compositae, (B&B, 3: 539-546).
*S. vulgaris* L. is the source of *senecine*, an alkaloid that in small doses can cause hemorrhaging; large doses can adversely affect the central nervous system[50] and cause ascites, an enlarged liver, nausea, vomiting, diarrhea, etc.[51] Culpeper uses it to induce vomiting, although he cites Dioscorides for many other uses.[52] *S. aureus* L., also a source of senecine, has been used as an emmenagogue.

**Gum Arabic.**        *Acacia Senegal*, and related species, Fabaceae.
The dried gummy sap exuded by *Acacia* species, used as a demulcent, emollient, and to make candy.

**Hart's horn.**

    **\*1-***Pulsatilla* species, Ranunculaceae, (B&B, 2: 102). Pasque-flower, Anemone, Wind-flower. *Pulsatilla* was once used as a sedative and for diseases of the reproductive organs; it is the source of *Anemonin* (a substance used additionally as an antispasmodic, and for asthma, whooping cough, and bronchitis[53]), and of *Ranunculin*, which breaks down to form toxic *protoanemonin.*[54] (*See Cowslip.*)

    **2-***Plantago* species, Plantaginaceae, (B&B, 3: 246-249). Gerard[55] shows a type of plantain which he calls Hart's horn. Plantains are used for salads and potherbs. (*See also Glossary, p. 256.*)

**Hart's-tongue.**        *Phyllitis Scolopéndrium* (L.) Newm., Polypodiaceae, (B&B, 1: 25).
       (*Scolopendrium vulgare* J. E. Smith).
A European evergreen fern with narrow tongue-shaped fronds. Culpeper[56] claims it is good for ailments of the spleen, liver, and stomach; it was also used in folk medicine for burns.

**Hops.**        *Humulus lupulus* L., Cannabinaceae, (B&B, 1: 633).
The dried cone-shaped female flowers of hops are used to flavor and preserve beer. Hops "opens obstructions of the liver and spleen... cleanses the reins from gravel and provokes urine."[57] Medically, hops are used as a bitter tonic, soporific, and diuretic. Hops are also used to flavor sherry and tea.

**Horehound, Hoarhound.** *Marrubium vulgare* L., <u>Labiatae</u>, (B&B, 3: 110). Culpeper (p. 157) uses it to cure earache, chest coughs, asthma, poison, jaundice, etc. It is still used in cough drops.

**Horse Mint.**

> **1-***Mentha longifolia* (L.) Huds. and *M. rotundifolia*, <u>Labiatae</u>, (B&B, 3: 150).

> **2-***Monarda* species, <u>Labiatae</u>, (B&B, 3: 131-134). Oswego Tea, Horse Mint. *Monardas* are native to the Americas, and are used for tea.

**Horseradish.** *Armoracia Armoracia* (L.) Britton, and related species, <u>Cruciferae</u>, (B&B, 2: 163). A common garden herb known best for the hot sauce produced from its roots. Medicinally, it is used as a digestive aid, an antiseptic, antiscorbutic, and diuretic.

**Hypericon.** (*See St. John's Wort.*)

**Hyssop.** *Hyssopus officinalis* L., <u>Labiatae</u>, (B&B, 3: 140). According to Culpeper, hyssop cures just about everything from epilepsy to head lice.[58] Oil of Hyssop is used to flavor the liqueur *Chartreuse*; hyssop is also used as a cough remedy.

**Jujube.** *Ziziphus jujuba*, and related species, <u>Rhamnaceae</u>. Chinese Dates. The jujubes called for here are fruits, and not the small jelly candies. Jujubes are about the size of a plum, and are usually candied.

**Juniper.** *Juniperus communis* L., <u>Pinaceae</u>, (B&B, 1: 66). Hackmatack. The berries, bark, and tips are used in medicine as diuretics; the berries (called Melmot berries) are used for flavoring gin and beer. Oil of Juniper is used as a diuretic and stomachic.

**\*Kill lamb.** *Kalmia angustifolia* L., <u>Ericaceae</u>, (B&B, 2: 683). Lambkill, Sheep-poison, Sheep-laurel. It is a small shrub with oblong-lanceolate leaves and pink 5-lobed flowers; it is poisonous to sheep.

**Lavender.** *Lavandula vera* De C., and related species, <u>Labiatae</u>. Fragrant plants used in perfumes and soaps, and for fumigating clothes; an oil of lavender is available. Lavender was used medicinally as a digestive aid and stimulant.

**\*Lemon.** *Citrus limon*, <u>Aurantiodeae</u>. Malaga lemons are one type called for here. The lemon did not come into common use in England until the late 16th century. (*See Peach for cautionary note.*)

**Lemon Balm.** (*See Balm.*)

**Licorice.** *Glycyrrhiza glabra* L., and related species, Fabaceae, (B&B, 2: 391).
The name comes from the Greek, meaning 'sweet root.' The root is used for flavoring, and as an expectorant. "[The juice of licorice] is drunk with wine of Raiſons againſt the infirmities of the liuer and cheſt, ſcabs or ſores of the bladder, and diſeaſes of the kidneies."[59]

**\*Lily-of-the-Valley.** *Convallaria majalis* L., Convallariaceae, (B&B, 1: 522).
Although the flowers of lily-of-the-valley smell sweet, ingestion of any part of the plant may prove fatal. It has been used medically like digitalis, as a cardiac stimulant, and as a diuretic, and has also been used as a flavoring in wines.

**Liverwort.** *Marchantia polymorpha* L., Marchantiaceae.
Liverworts are very small non-vascular plants which are either aquatic or inhabit moist areas; they are related to mosses and do not have true flowers, nor do they produce seeds. In the case of *M. polymorpha*, the plant is terrestrial, preferring moist soil in areas where the vegetation has been burned. It has a distinctive multi-rayed star-shaped archegoniophore (egg-bearing stalk) which arises from the thallus (green leaf-like part) of the female plant during the sexual phase of the plant's reproductive cycle. Culpeper's description of "...small green leaves...crumpled; from among which arise small slender stalks an inch or two high...bearing small star-like flowers at the top..."[60] fits *M. polymorpha* very well. Note that he specifies the female plant by his description; he probably thought the male plant to be a different species. (His illustration shows the plant with immature archegoniophores.) (*See note p. 84; see also Bold, pp. 239-248.*)

**Long Pepper.** It is "the half-ripe flower heads of ...*Piper longum* and *chaba*,"[61] Zingiberaceae.

**Lovage.** *Levisticum officinale* Koch, Umbelliferae, (B&B, 2: 635).
The aromatic stems and fruits of lovage are used for flavoring. "The whole plant and every part of it smelling strong and aromatically, and is of a hot, sharp, biting taste."[62]

**Lungwort.** *Pulmonaria officinalis* L., Boraginaceae.
Cowslips of Jerusalem.

A potherb, formerly used for lung diseases.

**\*Mace.** *Myristica fragrans*, Myristicaceae.
A fresh nutmeg has four layers: the outer *husk* (which is discarded); the *aril*, a fleshy yellow membrane between the husk and the seed coat, which when dried is the spice called *mace*; a thin seed coat (which is discarded); and the nut itself, which we call *nutmeg*. It is difficult to find whole arils of mace or even broken bits of arils called mace *blades*. Mace is generally sold powdered (as the dried arils tend to be brittle), and since the size of an aril varies according to the size of the nutmeg it surrounds, it is not possible to say *exactly* how much powdered mace one should substitute for an aril of mace. We may estimate 1/8 to 1/4 teaspoons of powdered mace per blade, and from 1/2 to 1 teaspoon powdered mace per aril. If ingested in large doses nutmegs can cause hallucinations, intoxication, and convulsions, but there is no danger in the small amounts called for in our recipes.

**Maidenhair.** This refers to a fern, and not the Maidenhair Tree, *Ginko biloba*.

**1-***Adiantum Capillus-Veneris* L., Polypodiaceae, (B&B, 1: 31). Maidenhair Fern.
Hartley says Maidenhair Fern was imported to 18th and 19th century England from Ireland for use both as a garnish, and as the main ingredient in a flavoring syrup called *capillaire*, which was added to various fruit drinks or barley water as a tonic.[63] The black ribs of the fern yield a mucilaginous liquid when boiled with water. (Her recipe for capillaire calls for 2 ounces fresh ferns, stewed in water for several hours. Strain out the fern and add 1 pound sugar to 1 pint liquid. When thick, add 1 spoonful orange-flower water and jar the mixture. Two similar recipes for *sirrup of Mayden haire* can be found in *Martha Washington's Booke of Cookery*, # 243 & # 242, the latter recipe includes licorice.)

**2-***Asplenium Trichomanes* L., Polypodiaceae, (B&B 1: 28). Maiden hair Spleenwort. It is closely related to the former and is commonly found in England. Culpeper claims it is good for "infirmities of the spleen," yellow jaundice and hiccups.[64]

**3-***Adiantum pedatum* L., (B&B, 1: 31). Maiden-hair, Capillaire du Canada. Introduced to England before 1640, *A. pedatum* is the source of a medicine used as an expectorant, a stimulant, and in tea for chronic respiratory diseases.[65]

**Mallow.** *Malva* species, Malvaceae, (B&B, 2: 514-6).
The name was applied to marsh mallows (*which see*), and hollyhocks, as well as to common mallows. Culpeper devotes 2 1/2 pages to the virtues of mallows, among which are cures for epilepsy, ague, pleurisy, poisons, tumors, dandruff, etc.[66] The leaves of *M. sylvestris* L. and *M. rotundifolia* L., used as tea, are demulcent and emmolient. Young plants may be eaten as a potherb.

**Maple.** *Acer saccharum* Marsh., Aceraceae, (B&B, 2: 496).
Sugar Maple, Sugarbush.
It takes about 30 gallons of maple sap to make 1 gallon of maple syrup.

**Marigold.**

**1-***Calendula officinalis* L., Compositae. The plant being called for in these recipes is the European Marigold, and **not** *Tagetes* (*see below*). "The flowers, eyther greene or dryed, are often vſed in poſſets, broths, and drinkes, as a comforter of the heart and ſpirits, and to expel any malignant or peſtilential quality, gathered neere thereunto."[67] Marigold is the source of *calendulin*, and has been used as a bitter stomachic and fever medicine, as well as externally for sprains and bruises.[68]

**\*2-***Tagetes* species, Compositae. "French," "African," or "American" Marigolds come from Mexico, and are the kind most often found in American flower gardens. Gerard thought them to be poisonous because they smelled "ranke and unwholesome" and because his cat allegedly died after eating some.[69] *T. minuta* L. causes contact dermatitis.

## APPENDIX OF HERBS & FRUITS

**Marjoram.**                                                        *Origanum* species, <u>Labiatae</u>, (B&B, 3: 140).
                                                                              Sweet Marjoram, Organy.
A common kitchen herb.

**Marsh-Mallow.**                                            *Althea officinalis* L., <u>Malvaceae</u>, (B&B, 2: 514).
                                                                          Mortification-root, Sweat-root.
Its thick mucilaginous roots were used in confectionery, and medically as a demulcent and emollient.

**Mastic, Mastick, or Mastich.**                          *Pistacia Lentiscus* L., <u>Anacardiaceae</u>.
The dried resin 'tears' of the mastic tree, mastic was used as an astringent, a cure for epilepsy, bad teeth,
etc. It is now used in chewing gum, incense, lacquer, etc.

**Meadssweet.**                                       *Filipendula Ulmaria* Maxim., <u>Rosaceae</u>, (B&B, 2: 249).
                              (*Spiraea Ulmaria* L.), Meadow-sweet, Herb christopher, Bride-wort, My lady's belt.
"...the flowers boiled in wine and drunke, do take away the fits of a quartaine ague, and maketh the hart
merrie. The leaues and flowers far excell all other ſtrowing herbes, for to decke vp houſes, to ſtrowe in
chambers, hals, and banketting houſes in the ſommer time; for the ſmell thereof maketh the hart merrie,
delighteth the ſenses..."[70] It contains *salicylic acid*, and has been used for rheumatism and arthritis.

**Medlar.**                                                                  *Mespilus germanica*, <u>Rosaceae</u>.
Small apple-like brownish green fruits, which, like persimmons, are eaten when partially decayed.
Culpeper (pp. 186-187) praises their astringent qualities, using them for stanching blood and preventing
miscarriage, etc.

**Mint.**                                                           *Mentha* species, <u>Labiatae</u>, (B&B, 3: 149-153).
Most likely *M. spicata* L. (spearmint), or *M. piperita* L. (peppermint), is being called for here.
According to Culpeper, "it [mint] stirreth up venery or bodily lust...,"[71] and cures everything from
rabies to leprosy. Mints are used as carminatives; *M. piperita* is also used for colic and diarrhea. Mints
are also commonly used for flavorings and teas.

**Mother of Thyme.**                                          *Thymus Serpyllum* L., <u>Labiatae</u>, (B&B, 3: 141).
                                                                          Wild Thyme, Creeping Thyme.
Culpeper says it is good for headache, gas, cramps, and inflammations of the liver, etc.[72]

**Mouse ear.**

   **1-***Myosotis* species, <u>Boraginaceae</u>, (B&B 3: 85-87). Relatives of Forget-me-not, *Myosotis*
   species have astringent properties and were used for tonic.

   **2-***Hieracium Pilosella* L., <u>Cichoriaceae</u>, (B&B, 3: 333). Mouse-ear Hawkweed. "The decoction
   of Pylosella [mouse ear] drunke doth cure and heale all wounds, both inward and outward."[73]

**Mulberry.**                                       *Morus nigra* L., and related species, <u>Moraceae</u>, (B&B, 1: 631).
Trees and bushes producing edible fruits used in jams and wines; the cooked shoots are used for
potherbs. Culpeper uses the leaves for treating burns, toothache, poisoning, and bleeding.[74]

**Muscovy**.

**\*1-**-*Muscari neglectum*, and related species, <u>Liliaceae</u>, (B&B, 1: 510-511). Grape-Hyacinth. Muscovy "which is an herb, that smelleth like Musk."[75] A familiar spring flower, mentioned by Parkinson as an ornamental. The only reference to its being eaten that I have found is in Leggatt,[76] with the cautionary note that you should not eat more than may reasonably be used as a garnish, or roughly one tablespoonful of blossoms on a dish for four people!

**2-**-*Ferula Sumbul* Hook., and related species, <u>Umbelliferae</u>. Musk Root. These plants are described as having roots with a musk-like odor. An alkaloid extract, *sumbuline*, was used formerly in medicines for diarrhea, cholera, etc., while the root itself was used to treat hysteria and spasms.[77]

**3-**-A third plant, called by Gerard "Musked Cranes bill, ...is planted in gardens for the ∫weete ∫mell that the whole plant is po∫∫e∫∫ed with." It appears to be a type of scented geranium.

**4-**-Many other plants, among them the Common Mallow, *Malva sylvestris*, are described as having a musk-like odor.

**Musk melon.**                                     *Cucumis melo* L., <u>Cucurbitaceae</u>.
A common garden fruit. (*See note p. 208.*)

**Mustard**.                          *Brassica nigra* (L.) Koch., and related species, <u>Cruciferae</u>, (B&B, 2: 193). Used medically for arthritis, bronchitis, etc., and in cooking as a condiment and potherb. Mustard seed is used by Digby, and others, in an attempt to cause fermentation, but it is doubtful that it performed this function. More likely, yeast present in the cask or the brew house initiated fermentation, and the mustard merely supplied a biting flavor.

**Myrtle**.                          *Myrtus communis* L., and related species, <u>Myrtaceae</u>.
Myrtle is not to be confused with the toxic Bog Myrtle (*see p. 289*). *M. communis* is the source of a volatile aromatic oil (its constituents include *d*-pinene, eucalyptol, and camphor) used medically for bronchitis, dysentery, etc. (Merck, p. 396).

**Nard**. (*See Spikenard.*)

**\*Nectarine**. A smooth-skinned cultivar of the peach. (*See Peach for cautionary note.*)

**Nettle**.

**1-**-*Lamium* species, <u>Labiatae</u>, (B&B, 3: 121-122). Dead Nettle or Archangel. Gerard describes a Red (*Lamium purpureum* L.), a White (*L. album* L.), and a Yellow Archangel, which were commonly eaten as sweets. "The floures are baked with sugar as Roses are, which is called Sugar roset: as also the distilled water of them, which is used to make the heart merry..."[78]

**\*2-**-Stinging Nettle, *Urtica* spp., <u>Urticaceae</u>, (B&B, 1: 634-6). Nettles are common weeds whose young shoots are sometimes used as potherbs. These plants have stinging hairs – wear leather gloves when picking them. Hooper identifies *U. dioica* as the nettle used in nettle beer.[79]

**3-** *Celtis occidentalis* L., Ulmaceae, (B&B, 1: 629). Nettle Tree, Hackberry, Sugar-berry. The nettle tree is mentioned by Parkinson;[80] it has small, sweet edible fruits.

**\*Nutmeg.** (*See Mace.*)

**Oak of Jerusalem.**                     *Chenopodium Botrys* L., Chenopodiaceae, (B&B, 2: 14).

**Orache.** (*See Arras.*)

**\*Orange.**                                         *Citrus* species, Aurantiodeae.
(*See Peach for cautionary note.*)

**Organ, Organy.**                          *Origanum vulgare* L., Labiatae, (B&B, 3: 140).
(*See Marjoram.*)                                                         Wild-marjoram.

**\*Orris-root.**      *Iris germanica* L., *I. florentina* L., and *I. palida* Lam., Iridaceae, (B&B, 1: 536-541).
                                                                              Fleur-de-lis, White Flag.
The violet-scented rootstock is poisonous causing nausea, diarrhea, vomiting, etc.[81] The distilled oil and powdered root are not safe to eat, but they can be used in perfumes and cosmetics. Orris roots were used in various folk remedies for snake bite, stomach ache, sore skin and sore eyes.

**Parsley.**                                 *Apium Petroselinum* L., Umbelliferae, (B&B, 2: 642).
Parsley is a common garden herb; the seeds were used as a diuretic.

**\*Parsnip.**                                 *Pastinaca sativa* L., Umbelliferae, (B&B, 2: 634).
A common garden vegetable with a sweet taproot. Contact may cause phytophotodermatitis.

**Partridge-berry.** (*See Winter Evergreen.*)

**Paul's-betony.**

> **1-** *Lycopus americanus* Muhl., Labiatae, (B&B, 3: 148). Cut-leaved Water Horehound. The related *L. virginicus* L. has been used as an astringent and tonic.

> **2-** *Veronica officinalis* L., Scrophulariaceae, (B&B, 3: 201-202). Common Speedwell.

> **3-** *Veronica serpyllifolia* L., Thyme-leaved Speedwell.

**\*Peach.**                                   *Amygdalus persica* L., Amygdalaceae, (B&B, 2: 330).
Peaches are delicious fruits; however, their kernels contain 2% to 4% Hydrocyanic acid,[82] *which is highly poisonous.* Cyanogens present in the seeds of peaches, cherries, apples, apricots, pears, plums, and citrus fruits[83] release hydrocyanic acid when the plant tissue is damaged, in this case, when the peach kernels are crushed. Commercial oil of bitter almond has had the poison removed and may be substituted in brewing and cooking recipes which call for crushed pits or kernels.

**\*Pear**.                                                   *Pyrus communis* L., Malaceae, (B&B, 2: 288).
Gerard, in 1597, said: "To write of Peares and Apples in particular, woulde require a particular volume:
the ſtocke or kindred of Peares are not to be numbred..." (*See Peach for cautionary note.*)

**Pellitory**.
**1**-*Chrysanthemum parthenium* Pers., Compositae, (B&B, 3: 519). Common Feverfew, Pellitory.
It has bitter leaves and its flowers resemble clusters of small daisies. "Feverfew dried and made
into pouder, and two drams of it taken with hony or sweet wine, purgeth by siege melancholy and
flegme; wherefore it is very good for them that are giddie in the head, or ...melancholike..."[84]

**2**-*Anacyclus pyrethrum* De C., Compositae. Pellitory, Spanish Pellitory, Spanish Chamomile. A
source of pyrethrum, it is used for toothache, rheumatism, etc.

**Pellitory of Spain**.
**1**-*Anacyclus pyrethrum* De C., Compositae. (*See above.*) This identification would tend to be
supported by the description in Culpeper, who describes a Composite rather than an Umbellifer:
"...It is one of the best purgers of the brain that grows...Either the herb or root dried and chewed
in the mouth ...[eases] pains in the head and teeth... [prevents] coughs... consumptions, apoplexy
and falling sickness."[85] Parkinson also agrees that his 'Pelletory of Spaine' is a Composite, but he
mentions a "true *Pyrethrum* of Dioſcorides, which is an vmbelliferous plant..."[86]

**2**-*Imperatoria Ostruthium* L., Umbelliferae, (B&B, 2: 638). Masterwort, Felonwort.

**Pellitory of the Wall**.                         *Parietaria officinalis* L., Urticaceae, (B&B, 1: 637).
"The decoction of the herb being drunk, easeth pains of the mother, promotes women's courses; it also
easeth those griefs that arise from obstructions of the liver, spleen, and reins."[87]

**\*Pennyroyal**.
**\*1**-*Mentha Pulegium* L., Labiatae. European Pennyroyal. It is probably what is being called for
in these recipes; it is the source of an aromatic oil used for repelling insects and is *not* safe to eat.

**\*2**-*Hedeoma pulegioides* (L.) Pers., Labiatae, (B&B 3: 136). American Pennyroyal. This plant
yields a volatile aromatic oil that can, in sufficient doses, bring on a spontaneous abortion.
"...drunk in wine it provoketh women's courses... and expelleth the dead child and afterbirth."[88]

**Philipendula**. (*See Meadssweet.*)

**Pinks**. (*See Clove Gilliflowers.*)

**\*Plum**.        *Prunus domestica* L., *P. insititia* L., and related species, Amygdalaceae, (B&B, 2: 322-326).
                                                                    Garden plum, Bullace.
Damsons are one variety called for here. (*See Peach for cautionary note.*)

**\*Pomegranate**.                                         *Punica granatum* L., Punicaceae.
The seeds are commonly eaten. The root bark is used medicinally as a cure for tapeworms, diarrhea, and
fevers; ingestion of the root bark may cause vomiting.

## APPENDIX OF HERBS & FRUITS

**\*Potato.** *Solanum tuberosum* L., <u>Solanaceae</u>.
The sprouts and green-skinned parts of the tubers contain toxic *solanine glyco-alkaloids*, which can be fatal to children.

**\*Primrose.** *Primula* species, <u>Primulaceae</u>, (B&B, 2: 708-709).
Common garden plants which have been used for salads, teas, and confections. Some species contain *arthanitin*, a hemolytic poison; for this reason, Creasy warns against eating primroses.[89]

**\*Prune.** *Prunus domestica* L., <u>Amygdalaceae</u>, (B&B, 2: 322-326).
Prunes are dried plums. (*See Plum. See also Peach for cautionary note.*)

**Quince.** *Cydonia oblonga* Miller, (*Pyrus cydonia*), <u>Rosaceae</u>.
The quince fruit is fragrant, fuzzy, and yellowish when ripe. It is roughly pear-shaped, but lumpier and typically larger than a pear. The fruit must be eaten cooked as it is very astringent raw; the cooked pulp has a pretty pink color.

**Raisin, Raisins of the Sun.** *Vitis* species, <u>Vitaceae</u>, (B&B, 2: 505-511).
Raisins are dried grapes. "The dried Malaga, or Muscatel raisins, which come to this country [England] packed in small boxes, and nicely preserved in bunches, are variable in their quality, but mostly of a rich flavour, when new, juicy, and of a deep purple hue."[90]

**Raisins of Corinth.** (*See Currants.*)

**Raspberry.** *Rubus idaeus* L., and related species, <u>Rosaceae</u>, (B&B, 2: 276-277).
The French for raspberry is *framboise*, which is also the name of a raspberry-flavored liqueur and beer. The dried fruit is used in folk medicine to cure biliousness.

**Red Sage.** (*See Sage.*)

**Red Sandalwood.** *Pterocarpus santa-linus* L., <u>Leguminosae</u>.
The heart-wood is used as a dye, and to color medicines; in medieval times it was used as the red food dye *saunders*.

**\*Rhubarb.** *Rheum rhaponticum* L., <u>Polygonaceae</u>.
Wine Plant.
Rhubarb is a common garden vegetable. <u>The leaf blades are toxic, ingestion may prove fatal</u>; the leaf stalk, or petiole, is edible. The roots are used in medicine as a bitter tonic, cathartic, and to relieve constipation, but may actually cause constipation.[91]

**Ribwort.** *Plantago lanceolata* L., <u>Plantaginaceae</u>, (B&B, 3: 246).
English Plantain.
"The juice of plantain clarified and drunk...[helps] all torments... in the bowels, stayeth distillations of rheum from the head, and stayeth all fluxes and profuse menstruation... plantain is a very good wound herb to heal fresh or old wounds or sores, either inward or outward."[92]

**\*Roman Wormwood**.
*Ambrosia elatior* L., <u>Ambrosiaceae</u>, (B&B, 3: 341).
Ragweed.
Described by Culpeper as having a spicy smell; "Mars eradicates all diseases in the throat by his herbs... and sends them to Egypt on an errand never to return..."[93] Gerard calls it "St. James his Wort."[94] Both agree it is very good for diseases of the throat. Ragweed can cause allergic reactions in sensitive individuals.

**Rosa-solis**.
*Drosera rotundifolia* L., and related species, <u>Droseraceae</u>, (B&B, 2: 203).
Ros Solis, Round-leaved Sundew, Youthwort.
Sundews grow in bogs, and hence are rare – do not pick them. Their leaves are hairy and exude a sticky liquid "dew" which the plants use to trap insects for food. *D. rotundifolia* and related species have been used medicinally as anti-spasmodics, and to ease coughs in pertussis, bronchitis, etc.

**Rose**.
*Rosa* species, <u>Rosaceae</u>, (B&B, 2: 282-286).
Well known plants with a great many cultivated varieties. The flower petals of certain varieties have been used for medicine, flavorings, puddings, perfumes, sauces, etc.; the hips of some roses are used for jellies and pies, and are a good source of Vitamin C. According to Gerard, infusions made of roses have a laxative effect.[95]

**Rosemary**.
*Rosmarinus officinalis*, <u>Labiatae</u>.
A common culinary herb. According to Culpeper, rosemary is a powerful herb which cures epilepsy, drowsiness, loss of speech, gas, poor eyesight, coughs, etc.[96] "Take the leaves and put them into wine and it shall keep the wine from all sourness and evill savours and if thou wilt sell thy wine thou shalt have goode speede."[97]

**\*Rue**.
*Ruta graveolens* L., <u>Rutaceae</u>, (B&B, 2: 445).
Can cause phytophotodermatitis (*see Agrimony*). Rue was used as an antispasmodic and emmenagogue. It was also thought to be useful against the Evil Eye, Plague, and all poisons.[98]

**Saffron**. *Crocus sativus* L., <u>Iridaceae</u>.
Saffron, the dried stamens of the saffron crocus, is a very expensive spice and yellow food coloring; it has a very odd bitter flavor. (Mexican Saffron, the safflower, may be substituted for it in most recipes with minimal expense.)

SAFFRON CROCUS

**Sage**. *Salvia officinalis* L., and related species, <u>Labiatae</u>, (B&B, 3: 128).
Sage is a common flavorful herb; it is slightly astringent and carminative. "It is good for diseases of the liver, and to make blood."[99] It was also drunk in ale as a spring tonic, and to aid conception.

## APPENDIX OF HERBS & FRUITS

**\*Saint John's wort.**  *Hypericum perforatum* L., and related species, Hypericaceae, (B&B, 2: 533).
Common St. John's-wort, Touch-and-heal, Cammock.
St. John's-wort is used in brewing beer and *aquavit*. The flowers and buds produce a red dye when crushed. "...boiled in wine and drunk it healeth inward hurts or bruises... The decoction of the herb and flowers, especially of the seed being drunk in wine... prevents vomiting and spitting of blood..."[100] and also was thought to cure ague, fits, sciatica, epilepsy, and palsy. It is poisonous to sheep, cattle, horses, and goats, causing photosensitization when eaten, eventually leading to the death of the animal.[101]

**Sandalwood.**  *Santalum album* L., Santalaceae, (B&B, 1: 639).
Yellow or White Saunders.
The heart-wood is the source of an oil which is used as an incense, medicine, and fumigant.

**Sanicle.**  probably *Sanicula* species, Umbelliferae, (B&B, 2: 623).
Snake-root.
Many plants go by the name "Sanicle." Culpeper describes it as having seeds with burrs, which tends to support the *Sanicula* identification. He claims sanicle cures "ulcerations of the kidneys," and it is boiled in wine as a cure for "running of the reins." Parkinson agrees that sanicles are "great healers."

**\*Sassafras roots.**  *Sassafras sassafras* (L.) Karst., Lauraceae, (B&B, 2: 134).
The root cambium, or growth layer, contains an aromatic oil which was used as a flavoring agent; it has since been found to be toxic, and commercial use of sassafras extract has been banned in the United States. (*See note p. 74.*)

**Saxifrage.**  *Saxifraga* species, Saxifragaceae, (B&B, 2: 221-222).
Culpeper lists a White and a Burnet Saxifrage. "There are not many better medicines to break the stone than this... The saxifrages are as hot as pepper..."[102] Many cultivated varieties of saxifrage exist, mostly as ornamentals, but some may be used as potherbs and salad greens.

**Scabious.**  (*See Blue-buttons.*)

**Scurvy-grass.**  *Cochlearia officinalis* L., and *C. danica* L., Cruciferae, (B&B, 2: 163).
Scurvy-grass, Spoonwort; Danish Scurvy-grass.
"The English scurvy grass is more used for its salt taste, which gently purges and cleanses; but the Dutch scurvy-grass is of better effect, and chiefly used by those that have the scurvy, and is of singular good effect to cleanse the blood, liver, and spleen, taking the juice in the spring every morning, in a cup of drink."[103] Both have antiscorbutic properties.

**\*Sea-wormwood.**  *Artemisia vulgaris* L., Compositae, (B&B, 3: 527).
Common Mugwort.
Described by Gerard as the weakest of the wormwoods, of which there are three; the seeds of this plant were given to children as a vermifuge. (*See Wormwood for cautionary note.*)

**Self-heal.**  *Prunella vulgaris* L., Labiatae, (B&B, 3: 115).
Heal-all.
Gerard says "the decoction of Prunell made with wine and water, doth joine together and make whole and sound all wounds both inward and outward..."[104] Self-heal has also been used as a diuretic.

**Service berries.** *Amelianchier canadensis* (L.) Medic., and related species, <u>Malaceae</u>, (B&B, 2: 292).
Juneberries.
The fruit is used fresh or in jellies.

**\*Sloes.**
*Prunus spinosa,* <u>Amygdalaceae</u>.
Sloes are the small bluish-black fruits of the blackthorn tree, which are used to flavor Sloe Gin. (*See Peach for cautionary note.*)

**\*Southernwood.** *Artemisia abrótanum* L., <u>Compositae</u>, (B&B, 3: 526).
Sweet Benjamin.
Southernwood is a shrubby plant, closely related to wormwood, used medicinally as a vermifuge and emmenagogue. (*See Wormwood.*)

**Spike Lavender.** (*See Spikenard.*)

**Spikenard.**

1-*Nardostachys jatamansi*, <u>Valerianaceae</u>, is native to India. A costly perfume was prepared from the roots of this plant in Roman times.

> "About the leaf, which is that of the nard, it is proper to speak at greater length, as it holds a foremost place among perfumes. The nard is a shrub, the root of which is heavy and thick but short and black, and although oily, brittle; it has a musty smell like the gladiolus, and an acrid taste; the leaves are small, and grow in clusters. ...Nard is also adulterated with a plant called bastard nard, which grows everywhere, and has a thicker and broader leaf and a sickly colour inclining to white; and also by being mixed with its own root to increase the weight, and with gum and silver-spume or antimony and gladiolus or husk of gladiolus..." (Pliny, Book XII, section XXVI, p. 31.)

2-*Aralia racemosa* L., <u>Araliaceae</u>, (B&B, 2: 617). American Spikenard, Spicebush. *A. racemosa* has been used for coughs, syphillis, and as a stimulant; it has aromatic roots and is used for teas and root beer. It is related to Wild Sarsaparilla.

\*3-*Inula squarrosa* (*I. conyza*), <u>Compositae</u>. Ploughman's Spikenard or Cinnamon Root. *I. squarrosa* is described by Gerard[105] as having a fragrant root. It was used as an insecticide, and for wounds, itching, and as an emmenagogue.

4-*Lavandula spica* De C., <u>Labiatae</u>. Spike Lavender. It is referred to by Parkinson as *Nardus Italica,* or Lesser Spike.[106] Gerard recommends its use for migraines, epilepsy, palsy, and fainting spells, although Parkinson says it is little used in physic (medicine), being primarily a perfume for clothing, etc.

## APPENDIX OF HERBS & FRUITS

**Spinach.**             *Spinacea oleracea*, <u>Chenopodiaceae</u>.
*S. oleracea*, our cultivated variety, is a native of S.W. Asia. In medieval times the name 'spinach' applied to at least six different potherbs: *Chenopodium album* (Lamb's Quarters); *C. Bonus-Henricus* (Good King Henry); *Blitum capitatum* (Strawberry Blite); *Atriplex hortensis* (Orache – *which see*); *A. rosea* (Red Orache); and *Salicornia* species (Chickens'-toes and Sea-grass).

**Spleen-wort.**             *Asplenium* species, <u>Polypodiaceae</u>, (B&B, 1: 26-30).
Spleenwort was, of course, used in medieval times for ailments of the spleen.

**Spruce.**
     **1-***Abies balsamea* (L.) Mill., <u>Pinaceae</u>, (B&B, 1: 63). Balsam Fir, Single Spruce, Balm of Gilead. The tender new branch tips and the resin are used for flavorings. (*See also Fir.*)

     **2-***Picea rubens* Sargent., *P. mariana* (Mill.) B.S.P., <u>Pinaceae</u>, (B&B, 1: 61). Red Spruce, Black Spruce. The inner bark is edible, and the resin is used for flavorings and gum.

**Squinanth, Squinance.**             *Asperula cynanchica*, <u>Rubiaceae</u>.
Squinance is a relative of Sweet Woodruff; it was formerly used in folk medicine.

**Star Anise.**             *Illicium verum* Hook., <u>Magnoliaceae</u>.
The large, brownish-red seeds come in star-shaped pods which are very pretty and flavorful when added to a mulled drink. They are used medicinally as a digestive aid.

**Strawberry.**             *Fragraria* species, <u>Rosaceae</u>, (B&B, 2: 259-261).
Strawberries are widely cultivated for their fruit; about 35 species occur naturally, but many more cultivars are available. "The leaves and roots boiled in wine and water, and drunk, likewise cool the liver and blood, and assuage, all inflammations in the reins and bladder, provoke urine, ...stayeth the bloody-flux, and women's courses, and reduces the swelling of the spleen."[107]

**Succory.**             *Cichorium Intybus* L., <u>Cichoriaceae</u>, (B&B, 3: 305).
           Chicory, Coffee-weed.
"A handful of the leaves or roots, boiled in wine or water...driveth forth choleric and phlegmatic humours, openeth obstructions of the liver, gall and spleen; cureth the yellow jaundice..."[108] ague, swooning, headache, sores, etc.

**Sundew.** (*See Rosa solis.*)

**Sweetbrier.**             *Rosa rubiginosa* L., <u>Rosaceae</u>, (B&B, 2: 286).
           (*R. eglanteria* Mill.), Eglantine, Hip-rose, Hip-brier.
Rose hips are rich in Vitamin C and were used for a variety of dishes. The leaves are used for tea. "The fruit when it is ripe maketh moſt pleaſant meates and banketting diſhes, as Tartes and ſuch like: the making wherof I commit to the cunning Cooke, and the teeth to eat them in the rich mans mouth."[109]

**Sweet Fern.**             *Comptonia peregrina* (L.) Coulter, <u>Myricaceae</u>, (B&B, 1: 586).
           Fern-gale, Canada sweet-gale, Spleen-wort-bush.
Sweet Fern is a shrub with fragrant leaves that are used to make tea.

**\*Sweet gale.**                    *Myrica gale* L., <u>Myricaceae</u>, (B&B, 1: 585).

Bog Myrtle.

The fragrant leaves of *M. gale* are sometimes used for tea, but they contain a toxic oil which has been used as an abortifacient.[110]  Sage may be used as a substitute for Sweet gale.

**Sweet-oak.**                    *Myrica cerifera* L., <u>Myricaceae</u>, (B&B, 1: 585).

Wax-myrtle, Candle-berry, Wild Myrtle.

Sweet-oak is closely related to bayberry. Gerard says of the Wild Myrtle, "the fruit is troubleſome to the braine being put into beere or ale whileſt it is in boyling (which many vſe to do) it maketh the ſame headie, fit to make a man quickly drunke."[111]  The leaves and seeds may be used for flavorings.

**Sweet Woodruff.**                    *Asperula odorata* L., <u>Rubiaceae</u>, (B&B, 3: 267).

**Tamarisk.**                    *Tamarix gallica* var. *mannifera*, <u>Tamaricaceae</u>.

The sweet dried 'tears' of sap are sold commercially. "The root, leaves, young branches, or bark boiled in wine, and drunk, stays the bleeding of the hæmorrhoidal veins, spitting of blood, the too abounding of women's courses, jaundice, colic, and the biting of all venomous serpents, except the asp..."[112]

**Thyme.**                    *Thymus vulgaris* L., and related species, <u>Labiatae</u>, (B&B, 3: 141).

Thyme is a common garden herb with a very strong flavor; there are about 50 naturally occurring species, plus many more cultivated varieties. Thyme is used to make the liqueur *Benedictine*. Culpeper says there is no better remedy for whooping cough; he also says it brings on menstruation and eases childbirth, "comforts the stomach and expells wind."[113]  An oil of thyme has been used even quite recently for coughs, skin diseases, as a diaphoretic, etc. In combination with an extract of *Monarda punctata* L., Wild Bergamot, it was used to cure various kinds of worms, including trichiniasis, and also bronchitis, coughs, and skin diseases such as eczema.[114]

**Tormentil.**                    *Potentilla* species, <u>Rosaceae</u>, (B&B, 2: 249-257).

Cinquefoil.

Culpeper claims tormentil is good for all wounds, internal and external.  The roots are astringent. Gerard describes a "Wall Cinkefoile," *P. argentea* L., "the decoction of the roots held in the mouth doth mitigate the paine of the teeth."[115]  (*See note p. 264.*)

**Turmeric, Turmerick.**          *Cucurma domestica*,
                                   <u>Zingiberaceae</u>.
The bright yellow powdered rhizome of turmeric is used as a spice and coloring agent.

**Turnip.**          *Brassica campestris* L., (*B. rapa* L.),
                     <u>Cruciferae</u>, (B&B, 2: 193).
A common vegetable with many cultivated varieties.
**Navew** turnip refers to the wild form of *B. campestris*.

*Sweet Gale.*

**\*Turnsole**. The word turnsole, or tournesol, means, literally, to turn toward the sun. In Greek the word is *Heliotrope*.

**\*1-***Heliotropium indicum* L., Boraginaceae, (B&B, 3: 75). Indian Heliotrope, Turnsole. *H. indicum* is a native of India, but has spread widely. It is mentioned by Culpeper, who says it is a foreign plant that is grown in gardens and is grown extensively in Spain and France. It is a small hairy plant with a flower stalk that "...turneth inwards like a bowed finger, opening by degrees as the flowers blow open..."[116] He uses it for medicine and does not mention its use as a dye, which is not unusual. *H. indicum* is poisonous;[117] the toxin is *pyrrolizidine alkaloids*. (*See Alkanet for a description of symptoms*.) It is possible that *H. indicum* is the *H. minus* or "Small Tornʃole" mentioned by Gerard: "the ʃame boiled in wine and drunke is good againʃt the ʃtinging of Scorpions or other venemous beaʃts..."[118]

**\*2-***Tithymalus Helioscopia* (L.) Hill., Euphorbiaceae, (B&B 2: 473). Turnsole, Wartweed, Madwoman's Milk, Devil's-milk, (*Euphorbia Helioscopia* L.). Ingestion may prove fatal.[119]

**3-**Litmus is "Lacmus, Turnsole, Lacca Musica, Lacca Coerulea. Blue coloring matter from various species of lichens, particularly *Variolaria, Lecanora* and *Rocella* [*tinctoria*] (Parmeliaceae)... Has been used, but rarely now, for coloring beverages, etc."[120] *Rocella* species contain *erithritol*, a substance used in medicines.[121] Adrosko mentions turnsole as a type of litmus used sometimes for dyeing Dutch cheese.[122] She says *Rocella* is the source of orchil, a popular commercial dye for cloth in the 18th and 19th centuries. Weigle, et al., discuss how to dye with lichens in some detail; *Rocella* is not mentioned specifically, but they do state that most lichens will produce dyes of various colors when treated with the proper chemicals. Orchils, they say, are any lichens that contain colorless acids which produce dyes when soaked in ammonia. *Umbilicaria proboscidea* and *U. mammulata* produce purple dye.

**4-(?)***Crozophora tinctoria*, Euphorbiaceae. According to the OED, turnsole is a violet-blue or purple dye obtained from the plant *Crozophora tinctoria*, a member of the Euphorbiaceae said to be cultivated in southern France; the dye is extracted by the addition of ammonia. (I have been unable to locate *C. tinctoria* in botanical or horticultural texts.)

Either *Heliotropium* or *Rocella* are good candidates for being medieval turnsole, but neither should be consumed. As with Alkanet, safe commercial food dyes are available, so why take the risk? (Turnsole is oftentimes confused with alkanet, but they are not the same thing. *See Alkanet*.)

**Violet**.                         *Viola odorata* L., and related species, Violaceae, (B&B, 2: 558).
                                                                    Sweet Violet.
Culpeper uses violets to cure swellings, epilepsy, lung diseases, etc. Also, "...the syrup of violets...being taken in some convenient liquor...giveth to the drink a claret wine colour, and a fine tart relish, pleasing to the taste."[123] Violets have been used in sauces, pottages, salads, candies, etc.

**Wall-flower**.                    *Cheirina* and *Erysimum* species, Cruciferae, (B&B, 2: 172-174).
Culpeper[124] and Parkinson refer to wall-flowers as winter-gilliflowers: "a Conʃerue made of the [wall-] flowers, is vʃed for a remedy both for the Appoplexie and Palʃie."[125]

**Walnut.**                                *Juglans* species, Juglandaceae, (B&B, 1: 578-579).
The growth layer or *cambium* is called for, not the nuts. The root cambium of *J. cinerea* L. (Butternut, White or Lemon Walnut), was used in medicine as a laxative and febrifuge.

**Wall-rew.**                         *Asplenium Ruta-muraria* L., Polypodiaceae, (B&B, 1: 29).
*(See Spleenwort.)*                                    Wall Rue Spleenwort.

**Watercress**                 *Sisymbrium Nasturtium-aquaticum* L., Cruciferae, (B&B, 2: 162).
                                                     Brook-lime.
Watercresses are common salad greens which "tasteth hot and sharp...they are more powerful against the scurvy and to cleanse the blood and humours, ...[they] break the stone, and provoke urine and women's courses."[126]

**Wild-sage.** *(See Sage.)*

**Wild-marjoram.** *(See Marjoram, Organy.)*

**Winter evergreen.**

**1-** *Gaultheria procumbens* L., Ericaceae, (B&B, 2: 693). Rheumatism weed, Checkerberry, Spicy or Creeping Wintergreen. *Gaultheria* leaves contain *methyl salicylate*, the active ingredient in oil of wintergreen, which is used both in medicines for rheumatism and for flavoring candy. The leaves and berries are edible. "The herb boiled in wine and water, and drunk by those who have any inward ulcers in their kidneys or neck of the bladder, doth wonderfully help them. It stayeth all fluxes, ...and taketh away inflammations and pains of the heart..."[127]

**2-** *Mitchella repens* L., Rubiaceae, (B&B, 3: 255). Partridge-berry, Checkerberry. *M. repens* is sometimes confused for *G. procumbens*. These two plants share many common names and look somewhat similar. Fruits of *Gaultheria* are 5-lobed, while those of *Mitchella* are 4-lobed. *M. repens* is used in folk medicine as a diuretic and astringent, as well as a tonic and cure for sore nipples, but Merck says there is "no evidence of therapeutic value."[128] The berries are edible.

**Winter Savory.**                        *Satureia montana* L., Labiatae, (B&B, 3: 137).
**Summer Savory.**                                     *S. hortensis* L.
Winter and Summer Savory are garden herbs used in sauces, stuffings, etc. Savory was used in period to cure gas, chest congestion, dull eyesight, ringing of the ears, sciatica, palsy, and just about anything else, including driving away evil spirits.

**Wood Betony.**                          *Betonica officinalis* L., Labiatae, (B&B, 3: 128).
Culpeper says Wood or Common Betony has reddish or purplish flowers, and a sweet and spicy taste in the leaves and flowers. *(See Betony.)* "The decoction made with mead and a little penny-royal, is good for those that are troubled with putrid agues, ...the decoction thereof made in wine...killeth...worms...openeth obstructions both of the spleen and liver..."[129]

**\*Woodbin(d)e.**     *Lonicera Caprifolium* L., and related species, <u>Caprifoliaceae</u>, (B&B, 3: 278).
Perfoliate Honeysuckle.
Used formerly to cure asthma, wounds, cramps, coughs, sunburn, to ease childbirth, to cause
perspiration, etc. The berries are toxic.

**\*Wood Sorrel.**     *Oxalis Acetosella* L., and related species, <u>Oxalidaceae</u>, (B&B, 2: 431).
Alleluia.
Wood sorrel is a source of *oxalic acid* (*see Dock*). Wood sorrel and *Rumex* species were used in
medieval times to make *Sauce Sorrell*, a sour sauce. It is "of a fine sour relish, and yielding a juice
which will turn red when it is clarified, and maketh a most dainty clear syrup."[130]

**\*Wormwood.**     *Artemisia Absinthium* L., <u>Compositae</u>, (B&B, 3: 525).
Absinth.
Wormwood was used formerly as a bitter stomachic, especially in France; it was used to make the
licorice-flavored liqueur *absinthe*. Wormwood contains *thujone*,[131] which can cause brain damage; it
is addictive, with habitual use also causing vomiting, tremors, vertigo, hallucinations, violent behavior,
and convulsions.[132] *Absinthe* was deemed responsible for many deaths, and has been banned in several
countries since the turn of the century. A wormwood-free version of *absinthe*, called *pastis*, is now
popular in France.

**\*Yarrow.**     *Achillea millefolium* L., <u>Compositae</u>.
Yarrow has been used as a tea, a wound herb, a bitter tonic to stimulate appetite, an emmenagogue, and
to sooth inflammations of the nose and throat. It has an anesthetic effect when chewed. "The
inhabitants of Dalekarlia mix it with their ale, instead of hops, in order to increase the inebriating quality
of the liquor..."[133]

**Yellow-Saunders.** (*See Sandalwood.*)

*A Dyer's Workshop.*
Buckets of dye are heated in the
furnace on the left. Workers on
the right mix the dye vats. Dyed
cloth dries on overhead racks.
(Hazen, 1836.)

## A PARTIAL LIST OF DYE PLANTS:

Why were certain known dye plants included in the preceding recipes? Was it for their color, medicinal properties, and/or their flavor? Many of the plants require preparation in pots of iron, copper, or tin to release their dye, yet curiously enough, many of our brewing recipes specify that cauldrons of certain metals be used for boiling the wort. It is quite likely that these dye herbs were deliberately chosen to add color, perhaps in an effort to simulate an expensive imported beverage. The evidence is here before you - you may draw your own conclusions.

(Sources: Weigle, Adrosko, Bemiss, etc.)


(The symbol "☛" indicates plants that have been listed in the text.)

| Common Name | Scientific Name | Color Produced |
|---|---|---|
| Actinospermum | *Balduina* spp. | yellows, greens |
| ☛ Agrimony | *Agrimonia Eupatoria* L. | gold |
| Alder (bark) | *Alnus* spp. | yellows, oranges, browns |
| ☛ Alkanet (roots) | *Alkanna tinctoria* | reds, lilac blue |
| ☛ Aloe | *Aloe* spp. | purples |
| American Chestnuts (burrs) | *Castanea dentata* Borkh. | browns |
| Annatto/Roucou/Otter (seeds) | *Bixa orellana* | oranges, reds |
| ☛ Apple (bark) | *Malus malus* (L.) Britton | yellow-tan |
| Artichoke | *Cynara scolymus* | greens |
| ☛ Ash (bark) | *Fraxinus excelsior* L. | blues |
| Aster | *Callistemma* spp. | yellows, green-yellow |
| ☛ Avens | *Geum* spp. | brown |
| Baneberry (frt) | *Actaea alba* | blacks |
| ☛ Barberry | *Berberis vulgaris* L. | yellows, reds |
| ☛ Bayberries | *Myrica* spp. | yellows, gray, gray-greens, blues |
| ☛ Bearberry/Bilberry | *Uva-ursi uva-ursi* (L.) Britton | brown, black |
| Bedstraw | *Galium* spp. | oranges, reds |
| Beggar-ticks | *Bidens* spp. | oranges, reds |
| ☛ Betony [lvs] | *Betonica officinalis* L. | yellows |
| ☛ Bilberry | *Vaccinium myrtillus* | cinnamon-red |
| Bindweed | *Convolvus* spp. | yellow-orange |
| ☛ Birch (bark, lvs) | *Betula* spp. | yellows, browns, black |
| ☛ Black Cherry (lvs, unripe frt) | *Prunus serotina* | yellows, oranges |
| Black Gum/Tupelo (bark) | *Nyssa sylvatica* | yellow-tan, khaki |
| Black Oak/Quercitron (bark) | *Quercus velutina* | yellows, oranges, gold |
| ☛ Black Walnut (hulls, bark) | *Juglans nigra* | browns, black, drabs, tans |
| Black Willow (bark) | *Salix nigra* | rose-tan, browns |
| Bloodroot | *Sanguinaria canadensis* | yellow-red |
| ☛ Blue-bottles (flrs.) | *Centaurea cyanus* L. | blues |
| Blue Flag | *Iris* spp. | browns, blacks |
| Braziletto | *Haematoxylon brasiletto* | reds, purples |
| ☛ Brazilwood/Sapan | *Caesalpinia* spp. | pinks, reds |
| Broomsedge | *Andropogon* spp. | yellows, greens |
| Buckwheat | *Fagopyrum* spp. | blue |

## APPENDIX OF HERBS & FRUITS: DYE PLANTS

| | | |
|---|---|---|
| Butterfly Weed | *Asclepias tuberosa* | yellows, greens, oranges |
| ☛ Butternut (hulls, rt, bark, lvs) | *Juglans cinerea* | browns, black, grays, green-tan, purple |
| Canadian Thorn | *Crataegus canadensis* | reds |
| Carrot (lvs) | *Daucus carota* | yellows, oranges, greens |
| Catechu of Bengal | *Acacia catechu* | olive, gray, browns |
| Catechu of Bombay | *Areca catechu* | olive, gray |
| Catechu of Gambia | *Uncaria gambir* | olive, gray, blacks |
| Celandine | *Chelidonium majus* L. | yellows |
| Celery-leaved-pine (bark) | *Phyllocladus trichomanoides* | beige, browns |
| ☛ Chamomile (flrs) | *Anthemis tinctoria* | yellows, khaki |
| ☛ Cherry [bark] | *Prunus* spp. | browns, blacks |
| Coffee (beans) | *Coffea arabica* | yellow-tan, browns |
| Common Reed-grass (lvs) | *Phragmites Phragmites* (L.) Karst. | greens |
| Coreopsis (flrs) | *Coreopsis* spp. | yellows, oranges, reds, browns |
| Cotton (flrs) | *Gossypium* spp. | yellows, tans |
| Cranberry | *Oxycoccus macrocarpus* (Ait.) Pursh. | reds |

"Cudbear" (a mixture of lichens patented 1758):

| | | |
|---|---|---|
| | *Ochrolechia tartarea,* | purple-red |
| | (or *Umbilicaria pustulata*), | |
| | *Urceolaria calcarea,* | |
| | *Cladonia pyxidata.* | |

| | | |
|---|---|---|
| Dahlia | *Dahlia* spp. | yellows, greens, oranges |
| ☛ Dandelion | *Taraxacum officinale* Weber | violet |
| ☛ Dock/Patience/sorrel | *Rumex* spp. | yellows, black |
| Dodder/Love vine | *Cuscuta americana* | yellow |
| Dog Fennel | *Eupatorium capillifolium* | yellows |
| Dyer's Broom | *Genista tinctoria* | green-yellow |
| Dyer's Buckthorn (frts) | *Rhamnus* spp. | yellows, oranges, browns, golds |
| Dyer's Savory | *Serratula tinctoria* | yellows |
| ☛ Dyer's Woodruff | *Asperula tinctoria* | reds |
| ☛ Elderberries | *Sambucus* spp. | blues, lavenders |
| ☛ Elecampane | *Inula helenium* L. | blues |
| Eucalyptus (dried lvs, bark) | *Eucalyptus* spp. | yellow, orange, red, greens, brown, grays, black |

| | | |
|---|---|---|
| False Indigo | *Amorpha fruticosa* L. | blues |
| Fenugreek | *Trigonella foenum-graecum* | yellows |
| Fetterbush | *Leucothoe fontanesiana* | yellows, browns, greens |
| Flaveria | *Flaveria linearis* | yellows |
| Fumitory | *Adlumia* spp. | yellows |
| Fustic/Dyer's Mulberry | *Chlorophora tinctoria* | yellows, gold |
| Gloriosa Daisy | *Rudbeckia* spp. | yellows, greens |
| Golden Aster | *Chrysopsis* spp. | yellows, browns, black |
| Goldenrod (flrs) | *Solidago* spp. | yellows, browns, blacks |
| Goldthread | *Coptis trifolia* (L.) Salisb. | yellows |
| Hemlock (bark) | *Tsuga* spp. | grays, blacks, browns, red-brown |
| Hickory (hulls, bark) | *Carya* spp. | yellows, grays, browns |
| ☛ Hops (lvs, flrs) | *Humulus lupulus* L. | browns |
| Horsetails | *Equisetum* spp. | gray |
| Indigo (lvs, twigs) | *Indigofera suffruticossa* | browns, blues, pinks, purples |
| Jerusalem Artichoke (flrs) | *Helianthus tuberosus* L. | yellow |
| Jointweeds | *Polygonella* spp. | yellows |

| | | |
|---|---|---|
| ☛ Juniper/Red Cedar (frt, bark) | *Juniperus* spp. | yellows, browns, khaki, blacks |
| Kawa Kawa (lvs, branches) | *Macropiper excelsum* | greens |
| Labrador Tea/*Cistus ledon* | *Ledum* spp. | yellows |
| Lichens: | | |
|    Iceland moss | *Cetraria icelandica* | yellow-brown, scarlet |
| | *Cladonia* spp. | tans, browns |
| | *Evernia* spp. | yellows, greens |
|    Oak Rag | *Lobaria pulmonaria* | rust-red, brown |
|    Litmus | *Ochrolechia tartarea* | red, blue |
| | *Parmelia* spp. | rust-reds, red-violets |
| | *Parmelia tinctoria* | magenta |
| | *Peltigera* spp. | yellow-tan, rose-tan |
| | *Pseudocyphellaria* spp. | yellows, oranges, browns |
| | *Ramilina* spp. | rose |
| ☛ ?  Orchil/Litmus | *Rocella* spp. | purples, reds, blues |
| | *Umbilicaria* spp. | pinks, purples |
|    Old Man's Beard | *Usnea* spp. | yellows, rusts, rose-tan |
| ☛   Turnsole/Litmus | ? | red, blue |
| Lilac | *Syringa* spp. | yellows |
| ☛ Lily-of-the-valley | *Convallaria majalis* L. | yellows, golds |
| Logwood (chips) | *Haematoxylon campechianum* | blue, gray, purple, brown, black |
| Lombardy Poplar | *Populus nigra* var. *italica* | yellows, browns |
| Loose strife/Willowherb | *Lysimachia vulgaris* L. | yellows |
| Madder/Garance (root) | *Rubia tinctorum* | oranges, reds |
| Magnolia (lvs) | *Magnolia* spp. | yellows, gray |
| Malacca (bean) | *Semecarpus anacardium* | black |
| Mangrove (bark) | *Sweitenia mahogani* | browns |
| ☛ Maple (bark) | *Acer* spp. | reds, browns, grays, drabs, brown-purple, blue |
| ☛ Marigold (flr) | *Calendula* spp. | yellows |
| Marigold (flr) | *Tagetes* spp. | yellow-tan, oranges, golds, greens |
| ☛ Marsh Marigold (flrs) | *Caltha palustris* | yellows |
| Milkweed | *Asclepias syriaca* | yellows, oranges, greens |
| Mistletoe | *Phoradendron* spp. | yellow |
| Mountain Ash/Rowan (frts) | *Sorbus aucuparia* | yellows, greens, browns |
| Mountain Laurel (lvs) | *Kalmia latifolia* | yellow-tan |
| Mountain Mahogany | *Cercocarpus montanus* | oranges, browns |
| Mullein | *Verbascum* spp. | yellows |
| Mungeet | *Rubia cordifolia* | reds |
| New Zealand Flax | *Phormium tenax* | browns, pinks, oranges |
| Oak (bark) | *Quercus* spp. | grays, blacks, browns, reds, tans |
| Oak Galls | infestation on *Quercus* spp. | grays |
| Onion (skins) | *Allium cepa* | yellows, browns, oranges |
| Orange-root/Golden Seal | *Hydrastis canadensis* L. | yellows |
| Oregon Grape (root) | *Mahonia* spp. | tans |
| Osage Orange | *Toxylon pomiferum* | yellow-tan, gold |
| ☛ Peach (lvs, bark) | *Prunus persica* | yellows |
| Pecan (hulls) | *Carya illinoensis* | browns, grays |
| ☛ Pellitory of the wall (lvs, stm) | *Parietaria* spp. | gray-olive, browns |
| ☛ Pigweed | *Chenopodium album* | greens |
| Plane tree | *Platanus acerifolia* | browns |
| Pokeweed (frt, lvs) | *Phytolacca* spp. | yellows, reds, tans, browns, blacks |
| Poinsettia (bracts) | *Poinsettia* spp. | lavender |

*295*

| | | |
|---|---|---|
| Poison oak (juice) | *Rhus toxicodendron* | black |
| ☛ Potato (lvs) | *Solanum tuberosum* L. | yellows |
| ☛ Puccoon | *Anchusa virginiana* | yellow |
| Prickly pear | *Opuntia* spp. | pinks |
| Privet (frt, lvs) | *Ligustrum vulgare* | gold, greens |
| ☛ | *Prunus* spp. | yellows, oranges, reds |
| Rabbit brush/Goldenrod | *Chrysothamnus* spp. | yellows |
| Raurekau | *Coprosma australis* | browns, reds |
| ☛ Red Currant (shoots) | *Ribes rubrum* | brown |
| Red Maple | *Acer rubrum* | browns, gray-blue, black |
| Rhododendron (lvs) | *Rhododendron* spp. | gray |
| ☛ Rhubarb (lf stalks) | *Rheum rhabarbarum* L. | lavender |
| ☛ Rue (stems) | *Ruta graveolens* | yellows |
| Safflower/Saffron (flrs) | *Carthamus tinctorius* | yellows, reds |
| ☛ Saffron | *Crocus sativus* | yellows |
| Sagebrush | *Artemisia tridentata* | yellows, greens |
| ☛ Sanders/Red Sandalwood | *Pterocarpus santalinus* | reds |
| ☛ Sassafras (roots) | *Sassafras* spp. | peach, oranges, browns, tans, grays |
| ☛ Scabious/Devil's Bit (lvs) | *Scabiosa succisa* L. | yellows |
| ☛ Self-heal | *Prunella vulgaris* | olive-green |
| ☛ Senna | *Cassia* spp. | yellows |
| ☛ Sloe (roots) | *Prunus sylvestis* | brown |
| Sophora | *Sophora* spp. | yellow, orange, browns, greens |
| Sorrel Tree | *Oxydendrum arboreum* DC | blacks |
| ☛ St. John's Wort | *Hypericum* spp. | yellows, greens, oranges, reds |
| Smartweed | *Polygonum* spp. | yellows |
| ☛ Stinging Nettle | *Urtica dioica* L. | yellows |
| ☛ Strawberry (roots) | *Fragraria vesca* | cinnamon red |
| Sumac/Sumach (frt, lvs, stem) | *Rhus* spp. | yellows, grays, blacks, tans |
| Sunflower | *Helianthus* spp. | gold |
| ☛ Sweet Gale | *Myrica gale* | yellow |
| Sweet Leaf (lvs) | *Symplocos tinctoria* L'Her. | yellow |
| Sycamore | *Platanus occidentalis* | browns |
| ☛ Tea (lvs) | *Camellia* or *Thea sinensis* | rose-tan, browns |
| Teasel (flrs, lvs) | *Dipsacus sylvestris* | yellows |
| Totara | *Podocarpus hallii* | browns, greens |
| Tulip Tree (lvs) | *Liriodendron tulipfera* | gold |
| ☛ Turmeric | *Curcuma* spp. | yellows |
| ☛ Violet (flrs) | *Viola* spp. | greens |
| Water Horehound (juice) | *Lycopus rubellus* Moench. | blacks |
| Weld (lvs, seeds, stems) | *Reseda lutea* | yellows |
| ☛ White Ash (bark) | *Fraxinus americana* | yellows, tans |
| Wild Basil | *Clinopodium vulgare* L. | yellows |
| ☛ "Wild Carrot"/sorrel | *Rumex hymenosepalus* | red-orange, oranges, browns |
| ☛ Wild Grape (frt) | *Vitis labrusca* | purple, blues |
| Wild Indigo | *Baptisia tinctoria* | blues |
| Wild Madder | *Galium mollugo* | reds |
| ☛ Wild Marjoram | *Origanum vulgare* | brown-purple |
| ☛ Wild Sage | *Salvia* spp. | yellows |
| Woad | *Isatis tinctoria* | blues |
| ☛ Wormwood | *Artemisia absynthium* L. | olive green |

## APPENDIX NOTES:

[1] Culpeper, p. 13.

[2] *AMA Handbook*, pp. 187–8, 199.

[3] Culpeper, p. 16.

[4] Grieve, v. 2, p. 442.

[5] Kingsbury, p. 298.

[6] Culpeper, p. 16.

[7] Parkinson, p. 490.

[8] Culpeper, p. 10.

[9] Adrosko, p. 27.

[10] Grieve, v. 1, p. 19.

[11] *AMA Handbook*, pp. 76–77.

[12] Culpeper, pp. 22–23.

[13] Woodward, p. 71.

[14] Culpeper, p. 30.

[15] Merck, pp. 59–60.

[16] Culpeper, p. 31.

[17] Grieve, v. 1, p. 74.

[18] Gerard, p. 560.

[19] Parkinson, p. 480.

[20] Culpeper, pp. 35–36.

[21] Woodward, p. 160.

[22] Culpeper, p. 49.

[23] *ibid.*, p. 286.

[24] Parkinson, p. 328.

[25] Culpeper, p. 54.

[26] *ibid.*, pp. 265–267.

[27] Woodward, p. 185.

[28] *ibid.*, p. 144.

[29] Culpeper, p. 64.

[30] *ibid.*, p. 139.

[31] Kingsbury, p. 314.

[32] Culpeper, p. 70.

[33] *ibid.*, p. 88.

[34] Bailey, p. 295.

[35] Culpeper, pp. 90–91.

[36] *ibid.*, p. 94.

[37] Gerard, p. 661.

[38] Culpeper, p. 96.

[39] Parkinson, p. 471.

[40] *ibid.*, p. 247.

[41] Hall, pp. 94–95.

[42] *AMA Handbook*, pp. 46–7.

[43] Grieve, v. 1, pp. 265–276.

[44] Culpeper, p. 120.

[45] Gerard, p. 1000.

[46] Culpeper, p. 121.

[47] Parkinson, p. 494.

[48] *ibid.*, pp. 180, 188.

[49] Gerard, p. 487.

[50] Merck, p. 495.

[51] Kingsbury, p. 432.

[52] Culpeper p. 145.

[53] Merck, pp. 41, 462.

[54] Kingsbury, p. 130.

[55] Gerard, p. 346.

[56] Culpeper, p. 147.

[57] *ibid.*, pp. 156–157.

[58] *ibid.*, pp. 161–162.

[59] Gerard, p. 1120.

[60] Culpeper, p. 174.

[61] Beeton, p. 192.

[62] Culpeper, p. 177.

[63] Hartley, p. 456–457.

[64] Culpeper, p. 276.

[65] Merck, p. 11.

[66] Culpeper, pp. 180–182.

[67] Parkinson, p. 298.

[68] Merck, p. 114.

[69] Woodward, pp. 169–170.

[70] Gerard, p. 887.

[71] Culpeper, pp. 190–192.

[72] *ibid.*, pp. 290–291.

[73] Woodward, p. 147.

[74] Culpeper, pp. 198–199.

[75] Digby #59, p. 65.

[76] Leggatt, pp. 112, 138.

[77] Merck, p. 540.

[78] Woodward, pp. 157–158.

[79] Hooper, p. 112.

[80] Parkinson, pp. 569–570.

[81] *AMA Handbook*, p. 98.

## APPENDIX
## NOTES, CONTINUED:

[82] Merck, p. 391.
[83] McGee, p. 159.
[84] Woodward, p. 150.
[85] Culpeper, p. 215.
[86] Parkinson, p. 292.
[87] Culpeper, p. 216.
[88] *ibid.*, p. 218.
[89] Creasy, p. 49.
[90] Beeton, p. 665.
[91] Merck, p. 480.
[92] Culpeper, pp. 225–226.
[93] *ibid.*, pp. 308–309.
[94] Woodward, pp. 62–63.
[95] Gerard, p. 1083.
[96] Culpeper, pp. 246–248.
[97] Bancke's Herbal.
[98] Culpeper, pp. 251–253.
[99] *ibid.*, p. 255.
[100] *ibid.*, pp. 162–163.
[101] Kingsbury, pp. 171–175.
[102] Culpeper, pp. 264–265.
[103] *ibid.*, p. 268.
[104] Woodward, p. 145.
[105] *ibid.*, pp. 182–184.
[106] Parkinson, pp. 447–448.
[107] Culpeper, p. 278.
[108] *ibid.*, p. 279.
[109] Gerard, p. 1089.
[110] Grieve, v.1, p. 88.
[111] Gerard, p. 1228.
[112] Culpeper, p. 282.
[113] *ibid.*, p. 290.
[114] Merck, p. 554.
[115] Woodward, p. 236.
[116] Culpeper, pp. 292–293.
[117] *AMA Handbook*, pp. 88–9.
[118] Gerard, p. 266.
[119] Kingsbury, p. 188.

[120] Merck, p. 322.
[121] *ibid.*, p. 217.
[122] Adrosko, pp. 44–45.
[123] Culpeper, pp. 298–9.
[124] *ibid.*, pp. 300–1.
[125] Parkinson, pp. 257–259, (*see his illustration #1.*)
[126] Culpeper, p. 100.
[127] *ibid.*, pp. 144–145.
[128] Merck, pp. 362–363.
[129] Culpeper, pp. 42–44.
[130] *ibid.*, p. 273.
[131] McGee, p. 160.
[132] Merck, p. 2.
[133] Miller, found in Favretti, p. 74.

From *The Shepherds Great Calendar*, 15th c.

# BIBLIOGRAPHY
# AND SUGGESTIONS FOR FURTHER READING:

Acton, Bryan, and Peter Duncan. *Making Mead, a complete guide to the making of sweet and dry Mead, Melomel, Metheglin, Hippocras, Pyment and Cyser.* The Amateur Winemaker, South Street, Andover, Hants, 1972. *Gives 44 recipes.*

Adrosko, Rita J. *Natural Dyes and Home Dyeing.* Dover Publications, Inc. New York, 1971.

American Medical Association. *AMA Handbook of Poisonous and Injurious Plants.* Chicago, Illinois, 1985. *Incomplete, but contains much useful information.*

Anonymous. *The Art of Confectionery.* (Collected from the best New York, Philadelphia, and Boston Confectioners, and include a large number from the French and other foreign nations.) 1866.

_____. *Le Menagier de Paris.* (The Goodman of Paris.) c. 1395.

_____. *A New System of Domestic Cookery, Formed Upon Principles of Economy, and Adapted to the Use of Private Families.* Andrews and Cummings, and L. Blake. Boston, 1807.

_____. *A True Gentlewoman's Delight, Wherein is contained all manner of Cookery.* W. I. Gent. London, 1653. Rpt. Falconwood Press. New York, 1991.

_____. *Bancke's Herbal.* Printed by Richard Banckes. 1525.

_____. *The British Jewel, or Complete Housewife's best Companion.* London, 1782.

_____. *The Family Receipt Book, Containing Eight Hundred Valuable Receipts in Various Branches of Domestic Economy; Selected from the Works of the Most Approved Writers, Ancient and Modern; and from the Attested Communications of Scientific Friends.* (Second American Edition.) Randolph Barnes. Pittsburgh, 1819.

_____. *The Forme of Cury.* A Roll of Ancient English Cookery, Compiled, about A.D. 1390, by the Master-Cooks of King Richard II, London, Printed by J. Nichols, Printer to the Society of Antiquaries, 1780. Rpt. Early English Text Society, Supplementary Series 8, 1985.

_____. *The Four Seasons of the House of Cerruti.* Tr. by Judith Spencer. Facts on File Publications. New York, 1983.

_____. *The Kitchen Directory, and American Housewife: Containing the most Valuable and Original Receipts, in All the Various Branches of Cookery; Together with a Collection of Miscellaneous Receipts, and Directions Relative to Housewifery. Also the Whole Art of Carving,* Illustrated by Sixteen Engravings. Mark H. Newman and Company. New York, 1844 and 1846.

# BIBLIOGRAPHY

_____. *The Practical Housewife: A Complete Encyclopedia of Domestic Economy and Family Medical Guide.* J. B. Lippincott and Company. Philadelphia, c. 1860.

Apicius. *Cookery and Dining in Imperial Rome.* Tr. by J. D. Vehling. Walter M. Hill. Chicago, 1936. Rpt. Dover Publications, Inc. New York, 1977.

Athenaeus. *The Deipnosophists, or The Sophists at Dinner.* Tr. by Charles Burton Gulick. Wm. Heinemann, Ltd. London. G.P. Putnam's Sons. New York, 1927. Ed. by E. Capps, T.E. Page, W.H.D. Rouse. The Loeb Classical Library. *7 volumes dating from circa 228 A.D., containing a great deal of information on the wines and foods of ancient Greece, Rome, and Egypt.*

Bailey, L. H., and Ethel Zoe. *Hortus Second, A Concise Dictionary of Gardening, General Horticulture and Cultivated Plants in North America.* The Macmillan Co. New York, 1930. Rpt. 1960.

Baugh, Albert C., ed. *Chaucer's Major Poetry.* Prentice-Hall, Inc. New Jersey, 1963.

Beecher, Miss Catherine E. *Miss Beecher's Domestic Receipt-Book: Designed as a Supplement to her Treatise on Domestic Economy.* Third Edition. Harper and Bros., Publishers. New York, 1857.

Beeton, Mrs. Isabella. *Mrs. Beeton's Book of Household Management.* S. O. Beeton. 1861. Rpt. Chancellor Press. London, 1982. *A wealth of information.*

Bemiss, Elijah. *The Dyer's Companion.* 1815. Rpt. Dover Publications, Inc. New York, 1973.

Benson, Evelyn Abraham, ed. *Penn Family Recipes, Cooking Recipes of Wm. Penn's Wife, GULIELMA.* George Shumway, Publisher. York, Pennsylvania, 1966. Contains the MS. cookbook: "My Mother's Recaipts for Cookerys Presarving and Chyrurgery – William Penn" signed "Here ends the book of Coockary in great hast transcrided by Edward Blackfan the 25th of October 1702." *Gulielma Penn died in 1694 at the age of 50, so this collection of recipes should rightly be dated circa 1664-94.*

Black, Penny. *The Book of Potpourri, Fragrant flower mixes for scenting & decorating the home.* Simon and Schuster. New York, 1989. *A beautiful book which contains color pictures of many of the herbs and spices called for in our recipes.*

Blue, Anthony Dias. "Bold Belgian Beers," *Bon Appétit.* June, 1994.

Bold, Harold C. *Morphology of Plants.* Third edition. Harper & Row. New York, 1973.

Boorde, Andrew. *The Regyment, or a Dyetary of Helth.* 1542.

Bradley, Richard. *The Country Housewife and Lady's Director.* Part 1 first printed 1727. Part 2 first printed 1732. 1736 edition. Rpt. Prospect Books. London, 1980.

Braidwood, Robert J., et al. "Symposium: Did man once live by beer alone?" *American Anthropology.* 55: 515-526. 1953. *(Symposium, noun: an ancient Greek drinking party.)*

Brainard, Douglas. "Oxford Braggot," *Scum*. Number 13, pp. 19-20. *"Scum" is a publication of the Brewers Guilds of the East and Athelmearc in the Society for Creative Anachronism. It is available by writing to Douglas Brainard, 45 Southwind Way, Rochester, NY 14624.*

Briggs, Richard. *The English Art of Cookery, According to the Present Practice, Being a Complete Guide to all Housekeepers, etc.* Circa 1788. Printed in America under the title: *The New Art of Cookery*. Philadelphia, 1792. By Richard Briggs, Many Years Cook at the Globe-Tavern, Fleet Street, The White-Hart Tavern, Holborn, and now at The Temple Coffee House, London.

Britton, Nathaniel, Lord, and Hon. Addison Brown. *An Illustrated Flora of the Northern United States and Canada.* 3 volumes. Second edition. 1913. Rpt. Dover Publications, Inc. New York, 1970. *An indispensable tool in plant identification. Referred to here as B&B.*

Brown, John Hull. *Early American Beverages.* Bonanza Books. New York, 1966. *A very useful collection of documented early American recipes.*

Bullock, Mrs. Helen. *The Williamsburg Art of Cookery or Accompliſh'd Gentlewoman's Companion: Being a Collection of upwards of Five Hundred of the moſt Ancient & Approv'd Recipes in Virginia Cookery, etc.* Colonial Williamsburg. Richmond, Virginia, 1949. Rpt. The Dietz Press, Inc. 1985. *A modern work cleverly and convincingly done in the style of Eliza Smith's 1742 "The Compleat Housewife," contains ±17 pages of documented recipes for shrubs, eggnog, wines, punches, syllabubs, etc., from 18th and 19th century Virginia.*

Butler, Charles. *The Feminine Monarchie or A Treatise Concerning Bees, and the Dve Ordering of Them, etc.* Printed by Ioſeph Barnes. Oxford, 1609. Rpt. Theatrum Orbis Terrarum Ltd. Amsterdam, 1969.

Carter, Charles. *The Receipt Book of Charles Carter.* Cook to the Duke of Argyll. 1732.

Carter, Susannah. *The Frugal Colonial Housewife or Complete Woman Cook.* London and Boston, 1772. Rpt. Dolphin Books. Garden City, New York, 1976. *11 recipes for wines and mead.*

Chase, Dr. *Dr. Chase's Recipes, or Information for Everybody: An Invaluable Collection of About Eight Hundred Practical Recipes.* Ann Arbor, Michigan, 1869.

Child, Mrs. *The American Frugal Housewife. Dedicated to Those Who Are Not Ashamed of Economy.* Twelfth edition. Carter, Hendee, and Co. Boston, 1832. Rpt. Old Sturbridge Village and Applewood Books. Box 365, Bedford, MA, 01739.

Cleland, Elizabeth. *The Receipt Book of Elizabeth Cleland.* 1759.

Cook, Albert S., ed. *Select Translations from Old English Poetry.* Ginn and Company. Boston, 1902.

Coon, Nelson. *Using Wild and Wayside Plants.* Dover Publications, Inc. New York, 1980.

Cornelius, Mrs. *The Young Housekeeper's Friend, or A Guide to Domestic Economy and Comfort.* Charles Tappan. Boston. Saxton and Huntington. New York, 1846.

Creasy, Rosalind. "Edible Flowers," *Organic Gardening*. February, 1990.

*301*

# BIBLIOGRAPHY

Culpeper, Nicholas. *Culpeper's Complete Herbal.* 1653. Rpt. Chartwell Books, Inc. Secaucus, New Jersey, 1985.

Dawson, Thomas. *The Good Housewife's Jewell.* 1585.

Digby, Sir Kenelme. *The Closet of the Eminently Learned Sir Kenelme Digby Kt. Opened: Whereby is Discovered Several ways for making of Metheglin, Sider, Cherry-Wine, &c. Together with Excellent Directions for Cookery: As alſo for Preſerving, Conſerving, Candying, &c.* Publiſhed by his Son's Conſent. Printed by E. C. for H. Brome, at the Star in Little Britain. London, 1669.

Dods, Margaret. *The Cook and Housewife's Manual: a Practical System of Modern Domestic Cookery and Family Management.* Fourth edition. By Mistress Margaret Dods, of the Cleikum Inn, St. Ronan's. 1829. Rpt. Rosters Ltd. London, 1988. *Contains a great many recipes for flavored brandies, liqueurs, wines, beers, cordials, etc. This inexpensive reprint is well worth having.*

*Epulario, Or, The Italian Banquet.* Translated out of Italian into English. London, 1598. Rpt. Falconwood Press. New York, 1990.

Farley, John. *The London Art of Cookery, and Housekeeper's Complete Assistant, etc.* By John Farley, Principal Cook at the London Tavern. 1804. (*The 8th edition of this book was printed in 1796.*)

Favretti, Rudy F., and Gordon P. De Wolf. *Colonial Gardens.* Barre Publishers. Barre, Mass., 1972.

Fernie, Dr. *Herbal Simples.* 1897.

Ferns, Catharine V. *The Kitchen Guide.* Chester Times. Chester, Pennsylvania, 1925.

Foley, Ruth H. "Snail Water," *Herb Quarterly.* Vol. 4. 1979.

Freedman, David, ed. *A Collection of Medieval and Renaissance Cookbooks.* Volume II. Third edition. Chicago, 1989. *This work has a chapter containing 32 non-alcoholic beverage recipes, Arabic in origin, from an anonymous 13th century Andalusian manuscript.*

Freeman, Margaret B. *Herbs for the Medieval Household.* Metropolitan Museum of Art. New York, 1943.

Frere, Catherine Frances, ed. *A Proper Newe Booke of Cokerye, declarynge what maner of meates be beſte in ſeaſon, etc.* 16th century. Rpt. Heffer & Sons, Ltd. Cambridge, 1913.

Frishman, Robert and Eileen. *Enjoy Home Winemaking.* Winemakers Ltd. Westport, Connecticut, 1972. *This small pamphlet has a useful chart specifying which yeasts to use for various fruit wines.*

Gelleroy, William. *The London Cook, or the whole art of cookery made easy and familiar.* London, 1762.

Gerard, John. *The Herball or Generall Historie of Plants.* London, 1597. Rpt. Walter J. Johnson, Inc. Theatrum Orbis Terrarum, Ltd. Keizersgracht 526, Amsterdam, 1974. *An enormous work – far superior to the Woodward edition (and consequently priced beyond reach).*

Glasse, Mrs. Hannah. *The Art of Cookery, Made Plain and Easy.* Originally published 1747. 1796 edition. Rpt. Randolph C. Williams. Richmond, Virginia, 1976.

Gleason, Henry A., and Arthur Cronquist. *Manual of Vascular Plants of Northeastern United States and Adjacent Canada.* D. Van Nostrand Co. New York, 1963.

Grieve, Mrs. M. *A Modern Herbal, The Medicinal, Culinary, Cosmetic and Economic Properties, Cultivation and Folk-lore of Herbs, Grasses, Fungi, Shrubs & Trees with All their Modern Scientific Uses.* Two volumes. Harcourt, Brace & Co. 1931. Rpt. Dover Publications, Inc. New York, 1971.

Hale, Mrs. Sarah J. *The Way to Live Well, and To Be Well While We Live.* Case, Tiffany and Co. Hartford, 1849.

Hall, Alan. *The Wild Food Trailguide.* Holt, Rinehart and Winston of Canada, Ltd. Canada, 1976.

Harrison, William. *The Description of England.* 1587. *A new edition by Georges Edelen, subtitled: "The Classic Contemporary Account of Tudor Social Life," is available from the Folger Shakespeare Library and Dover Publications, Inc. Washington, D.C., and New York, 1994. Edelen's edition has somewhat modernized spelling and is very well annotated. The book contains descriptions of most facets of Tudor life, including directions for cultivating saffron, brewing beer, etc.*

Harrison, Sarah. *The Housekeeper's Pocket Book.* 1739.

Hartley, Dorothy. *Food in England.* Futura Publications. London, 1985. *Contains a large section on brewing and period beverages; unfortunately, she neglects throughout the book, and in this section in particular, to provide proper citations for the sources being quoted. There is no bibliography. (She has a delicious-sounding recipe for a blackberry cordial which calls for half cider and half blackberry juice, p. 428.) This is a thoroughly engrossing and entertaining book, well worth adding to your library.*

Hayden, E. G. *Travels round our Village.* Circa 1900.

Henisch, Bridget A. *Fast and Feast – Food in Medieval Society.* The Pennsylvania State University Press. University Park, 1978.

Hess, Karen, ed. *Martha Washington's Booke of Cookery, and Booke of Sweetmeats: being a Family Manuscript, curiously copied by an unknown Hand sometime in the seventeenth century, which was in her Keeping from 1749, the time of her Marriage to Daniel Custis, to 1799, at which time she gave it to Eleanor Parke Custis, her grandaughter, on the occasion of her Marriage to Lawrence Lewis.* Columbia Univ. Press. New York, 1981. *The recipes contained in the MS. are dated 1550 to 1625 by the editor. The MS. contains many recipes for wines, mead, cordials, etc.*

Hill, Sir John. *The British Herbal.* 1772.

Hooker, Richard J., ed. *A Colonial Plantation Cookbook: The Receipt Book of Harriott Pinckney Horry.* 1770. Univ. of South Carolina Press. Columbia, South Carolina, 1984. *An unusual recipe for Spruce Beer can be found on p. 96: 1 quart of maize is boiled with 7 gallons of water, 1/2 pound of spruce or pine tops, 1/2 pound of China root (caution – see appendix), and 1/2 pound of sassafras (caution – see appendix), until the liquid is reduced to 5 gallons or the kernels crack open. The wort is cooled and 1 pint of yeast, and 3 pints of molasses are added. The spruce beer is bottled as soon as it begins to ferment.*

Hooper, Madge. *Herbs and Medicinal Plants.* Arco Publishing. New York, 1986.

Howland, Mrs. Esther Allen. *The American Economical Housekeeper and Family Receipt Book.* Worcester, 1850.

Katz, Solomon H., and Fritz Maytag. "Brewing an Ancient Beer," *Archaeology.* July/August, 1991, pp. 24-33.

Kingsbury, John M. *Poisonous Plants of the United States and Canada.* Prentice-Hall, Inc. New Jersey, 1964.

Leggatt, Jenny. *Cooking With Flowers.* Ballantine Books. New York, 1987. *A beautiful book with some useful information on edible flowers. Contains a short section on flower drinks, including elderflower champagne, and tisanes.*

Leslie, Miss. *Seventy-five Receipts for Pastry, Cakes, and Sweetmeats.* Tenth edition. Munroe and Francis, and Joseph H. Francis. Boston. Charles S. Francis. New York, 1838.

Lorwin, Madge. *Dining With William Shakespeare.* Atheneum. New York, 1976.

McCully, Helen, et. al., eds. *American Heritage Cookbook, and Illustrated History of American Eating & Drinking.* American Heritage Publishing Co., Inc. 1964. *Contains many undocumented colonial-era recipes for shrubs, bounces, sangarees, etc.*

MacGregor, James. *Beer Making for All.* Dover Publications, Inc. New York, 1967.

Mackenzie. *Five Thousand Receipts in All the Useful and Domestic Arts: constituting A Complete Practical Library.* James Kay, Jun. and Brother. Philadelphia, 1829.

Mac Nicol, Mary. *Flower Cookery, the Art of Cooking with Flowers.* Fleet Press Corp. 1967.

Markham, Gervase. *The English Huſ-wife, Contayning The inward and outward vertues which ought to be in a compleat woman; As, her skill in Phyſicke, Cookery, Banqueting-ſtuffe, Diſtillation, Perfumes, Wooll, Hemp, Flax, Dayries, Brewing, Baking, and all other things belonging to an houſhould.* Iohn Beale. London, 1615. (*The English Housewife*, collated and edited by Michael R. Best, contains the 1615, 1623, and 1631 editions. Queen's Univ. Press. Kingston, 1986.) *Markham devotes several chapters to wine, beer, distillation, the ordering of the brew house, etc. Chapter IV deals with the subject: "ordering, preserving, and helping (i.e. altering the color of, or adulterating) of all sorts of wines." He especially goes into great detail about the process of malting.*

Massaccesi, Raymond. *Winemaker's Recipe Handbook.* 1976. *A small pamphlet, apparently self-published, with over 100 wine recipes – many for odd wines such as tomato, onion, firethorn, watermelon, pumpkin, jelly & jam, etc. He also has a modern Perry recipe.*

May, Robert. *The Accomplisht Cook, or the Art and Mystery of Cookery.* Printed by N. Brooke for T. Archer. 1660.

McGee, Harold. *On Food and Cooking.* Charles Scribner's Sons. New York, 1984.

Mendelsohn, Oscar A. *The Dictionary of Drink and Drinking.* Hawthorn Books, Inc. New York.

Merck & Co., Inc. *The Merck Index.* Fifth Edition. Rahway, New Jersey, 1940.

Miller, Philip. *The Gardener's Dictionary.* Seventh edition. London, 1759.

Monckton, H. A. *A History of English Ale and Beer.* The Bodley Head. London, 1966. *He has an undocumented braggot recipe on p. 31.*

Murrell, John. *A Delightful Daily Exercise for Ladies and Gentlewomen.* London, 1621. Rpt. Falconwood Press. New York, 1990.

*The New York Gazette.* February 13, 1744.

Newington, Thomas. *M.S. Book of Receipts.* 1719.

Nims, Charles F. "The Bread and Beer Problems of the Moscow Mathematical Papyrus," *The Journal of Egyptian Archaeology.* Vol. 44, 1958, pp. 56-65.

Nott, John. *The Receipt Book of John Nott.* Cook to the Duke of Bolton. 1723.

Parkinson, John. *Paradisi in Sole Paradiſus Terrestris. Or A Garden of all ſorts of pleaſant flowers which our English ayre will permitt to be nourſed vp, etc.* Collected by John Parkinſon Apothecary of London. Humfrey Lownes and Robert Young. London, 1629. Facsimile rpt. Dover Publications, Inc. New York, 1976.

Partridge, John. *The good Huswifes Handmaide for the Kitchin.* 1594.

Penner, Lucille Recht. *The Honey Book.* Hastings House Publishers. New York, 1980. *A delightful book containing several old honey recipes.*

Peterson, Lee Allen. *A Field Guide to Edible Wild Plants of Eastern and Central North America.* Houghton Mifflin Co. New York, 1977. *Very useful if you intend to harvest wild plants.*

Phipps, Frances. *Colonial Kitchens, Their Furnishings, and Their Gardens.* Hawthorn Books, Inc. New York, 1972. *Well researched, contains many documented colonial-era recipes.*

*Pikestaff.* Arts & Sciences Supplement. December, 1991. *A pamphlet of articles containing several recipes for mead, horilka, braggot, hypocras; also how to grow hops. A reprint, or information leading to a copy might be available from the Stock Clerk, Society for Creative Anachronism, P.O. Box 360743, Milpitas, CA  95035-0743.*

Plat, Sir Hugh. *Delightes for Ladies, To adorne their Perſons, Tables, Cloſets, and Diſtillatories: with Beavties, Banqvets, Perfumes & Waters.* Printed by Humfrey Lownes. London, 1609.

Plat, Sir Hugh. *The Jewel House of Art and Nature.* 1594.

## BIBLIOGRAPHY

Platina. *On Honest Indulgence (De Honesta Voluptate).* Venice, 1475. Rpt. Falconwood Press. New York, 1989.

Pliny the Elder. *Natural History.* c. 77 A.D. H. Rackham, ed. Harvard Univ. Press. Cambridge, Massachusetts, 1938.

Pliny the Elder. *Natural History.* c. 77 A.D. H. Rackham, ed. Rpt. The Loeb Classical Library. Harvard Univ. Press. Cambridge, Massachusetts, 1983.

Pouncy, Carolyn Johnston, ed. *The Domostroi, Rules for Russian Households in the Time of Ivan the Terrible.* Cornell Univ. Press. Ithaca, New York, 1994. *A new book with at least 10 recipes for mead and beer.*

*The Queen's Closet Opened. Incomparable Secrets in Physick, Chirurgery, Preserving, Candying, and Cookery, etc.* By W.M., Cook to Queen Henrietta Maria. London, 1655.

Randolph, Mrs. Mary. *The Virginia Housewife: or, Methodical Cook.* E. H. Butler and Co. Philadelphia, 1856.

Renfrow, Cindy. *Take a Thousand Eggs or More, a translation of medieval recipes from Harleian MS. 279, Harleian MS. 4016, and extracts of Ashmole MS. 1439, Laud MS. 553, and Douce MS. 55, with nearly 100 recipes adapted for modern cookery.* By the author. Pottstown, Pennsylvania, 1990.

Rohde, Eleanour Sinclair. *A Garden of Herbs.* Circa 1922. Rpt. Dover Publications, Inc. New York, 1969. *Contains lots of old recipes.*

_____. *Rose Recipes from Olden Times.* Routledge. 1939. Rpt. Dover Publications, Inc. New York, 1973. *Some old recipes, including one for pastilles.*

_____. *The Old English Herbals.* Longmans, Green and Co. 1922. Rpt. Dover Publications, Inc. New York, 1971.

Rose, Giles. *A Perfect School of Instructions for the Officers of the Mouth.* By Giles Rose, one of the Master Cooks to Charles II. 1682.

Ross, James Bruce, and Mary M. McLaughlin, eds. *The Portable Medieval Reader.* The Viking Press. New York, 1949. Rpt. 1962.

Ruthen, Lord. *The Ladies Cabinet Enlarged and Opened...* By the late Right Honorable and Learned Chymist, The Lord Ruthen. Second edition. G. Bedell and T. Collins. Fleetstreet, London. Rpt. Falconwood Press. New York, 1990.

Salmon, William, M.D. *The Family Dictionary: or Household Companion.* London, 1710.

Sass, Lorna J. *To the Queen's Taste.* Metropolitan Museum of Art. New York, 1976.

Sibley, Jane. "Guide to Brewing," *The Compleat Anachronist.* No. 5, March, 1983. *(See note for "Pikestaff" above.)*

Simmons, Amelia. *The First American Cookbook, A Facsimile of "American Cookery."* 1796. Rpt. Dover Publications, Inc. New York, 1958.

Simon, André L. *How to Make Wines and Cordials.* 1946. Rpt. Dover Publications, Inc. New York, 1972. *Contains hundreds of documented old recipes.*

Smith, Eliza. *The Compleat Housewife: or, Accomplished Gentlewoman's Companion.* 1736.

Spalinger, Anthony. "Dates in Ancient Egypt," *Studien Zur Altägyptischen Kultur.* Band 15, 1988, pp. 255-276.

Spenser, Edmund. *The Faerie Queene.* Thomas P. Roche, Jr., ed. Penguin Books. New York, 1978.

Taylor, Raymond L. *Plants of Colonial Days: a Guide to One Hundred & Sixty Flowers, Shrubs, and Trees in the Gardens of Colonial Williamsburg.* Williamsburg, Virginia, 1952.

Thornton, R. *The Family Herbal.* 1810.

Tirel, Guillaume. *Le Viandier di Guillaume Tirel, dit Taillevent.* Jerome Pichon and Georges Vicaire, eds. Paris, 1892.

_____. *Le Viandier de Taillevent, 14th Century Cookery.* Tr. by James Prescott. Alfarhaugr Publishing Society. Eugene, Oregon, 1989.

Tritton, S. M. *Tritton's Guide to Better Wine and Beer Making for Beginners.* Faber and Faber. London, 1965. *Good how-to with British, U.S., and Metric measurements given for each recipe.*

Tryon, Thomas. *The Way to get Wealth, or a new Art of making above twenty-three sorts of Wine, equal to that of France.* London, 1706.

Vinaver, Eugene, ed. *Malory Works.* Oxford Univ. Press. Oxford, 1971. Contains Sir Thomas Malory's, *Le Morte D'arthur,* c. 1469.

Weigle, Palmy, et. al., eds. "Natural Plant Dyeing," *Plants & Gardens.* Vol. 29, No. 2, March, 1976. Brooklyn Botanic Garden, Brooklyn, NY 11225.

Wheaton, Barbara Ketcham. *Savoring The Past, The French Kitchen and Table from 1300 to 1789.* Univ. of Pennsylvania Press. 1983.

Winslow, Mrs. *Domestic Receipt-Book.* Jeremiah Curtis and Sons and John I. Brown and Sons. Circa 1875.

Woodward, Marcus. *Gerard's Herball, The Essence thereof Distilled by Marcus Woodward from the Edition of Th. Johnson, 1636.* Crescent Books. New York, 1985. *Mercilessly incomplete, but affordable.*

# INDEX

Absinthe (*See also Wormwood.*), pp. **225**, 274, 292.
    CREME d'ABSINTHE, BY M. BEAUVILLIERS' RECEIPT – 1829, p. 225.
African Marigold (*Tagetes* spp.), pp. 162, **279**.
[AFTER-WINE] – c. 77 A.D., p. 158.
Agrimony, pp. 53, 55, 59, 61, 62, 65, 67, 71, 86, 88, 93, 95, 101, 107, 115, 119, **266**, 293.
Ale, pp. **1-30**, 34, 62, 80-82, 91, 163, 187-191, 195, 197, 198, 210, 211, 214, 238, 247, 249, 250, 254, 256, 257, 259, 272, 273, 285, 289.
    ALE, HOMEBREWED – HOW IT IS MADE – 1869, p. 17.
    ALE, MULLED – 1860, p. 195.
    ALE WITH HONEY – 1669, p. 13.
    COCK ALE – 1780, p. 16.
    DIVERS EXCELLENT KINDES OF BOTTLE-ALE – 1609, p. 8.
    MR. WEBB'S ALE AND BRAGOT – 1669, p. 14.
    SCOTCH ALE FROM MY LADY HOLMBEY – 1669, p. 11.
    SMALL ALE FOR THE STONE – 1669, p. 12.
    SUMERIAN ALE – c. 1800 B.C., p. 2.
    TO BREW ALE IN SMALL FAMILIES – 1829, p. 18.
    TO MAKE ALE DRINK QUICK – 1669, p. 250.
    TO MAKE CAPON ALE – c. 1550 to 1625, p. 15.
    TO MAKE COCK-ALE – 1669, p. 15.
    TO MAKE COCK ALE – 1762, p. 16.
Alecost (*See Costmary.*)
Alehoof, pp. 54, 250, **266**.
Alexander, pp. 120, **266**.
Alkanet, pp. 189, **266**.
Alleluia (*See Wood Sorrel.*)
Almond milk, pp. 188, **189**, 243.
Aloe, pp. 244, **267**, 293.
Amber, pp. 183, **253**.
Ambered-sugar, pp. 196, **197**, 202, **253**.
Ambergris, Amber-greece, pp. 32, 48, 99, 105, 108, 154, 183, 194, 196-200, 216, 219, 241, 242, **253**.
Angelica, pp. 44, 51, 52, 61, 65, 76, 77, 88, 105, 107, 115, 172, **266, 267**.
Anise, pp. 15, 64, 93, 120, 208, 217, 220-223, **267**.
Anisette, pp. 207, 208, 267.
    ANISETTE DE BORDEAUX – 1866, p. 208.
    ANNISEED CORDIAL – 1839, p. 207.
    ANOTHER ANISETTE DE BOURDEAUX – 1866, p. 208.
Annys Seeds (*See Anise.*)
Apple, pp. 17, 125, 144, 193, 194, 204, 209, 227-233, 265, **267**, 293.
[APPLE BEER] – c. 1674, p. 17.
APPLE BRANDY, METHOD OF MAKING – 1815, p. 209.
Apple Cider, pp. 125, 138, 157, 198, 199, 203, **226-233**, 251.
    AFTER IT HAS FINED – 1796, p. 251.
    APPLE DRINK WITH SUGAR, HONEY, &c – 1669, p. 231.
    A VERY PLEASANT DRINK OF APPLES – 1669, p. 230.
    A WAY TOO MAKE CYDOR – c. 1674, p. 231.
    DOCTOR HARVEY'S PLEASANT WATER-CIDER, [etc.] – 1669, p. 230.
    FOR FINING CYDER – 1796, p. 251.

A Cider Mill and Press.
From *The Universal Magazine of Knowledge and Pleasure.*
London, September, 1747.

From *Das Kreüterbuch oder Herbarius*, 1534.

# INDEX

*317*

# INDEX

*Hyssop.*
From *Neues Paradeissgärtlein*,
by Conrad Rosbach, Frankfurt, 1613.

# SOURCES

**HEIRLOOM SEEDS:**

◆ SEEDS OF CHANGE, 1364 Rufina Circle #5, Santa Fe, NM 87501.

◆ OLD STURBRIDGE VILLAGE, 1 Old Sturbridge Village Road, Sturbridge, MA 01566.

◆ BOUNTIFUL GARDENS, 18001 Shafer Ranch Road, Willits, CA 95490-9626.

◆ NICHOLS GARDEN NURSERY, HERBS & RARE SEEDS, 1190 N. Pacific Hwy., Albany, OR 97321-4598.

**HERBS, ETC.**

◆ LORANN OILS, INC., 4518 Aurelius Road, Lansing, MI 48910. A source of distilled oils of spices.

◆ PENN HERB CO., Ltd., 603 North 2nd Street, Philadelphia, PA 19123-3098. 1-800-523-9971.

◆ APHRODESIA, 282 Bleeker Street, New York, NY 10014.

**HISTORICAL ROSES:**

◆ ANTIQUE ROSE EMPORIUM, Rt. 5, Box 143, Brenham, TX 77833.

◆ HISTORICAL ROSES, 1657 W. Jackson St., Painesville, OH 44077.

◆ ROSES OF YESTERDAY & TODAY, Brown's Valley Rd., Watsonville, CA 95076.

**BOOKS & MAGAZINES:**

◆ "*PETIT PROPOS CULINAIRES*," c/o Prospect Books, 45 Lamont Road, London, England SW10 0HU.

◆ "*SPECULUM, A JOURNAL OF MEDIEVAL STUDIES*," The Medieval Academy of America, 1430 Massachusetts Ave., Cambridge, MA 02138.

◆ THE WINE AND FOOD LIBRARY, c/o J. Longone, 1207 W. Madison , Ann Arbor, MI 48103.

◆ FALCONWOOD PRESS, c/o S. J. Evans, 193 Colonie St., Albany, NY 12210-2501.

◆ ALFARHAUGR PUBLISHING SOCIETY, 1908 Oak Street, Eugene, OR 97405.

◆ APPLEWOOD BOOKS, Box 365, Bedford, MA, 01739, dist. by The Globe Pequot Press, Box Q, Chester, CT 06412.

◆ "*SCUM*," c/o D. Brainard, 45 Southwind Way, Rochester, NY 14624.

◆ "*ZYMURGY*," The American Homebrewers Association, P.O. Box 1679, Boulder, CO 80306-1679.

**MEAD:**

◆ THE AMERICAN MEAD ASSOCIATION, c/o P. Spence-Allen, 41 North Street, Ostrander, OH 43061.

◆ BLACK FOX MEADERY, c/o R. Lasseter, Auburntown, TN 37016.

**HISTORICAL SOCIETIES:**

◆ MARKLAND MEDIEVAL MERCENARY MILITIA, Ltd., P.O. Box 715, Greenbelt, MD 20768-0715. Markland is a non-profit educational organization that attempts to recreate the Middle Ages through role-playing, emphasizing the years 800 to 1370 A.D.

◆ THE RICHARD III SOCIETY, 12 Bolfmar Avenue, Cranbury, NJ 08512, "is devoted to a reassessment of Richard III's reputation... and to research into the life and customs of England in the Yorkist and early Tudor eras."

◆ THE SOCIETY FOR CREATIVE ANACHRONISM, Inc., Office of the Registry, P.O. Box 360743, Milpitas, CA 95036-0743, is a non-profit educational organization devoted to researching and re-creating the art, music, crafts, etc., of pre-17th century Western civilization.

# TAKE A THOUSAND EGGS OR MORE

*A Collection Of Fifteenth Century Recipes*

## NEW! Second Edition

by Cindy Renfrow

# TAKE A THOUSAND EGGS OR MORE
## *A Collection Of Fifteenth Century Recipes*

### *NEW!* Second Edition

### by Cindy Renfrow

*TAKE A THOUSAND EGGS OR MORE* is a fascinating cookbook of 15th-century recipes for the student of history or the modern cook. This new two-volume set contains 400 medieval recipes (found in *Two Fifteenth Century Cookery Books*). *TAKE A THOUSAND EGGS OR MORE* is a completely usable cookbook featuring:

- ☛ over 100 easy and delicious modernized recipes;
- ☛ two glossaries;
- ☛ a complete index;
- ☛ a how-to section;
- ☛ bibliography;
- ☛ dozens of period woodcuts;
- ☛ and much more!

"...many Medievalist groups... have already hailed this book with great excitement. Many of these dishes will surely turn up at the ever-popular Renaissance Fairs throughout the country... For adventurous cooks and for anyone interested in life in medieval Europe." *–Academic Library Book Review*

"Friends, this is without doubt the most interesting, engaging and certainly unique cookbook I've come across in some time. The updated recipes cover everything from soup to nuts and they're terrific. *–The Gourmet Co-op*

"Cindy Renfrow... has taken a very scholarly subject and made it interesting, 'palatable' and informative for today's cook. *TAKE A THOUSAND EGGS OR MORE* is a set of books to read, to use and to savor." *–Cookbook Collectors Exchange*

"I was... completely thrilled with both volumes... Documentation has never been this easy." *–Tournaments Illuminated*

✂-----------------------✂------------------✂-------------------✂----------------------✂-------------------

Please send me ____ copies of *Take a Thousand Eggs or More* at $ 27.00 postpaid per Two-Volume Set.

| | |
|---|---|
| Name (please print)_____ | ____ 2 Vol. set(s)  $____.__ |
| Address_____ | NJ residents add 6% tax  $____.__ |
| _____ | Total enclosed  $____.__ |

Make check or money order payable to: Cindy Renfrow, 7 El's Way, Sussex, NJ 07461, USA.
All orders are sent 4th class Book Rate. Payment in full must accompany all orders. Dealer inquiries are welcome.